JOHN ARCHIBALD CAMPBELL

JOHN ARCHIBALD CAMPBELL, SOUTHERN MODERATE, 1811–1889

Robert Saunders, Jr.

The University of Alabama Press

Tuscaloosa and London

∞

The paper on which this book is printed meets the minimum
requirements of American National Standard for Information
Science–Permanence of Paper for Printed Library Materials,
ANSI Z39.48–1984.

Library of Congress Cataloging-in-Publication Data

Saunders, Robert, Jr.
    John Archibald Campbell, Southern moderate, 1811–1889 / Robert
Saunders, Jr.
        p.   cm.
    Includes biblographical references (p. 267) and index.
    ISBN 0-8173-0849-0 (cloth : alk. paper)
    1. Campbell, John Archibald, 1811–1889. 2. Judges—United States
—Biography. I. Title.
KF8745.C27S28   1997
347.73′2634—dc20
[B]
[B347.3073534]
[B]   96-31041

British Library Cataloguing-in-Publication data available

This book is dedicated to Shannon

Contents

Illustrations

Preface

Biographers risk choosing a subject whose life, although perhaps interesting, does not merit a full-length study. This is not the case with John Archibald Campbell, who served as an associate justice of the United States Supreme Court from 1853 to 1861 and whose life and labors reflect nearly every major development of nineteenth-century American history. Campbell participated either directly or indirectly in events ranging from the unconscionable Indian removal process of the 1830s, to sectionalism and the Civil War, to Reconstruction and Redemption. He lived during the most traumatic years in American history when the nation split and a civil war of unprecedented destruction forever changed its destiny. This was an era of increasing radicalism, of abolitionism, of Free-Soilism, of Know-Nothingism, and of southern nationalism disguising an inherent dread of social change. Fundamentally conservative, Campbell deplored social revolutions that promised rapid change and threatened his innate desire for order and stability. By midcentury, when abolitionism and sectionalism jeopardized Campbell's perception of an ordered society, he struck back at those forces and in many respects often appeared as radical and as reactionary as the so-called southern fire-eaters, an often irresponsible group of individuals who sought to separate the southern states from the rest of the nation. By the same token, though, Campbell vehemently disagreed with the southern fire-eaters, who maintained that secession was inevitable. Serving as an associate justice, Campbell sought to protect states' rights while maintaining the sanctity of the federal Constitution and the power and authority of the central government.

Campbell was not a defender of slavery, but he detested any person who demanded immediate and noncompensatory abolition, because he feared that the hasty removal of slavery from southern society would cause severe economic and social dislocation. But Campbell also felt strongly that, because human bondage was antithetical to American ideals of liberty and freedom, southern states had to reform their labor system. In the early 1850s he proposed a series of reforms to strengthen slave families and to educate the slaves so as to prepare them for assimilation into southern society as productive citizens. Campbell's moderate and progressive views distinguish him from many other southerners who steadfastly maintained the sanctity of the South's peculiar institution.

On 17 March 1857, shortly after the United States Supreme Court handed down its decision in the famous *Dred Scott* case, the *New York Tribune* printed caustic remarks about those justices who had voted with the majority. "Of Judge Campbell of Alabama," the article read, "he is more fanatical than the fanatics—more Southern than the extreme South from which he comes. . . . He is a middle-aged, middle-sized man, bald, and possessed of middling talents." Considering the furor surrounding the Court's decision, such remarks by vindictive antislavery editors were at least half expected. But it was a mistake to label Campbell a "fanatic." He was undeniably a staunch defender of southern rights who maintained that most political power should be vested in the states and that the federal government's principal role was to ensure that no one state or group of states gained political or economic hegemony over other states.

But Campbell's ardent defense of states' rights was profoundly tempered by his utmost respect and admiration for the United States. He believed that the American Constitution served as a shining beacon to innumerable victims of tyranny throughout the world and that it symbolized humanity's progression toward and realization of self-government. His perception of the nation was founded on an interpretation of the debates in the Constitutional Convention of 1787 that saw the federal government as fundamentally representing a conglomeration of semiautonomous states united in a celebration of freedom and democracy. As nearly all issues of import to most Americans involved local concerns with few truly national ramifications, Campbell reasoned that state governmental power should never become subservient or secondary to that of the federal government. Such a political philosophy was by no means unique during the nineteenth century, particularly throughout the antebellum period, when sovereignty was most often defined in terms of dual federalism—meaning that the federal and state governments encompassed entirely separate but coequal spheres of influence.

By midcentury, many Americans—Campbell among them—were concerned that the federal government's authority was being unconstitutionally enhanced at the expense of state authority. And during this period southern fire-eaters began to assert that the southern states no longer enjoyed a coequal position with either the northern states or the federal government. These southerners therefore concluded that the South must secede and unite in a new nation—one in which their peculiar institutions would not be threatened. Campbell joined these radicals on occasion, but he never became one of them. Though his anxiety for states' rights forced him to modify his fundamentally nationalistic philosophy and to adopt a decidedly more inflexible defense of state sovereignty, Campbell never advocated the dissolution of the Union.

When the sectional crisis reached fever pitch in 1860, Campbell counseled moderation. Secession was perfectly constitutional, he argued, but the mere election of a Republican by no means warranted such drastic action.

Detested in the North because of his defense of states' rights and distrusted in the South because of his moderate views on slavery and secession, Campbell blamed his alienation on radicals in both sections who he believed had led the nation toward civil war. In May 1861, he resigned from the bench and later became the assistant secretary of war for the Confederacy, an altogether thankless role that he retained until April 1865.

After the war, Campbell rebuilt his law practice and became a highly respected member of his profession. Disturbed by the fundamental changes ushered in during congressional Reconstruction, Campbell became an active critic of social revolution. He voiced his opposition to Reconstruction through largely ineffectual political activity and, more successfully, through court appearances during which he sought to weaken the Republican-controlled state governments. Campbell's moderate views contrasted sharply with those of the more radical members of American society. This book chronicles his life and career.

I thank a number of individuals for their assistance. First, Kim Cantrell Fabel, a colleague and a friend, suggested more than three years ago that Campbell would be an appropriate and an interesting subject for my dissertation. The faculty and staff at Auburn University's History Department lent constant support and certainly exceeded normal expectations. My major professor, Dr. James Lee McDonough, was truly an inspiration throughout this project. His advice was always sound and his patience unwavering. It was indeed an honor to study under a professor with such profound knowledge, insight, and understanding. I should be remiss if I neglected to thank his wife, Nancy, who always had encouraging words as well. I also thank Alfred Goldthwaite, an attorney in Montgomery, Alabama, and Campbell's great great-nephew, with whom I spent a wonderful afternoon discussing the Campbell-Goldthwaite family.

I was particularly impressed with the prompt and professional service that I received from the staff members of the Southern Historical Collection at the University of North Carolina, Chapel Hill. My time there was far more enjoyable and profoundly more enriching as a result of their efforts. Many thanks go to the interlibrary loan personnel of the Ralph B. Draughon Library at Auburn University, whose professionalism, patience, and expertise was always exemplary. Dr. Norwood Kerr and the entire staff at the Alabama Department of Archives and History made my frequent trips to Montgomery exceedingly worthwhile. Michael Musick at the National Archives was especially helpful, as was Eleanor Robin at the University of Southern Mississippi, Collette King at the Mobile County Probate Court Archives, and the staff of the John Archibald Campbell Federal Courthouse Archives in Mobile. I am grateful to the staff of the Mobile County Library and three very helpful staff members at the City of Mobile Municipal Archives.

The lifelong encouragement that I have been given by my devoted parents, Robert and Gloria Saunders, has, finally, borne fruit. Their support has been unwavering, and I will always be grateful to them. Dorothy J. Jones, a dear friend who just happens to be my mother-in-law, has never ceased to be supportive. Finally, I owe a debt to my wife, Shannon, that I shall never be able to repay. She accepted John Archibald Campbell as not only a disruption of our home and our lives for an extended period but also a source of enrichment— and she saw that he would draw us closer when his story was finally told.

JOHN ARCHIBALD CAMPBELL

1 | Ancestry and Antecedents

Campbell was descended from small farmers of the Scottish Highlands. Both the paternal and maternal sides of his family tree included individuals of marked achievement, and brief composites of these people reveal much about the character and background of John Archibald Campbell. In addition, a concise but detailed analysis of his father's career reveals many of the strong character traits that were so manifest within John Archibald. And though neither the father nor the son was without considerable faults and weaknesses, a strong character, a determination to succeed, a love of learning, a penchant for absolute thoroughness, and a deep, unbridled devotion to family were the hallmarks of their lives. These characteristics were perhaps John Archibald's principal legacy from those family members who had preceded him.

The story of Campbell's paternal family history begins with a group of Campbells who emigrated from the Highlands of Scotland to the shores of North Carolina and settled along the Cape Fear River in 1739. The first Campbell of note was Duncan Campbell, who was commissioned justice of the peace for Bladen County in 1740.[1] Duncan Campbell's grandson, Archibald, gained distinction during the American Revolutionary War. With the opening of hostilities in 1775, Campbell joined General Nathaniel Greene's forces and became one of the leading officers on the general's personal staff. He represented New Hanover County for nine terms from 1779 to 1794; as a delegate to the Hillsborough Convention of 1788 Campbell voted against ratification of the Constitution adopted at Philadelphia during the previous year. Like the majority of his fellow North Carolinians, he insisted on the inclusion of a Bill of Rights. When this was subsequently accepted, the Constitution was ratified by North Carolinians at the Fayetteville Convention of 1789.[2]

John Archibald married Rebecca Kirk of Guilford County, North Carolina, on New Year's Day 1784. On 16 February 1787, Duncan Campbell, the second of John Archibald's and Rebecca's sixteen children, was born.[3] His early education, though meager, was suitable enough to gain him entry into the state university at Chapel Hill. While attending college, Duncan and a classmate whose last name was Greene developed such a close friendship that Duncan adopted "Greene" as his middle name. For the remainder of his life

Duncan went by the full name of Duncan Greene Campbell. In late spring 1807 he graduated from college and soon thereafter moved to Wilkes County, Georgia.

In 1807, when Duncan Greene first arrived in Georgia, the territory that encompassed Wilkes County had been part of Georgia only thirty-five years. Through a series of treaties with the Creek and Cherokee Indians in 1773, Georgians acquired nearly 2 million acres that Governor James Wright dubbed the "New Purchase." Almost immediately, surveyors, speculators, and settlers made their way into the new lands. In December 1773, a group of about sixty Westmoreland County, Virginia, families began the arduous task of carving out a settlement in the thickly forested countryside. This community eventually became the town of Washington, which was incorporated by the state legislature in 1805.[4]

Two years later, freshly graduated from college and seeking to begin professional life in Georgia, Duncan Greene arrived in Washington. He accepted a position as principal of a female seminary in town, a job that provided sufficient income while he was engaged in reading for a legal career. Campbell had the good fortune to study under the tutelage of Judge John Griffin, one of the town's most respected citizens, who had built a well-established and lucrative legal practice. In 1808, Judge Griffin's wife, Sarah, introduced her youngest sister, Mary, to Duncan Greene. After one year's courtship, Duncan Green and Mary Williamson were married. Their union lasted twenty years and produced four children between 1811 and 1820: John Archibald, Sarah Greene, Lawrence Greene, and Mary Greene.[5]

Mary Williamson was born into one of Georgia's most prominent families. Her father, Micajah Williamson, owned a popular tavern that provided considerable wealth and enabled him to build one of the stateliest plantations in Wilkes County. Micajah is described as a spectacularly gallant soldier during the Revolutionary War who fought with distinction at the Battle of Kettle Creek and other smaller engagements.[6] While Micajah was fighting the British, his wife Sarah (Gilliam) Williamson courageously endured numerous depredations committed by Tories, who had temporarily gained control of the county. One source notes that "when her husband was at the front, she not only ran the plantation but also kept the looms and the ovens busy, furnishing supplies to the army as well as to her own household. Nor did she escape the perils incident to frontier life during the reign of terror in Upper Georgia. The Tories, incensed by the activities of her husband, took peculiar delight in annoying Mrs. Williamson. One day they made a raid upon her home, and, after gorging themselves with plunder, applied the torch. It is said that the Tories also hanged her eldest son [William] in her presence, compelling her by force to witness the murder of her own offspring."[7] Sarah Williamson's perseverance in the face of such hardships brought her the admiration of many Georgians.

During their years of marriage, Micajah and Sarah raised twelve children, many of whom became prominent members of their communities. For instance, Micajah, Jr., the third-born child, fought in the Revolutionary War at the Battle of Kettle Creek and later became a lawyer in Jackson County, Georgia. Micajah, Jr., was believed to have been poisoned to death by a Dr. William Wright in 1807. Nancy and Sarah, the two eldest daughters, married into renowned families, the former marrying John Clark, governor of Georgia from 1819 to 1823. Sarah married Judge John Griffin of Washington and, after Griffin's death, Judge Charles Tait, who from 1809 to 1819 served as United States senator from Georgia.[8]

Susan Williamson, Micajah's and Sarah's tenth child, married Dr. Thomas Bird in 1793. Their daughter Sarah married L. Q. C. Lamar of Georgia, whose son, L. Q. C., Jr., eventually became a leading Mississippi politician and was named to the United States Supreme Court by President Grover Cleveland.[9] Finally, Micajah's and Sarah's last child was Mary. Evidently she was also known to many of her friends as "Polly," for several sources identify her by that name. Mary, in 1808, was introduced to Duncan Greene Campbell by her older sister Sarah, the wife of Judge Griffin.[10] The Williamsons were unquestionably one of Georgia's most prominent families, and Duncan Greene's marriage to Mary substantially increased his prospects for success in a society where family connections were often more important than knowledge, skills, or abilities.

Soon after they married, Duncan Greene and Mary took up residence in Washington. Duncan Greene was admitted to the bar and had started to build a law practice when Judge Griffin decided to retire. Because of his fondness for and confidence in his former student, the judge passed his entire practice—one of the busiest and most lucrative in the county—to Duncan Greene. John Archibald Campbell's father was thus handed a well-established business, one that gave him considerable financial security.[11]

Between 1811 and 1821, Duncan Greene's law practice thrived, and he acquired considerable distinction as a talented attorney. As most of his clientele consisted of the county's wealthiest planters, his most active legal pursuits involved the disposition of land sales and the collection of debts owed to various clients. In 1816, as clear evidence that he had achieved distinction in Wilkes County, Duncan Greene was elected solicitor general of the western circuit.[12] This position carried considerable respect, although much of Campbell's caseload dealt with mundane issues of little consequence. In 1817, for instance, William Gartrell and Nancy Harris, two residents of Wilkes County, were prosecuted by Campbell for "living together in an unlawful intimacy at

Gartrell's house." During the 1818 term of the grand jury, Gibson Hopkins was charged with adultery, Betsy Ross with "fornication," and Abner Henley with maintaining a billiard table.[13] Such cases offer insight into the early nineteenth century Georgia society into which John Archibald was born.

Early in 1818, the year John Archibald turned seven, Duncan Greene purchased a "country place" about two miles west of Washington on the Lexington Road. Under Mary's watchful eye, the Campbell estate underwent extensive renovations; when completed, the main house resembled an Italian villa and was regarded as one of the finest homes in the county.[14] Susan Campbell Rowland, Duncan Greene's niece, explains that in the early 1820s when there was tremendous "love and gratitude to France for assistance in the war, . . . memories of Rochechambeau, Lafayette, and de Grasse were in every heart," Duncan Greene christened his plantation "Fontainbleau" in honor of the French soldiers who had fought in the American Revolutionary War.[15]

Having spent much of her youth at the Campbell estate, Rowland remembers that Fontainbleau was a plantation of singular beauty. She states that Mary Campbell worked diligently to make the estate "greatly adorned and cultured." "Near the front of the beautiful grounds, made lovely by flowing streams, lawns of Kentucky grass, and every variety of foliage and shrub," Rowland writes, "arose the capricious dwelling built in the style of an Italian villa with surrounding verandas." The fields and pastures were "well stocked with flocks and herds," and there were also "broad acres of grain and cotton." For the next decade, the Campbells hosted scores of travelers and visitors, who included "members of the bar from other circuits, delegates to conventions, [and] ministers of all denominations." The hospitality shown at Fontainbleau was exceptional, even in the "hospitable Southland."[16] Mary Campbell singlehandedly managed the estate whenever Duncan Greene's business and political activities kept him away from home, which occurred more often as his reputation spread and his business affairs improved.

By late 1818, Duncan Greene was recognized as one of Wilkes County's foremost citizens, and he had gained the trust and friendship of many leading politicians in the state who supported his bid for political office. In that year he was elected to represent Wilkes County in the state legislature. Harboring a deep appreciation for the value of education, Campbell attempted to inaugurate a statewide system of free elementary schools to ensure that all Georgians, regardless of financial condition, could receive at least a basic education and an ability to read and write.

In 1822, Campbell and other members of the legislature offered a bill to establish a "Regular Free School System." The measure failed, however, largely because of opposition from Georgia's governor. In its place Campbell presented a second bill to create a state-sponsored "poor fund" that would provide tuition money for parents who could not afford to send their children to academies. His efforts in this regard were likewise rejected. A third proposal Campbell offered that year would have provided state money for the construction of a college reserved exclusively for women. As the proposed college was to be funded on the same level as the main university in Athens, Campbell's bill provided that the state would clearly recognize the importance of women's higher education. The legislature's rejection of Campbell's third education bill made clear that most Georgia representatives were not as concerned with female education as with male education. In Georgia society education was intended for males only; females were to be taught the "higher" lessons of life such as child rearing and social graces. In contrast, Campbell strongly believed that women should receive the same education as men so that all society could benefit.[17]

In 1825 Duncan Greene was named chairman of the Senate Committee on Public Education and Free Schools and thus wielded considerable influence in the legislature. In 1827, Governor Troup recommended that Campbell issue a report on the most practical means of establishing a free elementary school system. Because of a protracted illness, however, he never sent this report to the governor, and the effort to improve education in Georgia languished for the next several years.

The one blemish on Duncan Greene's public record was his connection with the fraudulent Treaty of Indian Springs signed in 1825.[18] During the previous year, Secretary of War John C. Calhoun appointed Campbell and James Meriwether commissioners to negotiate land cession treaties with the Cherokee and Creek Indians, who retained thousands of acres in both Georgia and Alabama. Many such treaties had been arranged between the Georgians and the Indians since the end of the Revolutionary War, but as more and more settlers from Virginia and the Carolinas swelled Georgia's population, pressure to acquire the remaining lands relegated to the Creeks and the Cherokees mounted steadily.

Throughout 1824, Duncan Greene failed to persuade either the Cherokees or the Creeks to cede their territory to the United States. The Cherokees were unusually adamant in their refusal to consider the matter. The Creeks were largely unyielding as well; but there was a group of secondary Creek leaders under the influence of William McIntosh of Coweta—a principal chief in one of the Lower Towns within the Creek Nation—who seemed nominally receptive to relinquishing their lands and removing west to Arkansas. This schism within the Creek Nation forced two chiefs of the Upper Towns, Big Warrior and Little Prince, to call a private meeting at Polecat Springs to enact measures designed to discourage further dissension within the Nation. The resulting "Polecat Law" decreed that any Creek chief who pledged to relinquish Creek lands to the United States faced immediate execution.[19]

Despite this law, McIntosh remained eager to cede Creek lands in exchange for money and a predominant position in the Creek Nation once it relocated west of the Mississippi River. Duncan Greene was likewise anxious to negotiate a treaty, and though the Monroe administration had explicitly forbidden the signing of treaties with the Creeks unless the entire Nation was represented, Campbell chose to ignore these orders and to deal almost exclusively with McIntosh.

On 10 February 1825, the commissioners, the agents, and about 400 Creeks opened negotiations at Indian Springs. Significantly, none of the Tuckabatchee chiefs, those of the Upper Creek towns in Alabama, participated in these proceedings because, as they explained, "they were not ready, and were not disposed to meet in the room prepared for the council, but were disposed to hold meetings at their own camp."[20] Had Campbell been concerned with following Monroe's orders to the letter, he would have postponed the negotiations until he could have convinced the Upper Town Creeks to participate. Duncan Greene, however, impatient to acquire land and apparently willing to ignore what he perceived as the insignificant details of his orders, decided to proceed with the negotiations even though only the Coweta chiefs were present.

The resulting Treaty of Indian Springs ceded all of the Creek lands in Georgia that lay between the Flint and Chattahoochee Rivers. In return for this land, the United States agreed to provide the Creeks with an equal number of acres along the Arkansas River, to compensate them for improvements on their ceded lands, and to pay a total of $400,000 to those Creeks agreeing to emigrate. The Creeks assented to vacate all of their lands in Georgia by September 1826. Article 5, interestingly, stipulated that all monies paid to the Creeks had to be distributed by the commissioners, an entirely new precedent and one meant as the commissioners' parting shot at Creek agent John Crowell and subagent Henry Walker. Campbell in particular believed that these Indian agents sympathized with the Creeks and had diligently sought to obstruct treaty negotiations. Moreover, Campbell accused Crowell and Walker of goading the Upper Creeks into adopting the Polecat Law, the text of which had been transcribed by Walker in his own home.[21]

Though the Treaty of Indian Springs was ratified by the Senate and signed by President John Quincy Adams, complaints about the cession from the Tuckabatchee chiefs and from the Indian agents prompted a formal investigation into the negotiations. Secretary of War James Barbour dispatched Major T. P. Andrews and General Edmund P. Gaines to investigate the treaty and to determine whether it had been negotiated in good faith and with the entire Creek Nation.[22]

In December 1825, the United States Senate opened discussions on the abrogation of the Treaty of Indian Springs. The report presented to Congress by Major Andrews was most damning, for it showed that only eight of the fifty-six Creek towns were represented at Indian Springs, that thirty of the fifty-two signers were from Coweta, and that McIntosh had absolutely no authority to negotiate for the entire Nation. Moreover, Andrews reported:

> McIntosh was induced to sign the treaty, and to induce or compel his adherents to sign with him, from large *douceurs* or bribes offered or given to him by the Commissioners, at the same time remarking that he had forfeited his life in doing so, under the laws of his Nation. . . . No unprejudiced person, after reading the mass of testimony now submitted, can withhold the belief, that the treaty made at Indian Springs, in February last, was in fact agreed on in private in the nocturnal interviews between the commissioners and McIntosh at Broken Arrow in the preceding December.[23]

This report was the death knell for the Treaty of Indian Springs, which was summarily abrogated despite thunderous objections from Georgia's governor and legislature.[24]

The Treaty of Indian Springs was not invalidated because it provided for Indian land cessions; after all, that was clearly the objective in both Washington and Milledgeville. The treaty was rejected because the commissioners, and Campbell in particular, exceeded their authority by negotiating with a deputation unauthorized to make arrangements for the entire Creek Nation. The evidence shows that in his haste to acquire a treaty, any treaty, Campbell promised McIntosh huge monetary rewards and a predominant position within the Creek Nation once the Indians emigrated across the Mississippi River. Considering McIntosh's conspicuous greed and his waning influence within the National Council, Campbell's offers proved too tempting to reject.[25]

Historians generally agree that the Treaty of Indian Springs was an unmitigated fraud.[26] With all other avenues for negotiation apparently closed, however, Campbell resorted to possibly the only other means of negotiating a treaty. His objective was to acquire the Creek lands in Georgia, and he felt that it was only reasonable to treat with the Indians in actual possession of those lands. This practical approach, although outside the scope of his authority, was thoroughly acceptable to most Georgians, who were anxious to settle the vast and fertile Creek Territory. Nothing Campbell did in relation to the Creeks was viewed by Georgians as wrong or extraordinary; it was simply a means of achieving his objective. One can hardly refrain from condemning such activity today; yet viewed from the standpoint of most Georgians in the 1820s, Campbell's attempt to gain Creek lands was certainly expected and applauded.

During the late 1820s, Campbell was accorded great respect and admiration by nearly all Georgians. His role in negotiating the Treaty of Indian Springs further enhanced his already considerable political position and led his allies in the legislature to propose his name for the 1827 gubernatorial campaign.[27] Campbell's chances for victory were apparently good; yet he decided to withdraw his name from consideration. The reasons for his refusal to run are unclear, but his health may have been a factor. During the summer of 1827, he contracted yellow fever, which nearly killed him and kept him bed-ridden for three months. Another explanation might be that after two years away from Fontainbleau, he longed to return home and look after his family and business affairs.[28]

How should one judge the life and character of Duncan Greene Campbell? The Treaty of Indian Springs was a fraud negotiated by a man willing to resort to bribery, distortions, and malfeasance. Moreover, Duncan Greene showed little, if any, concern that the Creeks were being forced to move away from their ancestral homeland. And yet, despite the obviously deceptive nature of his treaty negotiations, he should not be judged by this one episode alone. We should also consider his substantial efforts to improve the state's education system and his legislative measures and committee reports in support of female education in Georgia.

In a closing assessment of Duncan Greene, former Georgia governor George Gilmer, who was sparing with praise for most of his subjects, writes that he

> had none of the rowdy habits of the North Carolina, Wilkes settlers. He avoided violence, and was courteous and kind to everybody. Though his talents were not of the highest order, nor his public speaking what might be called eloquent, he was among the most successful lawyers at the bar and useful members of the Legislature. He was very industrious, and ever ready to do the part of a good citizen. The amenity of his temper was constantly shown in the delight which he derived from pleasing the young. His house continued, as long as he lived, to be one of their favorite resorts.[29]

Finally, there is one other character trait that must be considered when assessing Duncan Greene Campbell—his enduring and unfaltering devotion to his family. In essence, he believed that a man was best measured by his off-spring and that the values one passes to his children greatly affect how they live their lives. Personal honesty, a devotion to hard work, a quest for knowledge, and a seemingly endless love for one's family were the hallmarks of Duncan Greene's heritage to his children.

John Archibald Campbell was born on 24 June 1811 at the family residence in Washington. During his early years, the strict Presbyterian upbringing and liberal education provided him by Duncan Greene and Mary Campbell instilled within him unwavering faith in Christianity, an uncompromising respect for learning, and a powerful desire to succeed. Campbell had an amazing memory coupled with an ability to digest vast amounts of material. He progressed rapidly through most of the extensive family library and was reading classical writings in ancient Greek before he was eight years old. His parents carefully cultivated his desire for knowledge. While Duncan Greene was most concerned that John Archibald concentrate on classical works, his mother insisted that he read passages from the Bible each morning and apply these lessons in daily life.[30]

Campbell's boyhood environment was characterized by markedly contrasting images. Wilkes County, with the exception of Washington and a few other small towns, was during the 1810s as frontierlike as it had always been. Just a short distance from Washington lay a wilderness densely filled with evergreen trees, where creeks and streams meandered toward the Savannah River, with backwater sloughs in which the various fevers bred that plagued Georgians during the summer months. Despite its wilderness setting, however, Wilkes County attracted many settlers soon after the Revolutionary War. With a burgeoning population, this county rapidly grew in importance both politically and economically. Seventeen counties were eventually named for men who had at various times lived in Wilkes. The county produced ten of Georgia's governors, scores of state legislators, and numerous judges—all of whom achieved prominence in the state.[31]

Three months after his tenth birthday, in September 1821, John Archibald began attending Wilkes Academy, located in Washington.[32] Under normal circumstances, male children attended this school for at least three years until they were prepared to enter the state college in Athens. Because of the substantial educational foundation given Campbell by his parents, however, he was sent to Athens after only one year at the academy. It was quite evident that he was already prepared for university study, and despite his youth his parents were eager for him to acquire a college education.

By June 1822, when Campbell first began classes at Franklin College—as the University of Georgia was then known—the school was considered the leading higher education institution in the state. It had not always enjoyed this reputation, however. Since its founding in 1785, Franklin College had tottered on the brink of financial disaster. The school's chief administrative organ, the Senatus Academicus, consisted of annually elected officials who sometimes allowed their personal ambition or drive for wealth to overshadow their dedication to the college. As a result, operating funds were woefully inadequate, the few buildings on campus were dilapidated, and faculty members often resigned in protest of their scant salaries and the meager educational facilities.

In 1819, Franklin College's prospects for success and longevity were greatly improved when Moses Waddel was hired as its president. Waddel had previously gained a sound reputation as the South's leading educator; two of his most famous students were John C. Calhoun and William H. Crawford.

Waddel's emergence at the helm in Athens lent great promise to the struggling school. When Campbell began college studies in Athens three years after Waddel's arrival, Franklin College was able to provide the education that both he and his parents hoped he would receive. Of course, while at Athens, Campbell lived in a strict, closely regulated environment but, under Waddel's leadership, one that clearly prepared him for a successful career.

Waddel instituted a highly regimented curriculum primarily based on religious instruction but coupled with intense classical studies. To be admitted to the institution, each student had to demonstrate an ability to "read, translate, and parse Cicero, Virgil, and the Greek Testament, and to write true [L]atin in prose." All students had to show that they had learned "the rules of vulgar arithmetic" and could provide "satisfactory evidence of a blameless life."[33]

In general, the average age of incoming freshmen was between sixteen and seventeen years. Before the 1830s, however, a considerable percentage of the students entered in their thirteenth year. For these youngsters, the college opened a special institution known as Meigs's Grammar School, where they studied until they were better prepared to enter the college. Many of the young students at the Grammar School became targets of ridicule by older students, and most were genuinely pleased when they were finally allowed to matriculate to the upper classes. President Waddel often sent students who fell behind in their studies to attend classes in the Grammar School. The mere threat of this humiliation normally kept most students in line.[34] Campbell attended the Grammar School for one year, and then he entered the upper classes well ahead of other students who had started in 1822.[35]

College life was overseen with great diligence by Waddel and the faculty members, who insisted that students maintain both "clean minds and bodies," who set reveille and curfew, and who taught a curriculum that required devotion to study and an ability to recall passages from classical works. Waddel and the faculty were no less adamant that each student excel in oratory. "Forensic disputation" was required of juniors; every two months each had to stand and recite long passages from one of the classical Greek or Latin writers.[36] These exercises, seemingly productive of little that could be used in a frontier environment, nevertheless proved most beneficial in developing a reliable memory and a superior ability to recall details. Failure to perform these exercises satisfactorily often led to humiliation before one's classmates or even suspension if there was no improvement over time.[37]

Campbell excelled in recitation and debate, and he won much praise for his efforts. His most active extracurricular pursuits involved the school's Demosthenian Society, a fraternal debate organization. George Gilmer relates an interesting anecdote concerning the Campbells and the Demosthenian Society. On one occasion while Duncan Greene was visiting Athens, the society asked him to address their meeting on a current topic of his choosing. "When he was done speaking," Gilmer states, "John asked leave to answer the gentleman, and so knocked all of his father's conclusions into *non sequiturs,* that it was difficult to tell which had the uppermost in the father's feelings, mortified vanity or gratified pride."[38] These were good years for John Archibald. He continuously impressed the faculty at Athens with his longing for knowledge and his intellectual abilities. "As a student," one lifelong acquaintance once remarked, "he was from early life rigorously severe, undertaking labors from which even those counted resolute would have shrunk."[39]

Yet Campbell seemed to have been somewhat troublesome for both the faculty and the debating society. There were apparently as many rules associated with membership in the Demosthenian Society as there were in the college. Campbell broke many of these; he was fined "three times for going out without permission, once for eating in the hall, eight times for being out too long, twice for disorder, once for moving his seat, and twice for reading in time of session."[40] Despite his mildly mischievous behavior, however, he earned high praise not only from Waddel but also from his entire class. "I have never known a class in my life," he wrote, "which included so much intellectual talent as the present Junior Class in this institution."[41]

Having excelled in all of his studies, Campbell graduated in June 1825 "with the first honors of his class."[42] If we are to gauge institutions of higher learning by the success of their alumni, then the strict and rigorous education young students received at Franklin College was superior. Throughout the nineteenth century, this institution educated many young men who later became influential politicians, judges, preachers, and doctors.

There is little doubt that the education Campbell received at Athens served him well throughout his legal career. Campbell had no intention of becoming a lawyer, however; his foremost ambition was to attend West Point Military Academy and to build a career as an officer in the United States Army. In early 1826 Duncan Greene requested that Secretary of War Calhoun nominate the young Campbell for one of the highly prized seats at West Point. Calhoun readily obliged, and by late August John Archibald was a new cadet at the Academy.

Unfortunately, Campbell's years at West Point were unhappy ones because of tragic and unforeseen events in Georgia. On 22 September 1826, just one month after Campbell had entered the Academy, his ten-year-old brother, Lawrence, and five-year-old sister, Mary Greene, died. Eleven-year-old Mary Ann McKenzie, Duncan Greene's niece, also died that day.[43] The cause of these deaths is unknown, but most likely all three children either were killed in a tragic accident or succumbed to yellow fever. Their deaths devastated the family and made the beginning of Campbell's military training most difficult. Considering how far John Archibald was from home when his siblings died, it is most unlikely that he was present for their burial.

Campbell attended West Point from August 1826 until November 1828 (see photo 1). During the summer before his final year at the Academy, tragedy once again struck the Campbell family. In mid-July 1828, Duncan Greene became violently ill. After lingering for a few weeks, he died at home on the thirty-first surrounded by his family.[44] Mary Campbell was widowed, and John Archibald and his only surviving sister, Sarah Greene, were left fatherless. Duncan Greene's premature death at age forty-one came as a great shock not only to his family but to many Georgians as well. He had served for several years as a trustee of Franklin College, where he was fondly remembered for his financial support and for his visits to the campus. The Demosthenian Society held a memorial meeting in Duncan Greene's honor on August 4 and resolved to wear black armbands for thirty days in his memory. They also drafted a letter of condolence to the family and expressed wishes that the "widow and orphan[s]" might soon experience happier days.[45]

But other calamities for the Campbells loomed on the horizon. In late August, Campbell returned to West Point and soon thereafter received troubling news from his mother that Duncan Greene's estate was in serious peril. Campbell later reported only: "[Duncan Greene's] affairs were in disorder and his family [was] in distress."[46] Evidently Duncan Greene had received government funds that were to be distributed to several Indian chiefs as gifts for signing the Treaty of Indian Springs. The money had mysteriously disappeared, and his estate was held liable for its recovery. As Susan Campbell Rowland explains, the "death of Colonel Campbell was followed by great and unexpected misfortunes to his family. During his protracted illness, the last government appropriation for the payment of the Indian claims had been left in the hands of several parties associated with [Duncan Greene]. These others misappropriated the funds, some of them fled the state, and the estate of Colonel Campbell, through no fault of his own, was made responsible. Nobly did the widow and children yield to the sacrifice of all their possessions."[47]

Learning of his mother's financial plight, Campbell returned home to Georgia to help his family. It was at once apparent that there was no other alternative but to sell Fontainbleau. "The hearth stone was broken and the house was sold in 1829," Campbell later wrote.[48] It was a cruel blow to an already devastated family to have to sell their house, their land, and practically all of their belongings.

With his father's death and the family's financial woes, Campbell was forced to acknowledge that further military study at West Point was impossible. With the family's care now his responsibility, he sought new career opportunities. When his uncle John Clark offered to tutor John Archibald in legal

John Archibald Campbell, ca. 1826–1828. This photograph, the only known likeness made of Campbell prior to the 1850s, was reproduced from a miniature that Campbell gave his mother. The jacket and neckwear suggests that he had this made for her while he was a cadet at West Point. (From Photo File, Box 7, Campbell Miniature, Alabama Department of Archives and History, Montgomery, Alabama.)

studies, he readily accepted. In January 1829, Campbell traveled to St. Andrew's Bay, Florida, and began reading law. This was obviously his second career choice and one upon which he decided only because of his father's death and the financial distress of his family. But once he had decided to become a lawyer, Campbell devoted nearly all of his time to his studies. His uncle, the former governor of Georgia who had lost the gubernatorial contest of 1825, had grown bitter over his defeat and had retired from Georgia politics altogether. Always eager to reward loyal friends such as Clark, President Jackson selected him to be the United States Indian Agent for Florida, a position that made Clark the custodian of all federal and Indian lands in that state. "It was not an office to which any high honor attached," one historian explains, "but the salary enabled him to live in comfort and to extend hospitality" to the many relatives and friends who often visited.[49]

To supplement his income while in St. Andrew's, Campbell tutored John Robert W. Clark, his second cousin.[50] The combination of John Clark's helpful instruction and Campbell's high intellect enabled the young student to complete his legal studies by the end of 1829. He was at once admitted to the bar in Florida and for a brief period considered establishing a legal practice in that state. In January 1830, he was offered the clerkship of the United States District Court in Key West. In Campbell's words, this position was "then lucrative" and would have provided a respectable salary and a comfortable life.[51] His ambitions, however, although by no means defined, nonetheless burned brightly, and to accept a position confined to the southernmost tip of Florida would have inhibited further professional advancement. He thus graciously declined the offer, as he often did throughout his long and illustrious career.

Campbell returned to Georgia, where he was promptly admitted to the bar. Because he was only eighteen when he was tested by the county magistrates, a special act was passed by the state legislature waiving the age restriction then in force. It is not known whether he established a law practice in Georgia; in all likelihood he never had the chance. With the family finances in utter ruin, and with little prospects for improvement, Campbell realized that professional life in Washington, Georgia, could not provide adequately for his family. By the late 1820s many Georgians were emigrating to the fledgling state of Alabama, where there was cheap land, ample labor, and golden opportunities. With a decent education, a willingness to work, and the right connections, professional life in Alabama could perhaps provide the wealth and prominence Campbell actively sought.

Though the Campbells had never been to Alabama, they were already related to or familiar with a substantial number of influential people in central Alabama. During the 1820s, several members of the Campbell family—including Campbell's paternal grandfather—migrated to Montgomery, Alabama, and these people probably suggested that Mary Campbell and her family move there as well.[52] Moreover, scores of Broad River residents, mostly wealthy planters who had operated plantations in the region just north of Washington and had relied on Duncan Greene for much of their legal services, moved to Alabama soon after the region was surveyed and opened for settlement. These people settled primarily in central Alabama near the town of

Montgomery. Most migrated with large numbers of slaves, and as the soil in central Alabama was extremely fertile and the climate exceedingly suitable for plantation agriculture, these Georgians became the founders of what was eventually known as the Cotton Belt. The majority of the Broad River settlers—or as one historian recently termed them, the "cousinry," for they were all related in one way or another—were from the upper classes in Georgian society and were accustomed to governing.[53] They naturally but erroneously assumed that they would dominate politics in Alabama as well.

Soon after their arrival, the Broad River emigrants to central Alabama competed for political hegemony with other residents, principally Tennesseans who migrated to north Alabama soon after the Creek War of 1814 and established small farms in that region. In 1819, while the territorial legislature diligently labored to attain statehood for Alabama, the Broad River residents temporarily gained dominance and were chiefly responsible for the framework and construction of Alabama's first constitution. Their political supremacy in the state was short-lived, but they reigned in the Cotton Belt throughout the antebellum years.[54] Thus, as many influential Montgomery residents had known Duncan Greene Campbell and had greatly respected him for his efforts in obtaining Creek Territory in Georgia, John Archibald was warmly received in Montgomery society upon his arrival in March 1830.

The journey to Alabama brought the Campbells down the newly opened Federal Road. This major southern thoroughfare stretched from Augusta, Georgia, to Mobile, Alabama, with the middle portion bisecting Creek Territory in Alabama. The Federal Road also extended through the region in western Georgia that had been ceded by the Treaties of Indian Springs and Washington and had since been formally annexed by that state.[55] After a brief stay at Columbus waiting for ferry passage, the Campbells crossed the Chattahoochee River and traveled by stage into Creek Territory. They then traveled the 100-mile route to Montgomery, arriving in town on 18 March 1830.[56] Having lived in a well-established and mostly cultivated town for so long, the Campbells were probably stunned when they first saw their new home: a rugged and largely lawless mudhole somewhere between wilderness and civilization.

During the early 1820s, Montgomery, Alabama, remained an isolated frontier village. There were but sixty-two houses in town, thirty-eight of which were crudely constructed of rough-hewn logs. The few cleared streets—present-day Dexter and Commerce Streets, for instance—were often so muddy that even the hardiest horse had difficulty trudging in the thick and foul-smelling sludge. Daily commodities such as dry goods and other items were usually imported from Charleston or Savannah; given the lack of passable roads, the only accessible route was by sea to Mobile and then up the Alabama River—the entire one-way passage could take as much as seventy days to complete.[57] With the opening of the Federal Road through Alabama, however, Montgomery experienced rapid growth. Emigrants from Georgia and South Carolina began swelling the village's population throughout the late 1820s and early 1830s, growth that enabled Montgomery to become central Alabama's commercial center.[58]

During the early 1830s, Montgomery County likewise made considerable progress; the population increased to nearly 12,700 people, of whom 6,500 were black slaves. About 1,500 people lived within Montgomery city, 650 of whom were slaves.[59] As these figures indicate, the slave-to-white population ratio was about even, and the large number of blacks clearly demonstrates that central Alabama was becoming the most prominent cotton-producing region in the state. So many slaves were transported into central Alabama that a traveler on the Federal Road counted 1,000 new arrivals in a single day.[60] This growth naturally led to exceptional career opportunities, especially for a young lawyer such as Campbell who could profit handsomely handling the affairs of the wealthiest planters.

Much like Washington, Georgia—but on an even grander scale—Montgomery abounded in contrasts. Civilization arrived in modest forms by 1830; there were a few private academies, but the tuition was extraordinarily high. Most people either home schooled as best they could or neglected to educate their children at all. From a practical standpoint, reading and writing might have been helpful in a more developed community, but in a rough, frontier town like Montgomery, rudimentary farming techniques and basic survival skills held priority for most people.[61]

Religion was also vitally important in Montgomery society. Frontier life, even within a town, was tenuous at best, and residents naturally looked to religion for comfort. During the 1820s, all Christians regardless of denomination worshiped at Union Church. By 1832, however, the Presbyterians, Baptists, and Methodists organized separate congregations to accommodate the burgeoning population.[62]

Even with these educational and religious foundations, there was a violent underpinning to Montgomery society that was very much a part of life in town. "The flavor of the frontier [still] lingered in Montgomery," as one historian recently wrote.[63] Alcohol was the root of most of the violence, and gambling—particularly at a local establishment known as the Montgomery Exchange—produced raucous brawls that sometimes ended with serious injuries or even death. By 1830, scenes of violence had become so common—and the city fathers were evidently unable to stem the disorder—that citizens' groups such as the Montgomery Regulating Horn and Jake Odum's Boys were organized to restore order, particularly during holidays or political rallies when tempers could become especially inflamed. In 1830 when the Campbells first arrived in the area, central Alabama remained more frontier than civilized.[64] Indeed, for a person generally accustomed to finer living, high culture, and polite conversation, Montgomery must have been something of a surprise and disappointment for John Archibald. Nonetheless, he quickly adapted to his new home and was soon socializing with the most influential citizens in Montgomery.

While attending church services at Union Church on the Sunday following his arrival, Campbell was introduced to Anne Esther Goldthwaite.[65] Though Anne was seven years older than her young suitor, the couple courted until the following winter and were married by Minister Robert Holman on 30 December 1830.[66] Their marriage lasted fifty-three years—until Anne's death in 1883—and was characterized by devotion, love, and respect that saw them through the most tragic and disastrous years in American history. Campbell later described Anne as "a woman of very rare cultivation and intelligence. Her judgement was exact and discreet. Her counsels exercised influence in the family of her mother and over her brothers. She had an innate sense of right and was habitually just in all of her relations among her equals and among her servants. Her husband had entire and implicit confidence in her management of the household and confided to her whatever concerned their domestic affairs."[67]

Anne Goldthwaite had been born in Dalton, New Hampshire, on 17 September 1804. Her paternal grandfather, Thomas Goldthwaite, and her father, likewise named Thomas, were British officers during the American Revolutionary War. Though their property was confiscated during the war, the elder Goldthwaite fought so gallantly for the British that the London government recompensed him for his lost property in America. Soon after hostilities ended, Thomas, Jr., returned to the United States and married Anne Wilson of Boston. The couple lived at various times in Portsmouth, Virginia; Hudson, New York; Dalton, New Hampshire; and Boston, Massachusetts. During their marriage, Thomas and Anne had four children: John, Henry, Anne, and George. For unknown reasons, Thomas abandoned his family and returned to England soon after George was born. His abrupt departure forced Anne to open a boardinghouse in Boston, where she eked out a living for her family.[68]

In 1817, Anne's eldest son John moved to Montgomery and opened a mercantile business. His store was one of the first retail outlets and few sources of dry goods and other products in central Alabama. In line with his financial success, when his sister Anne married Campbell in December 1830, John built a multicolumned, two-storied frame house on South McDonough Street and presented it to the newlyweds as a wedding gift.[69]

In 1819, Henry Goldthwaite decided to join his older brother in Alabama. For a few years after his arrival, Henry worked in his brother's store. In 1821, he and three close associates established Montgomery's first newspaper, the *Alabama Journal,* which he edited for the next three years. Goldthwaite meanwhile studied law and was admitted to the bar in 1823. Two years later, Henry Goldthwaite and Benjamin Fitzpatrick, a recent arrival in Alabama from Greene County, Georgia, began a law practice that was successful and provided both partners with substantial wealth. By the time the Campbells arrived in Montgomery, the firm of Fitzpatrick and Goldthwaite was one of the most prestigious law practices in the city.[70]

Henry Goldthwaite was elected to the state legislature as a representative from Montgomery County in 1829. He was recognized as "an active and efficient member" who established "a high character for talents and business qualifications."[71] Despite such accolades, Goldthwaite failed in his reelection bid, and he moved to Mobile and opened a new law practice in that city. His success at the bar brought him wide acclaim as one of Alabama's leading lawyers. This reputation led to his elevation in 1837 as an associate justice of the Alabama Supreme Court, where he served until his death from yellow fever in 1847. William Garrett writes that Judge Goldthwaite possessed a "gigantic mind, great research, superior reasoning faculties, [and a] cutting style of speech."[72] These qualities enabled him to become one of Alabama's most able jurists and well-respected citizens.

George Goldthwaite arrived in Montgomery in 1830 in time to see his sister marry John Archibald Campbell. He previously studied law in Boston and was admitted to Alabama's bar soon after his arrival in the state. Like his older brothers, George possessed a keen mind and was recognized for his talents and legal acumen. He practiced law throughout the Civil War, and in 1870 he was elected to the United States Senate.[73]

In sum, Campbell's affiliation by marriage to the Goldthwaite family gave him distinct ties to some of Montgomery's most influential citizens. In early 1831, Campbell and Henry Goldthwaite opened a new law practice in Montgomery; less than one year after his arrival, Campbell, who had not yet turned twenty, was a full partner in the city's most prestigious law firm. By virtue of very brisk business, he was introduced to some of the leading politicians of the state, and he gained recognition in the courts by successfully arguing cases for many of the wealthiest members of Montgomery society.

This, then, was the foundation for what became a long and highly successful legal career spanning nearly fifty years and culminating in Campbell's elevation to the United States Supreme Court, the highest honor a lawyer can achieve. Being blessed with a remarkable memory and profound intelligence, acquiring a respectable education at Franklin College, and marrying into a socially and politically prominent Montgomery family, Campbell launched his professional career on an extremely solid foundation. Of course, Campbell always presumed that he would be successful. His expectations were borne of the utmost confidence instilled by his parents, though it is difficult to determine whether it was Duncan Greene or Mary who had the most profound impact upon John Archibald's youth and development.

Mary Campbell's religious instruction and her insistence that the children maintain deeply Christian lives had a lifelong influence on John Archibald. Until her death in 1862, Campbell dearly loved and revered Mary Campbell, and he dutifully looked after his mother for the remainder of her life. Duncan Greene Campbell, on the other hand, exemplified the then common role of a caring yet sternly patriarchical father who strictly regulated his eldest son's education and development. There is some indication that Duncan Greene maintained considerable distance between himself and John Archibald and that he often shunned displays of affection. In fact, though John Archibald was seventeen years old when his father died, he knew surprisingly little of Duncan Greene's background. In a letter Campbell wrote in 1887 to a family friend inquiring about the family lineage, he erroneously explained that Duncan Greene "took the name of Duncan" because he greatly admired Duncan Cameron of North Carolina. Even more interesting is that instead of recounting personal memories and details of his father in this letter, Campbell merely quoted a secondary source describing Duncan Greene as "courteous."[74]

There should be little doubt that Campbell's extraordinary devotion to hard work and diligent study originated through Duncan Greene's influence. But the father's sternly patriarchical nature and reserved manner toward his son led to a less than loving relationship between them. John Archibald developed a similarly strained relationship with his son; Duncan Greene's approach to raising children thus did not die with him in 1828 but rather reemerged when John Archibald and Anne Campbell began having children in the 1830s. Whether he realized it or not, John Archibald shared many traits with his father. Similarly ambitious, Campbell hoped to emulate Duncan Greene—particularly in that he too aspired to political office. Though Campbell entered professional life in 1830 as an attorney, he had little intention of remaining in that profession any longer than was required to win political office. In this regard, as well in many others, Duncan Greene's influence was profound.

2 | Professional Career, 1830–1842

Having been born into Georgia's elite, Campbell felt more than obligated to assume a leadership role. His genuine desire for a career in public service originated in his intense ambition and his drive to become politically prominent and did not necessarily reflect any profound sense of duty. As the law was the most obvious and opportune avenue for a successful career in public life, Campbell expected to use his legal skills as a springboard into politics. By marrying into the Goldthwaite family, he gave himself ample opportunities to work and socialize with many powerful and politically influential men in the state. Between 1831 and 1836, Campbell associated with powerful Alabama politicians such as William Rufus King, Dixon Hall Lewis, Benjamin Fitzpatrick, and Clement Comer Clay, the four men who dominated state politics throughout the 1830s. By 1836, these connections enabled the young lawyer to parley his legal skills and social connections into a seat in the state legislature.

Upon assuming office in Tuscaloosa, however, Campbell quickly learned that being a politician was not something that he wished to continue; it took merely a few months in the state capitol before he came to detest the infighting and political back-stabbing endemic in Alabama politics. For most of the next twenty years, Campbell struggled to discover a place in public life appropriate for someone of his political persuasion and temperament. His internal struggle left him convinced that he could best serve the public interest by remaining outside politics. Only in that fashion, he reasoned, could he be considered an opinion maker within the state while aloof from day-to-day politics. This decision also enabled him to channel much of his energy into refining his legal skills, which during the next two decades became so well honed that he was known as one of the finest lawyers in the state.

The cases Campbell handled between 1831 and 1836 as a partner in Goldthwaite and Campbell, primarily dealing with land disputes and debt collections, are of little interest historically. But with this type of litigation Campbell developed a reputation as a lawyer who won cases.[1] His clientele included men whose fortunes were quickly rising in a period that some historians call the "flush times" in Alabama.[2] During the 1830s, central Alabama experienced remarkable economic growth, mostly on the backs of the thousands of slaves who were being imported into the region. Cotton had not yet been declared king, but it was quickly being granted at least princely status. With the rapid rise in cotton exports, wealth continually gravitated to the region and made the Cotton Belt increasingly important politically, socially, and economically. In this atmosphere it was little wonder that Campbell thrived as a lawyer. And as Campbell thrived, so too did his family.

To understand the complexities of John Archibald Campbell fully, one must study both his personal and professional lives, which he kept separate as a matter of principle. According to nearly every contemporary account, Campbell was cold, taciturn, and distant.[3] "No frivolous pursuits led him from that line of duty which he had marked out for himself," an associate once remarked, "and he was rewarded for his singular devotion to labor by the confidence, esteem, and veneration of all who knew him."[4] He kept to himself mostly, preferring to remain at home instead of socializing in town. He had few friends or relations outside his immediate family, and he normally sought to dissuade others from trying to develop too friendly a relationship with him. This reserved and businesslike personality left few people who remembered Campbell as warm or personable. But that was the way he preferred it. He drew a clear distinction between his personal and professional lives, and he made strenuous efforts to maintain the breach between them.[5]

In his personal life Campbell appeared the epitome of a loving family man and devoted much of his time to the happiness and security of his son and five daughters. He placed them well above any personal needs or professional ambitions, and he declined positions of great import solely because he did not want to leave his family.[6] Here, then, was the true John Archibald Campbell. He was perhaps the most serious and impersonal individual one might encounter in Montgomery, a person many considered it best to remain clear of. "Abstracted by contemplation," one observer noted, "and reserved in his manners, to the general public he seemed cold."[7] And yet, his wife, his children, and those few others who really knew him recount how warm and emotional he could be. Years later one personal friend remarked, "Judge Campbell was a man of deep feeling and of strong convictions; his manners were simple, and though austere to those who intruded, he was genial and kind in his family and among friends."[8] Another close associate stated, "As a profound lawyer, a wise judge, and a patriotic statesman, Judge Campbell has merited the admiration of all good men. In his family circle and among friends he was greater still. Here he was as tender, gentle, and affectionate as a woman. He neither knew nor saw any wrong in those he loved, and in return those who were nearest to him loved him past all understanding."[9]

Campbell soon realized that his talents as a lawyer could well provide for his family. Moreover, the law gave him an opportunity to demonstrate his vast mental capacity and remarkable memory. The years he spent in Athens memorizing and reciting long passages, formulating arguments and then delivering them with uncompromising clarity and forcefulness, and thoroughly researching a wide variety of topics well prepared him for a successful career. But with his political ambitions still burning brightly during the early 1830s, Campbell viewed his legal career only as a means to acquire political office and to provide for his family.

By the early 1830s, Campbell rapidly gained recognition as one of the most intelligent and talented members of Montgomery society. As William Garrett writes, "Indeed, his great ability and devotion to business would have commanded public attention and patronage anywhere."[10] His popularity with the electorate all but guaranteed success. The only assurance of political triumphs Campbell did not possess was active military service, but that too came his way early in 1836 when the last remaining Creek Indians in Alabama staged a minor rebellion known as the Creek War of 1836.

The backdrop for this uprising began in 1832 with the signing of the Treaty of Cusseta stipulating that the Creeks were to abandon their lands in Alabama and relocate west of the Mississippi. This treaty, signed by Secretary of War Lewis Cass and principal Creek chief, Opothleyoholo, was unique as it provided that those Indians wishing to remain in Alabama would receive land allotments from the federal Indian agent. They could either sell their land and remove west, or they could retain possession of their grant and become citizens of Alabama. The Treaty of 1832 also prohibited Alabamians from entering the newly acquired lands before the federal government completed land allotments to the Creeks and surveyed and subdivided the remaining lands.[11] Of course, white squatters already in "possession" of lands within Creek Territory were supposed to leave at once, but most simply refused to do so. To complicate matters further, Alabama's legislature promptly divided the newly acquired territory into nine counties and extended state jurisdiction over the entire area. This legislation served as ample justification for those whites eager to settle on the new lands even though the federal government had not yet fulfilled its treaty obligations. Unfortunately for the Creeks, Campbell later stated, "Simply, they were in the way."[12]

The treaty provisions ostensibly designed to protect the Creeks were generally ignored by land-hungry Alabamians and Georgians hopeful of acquiring as much land as possible for speculative purposes or to increase their personal landholdings. As one historian notes: "By January 1835 scenes of unparalleled fraud occurred daily in the Creek country. Speculators operating out of Columbus, Georgia, [and Montgomery, Alabama,] ignored regulations governing the sale and transfer of the Indian land to the whites and made 'stealing . . . the order of the day.' "[13] Between 1832 and 1835, scores of unscrupulous men, "jobbers," as Campbell called them, became quite adept at tricking the Indians out of their land allotments. According to Campbell, who vividly recounted the fraudulent nature of this pathetic affair,

> The Indian Treaty of 1832 provided for a reservation to Indians, of age, and to heads of families. A reservation might be sold by a reservee with the supervision and approval of an Agent appointed at Washington. The practice gave rise to the term, "stealing lands."
>
> The agent is corrupt. He certifies any *Indian* to be the Reservee, who is produced to be the Reservee. He hears the evidence of the value; the payment of the price to the Indian in his presence; and the making of a certificate of a fair sale. The Indian is paid in bank notes before the Certifying Agent, who makes an elaborate protocol. The Indian is carried out of sight, surrenders the bank notes to the purchaser, and receives whiskey [and] a few pieces of silver or calico. The reserve is sold.[14]

By Spring 1835, the Creeks had taken all of the abuse they could stand. "The privations, poverty, persecution of intruders and squatters," Campbell explained, "had driven the Indians to despair," and their hopelessness prompted small-scale violence against white homesteads and townships located along the Alabama-Georgia border.[15] When the Indian attacks became particularly acute in Macon and Russell Counties, white settlers petitioned Governor John Gayle for state protection. In late May 1835, the governor wrote to Secretary Cass, explaining that "it is certain [that] order cannot be maintained, and the laws executed, unless a military force be at hand to afford prompt assistance to the civil authorities." Troops would also be needed, he stated, to protect the citizens of Alabama and to ensure the peaceful transfer of Indian lands.[16]

Instead of dispatching federal troops to Alabama, however, Cass responded by sending John W. A. Sanford, the president of a company that had recently contracted with the federal government to distribute supplies the Creeks would need on their journey west. Sanford's principal assignment was to oversee the allotment of all Creek lands and to ensure that land sales were legitimate and legal. But Sanford was a poor choice; he was not beyond corruption and evidently engaged in fraud to enrich himself.[17] On 22 June 1835, though he refused to receive a deputation of Creeks led by Opothleyoholo, who wanted to complain about the fraud and abuse, and though he most certainly witnessed bogus sales on a regular basis, Sanford wrote Cass a grossly misleading letter, claiming that he could find "no facts . . . to discredit the proceedings which have hitherto taken place before me."[18]

Distraught that they could find no relief in Columbus, Opothleyoholo and a small number of Creek chiefs traveled to Montgomery and met with Campbell. It is ironic that the Creeks sought out Campbell's help, for it had been his father Duncan Greene, who had arranged the fraudulent Treaty of Indian Springs less than a decade earlier. The Creeks evidently never blamed the elder

Campbell for negotiating the treaty, however, and there was no animosity between the Creeks and John Archibald in 1835. In fact, these Upper Creeks obviously trusted him and believed that he could help. Campbell spent three weeks that summer in the Indian Territory, listening to the Creeks explain how they were being duped. He was genuinely concerned about the fraud, and yet there was little he could do to stop it.[19] The Indians with whom Campbell visited were not causing problems; they were peaceful and wished only to retain their property as provided by the treaty. A second group, however, independently engaged in violent acts that tainted the entire Nation.

The group of Creeks most responsible for the violence that occurred throughout 1835 and 1836 were led by Neamaltha, a renegade Seminole who had earlier been driven out of Florida by General Winfield Scott. Neamaltha was accompanied by Jim Henry, a twenty-year-old white man who at one time worked as a clerk for a Georgia land speculator but who, inexplicably, joined with Neamaltha's renegade Creeks in May 1835. By all accounts Henry was remarkably flamboyant, liked to wear "clothes of the finest broadclothe and cashmere," and "often looked more like a courtier than a warrior."[20] Despite his eccentric quirks and personal idiosyncrasies, Henry quickly proved his adeptness as a warrior when the Indian attacks intensified.

The immediate cause of the increased violence during the summer of 1835 was Sanford's refusal to acknowledge that most of the land sales were fraudulent. But the principal impetus for the violence of 1836 was the opening of the Seminole War in December 1835. The Seminoles' brave stand against a much larger United States force inspired the disenchanted Creeks, who sought to retaliate after their lands were stripped from them.[21]

During spring 1836, the Creeks attacked settlers at the Uchee Creek Bridge on the Federal Road. Several raids were also staged in Barbour County and at numerous locations in the Chattahoochee Valley. The most serious attacks occurred when the Creeks struck the towns of Irwinton (present-day Eufaula), Alabama, and, on 15 May, Roanoke, Georgia. Campbell wrote that the Creeks "were famished, miserable, and so pillagers—guilty of petty thefts. They burnt houses, stopped mails, and they were disorderly, unruly and injurious."[22] Panic erupted in the region as rumors of a general uprising spread throughout the white population. Some even believed, erroneously, as it turned out, that the infamous Seminole warrior Osceola had slipped into Alabama to lead attacks on white settlements.[23]

Meanwhile, Clement C. Clay replaced John Gayle as Alabama's governor in November 1835. Clay was determined not only to stop further Indian reprisals but also to ensure that all Creeks were expeditiously removed from Alabama.[24] For the first several months of his administration, Clay wrote Secretary Cass decrying the Indian attacks and demanding that federal troops be sent at once.[25] The Creek attack on Irwinton prompted the governor to order several divisions of the Alabama militia to assemble at Montgomery, and he placed General Benjamin Patterson in command of these forces.

When Clay summoned the militia, Campbell was attending federal court in Mobile. He immediately departed for Montgomery, and by the time he completed the 200-mile trip up the Alabama River, most of the militia had arrived and Clay had established a command center in town. The governor had become ill while traveling to Montgomery, however; Campbell later explained that he believed Clay had "a bilious fever of high type" brought on by "fatigue, exposure, and hard and exciting work." Campbell met with Clay upon his return to Montgomery "and found him delirious from fever." Unable to supervise military preparations, Clay appointed Campbell his aide-de-camp and charged him with organizing and supplying the troops then descending on Montgomery.[26]

By the middle of May nearly 1,500 men had arrived in Montgomery prepared to battle the Creeks. There was great excitement among the townspeople when rumors spread that large numbers of Indians were preparing to attack the town. Many people believed that the Creeks of the Upper Towns led by Opothleyoholo were also about to attack. To gauge the Upper Creeks' intentions, Clay issued a proclamation on 20 May, warning the Indians that when they "became subject to the laws of this state, [they] became bound" like all other Alabamians. Furthermore, he cautioned, the Creeks were by no means "permitted to carry on war against us, nor are you permitted to aid those who do carry on such war. If you do aid and comfort them, you are as guilty as if you had joined with them with arms in your hands."[27]

Opothleyoholo and the other Upper Creek chiefs must have been somewhat startled by Clay's proclamation, for they had not planned to join with Neamaltha's raiding forces, nor had they participated in any of the previous attacks. On 3 June, a deputation of thirteen chiefs led by Opothleyoholo rode to Montgomery and asked Campbell if they could meet with Governor Clay. Campbell readily agreed to make the arrangements at once. During their meeting held later that afternoon, the Upper Creeks consented not only to refrain from attacking white settlements but also to supply 400 warriors to fight with the Alabama militia against the Lower Creeks.[28] Two days later the governor ordered the militia to march to Tuskegee and prepare for an invasion into Lower Creek territory.

Meanwhile, the War Department in Washington finally decided to intervene before the Creeks engaged in additional hostilities in Alabama. Furthermore, because the belligerent Indians were located in present-day Barbour and Russell Counties, they had an easy escape route into the swamplands of Florida if they chose to flee. Cass was determined to prevent this occurrence, and so on 19 May he ordered Quartermaster General Thomas S. Jesup to Alabama "for the suppression of hostilities in the Creek country." "Your efforts," Cass informed Jesup, "will be directed to the unconditional submission of the Indians. . . . [T]hey must be disarmed, and sent immediately to their country west of the Mississippi." Cass posited that although most of the Creeks were peaceful and not involved in the current violence, they would most likely become hostile if not moved west as quickly as possible. The secretary was determined to remove the entire Nation by force if necessary.[29]

Within a few weeks, General Winfield Scott, who had recently been engaged in subduing the Seminoles in Florida, was sent to Columbus, Georgia, with seniority over Jesup and overall command. Scott initially decided that the most practical strategy to suppress the Creek uprising was to employ the federal forces in coordination with the Alabama and Georgia militia.[30] Scott ordered Jesup into Alabama to bivouac with the militia at Tuskegee and to form an advance line from the west. The original date for the beginning of operations was set for 5 June. The overall strategy was for the militia at Columbus to march westward while the forces at Tuskegee marched east. In this manner, General Scott reasoned, the entire army—which soon numbered over 12,000 men—could maneuver into a pincer designed to surround the Creeks and prevent their escape into Florida.[31]

Scott faced several irritating difficulties, however, that had to be overcome before he could implement his plan. First, rains so muddied the roads in the area that troops had considerable difficulty making their way to Columbus. Second, the Georgia militia had not been mustered into service as Scott originally thought, and valuable time was lost as the Georgians lumbered their way toward Columbus. A third problem for Scott was figuring out how to get Jesup to Tuskegee without being detected by the Creeks.[32]

Because of these obstacles, 5 June passed without any troop movement whatsoever. Scott informed Governor Clay that the entire operation had to be postponed until the fifteenth, but even that date was tenuous, for Jesup had not yet joined the forces in Alabama. Finally, during the early morning hours of 11 June, Jesup daringly crossed the Chattahoochee River with a force of 125 men and quickly rode the thirty miles to Tuskegee to assume command over the twelve companies positioned there. In light of the fact that Jesup traveled directly through the center of Creek Territory, his nighttime ride to Tuskegee was indeed bold. Campbell later describe it as "a very heroic achievement."[33]

When Jesup arrived in Tuskegee, he discovered that the Alabama forces mustered into service were hardly prepared for any major engagements. Governor Clay and Campbell labored diligently to supply the troops, but there were simply too few guns, rations, horses, and supplies of ammunition to provide adequately for the troops at Tuskegee. On 5 June Campbell left Montgomery and joined the militia to serve as the governor's personal representative and to coordinate supply shipments. He was assigned the full authority of an adjutant general.

Meanwhile Clay acted on his own initiative and ordered Major General William Irwin to Barbour County to ferret out the Creeks in the area. While at Claiborne, Irwin learned that the Indians had murdered a settler named Watson and were gathering in threatening numbers in a village near the town of Irwinton. He ordered a general assault on the Creek village but upon arrival found that the Indians had deserted their position and moved north into Russell County, where they joined the remaining renegade Creeks at Hatche-chubbee, Neamaltha's village.[34]

Jesup used the news of these "murders and conflagrations" in Barbour County as justification for bold and immediate action. Moreover, the constant and terribly vexing supply shortages convinced Jesup that he could not wait until the fifteenth before he moved against the Creeks; thus, he opted to march on the twelfth and if need be forage for food throughout Creek Territory. Perhaps Jesup was aware of the supply problems that had plagued Andrew Jackson's campaigns in 1814, and he knew the fickle nature of state militia with few supplies and hungry appetites. He therefore determined either to march at once or to dismiss the troops and return to Columbus without staging a single battle. Of course, to march before the fifteenth was a direct violation of Scott's orders. But Jesup was not the type of commander who allowed mere orders to interfere with his mission.[35]

Without consulting Scott, Jesup moved southeastward on the twelfth with twelve companies and 1,300 friendly Creeks "for the purpose," he later claimed, "of staying the tomahawk and scalping knife, and preventing the devastation of entire settlements."[36] Confident that he could end the Creek War within one week, Jesup moved rapidly into Creek Territory. As they entered Russell County, Jesup's forces happened upon a small band of Creeks led by none other than Neamaltha, who was captured without a struggle and was summarily imprisoned.[37] With the Creek leadership subdued, Jesup decided to attack Hatchechubbee and destroy all remaining Creek resistance.

On 17 June, Jesup ordered his forces to encamp a few miles west of Hatchechubbee alongside the northern fork of Cowikee Creek, and he planned to attack the village at dawn on the eighteenth. Word arrived from Columbus, however, that Scott had learned of Jesup's premature excursion and was irate. He then ordered Jesup to Columbus at once. Irked at his recall but not foolish enough to ignore General Scott completely, the insubordinate general ordered his troops to remain at their present location until his return. Later that evening Opothleyoholo, Big Warrior, and a Captain Walker, who, as Campbell explained, "was an Indian Country man with I don't know how many wives," met with Campbell and persuaded him to speak with the Creeks at Hatchechubbee.[38] The small deputation crossed Cowikee Creek and entered the village under flag of truce. Upon close inspection Campbell and the others saw that the Creeks were in a miserable state. Most appeared near starvation and were certainly no match for Jesup's forces.

The deputation asked to speak with the head chief, and they were escorted to see the Blind King, a very old Creek whose days as a warrior had long since passed. Campbell explained that the Creeks' cause was hopeless and that to protect their women and children, they must surrender as quickly as possible. He promised them "that if they would [surrender] quietly, when there was an old gun in their hands, a better gun should be given, that corn, corn-meal, bacon, [and] bread should be served. That calico clothes should be furnished to the ladies in the hostile branch and we would fight any who would harm them."[39] The Blind King told Campbell that he would discuss the offer with his warriors, and the deputation was led out of the village. Campbell and the others returned to camp to await the Creeks' answer.

Early the following morning a Creek messenger entered the militia camp and informed Campbell that the Blind King, who was waiting nearby, wished to speak with him. Campbell quickly mounted and rode across the Cowikee. As he approached the Creeks he saw the Blind King riding a pony. With daylight affording him a better view of this chief, Campbell saw that he was "shriveled and blind" and older than any person he had ever seen. When Campbell asked him his age, the old chief responded that "four generations of persons had been born and grown and passed away and he was here yet." Campbell noticed that most of the Creeks with the chief were women, some of whom carried "pickaninnies born within a day of the date."[40] This was no army of warriors; it was a pathetic group of worn and haggard Indians who had resorted to violence out of sheer desperation.

General Jesup returned to camp the following day and was surprised to learn that 300 warriors and 550 women had surrendered and were being fed and clothed. When Jesup met with Scott on 23 June, he informed the general that his campaign, although completely unauthorized, "broke the power of the hostile chiefs."[41] Scott was too good a commander to argue with success, and so he chose to ignore Jesup's earlier insubordination and unauthorized forays.

Campbell and the Alabama militia returned to Montgomery where jubilation over the victory swept through the city. The people were indeed proud of their fearless soldiers who subdued their "savage quarry" without quarter. Word quickly spread that the Creeks surrendered because Campbell had convinced them that they were defeated and their cause was hopeless. This much, of course, was true. Historians of later years, however, misinterpreted Campbell's role in the Creek War. For instance, L. D. Miller notes that Campbell "got them to surrender" and single-handedly ended the war. Miller fails to mention that the Creeks were already defeated and that Campbell simply told them what they already knew: they were completely surrounded, and there was no escape. The only choices remaining for them were surrender to or be slaughtered by Jesup's forces. In light of their predicament, nothing Campbell did should be given credit for "ending the war."[42]

Nonetheless, he arrived home to a hero's welcome. And in the mid-1830s war heroes often made successful politicians. Campbell's dreams of public service were still very much alive, and so he decided to run for a seat in the House as a representative of Montgomery County. He campaigned as a Democrat throughout July and August 1836, and he won the election with ease. At the young age of twenty-five, Campbell's dreams for political office were realized.[43]

In brief, politics in Alabama during the 1830s had already become about as nasty as anywhere in the country. During the 1820s, most of the leading men in the state avidly adhered to the principles espoused by Andrew Jackson. And in 1829 with the Hero of New Orleans in the presidential seat, most Alabamians were proud to have helped place him there. But very soon differences between Jackson and the several southern states surfaced. The Nullification Crisis in South Carolina, although seemingly parochial, sent tremors of discord throughout the South as people decried the danger to states' rights posed by increased federal authority. By 1830, Jackson's stance on nullification and his feud with Vice-President John C. Calhoun opened fissures within the state political machinery that changed forever the nature of Alabama politics.[44]

In Alabama, the vexing states' rights issue crept into state politics largely as a result of the ambiguities of the Treaty of Cusseta. When the state legislature divided the territory into counties and hordes of white settlers poured into Creek lands, the Washington government decided to use federal forces to oust squatters and to protect the Creeks' interests. Of course, this position angered many Alabamians, who assumed that the entire region was open for immediate settlement. Governor Gayle insisted that the federal government had no rights to intervene and that the legal disposition of lands within Alabama was a matter of states' rights. The Jackson administration was once again at odds with a southern state. Political factions quickly formed during 1832 and 1833 that either sanctioned or condemned Jackson's Indian policies and the increased concentration of the federal government's authority. A brief visit to Tuscaloosa by Francis Scott Key calmed tempers somewhat, but bitter antagonism still remained.[45]

Opposition to Jackson on the state and national levels lent impetus to the fledgling Whig party. With presidential hopeful Henry Clay at the helm, the Whigs gained considerable support throughout the country. During the 1830s, however, many southern Whigs were not in total agreement with the national party. Henry Clay's "American System," providing for internal improvements and higher tariffs, among other things, was at its core nationalistic. Yet southern concepts of states' rights were gradually overshadowing Clay's nationalism. What was becoming manifest in the South was a profound distrust of the central government—especially one that could not only usurp political authority from the states but could also pose a potential threat to slavery.

The adage that politics makes strange bedfellows certainly held true with regard to the anti-Jackson forces in Alabama. On the one hand, many disenchanted Democrats strayed from their party and proclaimed the sanctity of states' rights and nullification. These "nullies," as many contemporaries referred to them, were joined in their opposition by Whigs, who in fact favored states' rights as ardently as the nullies. With the nullies, the Whigs, and the pro-Jackson Democrats, there were in essence three parties in Alabama by 1835, the year before Campbell won election to the legislature.[46]

In mid-November 1836 Campbell arrived in Tuscaloosa and took his seat in the House of Representatives. Within one week, however, he seemed to have soured on any future political career. Politics was nasty business, and Campbell quickly became disgusted with the back-stabbing and petty politics in the statehouse. On 20 November 1836 he informed Henry Goldthwaite, who had moved to Mobile in 1832 and established an extremely lucrative practice: "The last week has glided away in doing nothing. We have passed no bills of genuine importance into law. We have discussed no matters of genuine interest. What will we do?"[47]

Campbell entered politics with an overly idealistic perception of the way business was transacted in Tuscaloosa. His attitude was remarkably naive, given that he normally kept abreast of events and voiced perceptions and judgments that were unusually astute. What Campbell did not seem to understand—nor ever fully comprehend—was the difference between a politician and a statesman. When he decided to enter politics, he genuinely hoped to serve the people of Montgomery County honorably. But he was not, nor would he ever become, a politician. He had little interest in or patience when it came to cultivating votes. Campbell certainly was not one to hobnob at dinner parties or barbecues—essential activities for any successful politician.[48]

What were Campbell's positions on the major issues and political divisions then tormenting the state? Two of his letters to Henry Goldthwaite in November 1836 answer this question. Campbell was a Democrat; he supported Jackson in 1828 and was genuinely pleased that Old Hickory had won the presidency. Echoing his innate nationalism, Campbell detested the "nullies"; he fervently believed that they were needlessly creating divisions within the state and throughout the country. He professed an uncompromising belief in the legitimacy of states' rights philosophy, yet he could never condone separate state action to nullify federal laws.[49]

At the same time, Campbell seemed to have developed a dislike for the Democratic leadership, particularly John McKinley of Madison County, whose nomination for United States senator in fall 1836 truly rankled Campbell. "He is an unspeakably weak man," he informed Goldthwaite, who "disgusts everyone" in the House with his demagoguery and rabble rousing.[50] "He is a feeble man," Campbell wrote in a second letter. "Not much superior to a common Methodist preacher."[51] Apparently, Campbell's loyalty to the pro-Jackson Democrats was less than absolute.

The contest for the United States Senate in November 1836 pitted pro-Jackson Democrat John McKinley against Arthur Francis Hopkins of Lawrence County, an ardent anti-Jacksonian who became one of Alabama's leading Whigs. Although he was a Democrat—and of course expected to vote for McKinley—Campbell complained that he "infinitely prefer[ed] Hopkins," who had earlier written a letter clarifying his views on a number of issues. According to Campbell, Hopkins "acknowledges the constitutionality of tariff laws, of internal improvements, and [of] the incorporation of a national bank."[52] The fact that Campbell "preferred" Hopkins suggested that he too held these views. Clay would have been proud to have Campbell join the Whigs; from an ideological perspective, his support of such nationalistic issues as protective tariffs and internal improvements would certainly have made him welcome among Whigs. Campbell also complained that he "felt degraded in voting for him [McKinley]."[53] Nonetheless, in this instance he disregarded his actual feelings and voted the party line.

Campbell informed Goldthwaite that when it came to a choice between the "nullies" and the "federalists," as he referred to the staunchly nationalistic forces, "I must be with the federalists." "My views [at] all time [are] in that direction," he explained, "and I am acting now with a party from all of whose tenets I feel I shall be opposed." Characteristically, he concluded by stating, "I do not wish, however, to criticize in public life."[54]

After only a brief period in Tuscaloosa, Campbell had become unquestionably disillusioned with politics. During the many debates in the House, he witnessed bitter arguments, lewd epithets, disorderly conduct, and on one occasion a brawl between two House members who had at least had the decency to carry their fisticuffs outside to the covered walk separating the house and senate chambers. Perhaps politics was better left to men who did not take life as seriously as did Campbell. "I keep out of all such scraps," he explained. By December he eagerly awaited the end of the session and hence an end to his political career. "I do not wish to continue in public life," he informed Goldthwaite. "[T]he law furnishes that kind of employment most congenial with my disposition."[55]

When he returned to Montgomery in the spring, Campbell was intent on quietly practicing law and providing for his family. The Panic of 1837, however, and the consequent financial chaos that swept the country produced such hardships in Alabama that a large portion of the population, saddled with debts it could not repay, faced economic ruin unless the state intervened and afforded relief.[56] Campbell wrote Governor Clay in early May urging him to summon a special session of the legislature to allay the financial crisis and to strengthen the state's banking system, which was on the verge of collapse.[57] Clay immediately heeded Campbell's advice.

In June 1837, Campbell returned to Tuscaloosa hopeful that a relief measure could be enacted, but he was not overly confident that the legislature could adequately respond to the crisis. Campbell supported a measure that he believed could bring relief to the farmers, namely repayment to the banks, which seriously—and chronically—overextended their lending capabilities, and an improved credit rating for the state.[58]

The relief bill approved that summer required the state to sell $5 million in bonds. All proceeds generated from the sale of these bonds were to be deposited in the several branches of the Bank of Alabama and used to provide emergency loans to farmers who could prove an inability to clear their debt. Campbell worked diligently in favor of the bill and on one occasion rose to address the House. He explained that he supported the bill because the farmers who received loans could easily repay them once they harvested their crops in August and September. The banks would receive their money, and the bonds would be paid before they reached maturity, thus saving the state interest payments.[59]

Campbell's speech "captivated the majority in the Legislature," and the bill was approved with little opposition.[60] Unfortunately, no one could have predicted the disastrous effects of the Panic of 1837, which all but crippled the state's economy. Consequently, when their crops ripened later that summer, many farmers were unable to sell them at reasonable prices. Borrowers were incapable of repaying emergency loans and the state was forced to remit interest on mature bonds. A second reason for the measure's failure was that the legislature relied on the state banks to distribute the funds. This arrangement proved problematic, because fraud and corruption so penetrated the banking system in Alabama that much of the money earmarked for debt-ridden farmers was invested irresponsibly and lost altogether. Campbell was more than simply disappointed that the relief measure failed. He became further convinced that it was perhaps best to steer clear of politics altogether.

Meanwhile, Governor Clay nominated Henry Goldthwaite to the Alabama Supreme Court. In August 1837, Campbell decided to assume Goldthwaite's share of the partnership and relocate his family to Mobile. Despite the economic mayhem produced by the Panic of 1837, the legal profession in that city was thriving, and Campbell expected to prosper in the new partnership.

"A growing family allowed of no diversion from professional prospects," he later wrote.[61]

Despite his reluctance to seek political office again, however, Campbell returned to the legislature during the 1842–1843 session after being persuaded to run by Benjamin Fitzpatrick. As noted above, during much of the 1820s and 1830s Fitzpatrick and Henry Goldthwaite had been partners in one of Montgomery's most active law firms. Fitzpatrick left the practice to seek political office, and his political career peaked in 1841 when he was elected governor. Fitzpatrick had won the election largely on promises of reforming the state's banking industry and bringing relief to thousands of Alabamians suffering from the economic chaos ushered in by the Panic of 1837.

By inauguration day for Fitzpatrick's first term in office, most privately owned banks throughout the state were near collapse, and the Bank of Alabama in Tuscaloosa, together with its branches in Montgomery, Mobile, Huntsville, Decatur, and Dothan, tottered on insolvency. Chartered by the state in 1823, the Bank of Alabama had enjoyed fourteen years of prosperity. In fact, the state bank had been so successful that in 1836 the legislature had abolished direct taxes and had relied solely on bank profits for the government's operations.[62] With the Panic of 1837, though, the bank's branches began experiencing financial difficulties, and in early May 1837 the Montgomery branch suspended specie payments. Two days later the branch of Mobile followed suit. Private banks, such as the Planters and Merchants Bank in Mobile, were likewise in serious jeopardy, and citizens throughout the state clamored for relief.[63]

During the next three years it became quite obvious to most Alabamians that their banking system was inherently weak and—as most people believed anyhow—thoroughly corrupt. There indeed was a profound underpinning of instability within the banking system that few people recognized until the Panic of 1837 and the near total collapse of the nation's economy. With little or no regulation, the several branches of the state bank had loaned money and had recklessly invested in railroads, real estate, cotton futures, canals, and many other financially risky ventures. Moreover, the bank was the willing financial agent for the hordes of land speculators in the state who hoped to reap enormous profits from land sales. With the revocation of direct taxes in 1836, the state's livelihood depended entirely on the bank's success. Thus, if the state bank failed, the state of Alabama would be obliged to declare bankruptcy and forced to default on all of its debt. As many Alabamians—including Governor Fitzpatrick—viewed this crisis, it portended disgrace and dishonor for the state and financial mayhem for its citizens.[64]

Fitzpatrick's first term as governor was successful in addressing the bank crisis primarily in that investigations into the bank's business affairs had uncovered an alarming number of corrupt legislators who owed money to the bank and who were determined that no potentially damaging legislation would be enacted. Soon after, the legislators summarily voted to adjourn without addressing the bank issue, and after reports of collusion and corruption reached the people, calls for immediate action were heard throughout the state. Recent research into the bank crisis has shown that the charges of corruption involving the state legislature were largely untrue and that most legislators actually owed little or no money to the bank.[65] Nevertheless, perception often being more powerful than reality, the mere charge of corruption was sufficient to arouse public sentiment firmly against the bank. Newspapers throughout the state, including the powerful and influential *Mobile Register,* printed inflammatory editorials chastising the banks and their directors and swelling the number of antibank reformers. Clearly, momentum for reform throughout the spring of 1842, however extreme, portended a dark future for the Bank of Alabama.[66]

In early summer Fitzpatrick "had long and earnest consultations" with Campbell and Henry Goldthwaite—both of whom were in Tuscaloosa for the Supreme Court's summer session.[67] The governor convinced Campbell that the administration urgently needed legislative allies if bank reform was to be realized, and so Campbell temporarily abandoned his self-imposed exile from state politics and on 29 June announced that he would stand for election as a representative from Mobile County. Campbell's opponent in this race was Robert C. McAlpin, a Whig who had abandoned his party's probank stance and, in a gesture indicative of bank reform's popularity with the populace, insisted that all state banks must be closed immediately. "Wind up! CLOSE up," he exclaimed at a political rally in Mobile. "Place the keys [to the banks] in the hands of the Commissioners."[68] Campbell, on the other hand, suggested closing merely banks that were obviously so insolvent as to make their recovery impossible. He insisted, however, that the state must divorce itself entirely from the banking business. Involvement in banking, he asserted, damaged the government's ability to govern. It had led to political corruption and held the potential for even greater corruption that could render the government little more than the pawn of the state's monied interests.[69]

With such speeches, Campbell revealed a deep anticorruption bias that clearly reflected Jacksonian ideology and sentiment. He saw no need to destroy the bank to save the state, however. As would become apparent many times throughout his career, Campbell was not antibusiness; he lived in what was during normal economic times the state's most thriving commercial center, and Campbell had extensive personal business and commercial interests. Still, he harbored deep aversion and distrust of corporations and monopolies whose economic clout held the potential for control of state and local governments. In Campbell's mind, this would be a flagrant usurpation of the sovereign power vested in the people, and thus, corporations, banks, and monopolies had to be closely regulated to ensure that their activities would in no measure undermine government's responsibility to the people.

Campbell's public speeches in Mobile apparently helped ensure a close victory in August. In fact, momentum for bank reform had grown so strong throughout the summer that many of the previous legislature's bank allies had been driven from office and replaced by antibank men hell-bent on the bank's complete destruction. Once the people of Alabama believed that their banking industry was hopelessly insolvent and riddled with corruption and that corrupt legislators deeply indebted to the bank were acting as its guardians, the citizens voted overwhelmingly to usher in sweeping reforms. During the four months between the election and the convening of the legislature, several branches of the state bank and the Planters and Merchants Bank of Mobile suspended specie payment and called in many loans in an effort to restore financial stability. This measure, however, did little else than further enrage a population already suffering the effects of the prolonged panic. Despite actions taken by the banks to restore solvency and to ward off potentially damaging legislation, bank reform was obviously to be the leading issue for the new legislature.[70]

Soon after the election, Campbell began investigating the bank, and he prepared reports and recommendations to the governor.[71] When the legislators convened in Tuscaloosa in early December, they were greeted with a lengthy message from Fitzpatrick unequivocally stating that bank reform would not succumb to the same political intrigues that had stymied such efforts in the previous legislature. Fitzpatrick reminded the assembly that the state was blessed with fertile soil and an industrious and educated population that could make it "one of the great producing states of the Union," but he noted that as long as the "population [remained] disenthralled from that load of debt and pecuniary embarrassment" brought on by "unprecedented bank expansions and contractions," a return to prosperity would remain an unrealized vision.[72]

Spearheading bank reform in the House, Campbell was named chair of the powerful Committee on the State Bank and Branches, and from this position he wielded considerable influence over committee reports and legislation regarding the banks. Campbell began his assault on the banks by issuing a report exceedingly damaging to the Planters and Merchants Bank of Mobile, which had suspended specie payments on 25 October. He asserted that this suspension was unwarranted in that it was "not occasioned by any sudden panic in the community in regard to [the bank's] condition." Instead, this action was a reflection that the bank was unable to meet its financial obligations due to extraordinary losses through unwise loans. For this reason Campbell recommended that "the franchise of banking should be withdrawn and the bank placed in a condition for liquidation and settlement." Campbell reported that the Planters and Merchants Bank was no different from other banks in

Alabama and that, due to "improvident loans, some blind practices, wild speculations, and great profusion," extraordinary and immediate measures were necessary to afford relief.[73]

Campbell recommended that every branch of the Bank of Alabama had to be investigated and its stability measured against its liabilities. To assist with this task, he suggested that a special Committee of Thirteen be appointed "to take into consideration . . . all questions in relation to the embarrassments that exist in a pecuniary condition of the citizens of this State" and to draft the necessary legislation that could ease the crisis.[74]

On 19 December Campbell and his committee issued a lengthy report to the assembly outlining the general recommendations in regard to the state banks. "The people of the state," the report stated, "bear at this time evils of no ordinary magnitude." The crisis, according to Campbell, had been instigated largely by "rash adventure and giddy speculation" and had nearly wrecked the state's economy. It was an "embarrassment [that] interrupts the transaction of civil and commercial intercourse." Campbell acknowledged that all businesses assumed varying degrees of risk as an accepted norm of conducting business. He cited the ill effects of reckless adventure and irresponsible investments, however, in which the banks had taken part with little or no effort to weigh the risks against the costs and the possible losses. The crisis affected not only the commercial interests but all of the state's people. Campbell wrote that the "effects on the laboring man" were even "more oppressive" than on the wealthy classes. "His [the wage laborer's] means of subsistence are exposed to danger." This in turn, he warned, could literally erode the character of the people like a cancer.

> Experience has shown [the working man] that a steady demand, and certain wages for his labor, is the condition most suitable to his condition in society. A variable and depreciated currency deranges all the regular operations of society. The capitalist refuses to make investments, because all is uncertain. He hopes that each day will afford a better market; hence, employment to the laborer becomes uncertain and difficult. The effect of this is to reduce his wages. His embarrassments are not ended, however, even when employment is obtained and his wages paid. The uncertainty in the value of the currency leads him into immediate and probably improvident expenditures. He does not know how long the bill he receives will retain its present value: hence, idleness and intemperance frequently result—for, confidence being destroyed, and confusion of mind substituted for it, the tendencies of the human character are to immorality, dissoluteness, and crime.[75]

The above passage shows not only that Campbell believed the crisis extensive but also that he believed economic crises in general produce societal deterioration. The passage reflects the thoughts and concerns of an extremely conservative individual who—in line with strict Presbyterian upbringing—

considered human nature at its core corrupt and prone to idleness. Unless the average working individual maintained employment and decent wages, Campbell asserted, he will most likely become lazy, seek solace in alcohol, or resort to criminal activity. Thus, the legislature was duty bound to ensure a sound economy and a stable employment environment. Otherwise the character of the people would erode to levels that could ultimately destroy society.

Considering the dire foreboding Campbell associated with the current crisis, it seems curious that he would recommend rather mild reforms. His report of 19 December included six recommendations for the legislature's consideration; yet none recommended that the banking system be dismantled altogether. Instead, Campbell proposed that the branch banks at Mobile and at Decatur be liquidated and that the main bank at Tuscaloosa and the remaining branch banks be closely regulated but open for business as soon as each was prepared to renew specie payments. In the final analysis, Campbell's report reveals that he was not guided by the extreme antibank rhetoric that had characterized the recent general elections. It was the legislature's duty, he advised, "[t]o move with no sudden, hasty, or violent effort, but with a calm and fixed purpose to attain" economic stability.[76]

Almost predictably, the harsh rhetoric and predictions of dire consequences uttered by Governor Fitzpatrick and Chairman Campbell and printed in many newspapers throughout the state greatly alarmed an already uneasy populace. With popular sentiment building strongly against the state banks, legislators—blindly responding to the demands of their constituents—formed an antibank bandwagon in the assembly that by late December reached fever pitch and was swirling out of control. In this environment Campbell's moderate bank reforms evaporated within a few weeks into more radical proposals requiring that the entire bank system be altogether abolished. Despite efforts to restore the initial proposals, the current against the banks became unstoppable, and both Campbell and the governor feared that the state would be left with no financial institutions whatsoever.[77]

Throughout the last two weeks of January several measures were enacted by the assembly that effectively liquidated each state bank. All that remained was the tedious work of "winding up" the affairs of the banks and ensuring that no future loans or investments be made. The process of liquidation, however, proved extremely complex and time consuming, so much so that the Bank of Alabama continued in operation reclaiming bad debts and selling real estate throughout the decade. In early 1847, Francis S. Lyon of Mobile County was commissioned by the legislature as "Sole Commissioner and Trustee" of the state bank and branches to assume control over all bank assets and to complete the final liquidation procedures.[78] According to Campbell, "The measures for liquidation were not perfected" until Lyon undertook the task of thoroughly investigating each branch and collecting as many of the bad debts as possible.[79] In 1853 Lyon presented a lengthy report to the House of Representatives informing the members that the liquidation process was complete and the banks could be officially closed.

More than a decade passed, therefore, between Campbell's last term as a state representative and final liquidation of the banks. His efforts as chairman of the bank committee were widely praised by his contemporaries and subsequently by historians chronicling the state bank crisis. Campbell had agreed to serve in the assembly solely to remedy what both he and Governor Fitzpatrick perceived as a crisis of far-reaching proportions. Once again Campbell had shown that he could be an extremely effective legislator. At the same time, however, he once again displayed mind-boggling naiveté about politics and politicians. Though he approached bank reform cautiously and wished to proceed slowly, his scathing reports to the assembly acted as a catalyst and reinforced pressure to liquidate the entire system.

Campbell was no doubt pleased when the session adjourned and he could return to Mobile, to his family, and to his thriving law practice, which he had been forced to neglect for the previous several months. He never again sought or served in any elected office. His focus in 1843 remained, as it had been in 1837, his family and his legal career. Campbell's dream of a political career evaporated when he realized that he was temperamentally unsuited to it. He moved his family to Mobile, in essence, to begin a new life more serene and more focused on his family.

3 | Submerged Lands and States' Rights

The 1830s and 1840s marked a period of genuine accomplishment in Campbell's career. His move to Mobile placed him amid a web of lucrative litigation, primarily concerning land disputes, that brought him recognition, wealth, and prestige. He was viewed as one of the most talented lawyers in the state, and his arguments before the state supreme court won him high praise and eventually national attention. To this point in his career he had been only indirectly involved in the volatile issue of states' rights, for example when the state of Alabama refused to recognize Indian titles according to the Treaty of Cusseta. But his sympathies then seemed more closely aligned with the Creeks than with either the state or the federal government. Beginning in the late 1830s, during a series of land dispute cases in Mobile, Campbell's courtroom arguments created the impression that he was one of the South's most indefatigable champions of states' rights philosophy. This widely held perception was, however, fundamentally incorrect. It was based solely on arguments Campbell had used to win cases and not necessarily on any personal convictions he held regarding states' rights and the authority of the federal government. Campbell unquestionably favored states' rights, but his sentiments were strongly tempered by a recognition that the federal government was vested with significant authority to regulate many aspects of American society.

In August 1837, the Campbell family boarded one of the many newly built steamboats that plied the Alabama and Tombigbee Rivers and made their way toward Mobile. Unlike Montgomery, which in 1837 was less than thirty years old and still retained much of its frontier infrastructure, Mobile had been established for over 120 years. Yet in many respects the port city languished for most of that period, experienced little growth, and appeared less than finished. Founded in 1701, Mobile had been governed by four sovereign nations during its existence: France, 1701–1763; Great Britain, 1763–1780; Spain, 1780–1813; and the United States after 1813.[1] This assortment of national ties produced a diverse population uncharacteristic of the nation as a whole. After James Madison ordered Major General James Wilkinson, the commander at New Orleans, to take possession of Mobile in February 1813, Alabama residents quickly swelled that city's population.[2]

By the early 1820s, when the cotton boom that was to define not only Alabama but the entire antebellum period took shape, Mobile was regarded by many south Alabamians as the most accessible port for shipping cotton to European markets.[3] Between 1813 and 1822 the city's population increased from 300 to 2,800 full-time residents. By 1824 there were 240 houses, about 40 streets—there had been only 8 streets in 1815—and 110 stores and warehouses, respectable figures for a small city.[4] Yet most of these structures presented a hodgepodge of architectural styles that hardly impressed European travelers who came to visit. Many of them contemptuously noted the lack of culture and high society in Mobile. One Englishman reported that he "saw more of men than of manners" at one of the local boardinghouses in town. He also marveled at the amazing swiftness with which residents gobbled their meals; ten to twenty minutes was apparently about as long as it took to satisfy one's appetite.[5]

Despite its lack of social graces, Alabama's "Metropolis by the Sea" was rapidly becoming one of the South's most important port cities. The old and dilapidated Fort Charlotte, built originally by the French in 1717, had by 1820 fallen into disrepair.[6] The city government ordered it razed in 1821 to improve the waterfront property. By 1824, residents had filled in the submerged lands just east of Royal Street and had constructed several new wharves soon to be congested with oceangoing ships en route to European ports.[7] These improvements allowed the city front along the Mobile River to accept deep-draft ships, and as the commercial interests in the city increased throughout the 1820s, Mobile experienced unprecedented growth.

Cotton exports from Mobile grew in proportion to the rise of cotton production in central and southern Alabama. In 1819, the year Alabama achieved statehood, only 10,000 bales were produced in southern Alabama. Ten years later over 100,000 bales were exported out of Mobile. During the next decade, Mobile surpassed Charleston and Savannah, with exports totaling over $66 million. In contrast, only $4.5 million in merchandise was imported during the same period.[8] This phenomenal rise in export and commercial activity certainly made Mobile one of the South's premier cities. There were many opportunities for wealth and prestige, particularly for lawyers who settled the many conflicting land claims then clogging the courts. This, of course, was the primary reason Campbell moved his family to Alabama's port city in 1837.[9]

When Campbell arrived in Mobile, he was accompanied by his wife, Anne, and their two children, Henrietta, born 21 February 1832, and Duncan Greene, born 7 November 1835. During the next decade, the Campbell family was enlarged by four girls: Katherine Rebecca, born 26 August 1839; Mary Ellen, born 1 August 1842; Anna, born 8 August 1844; and Clara, born 13 January 1847.[10] Even with such a large family, Campbell earned enough income through law practice in Mobile to provide a comfortable living. After Henry Goldthwaite's departure to Alabama's Supreme Court in 1837, Campbell established a partnership with Robert A. Gordon and they opened an office on Dauphin Street. Soon after Campbell and Gordon opened their office, however, the latter decided to retire. Campbell then invited his brother-in-law Daniel Chandler to join the practice.

Daniel Chandler and Sarah Campbell were married in Montgomery in 1832, and the couple soon thereafter relocated to Mobile. Chandler was originally from Georgia and was educated at the state university in Athens. Interestingly, Chandler, like Duncan Greene Campbell, championed education for women. Chandler's sentiments regarding the woeful condition of female education were evident when he was asked to deliver the commencement address at his alma mater in May 1835; he eloquently and forcefully reminded his audience that but one-half of white southerners had access to a full education. "The intellectual capabilities of females," Chandler stated, "have never been fairly developed." He argued that women were "by no means deficient in the sprightliness of imagination, quickness of perception, [or] originality of thought." "Give the female the same advantage with the male," Chandler urged. "Afford her the same opportunities for improvement."[11] His speech was so impressive that the university's Demosthenian Society ordered 5,000 copies printed and circulated.[12] Chandler's abilities as an attorney complemented Campbell's legal acumen and remarkable skills, and their partnership continued until March 1853.

One longtime associate commented that Campbell's "stature, his features, his look, his bearing—his whole presence was commanding."[13] Bernard Reynolds, a resident of Selma who regularly visited Mobile, remembered that Campbell was "above the common height" and was noted for nervously tugging at his ample eyebrows as he leisurely strolled along Mobile's streets. In recreating commonly viewed scenes in Mobile, Reynolds wrote:

> If you look at [the corner of Royal and St. Francis Streets], you will see a man coming north from Dauphin Street, walking quietly and leisurely. He stops at the corner, and after looking down St. Francis Street, he puts his left hand behind his back, and raising his right hand begins to pull at his eyebrows. He is above the common height and has a good figure; he is neatly dressed in black, which at once indicates that he is of the legal profession. But his face will attract your attention, and at the first glance you will recognize the fact that he is a man of mark. In his pale face, aquiline nose and quiet grey eye you see one of the lawyers who leave a deep trace on the road they travel, and also mark their names on the tablets of history with indelible fame. . . . It is almost superfluous to state that the notable person of whom we speak is Judge John A. Campbell, . . . the first lawyer of Alabama.[14]

A one-time editor of the *Mobile Register,* Erwin Craighead, wrote that Campbell's "apparent character was like the firefly's lamp: light, without heat." He continued that Campbell was "a master of reasoning, profound in logic and inspired by a commanding sense of justice." Craighead also quoted Rev. J. J. Hutchinson of Mobile, who once remarked that Campbell was "all head and no heart."[15] Of course, most people were acquainted with Campbell only on a professional basis—one that, as earlier shown, was indeed impersonal. Had they known more of Campbell's personal life, particularly his relationship with his daughters, perhaps they would have altered their impressions somewhat.

It is interesting to study Campbell's relationship with his children. By reading his personal letters, one discovers that he loved his daughters dearly. Nearly every note to Anne ends with the phrase "Kiss my daughters for me." But on those few occasions when he mentioned Duncan, he exhibited a stern disciplinary nature. Campbell clearly harbored a double standard with regard to his children. He placed women upon a pedestal and displayed a staunch belief in what some historians today term the "Cult of Domesticity." Women were to be protected, nurtured, and revered. The world outside the home was designed solely for men; women served to provide a safe haven from the outside world so that children could mature in relative bliss, while men could return each evening to a sanctuary far removed from the cutthroat, highly competitive business world. Young men, on the other hand, were to busy themselves in serious and productive study in preparation for professional life. This was the type of childhood that Campbell had experienced, and he reared Duncan in much the same manner. While his only son was young, Campbell's notions of childraising caused little grief in the household. When Duncan grew into his twenties, however, he rebelled against his disciplinarian father and sought solace in bottles of whiskey. As he watched his son grow into an alcoholic, Campbell expressed little pity or sympathy because he believed that a dependence on alcohol was but another indication of a weak constitution and a flawed character. As a result, John Archibald and Duncan remained all but estranged for most of their lives.[16]

Upon their arrival in Mobile, the family resided in Henry Goldthwaite's house, located at the corner of Government and Anne Streets. This was a modest, two-story dwelling that soon became too small for his growing family. In 1843, the Campbells moved to a larger, brick home at the southwest corner of Conception and Church Streets. Campbell's success at the bar allowed him to furnish his home elegantly and to collect one of the largest libraries in the country.[17] His decision to move to Mobile had indeed paid off handsomely.

Campbell's Mobile law firm specialized in the many land dispute cases brought before the state circuit court in Mobile and in Alabama's Supreme Court. And it was while he argued these cases that Campbell truly distinguished himself from most Alabama attorneys. Throughout the 1820s and 1830s Mobile became a veritable goldmine for attorneys, as ownership for much of the land in the city was in dispute. The most valuable land, of course, was located immediately adjacent to the Mobile River. Huge financial rewards could be had if one were to fill in the tidelands and construct wharves to accept the many ships seeking dockage. Throughout the 1830s, however, numerous disputes over title to those lands filled court dockets. Between 1838 and 1852, twenty suits of ejectment, collectively known as the "submerged lands cases," became Campbell's principal focus, although these cases were considered "unwinnable" by many of his colleagues.[18]

The litigation over submerged lands was no small matter for two critical reasons. First, considering the enormous acreage lying beneath tidewaters from Florida's northeastern border to, eventually, the northwestern tip of Alaska, the aggregate value of this real estate was astronomical. In Mobile, for instance, just one "water lot" that underwent substantial improvements was valued at $88,000 in 1842.[19] Second, these cases were largely argued by Campbell on the basis of states' rights versus the authority of the federal government. When the submerged lands issue was finally settled in 1845, it had been decided that states, and not the federal government, held exclusive proprietary rights over submerged lands and that Congress had erred when it granted titles to properties along Mobile's waterfront.

The background to the submerged lands litigation is relatively uncomplicated. During the Spanish period in Mobile's history, the Madrid government granted a large number of claims to persons living in the Mobile area. Many of these grants were for what were then called "water lots," meaning the land immediately adjacent to the Mobile River that received the ebb and flow of the daily tides, and each grantee was afforded full riparian rights and responsibilities. As much of this land was submerged daily, it was wholly unusable unless extensive improvements, that is, filling in, were made.[20]

Between the signing of the secret Treaty of San Ildefonso in 1800 and the Adams-Onis Treaty in 1819, the area then known as West Florida was claimed by both Spain and the United States. After the United States acquired the Louisiana Territory in 1803, Spain continued to occupy and grant lands in West Florida to various individuals, most of whom never made improvements to these lands but claimed full title nonetheless. On 22 February 1819, Secretary of State John Quincy Adams and Spanish minister to the United States Don Luis de Onis completed negotiations that recognized American ownership of both East and West Florida. Article 6 of this treaty stipulated that all Spanish subjects then residing in the ceded territory would immediately become United States citizens with full privileges, rights, and immunities granted under the Constitution. Most significantly, article 8 provided: "All the grants of land made before the 24th of January 1818 by his Catholic Majesty or by his lawful authorities in the said Territories ceded by his Majesty to the United States, shall be ratified and confirmed to the persons in possession of the lands, to the same extent that the same grants would be valid if the Territories had remained under the Dominion of his Catholic Majesty."[21] Clearly this treaty validated all Spanish grants made between 1803 and 1819 and afforded those persons holding land titles full rights to retain their property despite the transfer of ownership. Although seemingly an insignificant stipulation, the Adams-Onis Treaty also provided that each Spanish land grant had to be confirmed by an act of Congress.

Five weeks later, on 2 March 1819, Congress enacted legislation permitting the people of the Alabama Territory to draft a constitution and be admitted to the Union "on an equal footing with the original states, in all respects whatever." The Alabama Enabling Act further established Alabama's borders at their present location, including all lands "to the Gulf of Mexico." But this legislation made no mention of title to submerged lands along Alabama's southern coast, particularly those along the Mobile River.[22]

During the 1820s, few substantial improvements were made to the waterfront lots in Mobile. But several industrious individuals filled in their lots and constructed wharves that spanned to the river and allowed for the loading and unloading of cargo for a fee charged to ship owners. In 1823 the city government appropriated $400 to fill in the submerged lands between Church and Government Streets, and it constructed several wharves that generated considerable revenue. As a result, most waterfront properties appreciated far beyond their original value. The city further claimed title to the submerged lands immediately south of its newly built wharves situated between Water and Commerce Streets. On 20 May 1824, in accordance with the Adams-Onis Treaty, Congress enacted the Confirmatory Law acknowledging the City of Mobile's title to all water lots lying between Government Street and the southernmost tip of Water Street.[23] The city then contended that it held undisputable rights to those lots described above.

For the next several years the city operated its wharves between Church and Government Streets, but it neglected to improve the land situated between Water and Commerce Streets. Because of the various conflicting grants made by the United States and by Spain, however, several of these lots had more than one legitimate owner. In 1822 the Lot Company of Mobile acquired considerable properties bordering the river. It paid to have this land surveyed and subdivided into lots, one of which was sold to Charles L. Mathews of Mobile in 1823. From that year until 1833, Mathews paid taxes on this property and made several improvements at different intervals, including constructing a sidewalk around its perimeter as ordered by the city. In 1833, unable to afford the taxes on his property, Mathews leased his lot to Miguel D. Eslava, a wealthy real estate broker who owned several cotton warehouses in the city. In 1837 Eslava began making improvements to the lot, filling in most of it and beginning the construction of a wharf. At this juncture the city intervened, insisting that by the congressional act of 1824 Mathews's claim to the property was void and that consequently Eslava had no rights to construct a wharf.[24]

Seeking redress, Eslava went to the offices of Campbell and Gordon. The facts in this case suggest that neither Mathews nor Eslava had any rights whatsoever to the property. The Confirmatory Law of 1824 clearly stated that the disputed water lots were "vested in the Mayor and Aldermen of [Mobile], for the time being, and their successors in office, for the sole use and benefit for the [City of Mobile] forever."[25] Given the specific language of this act, it seemed that Campbell had undertaken an unwinnable case. Nonetheless, he agreed to represent Eslava, and he filed suit in the Mobile circuit court, which, to the astonishment of many observers, ruled in his client's favor. The city at once appealed to Alabama's supreme court, and the case of *Mayor of Mobile v. Eslava* was docketed for the January 1839 term.[26]

While Campbell was preparing a defense in the *Eslava* case, his services were requested for a similar dispute over a second conflicting land claim. The facts surrounding this litigation, which on appeal was heard by Alabama's supreme court as *Heirs of Pollard v. Kibbe*, differed slightly—but significantly—from those in Eslava's case. In 1802, John Forbes and Company had received a grant from the Madrid government recognizing title to several water lots extending as far south as Government Street. On 11 December 1809 William Pollard, a resident of Mobile, petitioned the Spanish intendant in West Florida, Cayetano Pérez, for the formal grant of a vacant water lot—part of the same grant that had been given to Forbes in 1802—situated along the Mobile River and just north of Government Street "to give more facility to his trading." Evidently Pollard made little improvements to his lot except for removing "some wreck and driftwood" in 1814.[27]

In 1823, a third party, Curtis Lewis of Mobile, assumed possession of the lot and filled in an area eighty feet eastward to the low water mark and about fifty feet north of Government Street, encroaching on the lot ostensibly owned by both Pollard and Forbes. As noted above, in May 1824 Congress granted the city of Mobile full title to all water lots between Government Street and the southern end of Water Street. As of that year, Pollard's heirs, Forbes, Lewis, and the city of Mobile all claimed demesne to the disputed lot.

Complicating matters even further was that in 1836 Congress enacted a second Confirmatory Law similar to that passed twelve years earlier and re-establishing the city of Mobile's title to most of the submerged lands bordering the river. But by then the city had already disposed of much of its land. In 1835, Gaius Kibbe purchased the city's, Forbes's, and Lewis's claims to the lot.

Only two parties remained in the dispute, and in 1837 the heirs of Pollard initiated a suit of ejectment to have Kibbe removed from the property. Representing Kibbe, Campbell used the same argument as in the *Eslava* case. The Circuit Court of Mobile ruled in favor of Kibbe's claim, and the case was appealed to the state supreme court, which heard arguments during the same January 1839 term, when the *Eslava* case reached the docket.[28]

Although Campbell's arguments in these cases were not recorded by the supreme court's clerk, the justices' rulings in Porter's *Alabama Reports* make his reasoning plain. Despite the laws passed by Congress in 1824 and again in 1836 confirming the city's title to the disputed lot, Campbell argued, Eslava was the only proper owner because Congress had no authority to give away land belonging to the state of Alabama. The act of 1819 enabling the inhabitants of the Alabama Territory to form a constitution and be admitted to the Union provided that the state would enter "on an equal footing" with the original states. And as each of the original states had full jurisdiction and sovereignty over the tidewaters within their borders, Alabama too had been given this right upon its admission in 1819. In all cases, original sovereignty passed to each state "on an equal footing" whenever a new state was admitted. The federal laws confirming grants to property in Mobile were therefore void, according to Campbell, because this property was solely within Alabama's domain. The phrase "original sovereignty," carried to its logical extreme, was indeed controversial. It could be construed as meaning that state sovereignty predated the Constitution, so that states might claim supreme authority in cases involving conflicts between the federal government and the states. Moreover, this construction portended future—and far more serious—disputes between the state and federal governments that would eventually lead to the dissolution of the Union.[29]

In delivering his opinion in the *Eslava* case, Chief Justice Henry W. Collier, a well-known states' rights Democrat,[30] noted that he would waive "a particular examination of the act of 1824 [and] proceed to consider an argument made for the defendant, which, if well founded, will render unnecessary an analysis of the act [of 1824]." Collier wrote:

> It was argued for the defendant that even if the act of 1824, according to a just interpretation of its terms, conferred upon the plaintiffs the interest of the United States of the property in question, yet the act was wholly inoperative, because no title was vested in the United States, which could be granted by Congress—That the act of 1819, to enable the people of the Alabama Territory to form a constitution, on an equal footing with the original states, dedicated, *in express terms,* to the free use of the citizens of this state and the United States, the navigable waters within the limits of the former. That this dedication embraced so much of the soil as was covered by water, not only at low, but at high tide, so as to place it beyond the just powers of

the Federal government to grant the same. . . . *And further*—that as the sovereign power of the State is the proprietor of the tide waters, in trust, for a public, it is incompetent, even by an act of legislation, to grant the space intervening between high and low water marks.[31]

This passage from the pages of *Porter's Reports* is quite remarkable. Campbell and Collier had in essence advanced a new and altogether novel expression of states' rights that might be viewed as an attempt to establish state judicial review over federal statutes. But even more to the point, Campbell expounded a theory of state interposition that well surpassed even Calhoun's version of nullification. Did Campbell mean for the Supreme Court of Alabama to assume the power to nullify federal statutes? In view of his earlier statements on the Nullification Crisis and his utter scorn for those individuals in the state who believed that state interposition was perfectly legitimate, Campbell could hardly be regarded as trying to strengthen the theory of nullification. On the contrary, he most assuredly hoped that the submerged land cases would be heard by the United States Supreme Court, the ultimate judicial authority in the interpretation of federal laws.

One of the most significant aspects of Campbell's argument in the submerged land cases was that he presented it exclusively for the benefit of existing states and made no mention of territories. Original sovereignty was applicable only after the people of a territory had been expressly granted permission by Congress to draft a constitution and apply for statehood. Once a new state entered the Union, Campbell claimed, it held all rights and privileges of the original states, including rights to define property and to grant lands. Implicit in his argument—and in agreement with his earlier statements concerning the powers of the federal government—was the assertion that in accordance with article 4, section 3 of the federal Constitution, Congress possessed extensive powers to regulate the internal affairs of territories, including the right to grant lands and to define what might or might not be held as property. The right of states to define private property was, therefore, inherited from the federal government at the time of their admission. Implicit in Campbell's argument was that had the federal government chosen, for instance, to abolish slavery in Alabama while it was a territory from 1817 to 1819, it would have been perfectly within its right to do so.

Justice Collier, on the other hand, went well beyond Campbell's reasoning and asserted that all lands ultimately belonged to the people and that Congress had no authority to issue land grants in either states or territories. The justice maintained that jurisdiction over private property rights was exclusively reserved to the states, and as any territory was in reality an embryonic state or group of states, Congress could not assume powers that would prospectively undermine property rights in those regions. All property rights, he insisted, derived originally from the British crown. "The rights of property in the *navi-*

gable waters," Collier wrote, "conferred upon the colonies by the royal char-
ters, have never been relinquished to the United States. . . . The right of property, which was given to the 'original states,' by the King of Great Britain,
when they were his colonies, is still retained."[32] As new states were to enter
the Union "on an equal footing" with other states, Congress could not enact
legislation that would in any way originate, define, or limit the people's right
to property.

Collier's 1839 ruling bore directly on the submerged lands bordering the
Mobile River. His version of the original sovereignty doctrine, however, was
as equally applicable to many questions involving Congress's powers to regulate the territories—the most volatile of which was whether Congress held
authority to regulate slavery in the territories. With the rise of the abolition
movement during the 1830s and 1840s—coupled with an almost universal demand from many quarters throughout the northern states that any new territory acquired by the United States be reserved exclusively for free labor—the
extension of slavery to the territories became the most divisive issue of the era.
In Collier's view, Congress could not pass legislation that would define what
may or may not be held as property in the territories. Any law, in other words,
barring slavery from United States territories was unconstitutional. Thus, the
Alabama justice used Campbell's argument as the foundation for an especially
forceful statement on states' rights. Campbell's political views as of 1839 were
far too moderate and nationalistic for him to have agreed with the concepts
expressed by Collier. Nevertheless, he was not one to argue with a judge who
had just ruled in his client's favor.

Campbell's second case heard before the state supreme court that term,
Heirs of Pollard v. Kibbe, also went before the United States Supreme Court.[33]
Before it reached that level, however, Campbell employed the same argument
for Kibbe's rights to the disputed lot that he had used in *Eslava.* In this case,
Justice John J. Ormond, a former Whig state representative from Lawrence
County, drafted the decision of the court—one that differed markedly from
Collier's ruling in *Eslava.*[34] After reviewing the title history of the particular
lot in dispute, Ormond ruled that Kibbe's claim was valid solely because it
passed originally from John Forbes, who had received a patent from Congress.
Ormond refused to consider Campbell's argument that Congress had no
authority to confirm land grants. He instead asserted that Spain had ceded West
Florida to France not by the Treaty of San Ildefonso but de facto. When the
United States purchased the Louisiana Territory in 1803, all lands situated between the Perdido and Iberville Rivers south of the Thirty-first Parallel con-
veyed with that transfer. As a result, Ormond asserted, Spain relinquished all
legal claims and had no rights to make land grants. Ormond ruled that as the
United States obtained physical control over West Florida in 1804, Congress
assumed sovereignty and could establish land grants at its discretion. If the

court were to grant validity to Pollard's claim, Ormond concluded, "this would be a concession by the United States that her pretension to the territory in dispute was unfounded."[35]

In respect to its legal reasoning and the international conventions then recognized, Ormond's ruling was extraordinarily specious. There should be little doubt that both the United States and Spain held joint possession of the region between the years 1803 and 1819. Ormond's astonishing declaration that all Spanish land claims had to be ruled invalid in order to justify American occupation of West Florida simply ignored the fact that Spain did not formally cede this territory until 1819. Before then, the disposition of the land was far from settled in any legal sense, and thus all claims, whether from Washington or from Madrid, held various degrees of validity.[36]

Ormond's ruling shows that he was eager to avoid a decision based on Campbell's argument. "In this case," he wrote, "both parties claim [title] under an act of Congress, and assert a grant for the lot in dispute, [but] *neither are in a situation to contest the right of Congress to legislate on the subject.*" With this summary dismissal of Campbell's argument that Alabama gained full rights to the land in 1819, Ormond affirmed the judgment of the circuit court.[37] Thus, Campbell won the case, but he lost the argument. Obviously, Ormond could not suggest that the court possessed authority to negate federal statutes; federal courts alone could do so.

Several of the submerged land disputes in which Campbell was involved and in which he had introduced his theory of original sovereignty proceeded to the United States Supreme Court beginning in 1840. Yet most of these cases heard in Washington and presented on the basis of original sovereignty were not argued by the original founder of that doctrine. Campbell did not appear before the Supreme Court until 1849, and by then the Court had already accepted the validity of the original sovereignty doctrine.

Pollard's heirs had hardly been satisfied with Ormond's decision, and an appeal was at once registered on writ of error with the Taney Court in Washington. During the 1840 term, *Lessee of Pollard's Heirs v. Kibbe* was argued in the nation's highest tribunal.[38] Associate Justice Smith Thompson delivered the opinion of the Court, which held that Alabama's supreme court had erroneously ruled in Kibbe's favor and that Pollard's heirs were entitled to undisputed ownership of the waterfront property. The Court refused to consider whether Spain had the power to issue land grants. Instead, it asserted that the Confirmatory Acts of 1824 and 1836 should stand because "Congress would not grant or even simply release the right of the United States to land confessedly before granted." The Court ruled that the filling in and eventual construction of Water Street in Mobile created a division of the disputed lot into two parcels situated on either side of the new road. Pollard, therefore, held perfect title to the land immediately adjacent to the river, while Forbes's grant was confirmed only for the parcel on the west side of Water Street that did not afford access to the Mobile River.

The Court refused to entertain any notion that Congress could not legally enact the Confirmatory Acts of 1824 and 1836. Such legislation was, according to the unanimous decision, well within the bounds of congressional authority. Thus, temporarily at least, Pollard's heirs received title to the disputed lot.[39]

In 1842, Campbell's original case in which he had represented Miguel Eslava was appealed to the federal Supreme Court and docketed as *Mayor of Mobile v. Eslava*.[40] Arguing for the defense was John Sargeant, a prominent Philadelphia lawyer hired to take the case before the Supreme Court. Sargeant's confidence in the soundness of Campbell's argument as presented in Alabama's courts is evident from the fact that he adopted it in full for his case in Washington. Thus, the doctrine of original sovereignty had its second hearing before the justices.[41]

Sargeant argued that Eslava held a more perfect title to the property first because it had been in his possession for the previous several years while the City of Mobile had done nothing to evict him and second because he had made improvements to the lot and had even paid all taxes as required by the city. Finally, Sargeant asserted that there "was no 'right or claim' *remaining in the United States,* and therefore there was none granted to the City of Mobile."[42] Any rights to grant lots, Sargeant insisted, were inherited by Alabama upon its admission in 1819.

Justice McLean delivered the Court's opinion, which reversed Justice Collier's ruling. In unmistakably blunt language meant as a judicial scolding, the justices declared that their decision had been reached solely on the basis of the circuit court's judgment and the established facts of the case. Because Alabama's supreme court did not "give a construction of the Act of 1824, under which the plaintiff's right is asserted; but [instead] consider[ed] the respective rights and powers of the federal and State governments arising under the federal Constitution, and the compact entered into on the admission of the State of Alabama into the Union, . . . and [because the court] decide[d] that the Act of 1824 is void, *their opinion constitutes no part of the record, and is not properly a part of the case.* We must look to the points raised by the exceptions in the Circuit Court, as the only questions for our consideration and decision."[43] Despite this rebuke of Alabama's highest tribunal, the Court ruled to affirm both lower court rulings in Eslava's favor because of the acknowledged ambiguities of the Act of 1824 and the conflicting claims that arose out of that legislation. Eslava's claim had been upheld, but Campbell's theory had once again taken a battering.

Meanwhile, the lot in Mobile ostensibly belonging to Gaius Kibbe changed hands once again and passed to Joseph F. Files. Pollard's heirs sued in Alabama's supreme court for Files's ejectment but were again denied rights to the property on the grounds that Congress possessed no authority to grant lands belonging to Alabama. In 1844, *Pollard's Heirs v. Files* was argued before the United States Supreme Court with the same result as in the earlier cases: Pollard's claim was held valid over Files's, and the Court refused to question whether Congress could enact the Confirmatory Laws.[44] Thus, within a four-year period, Campbell's theory of original sovereignty was argued before the nation's highest tribunal on four occasions but received little recognition other than an annoyed nod.

In the above described cases, the Supreme Court refused to rule on the validity of the theory of original sovereignty. This theory so obviously involved the volatile states' rights issue that the Court chose to sidestep the matter altogether and to render a decision based solely on the facts involved in each case. Thus, from 1837 to 1845 the United States Supreme Court and the Alabama Supreme Court passed the issue back and forth, with the federal court dodging the underlying question.[45]

During the 1840s the Supreme Court was by no means intent on reversing decisions investing the federal government with supreme authority. During the thirty-four years when John Marshall presided over the Court as chief justice, he carefully and skillfully rendered decisions designed to augment and define federal authority. By the 1830s, the power of the federal government had indeed surpassed that of the states, especially with regard to commerce and contracts. Landmark cases such as *Marbury v. Madison, McCullough v. Maryland,* and *Cohens v. Virginia* had placed the federal government in a superior position over state authority. But Marshall's death in 1835 created a vacancy, which was filled by Roger B. Taney of Maryland. A slaveowner and ardent Jacksonian, Taney had been President Jackson's principal henchman in the destruction of the Second Bank of the United States. It was widely perceived, therefore, that the judicial edifice constructed by Marshall was in serious peril. The subsequent naming of six new justices between 1836 and 1845 added further credence to the notion that the Supreme Court had experienced a fundamental shift in favor of states' rights.

What the submerged land cases in Mobile revealed, however, was that the Taney Court was by no means exclusively pro states' rights. Although the Court was undeniably leaning in that direction, its rulings provided the judicial justification not for a return to theories on which the Confederation was based but rather for the developing dual federalism that dominated American jurisprudence throughout much of the nineteenth century. In other words, leading constitutional scholars largely agree that the Taney Court's position with regard to states' rights was far more evolutionary than revolutionary in forging a delicate, if occasionally ill-defined, balance between the powers of the states and those of the general government.[46] Under these circumstances the Court's hesitancy to rule on original sovereignty reflects its ongoing concern with the nature of the federal union.

By 1845, however, several changes had taken place on the Supreme Court. Early that year, Justice Joseph Story, the last remaining member of the Marshall Court who steadfastly refused to strengthen the power of the states at the federal government's expense, died and was replaced by Levi Woodbury of New Hampshire. That same year yet another submerged land case was placed on this Court's docket. *Pollard's Heirs v. Hagan,* however, proved considerably different from all previous cases involving original sovereignty.[47] The only issue involved in this litigation, sent from Alabama's Supreme Court on writ of error, was whether Congress had the authority to enact the Confirmatory Act of 1824. In other words, the attorneys on both sides sought a ruling based solely on the doctrine of original sovereignty.

The principal issue in this case, as stated at the very beginning of the record, involved whether, "[w]hen Alabama was admitted into the Union it became entitled to soil under navigable waters therein, same as the original States—nothing therein remained to the U.S. but the public lands—these do not include lands below high water mark in navigable streams."[48] The facts of this case were closely related to those in many of the submerged land cases preceding it. Hagan gained title to a lot claimed by Pollard's heirs, who then sued for ejectment. John Sargeant, counsel for the defense, argued that the United States "had nothing to grant or to release" after 1819 and that the right to dispense land grants rested exclusively with the state government as a trustee of the people. Second, he argued, "the [1824] act of Congress could not operate as a release or confirmation, because there was no right *or color of right* for a release or confirmation to operate upon."[49]

After Sargeant's presentation before the Court, Justice John McKinley read the majority opinion. Ironically, this was the same McKinley elected to the United States Senate during the 1836 term of Alabama's legislature and the same man Campbell had called "unspeakably weak." McKinley was appointed to the bench by Andrew Jackson, and his presence added further strength to the Court's moderate but maturing pro states' rights disposition. In *Pollard v. Hagan* the Court ruled that a decision on the doctrine of original sovereignty had to be rendered as it was the only issue before the Court. McKinley recognized that this issue was of tremendous importance to the states—and particularly to those newly added to the Union. All one had to do, the justice explained, was to glance at a map of the United States and see how many millions of acres could rightfully be deemed submerged lands and how many, with proper improvements, could become valuable real estate, and one would understand the extreme significance of the submerged land cases.

"We think that a proper examination of this subject," McKinley wrote, "will show that the United States never held any municipal sovereignty, jurisdiction, or right of soil in and to the territory, of which Alabama and any of the new States were formed; *except for temporary purposes.*"[50] The "temporary purposes" mentioned by McKinley meant that the federal government's grants issued between 1817—when Alabama was given territorial status—and 1819 were valid but that those confirmed after the latter date were void. In other words, and of extreme significance with regard to future legislation, Congress held full sovereignty over Alabama's tidelands while the area was still a territory, but all sovereignty passed to the state once it achieved statehood.

Any congressional power to grant lands guaranteed to the states was, according to McKinley, "not only repugnant to the Constitution, but it is inconsistent with the spirit and intention of the deed of cession." The result of the 1845 *Pollard* ruling was an affirmation of the Alabama Supreme Court's ruling and a victory for Hagan. It also marks a clear break with past rulings and a fundamental shift toward states' rights philosophy.[51]

Justice John Catron of Tennessee, who was generally considered the Court's leading expert on land title law, wrote a vehement dissent in the Pollard case in which he disputed the validity of the original sovereignty doctrine. "Between 1840 and 1844," he wrote, "a doctrine had sprung up in the courts of Alabama (*previously unheard of* in any court of justice in this country) assuming" that the submerged lands "were part of the eminent domain and sovereign rights in the old states."[52] "An assumption that mud-flats and swamps," he continued, "once flowed, but long since reclaimed, had passed to the new states, on the theory of Sovereign rights, did, at first, strike my mind as a startling novelty; . . . A right so obscure, and which has lain dormant, *and even unsuspected,* for so many years, and the assertion of which will strip so much city property, and so many estates of all title, should as I think be concluded by long acquiescence, and especially in courts of justice."[53] Catron, who was normally pro states' rights and a staunch defender of slavery, lamented that the current ruling undermined the power and authority of the federal government, invalidated two congressional statutes affecting millions of acres, and reversed five previously decided cases. "[T]his is deemed the most important controversy ever brought before this Court, either as it respects the amount of property involved, or the principles on which the present judgement proceeds," he wrote.[54]

The *Pollard* case thus produced one of the most significant precedent-setting decisions rendered during the nineteenth century. The "*Pollard* rule," as it was thereafter known, established a series of principles governing the granting of lands once thought to be within the federal government's domain, and it recognized each state's sovereign rights to all lands bordering navigable waters and subjected to the ebb and flow of tides.[55]

This ruling was not only a landmark decision for the Supreme Court but also greatly enhanced Campbell's reputation in Alabama. As he was the first attorney to connect the original sovereignty doctrine with the submerged land cases, his stature as an attorney and as one of the South's leading proponents of states' rights soared. Though he had not personally argued these cases before the Supreme Court, Campbell benefited greatly once the Court had accepted his original argument as presented almost verbatim by John Sargeant.

In 1849, Campbell had the privilege of arguing his doctrine before the nation's highest court when a case, docketed as *Goodtitle v. Kibbe,* was filed testing the *Pollard* rule and the Confirmatory Act of 1836.[56] Once again, Pollard's heirs—who must be recognized for their persistence if for nothing else—sued to eject Gaius Kibbe, one of the defendants in an earlier case who had acquired a waterfront lot ostensibly deeded to Pollard. The plaintiffs in error argued that the *Pollard* decision of 1845 was based solely on the Confirmatory Act of 1824, so in essence the act of 1836 was still operational. Furthermore, the plaintiffs requested that the Court reconsider its 1845 *Pollard* decision and rule their title valid.

Campbell, who had only recently been admitted to the bar of the Supreme Court and was making his first appearance before that tribunal, maintained his earlier arguments and defended the soundness of the *Pollard* rule. On this occasion Chief Justice Taney delivered the opinion of the Court that upheld the decision of the lower court and reaffirmed its ruling of four years earlier. Commenting on Campbell's argument in the earlier Alabama Supreme Court decisions, Taney remarked that "it must be a very strong case indeed and where mistake and error had been evidently committed, to justify this court, after the lapse of five years, in reversing its own decision. . . . Upon a review of the case, we see no reason for doubting its correctness." The chief justice also insisted that the *Pollard* rule was recognized as a legitimate precedent that applied to the 1824 and the 1836 laws alike. Thus both acts were deemed invalid.[57]

Pollard v. Hagan and *Goodtitle v. Kibbe* established a precedent that remained unaltered until the 1950s. Throughout the remainder of the nineteenth century "a veritable flood" of decisions followed the *Pollard* rule and established state jurisdiction over submerged lands.[58] Before the Civil War, the doctrine of original sovereignty held distinct political significance, particularly for the proponents of states' rights. After the war and well into the twentieth century, the *Pollard* rule was cited generally in controversies involving state control over natural resources discovered offshore. Considering the potential value of this property, the decision produced an exceptionally reliable source of income for the states. The Court ruled that with the Confirmatory Laws of 1824 and 1836 Congress had assumed powers not delegated to the federal government but reserved specifically and exclusively for each newly added state.

Because of his role in the submerged land cases, Campbell became one of the most sought-after attorneys in the state. His income, as might be expected, increased in proportion to the success of his law firm in Mobile, and for the first time in his adult life Campbell was able to afford many of the luxuries available to wealthy members of southern society. Tax records from 1841 to 1863 indicate that Campbell used much of his income to purchase investment properties in and around Mobile. In 1841, for instance, he acquired an orange grove valued at $10,000 just outside the city limits. He also purchased a new frame house of approximately 4,000 square feet that was located on the southwest corner of Conception and Church Streets. This home, just a few blocks from the law offices of Campbell and Chandler and also from the courthouse, became the Campbell family's permanent Mobile residence. Daniel and Sarah Chandler owned a comparable home immediately adjacent to Campbell's but facing Church Street. This structure is still intact and today serves as the offices of a busy downtown Mobile law firm.[59]

By 1843 Campbell had acquired four vacant lots that started at the corner of Water Street and continued to the channel of the Mobile River. Campbell used this property as the site of a new wharf that he built between 1843 and 1845. After his work in connection with the submerged land cases, he was no doubt impressed by the profits that came from owning a wharf. Over the next seven years Campbell bought several additional rental houses. Most of these were wooden frame structures, but at least one was a red brick, two-story dwelling that included a large lot on Conception Street.

The most valuable of Campbell's investment properties was a cotton warehouse purchased in 1850, described only as "brown" and assessed at $20,000. The tax registry for 1851 documents Campbell's continued prosperity with his acquisition of one-half interest in a brick building on St. Louis Street, one-third interest in a second building on St. Anthony Street, five additional rental homes, a ninety-three-acre tract located in Mobile County, one structure listed simply as "kitchen" on Monroe Street that perhaps served as a restaurant, and a smith's shop and adjacent lot on Church Street. The aggregate value of his property that year was nearly $42,000, certainly an appreciable sum by mid-nineteenth-century standards.[60]

Campbell's legal career was indeed fruitful, and it allowed him to invest in an interesting assortment of properties. But Campbell was not only financially wealthy. He also enjoyed the prestige and respect afforded to the leading citizens of Mobile. Moreover, as he was considered by many to be a staunch defender of states' rights, his views on a number of issues were often solicited by leading politicians and jurists throughout the South. Despite this growing reputation, Campbell could hardly be considered obsessed with states' rights. It should be recalled that the two letters Campbell wrote to Henry Goldthwaite in 1836—as described in the previous chapter—reveal Campbell's all-but-Whig ideology, which encompassed support for internal improvements and higher protective tariffs. Viewed in conjunction with his arguments in the submerged land cases, one begins to see Campbell's conservative, nationalistic ideology, in which the federal government's power and scope figured prominently. In reality, throughout the 1830s and early 1840s Campbell's states' rights philosophy was quite moderate, tempered by strong nationalism, and critical of those who sought to diminish the powers delegated by the Constitution to the federal government.

Though Campbell disliked politics and dissociated himself entirely from that profession after 1843, he retained an especially keen interest in political affairs, particularly the enactment of legislation that he believed adversely affected the South. By the mid-1840s Campbell had become alarmed at the growing abolition movement, which he believed directly threatened the southern way of life. Assuming the role of social commentator in a series of published articles on slavery, abolitionism, and immediate emancipation, Campbell hoped to interject his thoughts on the South's peculiar institution. These articles are invaluable, for they more than any of his other writings reveal that he maintained surprisingly moderate and, in some respects, even progressive views on slavery and the South's eventual need to be rid of the institution.

4 | Campbell and the Peculiar Institution

Campbell's four publications appearing in the *Southern Quarterly Review* between 1847 and 1851—"Slavery in the United States" (July 1847), "Slavery Among the Romans" (October 1848), "British West India Islands" (January 1850), and "Slavery Throughout the World" (April 1851)—reveal that he devoted considerable thought to the issue of slavery and the likely consequences of the immediate, noncompensatory emancipation demanded by many of the nation's abolitionist societies. But this is not to say that Campbell defended the institution or that he believed it should last indefinitely. On the contrary, though he recognized that slavery was the chief pillar of southern agrarianism, Campbell believed that the institution prevented the South from realizing appreciable technological and industrial advances and that the region would best progress either by slowly abandoning slave labor altogether or by dramatically reforming the institution. He also recognized, however, that slavery was too entrenched in southern society to be ended without serious reflection on the consequences of immediate emancipation. As the South was by almost any measure intrinsically defined by slavery, Campbell reasoned that if the institution was hastily destroyed, so too would be the South's political position in the Union. As the attacks on slavery from many quarters in the North became increasingly hostile throughout the 1830s and 1840s, Campbell foresaw that the controversy surrounding it was sufficiently volatile to produce disunion and eventual national calamity.

The first article, "Slavery in the United States," contains most of Campbell's fundamental ideas on the South's peculiar institution. The remaining three publications echo much of what he wrote in 1847 and need only be examined to the extent that they differ from his initial article or further illuminate the evolution of Campbell's thoughts on slavery. "Slavery," he wrote, "was the ultimate solution which the ancient world afforded to the difficult and complicated questions that arose from the relations of parent and child; creditor and debtor; the State and its offenders against penal laws, and the conqueror and the captive."[1] Under these circumstances slavery not only was acceptable but also constituted a useful component of ancient societies, particularly in Rome.

The practice of enslaving vanquished peoples was as old as civilization, Campbell wrote, and it too was sanctioned in the ancient world. This acceptance, although tinged with Christian overtones, continued after the fall of the Roman Empire and the rise of medieval Europe. Pope Alexander III prohibited the sale of Christians into slavery during the twelfth century, but "[t]he African was not comprehended within the benignant principle of the papal decree. He was an infidel." Thus, as Campbell explained, African slavery was sanctioned by the early Christian church and had long been a common practice among Europeans. African slaves were introduced to the New World soon after its discovery because it was believed that "one Negro could do more work than four Indians." With the advent of the slave trade, blacks were transported across the Atlantic Ocean in increasingly large numbers. The horrors associated with this trade precipitated demands for its eradication, which began in England and in France and culminated in the abolition of the institution in Europe and in many colonies belonging to European nations. The antislavery movement in England was exported to the United States soon thereafter. Since the 1830s, with the advent of the various antislavery organizations in northern states, he wrote, "The agitation in the United States has increased with fearful rapidity."[2]

Campbell believed that slavery, for all its accompanying evils, was a reality in the South that could not be eradicated overnight. Southerners had inherited the institution from their colonial forefathers, and as westward-migrating emigrants peopled the southern states, they transported their slaves with them, established plantations and small farms, and constructed a society deeply rooted in slave labor. Nearly all facets of southern life were based on the institution, and to abolish slavery hastily would destroy the social, political, and economic underpinnings of the South. This was the ultimate peril associated with the abolition movement. Campbell did not deny that slavery could be an exceedingly cruel institution. He further believed that it kept the South in a state of perpetual commercial limbo. But he emphatically stated that as it was a southern institution to be regulated exclusively by the states that sanctioned its existence, neither other states nor the federal government could abolish slavery. An action of that magnitude was revolutionary in scope and could only be accomplished internally and gradually if the South's social fabric were not to be destroyed. Before southerners could abolish slavery, in other words, they had to prepare the slaves for freedom.[3]

Campbell then began a discourse on the various abolition decrees enacted by France and England and the results of instantly emancipating entire populations of slaves. He began with a discussion of France's laws in relation to Haiti. Campbell asserted that most of the civil strife that paralyzed France's colonies occurred directly as a result of the French Revolution. White slave-owners staged a rebellion in an effort to break colonial ties to France; slaves and mulattoes, on the other hand, were imbued with the more lofty ideals put forward by the revolutionaries. After several years of fighting between these two groups, Toussaint L'Ouverture gained political supremacy and endured French invasions for the next several years. Campbell remarked that under L'Ouverture's leadership, black Haitians "displayed great courage and desperation, and awed the invaders." By 1804, after a terrible "war of extermination," the French army had been completely driven from the island, and the former slaves retained control over their own domain.

Campbell informed his readers that his objective was not to judge the Haitians by their actions during the revolution but rather "to ascertain from their present state and condition, whether [they] are capable of taking [their] place as members of a well-organized society." In other words, he pondered whether Haitians could form a benevolent society, with an effective government, and could live within the confines and conventions of civilized nations.

By examining French emancipation laws and the policies that were adopted after the slaves had been freed, Campbell concluded that these decrees had created utter chaos in Haitian society largely because the French did little beforehand to educate the slaves and to teach them how to be productive and responsible citizens. He quoted numerous sources indicating that soon after emancipation, hundreds of stately plantations fell into disrepair, crops rotted in the fields, sugar production diminished dramatically, and general anarchy reigned throughout the island.

This situation prevailed until the government passed laws in 1826 establishing strict labor codes to govern the relationship between laborers and the proprietors of agricultural estates. Haitian laborers were bound to the soil, refused education, could not cultivate their own farms without special permission, and were required to enter into labor agreements with the owners of the large estates controlled by the mulatto class.

In essence, therefore, a caste system had developed on the island whereby the mixed bloods dominated those of pure African descent who, through the legislation of 1826, were relegated to the status of serfs. "We know of no evidence that is better calculated to reduce [to] silence and soberness the enthusiastic abolitionist." Immediate emancipation in Campbell's estimation undeniably led to anarchy in society and was an impetus for the reestablishment of serfdom. Practically all aspects of Haitian society had been destroyed as a result of the emancipation decree. The education system nearly vanished; the country was dominated by the army; roads, bridges, and estates had fallen into ruin; and the population had been reduced to living in squalor. Despite underpinnings of civilization such as a constitution, judicial organization, trial by jury, and a solid body of laws, the regeneration of the Haitian people had not transpired. "The forces that serve to exalt and to improve a nation are not in its paper systems, but in the character of the population," Campbell wrote. He warned that enacting abolition laws before the character of the slaves could be substantially improved would only reproduce the horrid events and conditions prevalent in Haitian society. The French erred in their hasty actions because their decrees

> were made upon the impression that mighty reforms in the condition and the character of the human race could be accomplished by the simple fiat of a tumultuous and excited [Legislative] Assembly. They proceeded on the notion that a magical influence belonged to the expressions of public authority, and that this sufficed to effect a complete transformation of those who were the subjects of their will. History teaches no such blind confidence in the efficiency of human decrees. History records many instances of measures for the liberation of slaves adopted in a sudden emergency to answer a transitory purpose, but such measures have left no impression, except to warn us of their own imbecility.[4]

"The conclusion" reached from a study of French abolitionism, Campbell wrote, "is that freedom, even when it can be peacefully and quietly communicated to the black, and when he is subject to no invidious distinctions in consequence of color or condition, is very far from securing to him the fruits of civilization."[5]

Campbell believed that an examination of the situation in Haiti was imperative because slavery was increasingly under assault from northern abolitionists, and southerners must be made aware of the possible ramifications of immediate emancipation. "In the Southern States, we cannot . . . incur the peril of such precipitation." "We cannot with indifference, visit evils upon either class without disturbing all the arrangements of society." "The Southern people find [slavery] penetrating their entire social system. Their industrial pursuits, business relations, investments of capital, family arrangements, and political organization, are constituted with reference to its existence." Campbell further explained that it was vitally important that southerners take initiatives to offset the perils involved in immediate emancipation should the South ever be forced to accept such legislation.[6]

One senses from reading this article that Campbell was convinced that slavery was disappearing gradually. His principal purpose in drafting "Slavery in the United States" was to recommend measures that could be taken to ameliorate social degeneration once emancipation had occurred. He stated that the only legitimate emancipation that would not destroy southern society was voluntary manumission, which occurred more often with each passing year. But in light of the pressure from the North to outlaw slavery altogether, Campbell proposed that southerners prepare blacks for freedom so that they could better assimilate into southern society and become responsible and productive citizens.

As Campbell held that blacks were indeed "susceptible of great improvement, and thrive by liberal and indulgent treatment," some of the more harsh slave codes—which he suggested were rarely enforced—should be weakened so as to promote more cordial and trusting relations between the races. The codes under which slavery operated in the South, Campbell contended, were largely devised during the colonial period, when "blacks were fresh from their native Africa, with gross appetites and brutal habits." Over the course of time, slaves had become more civilized and formed an important part of the southern community. Campbell estimated that by the end of the nineteenth century, the black population in the South would exceed 10 million. Southerners, he advised, "must not expect that the regulations that suited their first condition can continue or will be appropriate." Southern leaders "could fulfill no task more useful than that of adapting our laws to the varying wants of our society." As the black population was growing at unprecedented rates, the South had to adopt laws and social traits more conducive to blacks' well-being.[7]

Second, southerners should refrain from destroying slave families. "The connections of husband and wife," he wrote, "and of parent and child, are sacred in a Christian community and should be rendered secure by the laws of a Christian state." Slave marriages should be recognized by law so that blacks could provide stable homes for their children. Without the benefit of a loving, Christian family, he warned, former slaves would degenerate into "thuggery" and "banditry."[8]

A third reform Campbell proposed involved strengthening the relationship between masters and slaves. The current system that allowed for the sale of slaves was based largely on "the pecuniary condition of the master." This had created a deterioration of the master-slave relationship and had stripped the institution of its "patriarchical nature." "The condition of families should be permanent," he wrote. "Those domestic ties which contribute so much to the happiness of the members, should not be severed at the pursuit of a creditor. The great end of society, the well-being of its members, would surely be promoted by withdrawing slaves in some measure from the market, as a basis of credit."[9] Campbell also suggested that slaves be allowed to engage in a "diversity of employment" that would afford them fair salaries with which they eventually could purchase their freedom. This would also teach them useful skills that would benefit the entire South. He recommended that slaves be better educated and that they be taught to read and write and to perform basic arithmetic. Last, slaves should be diligently schooled in moral and religious instruction. Only through pure Christian living could the slaves truly feel part of southern society.

Such reforms were of the utmost necessity to maintain cordial relations among the races. Given the large population of slaves in the South, immediate emancipation would produce disastrous results for all southern society. "We cannot afford to be the subjects of experiment," he insisted. Campbell concluded with a stern warning to southerners: "The masters of these millions—considered alone in their capacities as guardians,—must not yield the destinies of this people to the enterprises of even well-meaning projectors;—much less to visionary and unreasonable fanatics;—and least of all, to politicians not responsible to themselves. . . . If we submit to take a lower place than that which the constitution assigns us, we must expect that the future control of this institution will fall from our hands into those of its enemies and our own."[10]

The subsequent three articles Campbell contributed to *Southern Quarterly Review* during this period reemphasized many of the points he made in "Slavery in the United States." Appearing in the October 1848 edition of the journal, "Slavery Among the Romans" was written principally to counter the antislavery argument that southern slavery was unique in the annals of history. The article reveals Campbell's breadth of knowledge of the ancient world, and it shows that he had mastered not only Roman law but also the social and political foundations of the Empire, which he gleaned principally from the writings of preeminent nineteenth-century historians. "The Roman law treated slaves as property," Campbell stated. Moreover, Roman slaves could hold no official positions in the state, were not permitted to bring suit in Roman courts, and were viewed as "incompetent witness[es]." "The slave could make no contract on his own account . . . [and] was the subject of sale, pledge, exchange, donation, bequest, distribution, and all other civil transactions." Under these circumstances, Campbell averred that there was little difference between the slaves' legal status in the Roman Empire and that in the southern states.[11]

According to Campbell, slavery among the Romans developed from two sources: war and debt. As the Romans became increasingly ambitious for greater territory, their propensity for war led to the enslavement of thousands of conquered people. Furthermore, the great disparity of wealth that evolved in Rome during the early years of the Empire meant that the number of people living in poverty grew enormously. Without any substantial means of subsistence, then, many people living in poverty had to sell themselves into bondage in order to provide for their families.

Campbell refuted the then common theory that slavery was the principal cause for the decline of the Empire, and he claimed that "the ruin of the free classes of Rome, and the consequent depopulation of the Empire" was "the specific malady of the state." Campbell wrote that as the Roman Empire stretched into nearly all of the civilized world, the city of Rome became increasingly reliant on the various parts of the Empire for its survival. The large estates that once produced food for the city with large numbers of slaves switched from growing corn to raising cattle, which was less labor intensive. Large numbers of slaves were consequently employed in Rome and served as the basic labor force of the city. The freedmen were then "indisposed" to work at all. As slaves were employed more and more in nonagricultural pursuits, the value of all labor plummeted, so that increasing numbers of unemployed workers in the city relied on the dole. This situation continued through many generations until the financial burden overwhelmed the state and created economic and political instability, which eventually led to a weakening of the entire Empire.

Campbell thereby conceded that an overabundance of slaves dramatically devalues labor for all society and in turn leads to economic depression and high unemployment. He also believed that the people of the Southwest would restrict the importation of slaves for this reason. "The law of self-preservation" would compel the people living in the Mexican cession "to maintain a distribution of Negro population." "A firm determination on the part of those [individuals] would be contagious," and the result would be "that the Negro population in the Union will maintain its existing location."[12]

Campbell predicted that, as slavery would be confined to the southern states, slaveowners would increasingly employ slaves in nonagricultural labor. This development would in turn lead to a decrease in the value of labor in the South and a prolonged era of gradual emancipation, such as had occurred in ancient Rome. To offset the dangers of eradicating slavery without a suitable substitute, southerners should employ greater diversity of manufacturing and commerce. Capital that had been reserved for agriculture should be diverted to entrepreneurial and industrial enterprises. Not only would this provide the South with a much needed labor safety valve, it would afford an economic position more on a par with that of the industrialized North. To Campbell, slavery was a dying institution and the South had to recognize this fact and prepare for the emancipation of all slaves. As the immediate threat to the South's labor institution was strengthened greatly by the Free Soil movement and by the federal government's assistance to northern manufacturing, the South would eventually have to prepare the slaves for freedom and to construct a manufacturing and commercial base for their economy. Failure to do this would surely reproduce the tragic events in Haiti.[13]

Campbell's third article, "British West India Islands," examined British emancipation decrees in comparison with those enacted by the French. He asserted that the economy of the British West Indies was in shambles as a direct result of emancipation. The British, like the French before them, had taken inadequate measures to prepare the slaves for freedom, and they also had not provided the estates with an adequate labor supply to replace the newly freed slaves. The great estates, therefore, crumbled into decay, unemployment and "idleness" permeated society, and general anarchy ensued. Former plantation owners faced with economic ruin fled the islands, leaving their former slaves to fend for themselves. The degeneration of the population naturally followed and a precivilized state emerged as a result of England's ill-conceived, hasty, and wholesale emancipation.[14]

In his last article, "Slavery Throughout the World," Campbell employed a retrospective glance "into the various forms of slavery, and the conditions of society in which the institution had heretofore existed." The purpose of the article was to investigate the various forms of slavery that had existed in different parts of the world and to ponder whether that which existed in the South could not be better "meliorated" to coincide with man's natural progression toward freedom and democracy. Campbell explained that life before the creation of organized societies was especially brutal. The bonds of family necessarily arose as a means of protection, and groups of families formed communities for even greater safety. As communities prospered, many of them engaged in wars of conquest. Campbell then traced the development of slavery in the ancient world and suggested that this development was a natural outgrowth of a warriorlike mentality that prevailed in many ancient societies. With conquests came greater wealth, and this subsequently led to a division of society into laboring and idle classes. This situation continued well into the present time when southern slaveowners were overly reliant on slave labor to provide their economic well-being. "We have noticed," he wrote with exasperation, "that in the Southern States, the general opinion is that [slavery] can exist in but one form; that great impatience is expressed at any attempt to depart from the absolute and rigid regulations adopted in colonial times; that no toleration of any opinion or any practice is manifested which implies the least doubt of the perfection of the model which we have established."[15]

"It is apparent," Campbell wrote, "that any revolution in society such as a general emancipation of slaves would effect, must be preceded by the introduction to them of the laws of the family. They must learn the performance of civil duties, and imbibe notions of the civil responsibilities of the domestic relations. Hence, in every inquiry concerning slaves, the structure of the family relation is of importance."[16] Southern slaves had to be schooled in the virtues of the family—only along those lines would southern society better survive wholesale emancipation. Campbell projected that the South must prepare for emancipation decrees as the forces of abolitionism, Free-Soilism, and industrialization were slowly overwhelming worn-out southern institutions. He recognized that the era in which he lived experienced an unprecedented faith in personal freedom and individual liberty, and that these forces, the very foundation of the United States, were becoming so powerful that they would surely overwhelm southern society and southern institutions. Society had changed, he counseled, and "ideas and employments on the part of the masters and the dominant classes of society" once considered perfectly natural had become disreputable. "The priestly and military classes," he wrote, "who formed the privileged *castes* in Asia, and the predominant classes of Europe, and who, in the 'pre-eminence and primogeniture' of birth and profession, felt they were entitled to service, have lost their sway over society."[17]

Campbell believed that the years of the American and French Revolutions had ushered in this new era and had produced within civilized populations an overwhelming passion for individual freedom. These forces that Americans greatly respected and incorporated into their Constitution had rendered the South's labor system incompatible with the times and obsolete in an era of personal freedoms and rapid industrial growth. Campbell worried: "Those ideas of a fundamental and radical difference in the races of men which determine their social position and duties, have lost their place in the religion of mankind. The predominant idea of this age is to raise, from their inferior position *all* classes of society; and to form governments on the recognition, if not of equality among the members, at least that there should exist no fundamental distinctions between them."[18] Southerners should therefore dispense with their outmoded notions of a laboring class and a ruling class. Those ideas had vanished and had been replaced by the concepts on which the United States was created. Moreover, the rise of democracy in the first half of the nineteenth century produced a revolution in labor. "[T]he dignity attached to particular employments" such as commercial agriculture "has proportionately diminished." As a result of the industrial revolution, he wrote, "labor, which constituted the degradation of the slave, is now the mark and characteristic of the freeman. Idleness, ease, luxury, and the pursuit of sensual enjoyments, have become disreputable. Science, literature, policy, arts, professions, all acknowledge a subordination to the commercial ideas of the age, and direct their activity and effort to useful enterprises. Every man is held to contribute his quota of mental or physical labor to society: The sweat of the body, or [the] mind is exacted from all, as the price of public estimation."[19]

In all of these articles, Campbell concluded that the South should welcome a social revolution in which all members of society could be usefully employed in various capacities. In order for southerners to maintain control over any potential social revolution, family structures, religious organizations, and educational facilities must be reinforced and utilized effectively to incorporate slaves into southern society. He held that the institution of slavery was disappearing because it was no longer acceptable in the modern world. Consequently, southerners needed to distance themselves gradually from their current labor system and invest their wealth in commercial interests.

One overriding theme present in all four articles, however, was his insistence that gradual emancipation voluntarily undertaken by southerners was the only method whereby slaves could gain their freedom without a subsequent destruction of southern society. Therefore, southerners could abide no further intermeddling from northern abolitionists or politicians who demanded immediate abolition. "The examination we have made illustrates the difficulty of accomplishing changes in the structure of society." Campbell advised that Northerners should exhibit patience with regard to slavery, and it would eventually disappear altogether. Southerners, on the other hand, should make every effort "to maintain, without obstruction or interference, their absolute control over" slavery.[20]

Campbell's writings and speeches during this period reveal the depth of thought that he devoted to slavery, to the Union, and to the South. As for Campbell's personal relationship with slavery, he owned a small and varying number of slaves throughout the antebellum period. Interestingly, in July 1865 Campbell wrote that he had "voluntarily liberated all of my slaves before the war some years."[21] Later historians who wrote on Campbell's life note that he freed his slaves, and they use this "fact" as evidence that the Alabamian held liberal and surprisingly progressive thoughts on slavery, emancipation, and abolition. What is often suggested is that Campbell put his liberal beliefs on emancipation into practice and that he freed his slaves as an example of how the South could reform its labor institutions and eventually rid itself of slavery. Also implicit is that Campbell manumitted his slaves before he was nominated to the United States Supreme Court in early 1853, thus suggesting that he did not do this merely to render his nomination more palatable to northern opponents of the South's peculiar institution.

Investigations into this matter reveal that Campbell was not entirely truthful in his letter to Curtis and that he did not free "all" of his slaves "some years" before the war. In fact, Campbell's affiliation with slavery was quite extensive, and though he honestly expressed personal misgivings about the institution of slavery and how it fundamentally weakened the South, he was not averse to owning house servants and general laborers. The most complete record of Campbell's personal slaveholdings can be established from the City of Mobile tax records. As previously stated, these records indicate that Campbell's personal wealth increased considerably throughout the 1840s and that he accumulated profitable investment properties in Mobile. These records also include an entry for the number of slaves each citizen owned, and they provide an accurate account of Campbell's personal history with regard to slave ownership.

The City of Mobile's 1841 tax list shows that Campbell owned eight slaves whose assessed value totaled $2,000. By 1846 he had increased his holdings to fourteen slaves, most of whom probably worked loading and unloading ships at the wharf Campbell had earlier constructed. This was the largest number of slaves he owned at any one time. After 1846, Campbell owned various numbers of slaves—twelve in 1848, for example, and seven in 1850, the year he bought the cotton warehouse in Mobile. Perhaps because he needed extra labor in this warehouse, Campbell purchased five additional slaves sometime during 1850–1851.

The records for 1852 and 1853 provide rather interesting information. The initial assessment shows Campbell owning eleven slaves with an aggregate value of $6,000. A second tax register on the same microfilm roll, however, includes a reassessment of his estate and a reduction in the number of slaves to six who were valued at $2,500; evidently Campbell had sold or manumitted five of his slaves.[22] The following year's tax registry for 1853 lists under his name six slaves, all of whom appeared on the same line as his warehouse. The records for these two years are especially intriguing when one considers that Campbell was nominated to the Supreme Court during the winter of 1852–1853. That he reduced the number of slaves he owned—and "transferred" the remaining slaves to his warehouse—perhaps indicates that he took measures to disassociate himself from slavery to protect his candidacy from abolitionist attacks.

Campbell owned no slaves between 1854 and 1856, and he employed wage laborers at his warehouse, on his wharf, and in his orange grove. In 1857, however, after he had been on the bench for four years, he purchased three slaves who were most likely used exclusively as house servants. Two documents registered in the Mobile County Probate Court in the spring of 1858 provide further evidence that Campbell continued to buy and sell slaves even while he sat as an associate justice on the United States Supreme Court. On 1 April of that year he purchased seven slaves at a public auction. The slaves' names were listed as Janus, Thompson, Meshad, Delpha, Lizzy, and Peggy and her two children, and Campbell paid a total of $2,200 for all of them.[23]

A second bill of sale written three months later, on 22 June 1858, and registered in the same court indicates that Campbell sold these same seven slaves to Daniel and Sarah Chandler. It is interesting to note that he maintained a trusteeship over these slaves even though Daniel and Sarah were granted rights to "sell, transfer, and bequeath" Janus and the others at their discretion. Sarah was granted permission to accept the slaves "unto her possession, and to use the same for her exclusive use subject only to my legal title as trustee."[24] Thus Campbell could rightly claim after June 1858 that he owned no slaves whatsoever. But the bill of sale clearly indicates that he maintained considerable control over these slaves whose possession had been legally transferred to Sarah.

It is impossible to know exactly why Campbell sold Janus and the others so soon after the initial purchase; perhaps he worried that owning them could further tarnish the Court's image—which certainly had not improved after the *Dred Scott* decision—and could provide antislavery newspapers additional grounds on which to berate the Court. Campbell was acutely sensitive to any attacks on slavery and on slaveowners, and he most assuredly would not have wanted to invite direct, personal attacks on himself and on his family. For whatever reasons, he discreetly sold the slaves to the Chandlers.

From 1858 until he sold most of his property in Mobile in 1863, Campbell owned just one slave whose value was originally assessed at $300 but—reflecting the uncontrollable inflation that plagued the South throughout the Civil War—was increased to $600 in 1862 and in 1863. In October 1862 Campbell agreed to serve as the Confederacy's assistant secretary of war, and he soon thereafter sold most of his Mobile property.[25]

The tax records, therefore, clearly indicate that Campbell had not "freed" his slaves "some years" before the war. At the same time, however, these tax records show that he substantially reduced the number of slaves he held after 1853 and owned only one to three house servants until 1863. That he owned slaves at all shows that he did not believe slavery immoral. If he had held that conviction, he was too devoutly religious to engage in any activity that he might have regarded as sinful. Inasmuch as slavery was a legally sanctioned institution, Campbell had a perfect right to own slaves.

Likewise, the fact that Campbell owned slaves should not diminish our perception of him as one who viewed the institution as inherently destructive to southern society and as a person who sought to reform slavery and prepare slaves for eventual freedom. Campbell's *Southern Quarterly Review* articles provide clear evidence that he regarded slavery as a doomed institution. But they also demonstrate that he predicted nothing less than the South's complete economic and societal ruin if the slaves were emancipated prior to being properly educated and prepared to enter American society as freedmen.

From an examination of these essays and other writings of this period, we may conclude that Campbell was greatly disturbed by the hostile attacks on slavery from the abolitionists, who were determined to rid the nation of the institution regardless of the cost to the South and to southerners. Of far greater concern to Campbell as the nation neared the midcentury mark, however, was the increasingly bitter sectionalism that was generated by the advent of the Mexican War. The internal struggles that rose to the forefront of American politics after 1846 created such a severe crisis by 1850 that many southerners felt compelled to reassess the South's continued relationship with the Union. The political philosophy Campbell had maintained throughout his professional career was thus fundamentally nationalistic and conservative. Yet the crisis at midcentury, defined by a great internal struggle over territory acquired from Mexico, was a veritable watershed event in his life and provided the impetus for a dramatic shift in Campbell's states' rights philosophy that was especially clear by the summer of 1850.

5 | The Crisis at Midcentury

Thus far in Campbell's public career, his political philosophy as revealed in personal letters and during court appearances was centered on a moderate version of states' rights. During his tenure as a state representative in 1836–1837, Campbell's letters to Henry Goldthwaite show that he despised the proponents of nullification, supported internal improvements, and approved of a high protective tariff. In any final evaluation of Campbell's first fifteen years in professional life, his states' rights philosophy must be viewed as strongly tempered by an absolute devotion to the federal union and to an apparent understanding that the Constitution vested the central government with extensive powers to govern the internal affairs of the nation. It had been Justice Collier after all, and not Campbell, who remarked that the federal government could not grant land titles to citizens, even when the land was situated in a territory under the protection and auspices of Congress. According to Collier's states' rights argument, original sovereignty was just as applicable in the territories, because these regions would one day become states. Thus the federal government had no constitutional authority to enact legislation that might prospectively undermine state authority.

As shown earlier, Campbell did not carry his submerged land cases argument to Collier's extreme position, and he most likely maintained, perhaps in accordance with article 4, section 3 of the federal Constitution, that Congress had the power "to make all needful Rules and Regulations respecting the Territory" belonging to the United States. Campbell's version of original sovereignty was applicable only to the states; Congress held exclusive domain over all United States territories and could enact legislation for these regions at its discretion, including abolishing slavery if it chose to do so. This was Campbell's position as late as March 1848, but he soon altered his opinions and, as will be shown, he adopted a far more aggressive states' rights philosophy that was as applicable in the territories as it was in the states.

Since his voluntary departure from state politics after the 1842 legislative session of Alabama's House of Representatives, Campbell had devoted himself exclusively to his law practice. He would perhaps have spent the remainder of his life as a successful but mostly obscure figure in American history had it not been for the onset of the Mexican War. This conflict, which held out the promise of nearly doubling the nation's size if Mexico could be defeated, also brought previously latent sectional jealousies to the forefront of national politics. Likewise, some political machinations in Washington in connection with the Mexican War convinced many southerners, Campbell among them, that northerners were conspiring to abolish slavery and to reduce southern society to anarchy and chaos. More ominously, Campbell became increasingly concerned that the South's political and economic position in the Union was waning before the rising tides of abolitionism and industrialization, and he worried that those forces would overwhelm southern agrarian society and leave his beloved South politically, economically, and socially subservient to the North.

While the South prided itself on its ability to raise extraordinary amounts of cotton, many regions of the North and Northwest were undergoing a market revolution of truly remarkable dimensions. As a result, the South was lagging dangerously behind the rest of the country in manufacturing, railroads, banking, and industrialization. Campbell surmised that southerners' implacable resolve to remain principally agrarian at all costs contributed to the South's chronic political and economic deterioration. The prospect of adding vast new territory to the nation in many respects underscored the growing differences between North and South as competition for this territory pitted the advocates of southern slavery and agrarianism against northern industrialization and a free labor force that could in no manner compete with slavery. Because of the war, or rather because of the sectional jealousies generated by the war that created the crisis at midcentury, Campbell felt compelled to end his self-imposed exile from public life and to exert as much influence as he could muster in an effort to combat what he perceived as a genuine threat to the South and to southern society.

On 8 August 1846, when David Wilmot, a freshman Democrat from Pennsylvania, introduced a proviso to Polk's military appropriations bill requiring that any territory taken from Mexico be forever free of slave labor, Campbell's fears reached fever pitch. The unthinkable had happened; the assault on slavery limited primarily to literary society meetings and a few pulpits was suddenly thrust into national debate in the halls of Congress where, Campbell feared, policies and statutes designed to abolish the institution would be enacted. Wilmot's amendment, although failing to pass, symbolized northern aggression toward southern institutions and southerners' extreme sensitivity to any attack on slavery.[1] With increased demands throughout the 1840s that all newly acquired territory be reserved solely for free labor, Campbell believed that the South was in danger of being surrounded by a cordon of free states and that southern institutions were in great peril. Far more serious, however, was his conviction that the South would lose nearly all political power if guarantees of state equality were not forthcoming. Campbell's apprehension far exceeded mere concerns about slavery; he was increasingly alarmed that the nation could be split into two opposing sections battling, first, for control over land prospectively acquired from Mexico and, ultimately, for economic and political hegemony. "I have great fears that the existing territories of the United States will prove too much for our government," he wrote.[2] Wilmot's proviso was, borrowing a famous phrase, Campbell's "firebell in the night."

The Wilmot Proviso and its author were categorically denounced throughout the South. Some of the more impetuous—and politically ambitious—members of southern society began insisting that the southern states no longer enjoyed an equal position in the Union and that unless Congress enacted measures guaranteeing southern rights, it would be necessary for the South to secede and to form a nation separate from the United States.[3] There was nothing in Campbell's past to suggest that he would have agreed with these southern radicals' claims that there was no alternative for the South but to secede. Nonetheless, he too believed that the South and its institutions were under assault and that southerners' political power was jeopardized as never before. Though he preferred to remain outside politics, Campbell was jolted into action to protect southern interests in the territories.

Aside from his discussion of slavery, Campbell's article "Slavery in the United States," published in July 1847, clearly shows that he was apprehensive about the Mexican War, and the article reveals that he could no longer remain idle while such a threat to southern society festered.[4] "The agitation on [slavery], every succeeding year," Campbell warned at the outset, "wears an aspect more and more threatening to the stability of [the South's] institutions." "From an obscure sect," he wrote, the abolitionists had become a strong and influential political force in many regions of the North, particularly in Massachusetts, "with sufficient influence to control important elections, and with sufficient authority to make a deep impression upon the councils of government."[5] Campbell recognized that abolitionists remained relatively isolated from the general population, but he complained that during the previous few decades abolitionism had gained more adherents. He believed also that neither slavery nor its abolition was of paramount importance to most people of the nonslaveholding states. A disturbing trend had recently become manifest, however, that wedded northern opinion to abolitionist dogma. "There is an indication that a principle will be found," he wrote, "upon which the conflicting portions [of the North] will harmonize, and that a unity of purpose and conduct will be attained."[6]

When Campbell spoke of a rising "unity of purpose" in the North, he referred to the Free Soil movement, which demanded that all lands prospectively acquired from Mexico remain devoid of slavery so that free labor would not have to compete. The abolition of slavery, therefore, was secondary to what he termed the Free-Soilism that, when coupled with abolitionism, created a political alliance too powerful for northern politicians to ignore. Hence Campbell surmised that this combination served as the primary impetus for Wilmot's proviso. The recently created fusion of the abolition and Free Soil interests had in Campbell's opinion arisen solely as a result of the Mexican War—and the leading culprit who had instigated that conflict was James K. Polk. "The war, if not solicited [by Polk] has not been eschewed; if not directly provoked by the actions of the government, it has done nothing to avoid it." "Sectional jealousies and mutual criminations" arose as a result of the war and the prospect of attaining vast new territories. The hostilities in Mexico exacerbated sectionalism, which had remained mostly dormant in American politics for the previous twenty-five years but was quickly coming to dominate public thought and, more ominously, debates in Congress.[7]

Meanwhile, in response to the Wilmot Proviso the South's leading politician, John C. Calhoun, inaugurated a campaign to organize an all-southern political party as a countervailing force against what he perceived as a menacing and growing abolitionist influence in Congress. The principal thrust of Calhoun's thoughts on slavery and the territories was his theory of nonintervention. According to this theory, Congress had absolutely no authority to legislate with regard to slavery in the territories and could adopt no measures that impeded southerners from emigrating to United States territories with their slaves. Throughout 1847 he wrote numerous influential southerners, including Campbell, requesting their opinions on Wilmot's proviso, nonintervention, current politics, and a number of other volatile issues.[8]

Between November 1847 and March 1848 Campbell responded with three letters to Calhoun in which he stated his views with staggering frankness and in which he most clearly revealed his moderate states' rights philosophy. Campbell began his 20 November letter by explaining that he had only recently returned from a "summer's excursion" to Boston for a visit with his wife's relatives. But, Campbell informed the South Carolinian, he had also called on several abolitionists' offices, inspected their operations, and decided that these people were not as great a threat as many in the South feared. Though his views on abolitionism would change dramatically over the next three years, Campbell stated in late 1847 that southerners should have no concerns about a few fanatics such as William Lloyd Garrison and Theodore Weld. But the Wilmot Proviso, on the other hand, portended dire consequences for the South unless immediate measures were taken to ensure southern rights in the territories.[9]

Campbell then lashed out against the Mexican War. "The folly of that proceeding was so stupendous," he wrote, "that one has hardly an opportunity to contemplate its wickedness." He predicted that the war and the subsequent cession of Mexican territory would prove so divisive that the Union could be destroyed. "I regard the subject of the acquisition of New Territory mainly as it may affect the *balance* of power in the federal government." Campbell surmised that the Mexican War "could only increase the strength of the non-slaveholding states" and produce "a corresponding diminution" of the South's influence and authority in Congress. As he expressed a belief that the majority of the Southwest was wholly unfit for slavery and would eventually be divided into Free Soil states, "I cannot see any ground for a hope that we should receive an equal share of advantage." Thus, the South should demand that absolutely no territory be taken from Mexico.[10]

But Campbell was sufficiently realistic to recognize that land would be added to the United States in the event of Mexico's defeat. Therefore, he informed Calhoun that to offset any potential inequities inherent with land acquisitions, "I wish a counter proviso to the Wilmot Proviso with a definition of property [which would provide that] . . . the laws of the state from which a citizen may remove may define as property [in the territories]. And that this condition shall so remain until the people of the territory shall form a State and be admitted to the Union, and this I would like to see a part of the Treaty of peace."[11] He was asking Congress not for a definition of property in the territories but rather for recognition that state laws governing property rights would remain in force throughout American territories. On the other hand, Campbell did not deny that Congress possessed authority to define property in the territories. And if it possessed such power, Congress could not only legislate with regard to slavery in the territories, it could enact an outright ban on slave labor. Here, then, was why the crisis was so severe and why an immediate southern response to Wilmot's proviso was necessary. Campbell hoped to garner treaty guarantees that Mexican emancipation laws would be automatically void with the formal transfer of territory. Furthermore, every citizen of the United States, he advised, must be guaranteed rights to settle in the territories with their slaves, and all property rights must remain as protected in the territory as in their home states.

Campbell also informed Calhoun that he vehemently opposed Michigan senator Lewis Cass's theory of popular sovereignty—a doctrine based on the premise that only the people of a territory should decide the slavery issue. In late 1847, the publication of what was known as the "Nicholson letter" confirmed Cass as the leading proponent of popular sovereignty. But this doctrine left obscure precisely *when* the people should vote on the slavery issue: *during* the territorial stage or *after* the population had reached sufficient numbers for statehood. The people of a territory, Campbell maintained, should not be allowed to ban slavery until *after* their territory had achieved statehood so that by then slave labor would be well established and relatively safeguarded from hostile legislation.[12] He thus sought to alert southerners to the inherent dangers of Cass's popular sovereignty in an editorial published in the *Mobile Herald* titled "The Prospect Before Us."

The editorial began with extracts from two letters: the first was a segment of the Nicholson letter in which Cass had written that due to geography and climate the Mexican cession was entirely unsuitable for slave labor and plantation agriculture. The second quotation was from Secretary of State James Buchanan that was in agreement with the sentiments Cass had expressed and included that it was "morally impossible" for slavery to exist in California and New Mexico. Campbell also asserted that Vice-President George M. Dallas and Secretary of the Treasury Robert J. Walker held similar beliefs. He therefore warned that the most influential members of the national government believed that "'a cordon of free states' by a moral and legal necessity must be constituted out of the new acquisitions from Mexico." Campbell may have been overly consumed by the Mexican War and suffering from clouded judgment and irrational thought; for whatever reason, he suggested that the war was but part of a much larger conspiracy by abolitionists and their political allies to create a crisis over territorial acquisition that could destroy slavery and the South's political position in the Union.[13] He informed Calhoun in November 1847 that Lewis Cass should not be considered for the Democrats' presidential nomination.

Much to Campbell's chagrin, however, Cass was the leading Democrat for the upcoming 1848 presidential campaign. And as he perceived that no southern Democrat would be acceptable in the North, Campbell worried that the South would become politically isolated if Cass were to win the election. The crisis over slavery and the territories so prostrated the Democratic party, Campbell reasoned, that he did not expect that it could resolve the growing crisis over the extension of slavery. "It is a very great error, it appears to me, to suppose that we have any party at the North, or that we shall ever have one." The northern Democrats, he explained to Calhoun, "do not guide public opinion on [slavery]. They follow after in obedience to it." Furthermore, he stated that the "union of the Democratic Party with the abolitionists [was] far more dangerous" than an abolitionist alliance with the Whigs because they were generally guided by their "leading and reflecting men," whereas the Democracy was full of ambitious newcomers hell-bent on national recognition. These new-generation Democrats, and men like David Wilmot in particular, were governed by "few restraints and ready to go [to] farther lengths to carry their ends."[14]

Hence, partisan and calculating opportunists willing to use slavery as a stepping-stone to political power were the great menace confronting the United States. Campbell warned that these opportunists' "notions are freer, impulses stronger, [and] wills less restrained."[15] And because abolitionism had so permeated northern churches, literary societies, and the press, it "had grown to embrace a very large proportion of the population." "The things which do affect the thoughts of men," Campbell surmised, ". . . are the continual condemnations that [slavery] receives. The Legislatures, anniversary orators and poets, ministers of the Gospel, [and] teachers, all combine in impressing a fixed sentiment in the people." Northern politicians, Campbell asserted, could not be trusted to protect southern interests because they were heavily influenced by the abolitionism and Free Soil movements. "I confess a profound indifference to the election of any Democrat [from] north of the Potomac," he wrote.[16] Consequently, the only strategy he believed that might work to the South's advantage was to find a more acceptable presidential candidate.[17]

In late December Campbell wrote a second letter to Calhoun. He once again informed the South Carolinian that he could not support Cass's bid for the party nomination because popular sovereignty would be the cornerstone of his platform. Campbell lamented, however, that there were no other Democrats capable of winning. He stated that he therefore had no alternative but to support Zachary Taylor, who at least *appeared* more friendly toward the South and who was not necessarily bound to any party, platform, or ideology. "We must find a man who will not accept a party nomination," Campbell informed Calhoun. "General Taylor is that man." Campbell had never been absolutely loyal to the Democratic party, and he had no qualms about supporting Taylor who, although a Whig, seemed less dangerous to the South than did a Democrat who might very well ignore southern grievances.[18]

Campbell advised Calhoun that he was not concerned about the spread of slavery per se, but he realized that if new states were added to the Union under Free Soil pretenses, the South would hold a minority position in Congress. Because of the differences in the populations of North and South, northerners controlled the House of Representatives. Representation in the Senate was equally divided between North and South, but Campbell feared that with the acquisition of Mexican lands, the South would lose its last bastion in Congress and would be left economically and politically subservient to the North. "In having peace with Mexico," he explained, "we must not transfer the war so that it shall reach our homes."[19] "It appears to me that the southern people will be found in a weak position if they insist on the acquisition of territory." The best course, Campbell advised, was to "desire no [territory] and ask for none for the purpose of strengthening our institutions." "We require a moderate and even a self-denying course of conduct in all matters connected with the settlement of the terms of the peace," he wrote. "Let us have peace, we shall not quarrel about the terms." "I say," he continued, "[that] we shall have the northern people settle the peace as they like and to arrange the questions of territory. But always with the PROVISO that no inequality should result. We should be the *proviso* men, and on that ground we should make our stand."[20]

On 1 March 1848, Campbell sent a third and most remarkable letter to Calhoun, who must have shuddered with disbelief as he read Campbell's opinions. This letter deserves close scrutiny, for it has been at the heart of much discussion concerning Campbell's 1857 *Dred Scott* decision while he sat as a United States Supreme Court justice. The *Dred Scott* decision rendered the Missouri Compromise line unconstitutional and in essence established that Congress had no authority to ban slavery from any United States territory. In contrast to this Supreme Court decision, with which Campbell agreed in substance, in March 1848 the Alabamian told Calhoun in unmistakably clear and frank language:

> I think Congress has the power to organize inhabitants of a territory of the U.S. into a body politic, and to determine in what manner they shall be governed. As incident to this power I think that Congress may decide what shall be held and enjoyed as property in that territory and that persons should not be held as property. I think further that when territory is acquired by conquest or by treaty and the municipal laws in force in the territory are not changed by the treaty of cession or by an act of [C]ongress that they remain in force. . . .
>
> When you admit that Congress may form a *government* you concede the right to it to define what shall be property and how it may be enjoyed, transferred, or inherited. It may decide that persons shall or shall not be property. There is nothing about Slave property that I know of that takes it from the sway of legislative authority.[21]

Campbell informed Calhoun that Congress had clearly established several precedents for the power to regulate slavery in the territories, and that these antecedents could not be overlooked. "Allow me to call your attention to the weight of authority and precedent" established throughout American history: "the repeated sanctions to the Ordinance of 1787 by Congress; the implied sanction in the compacts of Georgia and North Carolina ceding territories and stipulating for the extension of the ordinance except in one particular; the Missouri Compromise; [and] the admission of Texas with a restriction."[22]

The striking contradictions between Campbell's March 1848 letter to Calhoun and his decision in *Dred Scott* are unmistakable, and these certainly have not passed unnoticed by historians—some of whom claim that Campbell dramatically shifted his political philosophy in 1857 to concur with the majority in the *Dred Scott* decision. Several historians suggest that in light of his assertions to Calhoun in 1848, Campbell completely disregarded his actual feelings concerning congressional power to regulate slavery in the territories and instead ruled with the majority in an effort to perpetuate and to extend slavery throughout all United States territories.

The first historian to address this issue was E. I. McCormac in a 1933 article titled "Justice Campbell and the *Dred Scott* Decision."[23] The entire March 1848 letter is reprinted in McCormac's article to show Campbell's contrasting views. McCormac states that Campbell "executed a 'right about face' when he prepared his opinion in the *Dred Scott* case," and argued that Congress had no authority "to prohibit slavery from the territories." McCormac raises the question whether Campbell simply changed his mind on this issue, but he doubts whether a sincere change of opinion occurred. Jurists are normally "slow and reluctant to alter their opinions," McCormac writes, and as Campbell was one of the nation's leading legal minds, it is not likely that he would have so radically departed from the position he took in 1848. Thus despite his concurrence in *Dred Scott,* Campbell actually believed that Congress had full authority to establish the Missouri Compromise line and that it could regulate slavery in the territories at its discretion. McCormac concludes that in 1857 Campbell was obviously influenced more by political considerations than by any fundamental tenets of constitutional law.[24]

In 1966, James P. McPherson's article on Campbell appearing in the *Alabama Review* was in agreement with McCormac's assessment that Campbell changed his mind on this issue.[25] McPherson notes that it was impossible to determine why Campbell reversed his position on the powers of Congress to regulate slavery in the territories. He, like McCormac, doubts whether the Alabamian experienced an honest change of opinion, though, and he conjectures that perhaps Campbell maintained such highly conservative opinions in 1848 because he was "a young and ambitious Southerner and his goal in life was to serve on the United States Supreme Court." This supposition is completely without merit. In 1848 Campbell had no grandiose notions of joining the nation's highest tribunal; such pretensions had no place in his character. Besides, when he wrote the letter to Calhoun in 1848, he had never even appeared before the Taney Court. Why McPherson suggests that Campbell thought he could one day be a Supreme Court justice is somewhat baffling.[26]

Later historians who wrote more extensive accounts of the *Dred Scott* decision likewise adopted the view that Campbell either changed his mind on Congress's power to prohibit slavery in the territories or that he simply chose to ignore his earlier—and most heartfelt—opinions on the matter. For instance, Carl B. Swisher, clearly the most learned scholar of the Taney period, writes that when Campbell drafted his 1857 decision, "he showed a commitment to slavery hardly less fervent than that of Justice [Peter V., of Virginia] Daniel." Moreover, Swisher asserts, "[Campbell] ignored the position he had taken nine years earlier in a private letter to . . . Calhoun."[27] In one of the standard works detailing the political history of the 1850s, David Potter states,

"It was ironical that Campbell should have" ruled as he did in *Dred Scott*, "for he had written a letter to Calhoun in 1848, arguing that Congress possessed full power to exclude slavery from the territories."[28]

This issue is no insignificant matter, for it strikes at the very core of Campbell's character. If in 1857 he was willing to disregard his actual feelings regarding congressional authority to regulate slavery in the territories, it would certainly indicate abject hypocrisy on Campbell's part. Moreover, such a situation would suggest that he was guided more by political considerations and by what he saw as a diminution of the South's political power. But this was not the case. Though it would be wrong to conclude that political considerations played no role in Campbell's *Dred Scott* decision, it would be similarly incorrect to assert that he was driven singularly by current politics. As will be shown, Campbell's *Dred Scott* decision was based fundamentally on constitutional issues, and though in 1848 he had held that Congress could obstruct the expansion of slavery to the territories, he had long abandoned that position several years before *Dred Scott*.

The question that all of these historians tacitly raise yet do not address is *when* Campbell's change of opinion occurred. Their accounts of the *Dred Scott* decision leave readers with the impression that Campbell either ignored his true feelings or that he changed his mind *as the* Dred Scott *decision was being written*. Both suppositions are incorrect. Campbell did in fact change his mind and in effect repudiate much of what he told Calhoun in 1848. But this change did not occur in 1857 during the *Dred Scott* case. Nor did this happen in 1853 when Campbell was nominated to the bench. Instead, when one examines all of his papers, speeches, and writings, one sees that Campbell gradually began to alter the opinions he had expressed to Calhoun as early as summer 1848. Although it is impossible to pinpoint the exact moment when this change of opinion occurred, there is clear evidence to suggest that it was complete by June 1850 when Campbell served as a delegate to the Nashville Convention. Thus a narrative of Campbell's political activities from 1848 until 1852 provides considerable insight into his evolving political philosophy.

Campbell's third letter to Calhoun revealed that he was suffering no small measure of quiet desperation. He fully understood the serious ramifications of the crisis, and he was deeply pained for the Union and for the South, both of which he loved dearly. "I see we are on the eve of collisions and conflicts worse than those with Mexico."[29] To Campbell, the only proper remedy for the crisis over the Mexican cession would be a provision in any future treaty ceding the California and New Mexico territories from Mexico that would nullify all emancipation decrees formerly passed by the Mexican government and operative in the territories. "I think," he told Calhoun, "that when a territory is acquired by conquest or by treaty and the municipal laws in force in the territory are not changed by the treaty of cession or by an act of Congress that they remain in force." Mexican abolition laws would, therefore, remain operative after the territory passed to the United States unless the treaty specifically nullified these laws or the United States Congress passed laws to protect slavery and to supersede any previous emancipation decrees enacted by the Mexican government. "With these opinions," he wrote, "I hold Mr. Polk's war, as likely to produce the most disastrous consequences to the Southern States."[30]

In Campbell's view, the only measures sufficient to remedy the crisis would be based on assuring an equal share of the Mexican cession for the South. In January 1848, while he was in Montgomery preparing an argument for the state supreme court, Campbell sought to convince influential Alabama politicians that the crisis over the Mexican cession would be disastrous for the South and that immediate measures were necessary to offset any potential inequities that could result if the nation nearly doubled in size. Unquestionably, the most significant of these politicians with whom Campbell held informal discussions that January was William Lowndes Yancey.

Yancey's life has not been satisfactorily chronicled.[31] Nonetheless, enough is known to describe him as Alabama's premier fire-eater. As a moderately wealthy plantation owner and editor of the Wetumpka *Argus,* Yancey rose in the ranks of Alabama's democracy with an uncanny ability to rouse his audiences into a frenzy. One historian notes that Yancey "was a uniquely passionate orator in an age when passionate oratory was the standard; his vocal range was able to keep a staid conversational cadence and then leap into high tones of fervid declamation. . . . Yancey was deadly with his voice, and it was injurious to cross him on the speaker's platform."[32]

Like Campbell, Yancey had earlier grown disillusioned with American politics. Also like Campbell, he disagreed with Calhoun in 1848 that the Democratic party could settle the mounting sectional crisis. Unlike Campbell, though, Yancey maintained that the South had no other recourse but to abandon the Union and to establish a separate nation. By the late 1840s, as neither Yancey nor Campbell were in agreement with the Jacksonian branch of Alabama Democrats, principally in the northern regions of the state, and as they did not concur with the Calhounites in central Alabama holding firm to nonintervention, they were men without strict party affiliation. Both of these Alabamians who viewed the crisis at midcentury as a dramatically serious assault on southern institutions were drawn in January 1848 into what became a temporary political alliance that culminated in the drafting of the Alabama Platform.[33]

The Alabama Platform, adopted in February 1848 by delegates attending the Democrats' state nominating convention, was one of the most forceful statements of southern grievances to date and was considered by its authors to be a direct challenge to the Wilmot Proviso. It was in essence a sharply pointed threat to the northern people: southerners should be allowed to settle with their slaves in any new territory, it said, or the Union would be in serious jeopardy.[34] Consisting of twenty-four resolutions, or "planks," the platform was indeed a radical "line-in-the-sand," and it eventually contributed to destroying the unity of the Democratic party thirteen years after its inception. One of the principal resolutions required that Alabama's delegates to the National Democratic Convention scheduled for May in no way "support for the offices of President and Vice-President of the United States any persons who shall not openly and avowedly be opposed to either of the forms of excluding slavery from the territories of the United States." The next resolution established that the entire document serve as instructions to Alabama's delegates, "to guide them in their votes in that body."[35]

In his third letter to Calhoun, Campbell wrote that in light of the fact that Congress could legitimately ban slavery in the territories, "I wrote the resolutions offered by Mr. Yancey to the Montgomery Convention *requiring the rejection of territory unless the treaty or an act of Congress provided guarantees against Mexican and abolition legislation and laws.*"[36] The "guarantee" Campbell hoped to attain was a clear recognition of the doctrine of positive protection. The resolutions of the Alabama Platform that should be attributed to Campbell are:

> *Resolved:* That the treaty of cession should contain a clause securing an entry into those territories to all the citizens of the United States, together with their property of every description, and that the same should remain protected by the United States while the territories are under its authority.
> *Resolved:* That if it should be found inconvenient to insert such a clause into the treaty of cession, that our Senators and Representatives in Congress should be vigilant to obtain before the ratification of such a treaty ample securities that the rights of the Southern people should not be endangered during the period the territories shall remain under the control of the United States either from the continuance of abolition laws of Mexico, or from the legislation of the United States.[37]

These two resolutions unmistakably reflect Campbell's sentiments as expressed in his letters to Calhoun and especially the description of his contribution to the platform he presented in his 1 March letter. If it proved impractical for a clause to be inserted into the treaty guaranteeing southern rights, Campbell wrote, Congress should prudently, and for the good of the entire nation, enact laws designed to placate the South.

As noted earlier, neither Campbell nor Yancey believed that Cass should receive the Democratic nomination for the upcoming presidential contest because of his support for popular sovereignty. In an effort to defeat Cass's bid, Yancey and Campbell incorporated resolutions into the platform that both men knew were unacceptable to northern Democrats. As early as December 1847, Yancey decided that Levi Woodbury of New Hampshire, who was appointed to the United States Supreme Court in 1845, would be an acceptable candidate favorable to southern interests and a northerner capable of carrying crucial northern states.[38] Campbell, on the other hand, did not consider Woodbury a suitable candidate at all. "Mr. Woodbury has reached quite as high a place as Nature ever intended he should fill," Campbell wrote. He recognized that Woodbury was a loyal party man, but he inquired: "Looking above the party can we hope any good from his nomination? It would create a schism in every northern state in the democratic party," along the same lines that had been drawn at New York's nominating convention that ended with two delegations—Hunkers and Barnburners—both planning to attend the national convention.[39] Campbell believed that the crisis was so severe that it required men to "look above the party" and to consider with all seriousness the folly of ignoring the increasing animosity between the sections. He harbored few positive feelings for organized political parties, and he would not lament a schism in the democracy if the northern wing insisted on Cass's nomination. He conjectured that if by chance Woodbury received the nomination, the Democrats would lose the election. If the party split over the Alabama Platform, this too would ensure a Taylor victory. Either way Campbell's man would win, and popular sovereignty would be rendered politically moot. In any event, Campbell was confident that the Alabama Platform would candidly and unequivocally alert northerners that the South had legitimate grievances that needed to be addressed. Second, he believed that the platform could defeat Cass's nomination and ensure a Taylor victory.

Yancey was likewise interested in ensuring that the Democrats not nominate Lewis Cass. Brazenly confident that all of Alabama's delegates would follow his lead and bolt the national convention if Cass were nominated and the Alabama Platform rejected, Yancey arrived in Baltimore on 22 May armed with his platform that he hoped to force on the convention.[40] His dreams of nominating the dark horse Woodbury or producing a schism within the Democratic party, however, quickly evaporated into one of the more humiliating experiences of his life: when the platform was repudiated by the majority of delegates, only one Alabamian followed Yancey out of the convention hall. The outright rejection of the platform and its most vociferous proponent merely underscored the naiveté with which the entire episode was conceived.[41] That Yancey and Campbell expected their scheme to work revealed that each still had a tremendous amount to learn about the nature of American politics.

Of course, the problem was that as the years passed Yancey learned those lessons all too well, and his constant speech making in support of states' rights, coupled with the dramatic events that led the nation toward Civil War during the 1850s, lent increased credibility to the Alabama Platform. Seismic events such as Bleeding Kansas, the *Dred Scott* decision, and John Brown's raid at Harper's Ferry, made even more severe by Yancey's and other fire-eaters' incessant rhetoric, transformed the Alabama Platform into the radical document that it had become by 1860, when it served as one of the final wedges dividing the Democratic party.[42]

In 1848, Campbell's portion of the platform was an altogether misguided attempt to answer Wilmot's proviso with the doctrine of positive protection. It indicated that despite his objections to holding public office, he nevertheless wished to be politically influential. The crisis at midcentury boded such dire consequences for the South that Campbell felt compelled to depart radically from his earlier political inactivity and to engage in political chicanery unbecoming to someone of his social standing and high intellect. Campbell was one of the most intelligent and talented jurists in the nation, but his connection with the Alabama Platform revealed that he was exceptionally naive about American politics and American politicians. We can only speculate as to why he could not see the futility of joining Yancey in the attempt to disrupt a national convention. Obviously Campbell believed the crisis sufficiently severe to necessitate extraordinary efforts to ensure southern rights.

Still, Campbell was no fire-eater. He never suggested that the South secede, though he consistently maintained the constitutionality of secession. He could not imagine any scenario, however, short of an invasion from the North that would justify a dissolution of the Union. Campbell was a well-intentioned but impractical idealist who felt in 1848 that the nation was in serious peril and that extreme measures had to be taken to avoid catastrophe. His desire to preserve southern political and social interests was genuine, understandable, and in some respects honorable. Yet his attempt at playing politics from the periphery was woefully misguided, and the platform to which he contributed in 1848 was hopelessly unrealistic.

It is difficult to pinpoint the exact date when Campbell realized the futility of supporting positive protection as outlined in the Alabama Platform. It is tempting to conjecture that he began to reevaluate the political climate and crisis over the territories as early as June 1848. He most certainly would by then have realized that Yancey's use of the Alabama Platform was much more than an attempt to garner guarantees of southern rights in the territories and that the principal architect of this platform had secession as his ultimate goal. In other words, perhaps Yancey's actions in Baltimore convinced Campbell that the Alabama Platform was not a political document and a mechanism for rationally outlining southern grievances but an ultimatum to the North by a southern fire-eater fully intent on destroying the Union.

Moreover, Campbell realized that positive protection was an inadequate doctrine for protecting southern rights because it was politically unrealistic and potentially disastrous to North-South relations. He therefore began to seek other avenues to guarantee that the southern states would receive an equal share of the territories and that the South's political power within the federal government would not diminish further. This led him to revise his states' rights philosophy considerably and, in essence, to repudiate most of what he had written to Calhoun in March 1848.

Campbell turned thirty-nine years old in 1850. Throughout most of his life he had demonstrated nothing but profound respect for the federal government. He had been an ardent defender of states' rights, but at the same time his version of this doctrine was quite moderate, and more often than not Campbell defended the rights, power, and increased jurisdiction of the national government. The crisis at midcentury, however, changed much of this in Campbell. He reassessed what he perceived as the fundamental meaning of the Constitution, the respective roles of the state and federal governments, and the federal-state relationship. And by mid-1850 his political philosophy was decidedly more radical than it had been in 1848 when he acknowledged substantial congressional authority to govern the territories. As with many southerners—John C. Calhoun in particular—Campbell's early nationalism evaporated when he began to believe that the threats to the South were severe enough to destroy southern society.

6 | States' Rights Triumphant

Campbell was pleased that Zachary Taylor won the 1848 presidential contest. He was evidently under the impression that the new president would protect southern interests during a time of increased hostility between the northern and the southern states and when, as Campbell viewed the situation, Congress was coming to be controlled by radical abolitionists and Free-Soilers. He was also concerned that the waning months of the lame-duck Polk administration offered little hope of any abatement in the heightened sectional antagonisms. When Johann Sutter struck gold in California, the territory rapidly filled with settlers, so that there was an immediate need for organized government. Not a few southerners feared that California had slipped from their grasp, as the majority of settlers streaming into the territory were Free-Soilers. Henry Clay, the formidable Kentucky senator and spiritual leader of the Whigs, assumed that with Taylor safely in the White House, he could dominate national affairs and stifle internal discord. After the President insisted that Congress approve Californians' demands to enter the Union with an antislavery constitution, however, Clay's worst fears became reality.[1] By December 1849, the country faced a real possibility of disunion, and Americans looked nervously to the upcoming Thirty-first Congress to settle the growing crisis.

During the 1849–1850 congressional session, several key issues severely threatened the Union: California's request for admission to the Union with a constitution prohibiting slavery; the question of whether to apply the Wilmot Proviso to the remainder of the Mexican cession, comprising the Utah and New Mexico Territories; the question of whether to ban the slave trade in the nation's capital; a dispute over the boundary separating the New Mexico Territory and Texas; and last, southerners' demands that Congress enact a more effective fugitive slave law.[2] Fully comprehending the profound significance of these issues, Clay referred to them collectively as the "Five Bleeding Wounds." When southerners concluded that the crisis would not be settled to the South's satisfaction with existing party alignments, the gathering storm of disunion darkened the nation's political future as southern fire-eaters insisted that the South must secede at once. Secession—the word had been so often used in the past that by the 1840s it was generally viewed as little more than a veiled threat—was now being seriously considered by many southerners as the only viable alternative to economic ruin. Public meetings were organized at which hotheaded orators chastised the North and insisted in the best fire-eating rhetoric of the day that the South must secede or face destruction.

Calhoun too believed that the Union, which he loved and hoped to preserve, was seriously endangered because of the inflammatory nature of these problems. At the same time, however, he felt that the issues facing Congress could not be settled to the South's satisfaction. He thus continued to support the formation of a third party to serve as the voice and power of the southern states in Congress. Calhoun also urged a general convention of influential southerners to meet and discuss what the South's response should be if Congress enacted legislation unfavorable to southern interests. Largely to avoid charges of radicalism, the South Carolinian suggested that a southern state other than South Carolina should lead in the call for an all-southern convention. Nonetheless, he played a substantial role through letters to many influential southerners.[3]

In October 1849, a bipartisan convention held in Jackson, Mississippi, heeded Calhoun's advice and issued a call for a southern convention to meet in Nashville in June 1850. Initial reaction throughout the South was favorable, especially after Congress convened in December and found itself unable to elect a Speaker of the House without heated debate and numerous ballots. Sentiment toward the proposed convention was generally favorable in Alabama as well, particularly among Democrats. Many Whigs, on the other hand, preferred to avoid inordinate and impetuous acts; they declared that no action by Alabama should be taken unless Congress enacted strict antislavery legislation. In such an event, the Whigs maintained, a state convention would suffice as a show of Alabama's displeasure. Several attempts were made by Democrats to bring the issue to the floor of the House in late January. But the Whigs managed to stall any action and largely succeeded in blocking further proposals to elect delegates to the convention. Finally, on 6 February 1850, in an informal (actually extralegal) meeting called by a bipartisan majority, Alabama's legislature named thirty-six delegates to attend the Nashville Convention.[4] Among the prominent Alabama leaders selected to represent the state in Nashville were former governor Benjamin Fitzpatrick, state representative Leroy Pope Walker, state circuit court judge George Goldthwaite, and John Archibald Campbell, who was named one of eight delegates at large.

After several additional southern states had agreed to send representatives to the Nashville Convention, Americans in both the North and the South conjectured about the purpose of the planned meeting. Few people knew exactly what the delegates intended to do once they assembled in Nashville; some northern Whigs and other opponents declared that the delegates' objective was to excite emotions in the South and to coerce states to secede from the Union.

Lewis Cass announced that the convention would be composed "of the most violent men." "The future is all dark," he lamented.[5] Nathaniel Beverley Tucker of Virginia, a half brother to the often acrid John Randolph of Roanoke and a fanatical advocate of secession, was jubilant when he was selected to represent Virginia at Nashville. Tucker at once insisted that the convention demand impossible conditions from the North and thereby necessitate the South's secession.[6] Such rhetoric confirmed northern suspicion that the Nashville Convention's primary purpose was to orchestrate the South's withdrawal from the Union. Throughout the first half of 1850 the country remained in grave danger largely because the inflammatory speeches and letters of southern radicals temporarily found favor with many southern people.[7]

Henry Clay was certainly not blind to the danger, and as in 1820 and 1833, he began to construct compromise measures to defuse hostilities. The odds of orchestrating a settlement in 1850 were certainly stacked against the Kentuckian, however, especially considering that the House of Representatives was deadlocked in unprecedented sectional bickering and shameful political posturing. Even after fifty-nine ballots, none of the candidates for Speaker was able to muster a majority. Hence House members settled for Howell Cobb, who was elected with a mere plurality. But legislation could not be passed on that basis, and southerners watched with growing alarm as Congress sank further and further into virulent squabbling. Throughout most of January 1850, serious and conciliatory debate in the House ceased as members, many of them armed, resorted to shouts, retorts, and accusations.[8] The nation was on the verge of disaster.

On the night of 21 January, Clay called on Daniel Webster. Clay, Calhoun, and Webster comprised what historians often call the Great Triumvirate, for these three statesmen had dominated Congress for thirty years and had avoided disunion and disaster twice before 1850. On this occasion, however, battle lines divided the Triumvirate, as Calhoun stood defiantly in support of his beloved South. If a compromise could be reached, Clay reasoned, he had to have Webster on his side. At their meeting, the Kentuckian explained his ideas to Webster, who then agreed to support the bid for a compromise.[9] Clay's Omnibus Bill, as his collective compromise measures were dubbed, brought some measure of relief from the heightened tensions and flared tempers paralyzing the Thirty-first Congress.

With Clay's compromise measures then in Congress, Campbell believed that there was no compelling reason for the Nashville Convention to be overly radical or threatening. Yet he remained decidedly cautious; in reality, Clay's compromise measures did little to assuage the crisis and soothe tempers. Moreover, in Campbell's view the Omnibus Bill dodged the main issue: whether Congress could exclude slavery from the Mexican cession. Without this point being settled in favor of states' rights, Campbell reasoned that the five principal issues dividing the nation could easily be decided to the North's political advantage. He therefore adopted a wait-and-see policy; the convention resolutions should be moderate yet resolute, conciliatory yet concrete. Unless Congress enacted legislation diametrically contrary to slavery and southern interests, hasty, ill-advised radicalism should be avoided. Such rhetoric and posturing, he concluded, would only needlessly aggravate sectional tensions.

In late May, Campbell rode by stage through North Alabama toward Nashville. He used his time on the road constructively by drafting sixteen resolutions that he hoped would be adopted by the convention. In essence, these resolutions reveal Campbell's newly revised and strengthened states' rights doctrine. Whereas to 1848 Campbell had held to a moderate version of states' rights in which the federal government could constitutionally exclude slavery from the territories, the mounting sectional crisis coupled with attacks on slavery had so shaken him that he adopted an unquestionably more far-reaching version of states' rights in which the federal government's powers were greatly diminished. In June 1850 Campbell's new states' rights philosophy was first revealed. The Alabamian was certainly aware that his participation in the convention afforded a second opportunity to articulate southern grievances and demands; his first attempt with Yancey in 1848 became a comic opera that had unfolded in Baltimore and had revealed the dangers inherent in positive protection. The convention, he hoped, would produce more constructive results.

Nashville had been bustling for weeks as delegates and observers from throughout the South arrived. There was an air of excitement rarely seen in that town when the first session convened at Odd Fellows Hall on 3 June. During the first day of deliberations, William Sharkey of Mississippi was named president of the convention. Thereafter the meetings were moved to the McKendree Church because Odd Fellows Hall was not large enough to accommodate the delegates and the growing number of curious spectators.[10]

Campbell and the other Alabama delegates attended every session. On 5 June, the first order of business involved consideration of the Alabamian's sixteen proposals, which were referred to the Committee on Resolutions for further attention. The first resolution bluntly and decisively affirmed that all territories of the United States "belong to the people of the several states of this Union as their common property." Every American citizen, furthermore, had equal rights to migrate with their property to any territory, "and are [all] equally entitled *to the protection of the federal government* in the enjoyment of that property so long as the territories remain under the charge of that government."[11]

Campbell's first resolution was lifted directly from the Alabama Platform, particularly its reference to positive protection. The most significant clause of this resolution, however, was its reference to property rights. Campbell, who had by June 1850 adopted Justice Collier's version of original sovereignty, maintained that Congress had no authority to determine what property may be held by any American citizen. This role was exclusively reserved for the states. Therefore, Congress had an obligation to protect each state's right to define property. And in accordance with the logical extreme of the original sovereignty doctrine, all territories were in reality states waiting to be created, and thus Congress could not define property in territories, as doing so would unconstitutionally undermine the sovereignty of prospective states. Congress was not necessarily obligated to protect slavery in the territories, but it had to protect any citizen whose property was titled, legally sanctioned, and protected in his home state.[12]

Resolutions 2 and 3 stated that all laws passed by Congress "for the purpose of excluding [slavery] from the territories" were unconstitutional. Congress also had the duty to "refuse a recognition of foreign laws in American territories." The third resolution was, of course, aimed directly at the international convention, which held that laws, such as Mexican abolition statutes, remained in force even though territory might be transferred to the jurisdiction of a different sovereign nation. The purpose of the fourth resolution was to articulate Campbell's perception of the powers of the federal government and the limits that were placed on its power with the adoption of the Constitution. "That for the protection of the property recognized in the several States in the Union," Campbell wrote, "the people of those states invested the federal government with the powers of war and negotiation, of maintaining armies and navies, and of forming alliances and compacts, and denied to the State authorities these powers."[13]

He had changed his mind since speaking with Calhoun in March 1848, however, for he wrote: "[N]o discrimination was made in the federal constitution as to the extent of the protection to be afforded, or the description of property to be defended. . . . *Nor was it permitted to the federal government to determine what is property.* Whatever the laws of the States constituted as property the federal government is bound to protect as such."[14]

Here, then, was Campbell's fundamental view on property rights. He recognized a clear division between the powers of the federal government and those of the states. Whenever a conflict arose between these powers, particularly with reference to property, state definitions of property should be upheld. With these principles established as one of the cornerstones of the Constitution,

> It is therefore the sense of this convention that every act of the federal government which places any portion of the property lawfully held in the States of the Union out of the protection of the federal government, or which discriminates in the nature and the extent of the protection to be given to different species of property, or which impairs the title of the citizen in any of the territories of the Union, without affording just compensation, is a plain

and palpable violation of the obligations of the government, and is contrary to the spirit and meaning of the constitution of the United States.[15]

From a reading of these four resolutions, one gains a clear understanding of how sharply Campbell's version of states' rights doctrine differed from that which he had disclosed to Calhoun two years earlier. In all cases whatsoever, Congress indeed held extensive powers to establish governments for the territories, but it could neither pass laws to discriminate against slavery nor in any measure alter property titles that had originated in states. In fact, Congress was obligated to protect state definitions of property. Clearly, Campbell must have recognized the inherent contradictions between resolutions 1 and 4. He insisted that Congress had no authority to legislate with regard to slavery in the territories while he concurrently argued that sufficient authority existed for Congress to protect state definitions of property. Apparently, Campbell wanted it both ways—the assurances of positive protection coupled with the doctrine of nonintervention.

Resolutions 5, 6, and 7 were mostly reiterations of the preceding resolutions but included a clear statement that any recognition of inequality among the states would not be tolerated in the South. Campbell predicted in resolution 8 that, if the principles outlined in the first seven proposals were acknowledged, "the difficulties that environ the country would be removed." Moreover, "[t]he territories of the union would be gradually settled and the population disciplined and improved without interference from wily politicians. Their institutions would be adjusted by the wants and opinions of the immigrants and their constitutions as States would be the result of deliberate choice and not extraneous intermeddling—a people thus formed might properly claim an admission to the Union and all would admit the sufficiency of the claim."[16]

Basically stated, the people of a territory could in no manner ban slavery from their borders until they were prepared to adopt a state constitution. Thereafter, Campbell advised, "the wants and opinions of the immigrants" would form the basis of their constitution and all subsequent legislation regarding slavery. Any application of popular sovereignty—or, as Campbell called it, "extraneous intermeddling"—would produce further dissatisfaction in the South because it could lead to a premature and artificial exclusion of slavery from outside influences before there was sufficient population in the territory to protect southern property rights.

Campbell asserted in the ninth resolution that the Texas boundary dispute would likewise be magnanimously settled if the above principles were fully recognized, and as stated in resolution 10, a "spirit of conciliation would be infused into a discussion of every question which has grown out of the" territory crisis. The eleventh resolution declared, however, that southerners could in no manner accept further egregious assaults on their institutions, character, morals, or lifestyle by radical northern abolitionists. According to Campbell, southerners would not abide proposals in Congress to surround the southern states with free territory. All claims that Congress had the power to abolish slavery would be seen as an open attack on southern institutions. Furthermore, southerners would take extreme offense at resolutions suggesting that Congress could rightfully enact laws restricting slavery in the territories or at resolutions holding that slaves were automatically freed upon entering a free state. Last, Campbell insisted that tempers would again flare with statements that southern congressional representatives should be "cured of [their] propensity" to look outside the United States for the addition of future slave states.[17]

Such statements by northern radicals were, Campbell remarked, "alarming manifestations of hostility to the equal positions of the slaveholding States in the Union, dangerous declarations against their peace and tranquility, and demand from this Convention a special notice and unmixed reprobation." Campbell's statements in this resolution closely mirror the principal issues before the Supreme Court in the *Dred Scott* case of 1857, particularly with reference to congressional authority to restrict slavery in the territories and the question of whether a slave's temporary sojourn into a free state negated his or her legal status as a slave. As of June 1850, therefore, Campbell's position on these issues was well established, and it was—or it should have been—clear how he would rule when confronted with a case before the Court in which these issues were to be decided.

Resolution 12 stated that as the Mexican cession was acquired "by the blood and treasure of the people of all the states," southerners insisted on their fair share of the territory. "Whether the political ties which bind the parts of the Union together" could withstand an uneven distribution of territory, "this convention will not enquire." But he warned that the spirit of patriotism and nationalism that had in previous years permeated all of American society would be destroyed in the South and that southerners would lose all confidence and faith in the central government unless the South's rights to the territories were recognized. Any laws or regulations to the contrary would be "a triumph of fanaticism, party spirit, sordid and selfish ambition, and sectional hate" over the spirit of compromise that had prevailed since the drafting of the federal Constitution.[18]

In resolution 13 Campbell suggested that if Congress continued to deny the validity of southern rights in all the territories, southerners would be willing to "acquiesce" and equally divide the Mexican cession at the Missouri Compromise line. What is most remarkable about this resolution is that within seven years Campbell sat on the Supreme Court, which ruled the division at 36 degrees 30 minutes unconstitutional. For the present, though, he was not on the bench and was certainly in no position to influence national policy or to declare federal laws unconstitutional. From a practical standpoint, resolution 13 reveals that Campbell was willing to employ a small measure of flexibility with his political philosophy, particularly because he and all other delegates to the Nashville Convention were powerless to do otherwise. As will be shown, however, Campbell had already determined that the Missouri Compromise line was unconstitutional; with a strict application of the doctrine of original sovereignty, Congress, acting within what Campbell perceived as the confines of the Constitution, should not have passed a Missouri Enabling Act that defined property by either permitting or excluding slavery in Missouri or in the remainder of the Louisiana Purchase. That was a right limited exclusively to Missouri's legislature or to the legislatures of any future states carved out of the purchase.

The fourteenth resolution, which indicates how deeply Campbell was repelled by sectional jealousy, stated that "the spectacle of a confederacy of States, involved in quarrels over the fruits of war . . . [was] humiliating." "A termination to this controversy by the disruption of the confederacy, or by the abandonment of the territories" merely to stymie secession sentiment, "would be a climax to the shame which attaches to the controversy" that Congress was obliged to avoid.[19]

The final two resolutions are the shortest in length, but they are historically the most significant. Resolution 15 reflected the conciliatory atmosphere that Campbell attempted to create in the convention, and it underscored the wait-and-see posture that he felt the South must adopt until Congress completed deliberations on the compromise measures. Moreover, this resolution was written in direct response to southern radicals such as Yancey, Tucker, and Robert Barnwell Rhett—the fiery editor of the *Charleston Mercury*—who insisted on immediate secession. In the event that Congress should enact legislation contrary to southern interests, Campbell wrote, "this convention does not feel at liberty to discuss the measures *suitable for resistance* to laws involving a dishonor of the Southern States." Thus he believed that it was best to refrain from reckless and ill-advised demands for secession. There was no need to present an ultimatum that might be ignored in the North. Such an occurrence, Campbell believed, would only force southerners to dissolve the Union. Therefore, as stated in resolution 16, the South would bide its time for the present, and a second convention would be called if the South's grievances were not satisfactorily addressed.[20]

Campbell's influence at the Nashville Convention was indeed exceptional. Of the final twenty-eight resolutions adopted by the entire convention, the first thirteen were from those originally submitted by Campbell on 5 June. Most important, the convention's thirteenth resolution reaffirmed that "in the condition in which the convention finds the questions before Congress, *it does not feel at liberty to discuss the methods suitable for a resistance to measures not yet adopted.*"²¹ To this extent, and largely as a result of Campbell's resolutions, the Nashville Convention was far less dangerous than southern radicals had hoped and moderate unionists had feared.

The convention was also politically insignificant, however, as it became thoroughly overshadowed by the compromise measures that were adopted during the summer of 1850. Much to Campbell's relief, the secessionist sentiment that festered throughout the first half of the year waned considerably during the remaining months of 1850. Public opinion in the South was decidedly against extraordinary or radical acts by southern leaders.²² The fire-eaters failed to recognize the southern people's willingness to acquiesce on most points of the dispute. Generally speaking, southerners wanted to be left alone with their slaves; as long as Congress took no action to deprive them of their property in their own state, they were mostly pacified.

But Campbell was not pacified. Although the Compromise of 1850 became law, Congress failed to recognize each state's—and prospective state's— exclusive right to define property. During late 1850, he was invited to speak before a meeting held in Prattville in honor of Representative Sampson W. Harris.²³ Campbell agreed to attend the meeting and to speak on various issues of concern. Although his speech is no longer available, a letter written by Campbell accepting the invitation reveals much of what he thought of the Compromise of 1850. Campbell remarked that the South could in no manner remain pacified. California, "by an infamous juggle," he chided, was admitted to the Union as a free state. Moreover, "Southern property in New Mexico and Utah is subjected to litigation and embarrassments from Mexican laws, and their ignorant and mixed population have been empowered to legislate against it." Campbell also lamented that the "slave trade has been abolished in the District of Columbia in the acceptable form for the abolition taste." The Compromise of 1850, he wrote, "leave[s] the Southern States under a strong sense of their injustice and incapable of making an effort for a government that has wronged them—while the abolitionists [in the] North are incensed that all of their demands were not yielded, thinking with Charles VII [that] 'nothing gained while aught remains.' "²⁴ Harboring these sentiments, therefore, and being so apprehensive about the political and economic demise of the southern states, Campbell believed that his fellow southerners needed to be more fully enlightened on the heightened nature of the crisis and the struggles that he felt they would eventually have to endure.

As a result of his anxiety over the sectional crisis, and also at Yancey's urging, Campbell founded the Mobile chapter of the Southern Rights Association upon his return to Mobile after the Nashville Convention. He published articles and delivered speeches through this organization designed to alert southerners to the dangers of sectionalism, abolitionism, and the loss of the South's political power. As the publications of this association were meant for a general audience, Campbell structured his speeches and pamphlets largely to appeal to people's fears and emotions, intending to educate the masses about the assault on southern society, institutions, and way of life. His affiliation and activities with this organization unveil a less than appealing side of Campbell's character and demonstrate that he could be a firebrand on occasion.

At the inaugural meeting in Mobile, Campbell delivered the opening address outlining the need for such an organization and explaining how it intended to protect southern rights. "The institution of slavery has been a source of division between the two sections of the confederacy from the first days of its existence," Campbell informed his audience. During the debates over the Constitution in 1787, a compromise had been reached requiring that five slaves be counted as three freedmen for apportionment purposes. Campbell remarked that this arrangement had been satisfactory to most southerners in attendance at Philadelphia, but it should not have been. Though the three-fifths compromise had been reached in apparent deference to southern demands, Campbell asserted that it had actually been a lever used by northern representatives to placate the South and to gain an economic advantage. To Campbell, the most regrettable aspect of the constitutional debates was that they left the powers of the federal government too vague and subject to wildly differing interpretations. Therefore, the only means of ensuring states' rights and of arresting the trend toward a concentration of political power in the federal government was to employ an absolutely strict interpretation of the Constitution. In Campbell's opinion, such an interpretation would clearly establish that "states have the power to settle their domestic institutions, and Congress cannot acquire by compact the power to restrict state authority."[25] As slavery was a purely municipal institution, and as each slave was legally held property titled by the various states that sanctioned the institution's existence, Congress could not enact legislation that could potentially alter any master-slave relationship that had been created by state legislation.

Campbell then began a lengthy discourse on the history, composition, and aims of the various antislavery organizations that had been formed in the 1830s. He informed his listeners that the Anti-Slavery Society claimed as its mission, "to endeavor by all means sanctioned by law, religion, and humanity *to effect the abolition of slavery in the United States.*" This group disavowed all use of violence and "its modes of operation were declared to be moral and peaceful." The American Anti-Slavery Society, however, "had more definite political ends." The abolitionists planned to convince all Americans that slavery "is a *heinous crime in the sight of God;* and that the duty, safety, and best interest of all concerned, require its immediate abandonment, without expatriation."[26] This group also was determined that all new lands added to the United States remain free of slave labor. "You will thus see, gentlemen, that this society had its religious as well as its political creed," Campbell asserted.

A proper examination of these societies revealed "how direct and powerful an influence they have exerted in the politics of the country." "Their policy was agitation," he contended, and abolition societies forced northern politicians to address slavery, particularly with regard to the slave trade in Washington, D.C., and to the possibility of adding new slave states to the Union. "They recognized the power of Congressional action as the lever to move the States, and to form an opinion of mankind" more conducive to abolition. Abolitionists gained the right to petition Congress through diligent agitation, and he remarked, "The right to petition was practically a right to inflame, exasperate, and gall the representatives of one half the country." If the abolitionists received but "one favorable vote in Congress, [it would] speak to the whole world against the institution." As a result of the antislavery campaign, slavery had become a topic of national debate "more operative than all other influences." "In consequence of [the agitation], Congress has become a common nuisance," he remarked.[27]

As Campbell viewed the situation, the compromise legislation of 1850 in effect was a singular victory for Free-Soilism, and he determined that the South's political position in the Union would continually weaken as more and more western states were admitted to the Union. He never asserted that southern rights to the territories must be upheld solely for the protection of slavery. As shown earlier, he cared little for the institution and felt that slave labor was preventing the South from realizing its industrial and commercial potential. On the other hand, as the South's political power in Congress was all but tied to slavery, the institution had to be protected—and expanded—if the southern states were to retain political equality.

Here, then, was the real threat from the abolitionists. Campbell surmised that because Congress yielded to their demands with regard to the Mexican cession, the complete eradication of slavery throughout the nation would surely follow. "This condition of things it is obvious must be terminated, or our ruin will be complete."[28] He suggested that what the South needed first and foremost was the same unity of purpose that had permeated northern society as a result of antislavery agitation. Thus, the formation of the Southern Rights Association was but the first step in creating a renewed sense of community throughout the South that could overwhelm abolition sentiment in Congress and facilitate a restoration of the political equilibrium present before the admission of California.

"The object of this association," he stated, "is to defend southern institutions. We declare to one another the first object of our affections, the dearest object of our care, are the institutions of that section of country in which our lines are cast. We place the repose, the security, the interest and honor of the South as paramount to all other considerations."[29] One might assume that these statements meant that the South's honor was more important to the

Southern Rights Association than was maintaining the Union. "I am asked if this is a disunion association," Campbell said. "I answer, no. Disunion, whenever it comes, should be accomplished by the voice and votes of the people, after a considerate and enlightened view of all the circumstances and consequences that surround it. It is not a measure to be approached in a light, angry, or capricious temper. It should be a calm and resolute act of an entire people, exercising their powers of self-government upon just considerations of their welfare and that of their posterity."[30]

Campbell neither condemned nor condoned secession. The above phrase "whenever it comes" is quite revealing, though. It shows that Campbell perhaps believed secession inevitable but that he also thought it impossible without the full consent of the southern people or without a spirit of community transcending state lines and focused on maintaining southern rights in the Union. "To accomplish a disunion . . . would not be an appropriate office for such an association, and I feel no hesitation in saying that we have no such end in view." "While I say this," he added, "let me not be misunderstood. Whenever disunion is at all essential to the security of the institutions of the South, for one, I am in favor of embracing it. There is no competition in my mind between the union of the States and the rights of the South. My heart and hand are on the side of the last, whenever an incompatibility is established between them."[31]

One object of the association was, Campbell explained, to promote a close and cordial union of all southern men "for the defense of the constitutional rights of the South." Constitutional rights "were violated in the abuse of the right of petition; in the Oregon proviso; in the legislation for the Mexican conquests; and are menaced in points equally essential." It was most important, he exclaimed, that southerners band together to offset antislavery agitation and any future congressional attempts to usurp states' rights.

Finally, Campbell outlined the most imperative course for the South to follow. "We wish to rouse the attention of the people of the state to the rearing of domestic interests." The exportation of cotton, although extremely profitable, had left the South industrially weak and overly reliant on northern manufacturing. "We have leaned upon the North in too great a degree. We have neglected our duties at home to our own people. We have fostered enemies who have become strong enough to smite us." What the South needed most of all, therefore, was to promote its own industry and commerce and to reduce the region's reliance on agriculture. "Let us invigorate industrial pursuits in Alabama," Campbell advised. "Let southern men have the support of the South in their praiseworthy undertakings. Let us stimulate our mechanic arts and manufacturing enterprises. Let us find out in our business what will strengthen the hands of the South and of men true to the South. This association will assist in this."[32] Campbell's desire to bolster southern commerce was reflective of South Alabama's diverse economy where mercantile and shipping interests were of paramount concern, particularly in Mobile. And he well understood that the South, if it were to regain political parity in the Union, had to undergo the same economic and industrial transformation that had in recent decades become increasingly manifest in many northern states.

Campbell wrote a second article in 1850 entitled "The Rights of the Slave States by a Citizen of Alabama" that was distributed by the Southern Rights Association in pamphlet form and published in the January 1851 issue of *Southern Quarterly Review.* Southerners maintained that they had been denied justice with regard to the Mexican cession, Campbell wrote, "and that principles have been declared [by abolitionists and northern politicians] which strike at the foundations of political equality in the Union and social security at home." In his inaugural speech to the association, Campbell presented a brief history of the abolition movement. In this essay, he offered a retrospective glance at federal-state relations as they pertained to slavery. Furthermore, he emphasized the indispensable duties "which rest upon" southerners, "who, for weal or wo, are associated with [slavery]."[33] This article is fundamental to understanding Campbell's political and constitutional thought and hence must be explored in some detail.

After briefly tracing the debates during the Constitutional Convention that touched on the slavery issue, Campbell deduced that the South's labor institution was a major concern to the delegates and that sectional differences were readily apparent among them. This discord produced an intense need for compromise, but "the largest concessions were made by the Southern States. The moving spring of the Northern States was to command the *commerce* of the country, through the federal government." Northern domination of the nation's commercial interests was achieved in the convention, and southerners had little alternative, he lamented, but to rely most exclusively on agricultural pursuits. Campbell, of course, failed to mention that southerners were more than willing to base their economy solely on agriculture as long as they could do so on the backs of their slaves.[34]

Southern delegates to the Constitutional Convention made several dreadful errors, Campbell explained, that rendered the South nearly powerless. First of all, they "acted without concert, . . . and left the draught of the Constitution to their opponents." Second, southerners mistakenly agreed to grant the federal government exclusive control over the nation's military. A third mistake made by southerners was to deny states the right to create alliances with foreign nations, to enter into commercial or military compacts, or to issue paper money. Lastly, and most ominously, southerners failed to insist on "a guarantee to them against the exertions of the power of the federal government."[35]

Campbell remarked that these mistakes, although made in the spirit of conciliation, had cost the South dearly. While the South concentrated on cotton production, southerners were lulled into a false sense of security. It could not be denied that cotton production had blessed the South with much prosperity. But, Campbell stated, the South's agricultural and economic growth was infinitesimal when compared with the industrial and commercial expansion in the northern states.

The Alabamian nonetheless recognized that the delegates in Philadelphia were less concerned with preserving states' rights than with creating an effective central government. "The apprehensions of the convention," he wrote, "seem to have been confined to the centrifugal tendencies of the States, and were never directed to the monopolizing and absorbing quality of the central authority. Apparently, the faith of the convention was given implicitly to the creation of its will; or, they might have supposed the cobweb chains of paper constitutions, upon the strong hand of legislation, would prove a delusion and a snare, and they would not stoop to provide them."[36] To Campbell, the "chains" ratified in 1787 might have benefited the nation as a whole, but they mostly served to constrict the South and to facilitate northern economic expansion. Sectional antagonisms continued after the ratification of the constitution, and "[i]n matters of representation and revenue—that is, the arrangements of political power, of commerce and navigation: that is—all intercourse—these divisions were conspicuous."[37]

Campbell explained that sectional jealousies were again evident in the early nineteenth century during the debates over the Louisiana Purchase and during the Hartford Convention held as a protest to the War of 1812. On these occasions northerners complained about the lack of political balance in the Union, and their dissatisfaction generated demands that the New England states secede from the Union. But he insisted that these controversies were little more than the creations of unseemly politicians and should be viewed as interparty controversies. The population in each respective section of the nation was but little involved in these matters, because "Democratic ideas had not taken so firm a hold of the popular mind." Campbell asserted that, in the opening decades of the nineteenth century, "One community did not look upon the representatives of another as agents or machines; but as rulers giving mould and form to the policy of the State." By midcentury, however, the political and democratic environment had changed. The general population was more involved with issues that they believed profoundly affected themselves, their state, and the nation.

Campbell further maintained that not only had the nation's population grown more democratic, but that people's overall perceptions of politicians had also changed. During the country's early decades, politicians were viewed with great respect as individuals working without regard to party or self-interest. By 1850, however, many northerners accused southern politicians of being little more than dupes of a slave power conspiracy struggling to destroy northern prosperity and to protect slavery. Southerners likewise viewed northern politicians as the patsies of the abolitionists who, in Campbell's estimation, mollified the northern people's grandiose and often whimsical notions of freedom so that they could continue in office. This spirit of mistrust that so permeated the nation by midcentury, he concluded, weakened the two dominant political parties and rendered them incapable of overcoming crises that threatened the Union.

The Alabamian recalled that in 1831 "an insignificant disturbance" orchestrated by Nat Turner lent great impetus to northern antislavery societies. He then included a brief account of the origins and activities of the various abolitionist organizations in much the same manner and indignant tone that appeared in his earlier writings and speeches. Campbell explained that these societies continually expanded and became a compelling force that altered public opinion in northern states. The abolitionists eventually recruited politicians who introduced the struggle in the federal government. No politician in the 1830s, Campbell asserted, was as important in elevating slavery to the forefront as John Quincy Adams, whose influence as a former president was powerful and carried immense weight with his congressional colleagues.[38]

The Mexican War and Wilmot's proviso, coupled with what Henry Clay called "the five bleeding wounds" necessitating the Compromise of 1850, established the backdrop for the current crisis. Campbell recognized that the leading statesmen who had orchestrated the compromise measures in 1850 acted for the good of the nation and should be commended. He insisted, however, that the compromise was wholly without effect, for it did not include protection of state property rights. Only "the recognition of slavery, as an institution of property, in the States, entitled to the same rank, privilege, and protection as every other institution of property," could satisfy the South and "secure the tranquility of this section of the Union." "The powers of the general government were given to it for the 'common defense and for the general welfare.'" In other words, the federal government's chief concern should have been to ensure that its policies affected each state equally and that no state or collection of states benefited disproportionately. "The government can perform no *passive neutral part* in the concerns of the States or [the] people," he stated. It must, in other words, use its power to protect property and to settle disputes among the states.[39]

"The part of *non-intervention* in reference to a single interest," he stated, "involves an accumulat[ion] of unequal *protection* to antagonists or rival interests. The sovereign powers conceded to the federal government are essential to the well-being of every state; and if [these are] neutralized or deadened, the

State must undergo decay or dissolution."[40] To Campbell, the doctrine of non-intervention did little other than recognize the status quo and give the abolitionists free rein to continue their diatribes against slavery. He was particularly insulted by the abolitionists' claims that they answered to a "higher law," which insinuated that southerners were ungodly infidels incapable of perceiving the difference between virtue and sin. Furthermore, as several northern states had passed personal liberty laws that were, in Campbell's opinion, inconsistent with the Constitution because of their disregard for property rights, the central government needed to respond with diligence. Slavery had to be afforded property right protection because congressional inactivity was tantamount to legislative emancipation and the complete and irreversible destruction of the South. "*Protection* is the price paid by government for the support of its citizens, and we can conceive of no disgrace more heavy than the denial of this right of protection," Campbell asserted. If the doctrine of nonintervention was applied strictly, "*Northern* consciences" might be secured, but southern rights would be trampled. Moreover, "if [non-intervention was] carried out, it [would] overturn all legal and constitutional barriers against abolition, and submit [southerners] to the "higher law." Slaveholders' property "would then become prey to rapacity of fanaticism."[41]

Campbell asserted that the federal government possessed sufficient authority and had a solemn duty to protect the interests of the people from internal or external attacks on municipal institutions. "That government which fails to secure, fully and impartially, the *legal* rights of its citizens, within the range of its jurisdiction, is unworthy of support." Campbell then stated what he believed to be the central government's most fundamental role: "The end of government is to remove the confusion and anarchy that attend uncertainty and misgiving." The federal government was created solely to ensure security in property and to protect all citizens' rights to their property. This was the foundation for the compact that the states had entered in 1787.[42] "If Congress does the people of the Southern states wrong, their appeal must be to a higher authority—" he had stated to Calhoun in 1848, "and in the last resort—*we may overthrow the Congress.*"[43]

Campbell maintained that within the realm of human affairs there was no higher authority than the sovereignty of the people. Clearly influenced by political theorists such as Thomas Hobbes and John Locke, he postulated that society without government produced anarchy and that individuals constituting a society must concede certain freedoms to a central government for the common benefit of all. But people must also strictly limit those powers afforded to the central government to ensure against tyranny and dangers to man's natural rights.

But where exactly was the locus of sovereignty to the Alabamian? Campbell's reading of the debates in the Constitutional Convention convinced him that the sovereign people of each state, in seeking to form a centralized, representative government while simultaneously wanting to strictly limit that government and ensure against usurpations of power, entered into a social and political compact whereby their common security and collective interests could be protected. The people voiced their assent to this compact through the various states that were vested with the obligation of maintaining and protecting sovereignty. Therefore, ultimate power rested with the people but was expressed through the states that could best govern in matters purely local or municipal. In 1819, for instance, when Alabama was admitted to the Union, the state "was endued with powers to maintain personal and political rights," and this was "appreciated as the main aim of [state] government."[44] And as Campbell considered slavery an intrinsically local institution that should only be governed by those states in which it existed, the central government's duties and obligations in connection with the institution must be clearly understood.

Campbell held that the duties of the federal government included maintaining a political environment in which states could protect their own local interests. By allowing debates on slavery that even suggested the institution's immediate termination, the federal government failed in its duty to provide an unprejudiced political arena in which national issues could be addressed. If, for instance, the state of Virginia decided that slavery should no longer exist within its borders—as it had nearly done after the Nat Turner rebellion—then so be it. But the federal government could by no means commandeer this right from the states. Under these circumstances the social compact would be rendered void, and the states, or the people of those states, would have the unequivocal right to overthrow the government and to replace it with one that would better respect the balance of power in the Union.

By stating that the people retained the right to overthrow the central government, Campbell was not proposing anything that was either new or radical. This notion was a fundamental assumption of the founding fathers. To Campbell, the federal government could not be culpable for any infringement of states' rights; only a particular government or a specific branch of government, such as the Thirty-first Congress or perhaps an abolitionist president, for instance, should be "overthrown." This objective could most fastidiously be accomplished through the democratic process, whereby the people could refuse to reelect representatives whose philosophies and personal beliefs were deemed antithetical to the interests and well-being of the states. Of course, the democratic process produced an increasingly insurmountable quandary for southerners, who, in Campbell's opinion, were rapidly losing the political power necessary to counter attacks on their local institutions. His concern that the South was relegated to minority political status, and that its rights were being summarily trampled by the majority population in the North, convinced him that the locus of sovereignty was shifting from the states to the federal government. And to Campbell this was the greatest crisis facing the nation.

Campbell concluded "The Rights of the Slave States" with recommendations to the southern states on how best to reverse the weakening of their political power. He declared that the time for a proper southern response to the Free Soilers and the abolitionists had arrived and that further delay would only weaken the South and place it in an even more untenable situation. "The question was only one of time" before the two dominant sections of the country sparred for political supremacy. He continued, "The marvelous increase of the facilities of intercourse, the multiplication of commercial and social ties between the sections, the formation of national parties, and the habits of free discussion, and the irritating controversy they engender, have hastened the current of events. To these powerful and all-sufficient causes, the revolutionary and innovating spirit of the times must be added." He believed that the animosity between the sections became especially evident with the onset of the Mexican War, and that "we should have greatly preferred another field for the contest" over slavery. But as the contest was destined to occur, "and as the struggle necessarily involved the fate of our institutions," it was perhaps best that the struggle commenced before the South was rendered politically and economically impotent.[45]

The southern states' "first duty" was "to combine to meet the common danger." All southerners must acknowledge their common social structure, local interests, and institutions. What had to be formed was a "community of sentiment and institutions." He urged southerners "to take counsel together, for a calm, deliberate, disinterested and honest inquiry concerning" the future of the South's position within the Union.[46] Moreover, the southern states must unite "for their common defense." The crisis to the Alabamian had grown so ominous that he foresaw the possibility of an invasion by federal troops sent to enforce emancipation laws passed by a federal government completely dominated by abolition and Free Soil interests. "A war by the federal authorities upon a State of the Union, would be an anomaly so extraordinary, with consequences so direful," that all southerners must scorn anyone "who could maintain the lawfulness for a moment." "Independent nations may settle their disputes by war, but confederates must dissolve their confederacy, before such a result could be legitimate or proper."[47]

"The Rights of the Slave States" is disturbing to read when one considers that nearly all of Campbell's letters, speeches, and articles were normally written and delivered with remarkable dispassion. In contrast, this pamphlet is replete with overemotional, often acrid rhetoric. Campbell obviously understood the power of words and knew that his fellow citizens were often more inspired by rhetoric that inflamed passion and fear than by appeals to reason and civility. Pamphlets published by the Southern Rights Association were meant for general consumption, and as this organization felt obliged to "awaken" southerners to the dangers that lurked on the horizon, it was understandable that Campbell employed melodramatic arguments designed to stir southern sentiment. Despite his complaints that many northern politicians engaged in demagoguery for their personal or political aggrandizement, Campbell's affiliation and publications with the Southern Rights Association indicate that he too was similarly capable of producing incendiary propaganda designed to sway public opinion.

But Campbell's often cacophonous rhetoric notwithstanding, he was not a radical. While he may often have spoken caustic and belligerent words, his message was constantly tempered by his moderate position that secession by individual states or by a collection of states without the consent of the southern people was both ill advised and inherently wrong. Thus, in a broader sense, Campbell and Yancey were operating on divergent paths, and the Southern Rights Associations that each man commanded reflected the general disunity among Alabama Democrats. By the end of 1850, while Yancey maneuvered the Montgomery chapter of the Southern Rights Association into an increasingly radical posture, Campbell quietly repudiated radicalism and called for sober and civil discussions on the South's grievances.[48]

Meanwhile, tempers often flared in Congress, particularly when the Fugitive Slave Law entered into debate. Southern congressmen were acutely sensitive to any northern attacks on this measure, and threats from northern state governments that enforcement of the Act would not be tolerated within their state boundaries brought uproarious objections from radical southerners. The furor thus raised generated repeated calls for secession, especially from southern fire-eaters. Radicals in South Carolina in particular regarded any discussion of this law as an unmitigated attack on the South, and these individuals sought to separate South Carolina from the Union under the deluded notion that other southern states would follow her lead. In December 1850 the state legislature summoned a convention with the intention of initiating an ordinance of secession. Though such sentiment generally found favor with South Carolinians, there was considerable division among them on how best to proceed. It was quickly evident that not all South Carolinians approved of separate state action, and these "cooperationists" hoped that secession, if it were to occur at all, would result from an all-southern movement that would prompt the southern states to secede in unison. Events in the Palmetto State that winter reverberated throughout the South, and in Alabama support for South Carolina was voiced largely through the Montgomery and Mobile chapters of the Southern Rights Association.[49]

On 10 and 11 February 1851, a southern rights convention was held in Montgomery. Its purpose was to present a united front in support of those

Carolinians seeking separate state action and in opposition to the southern cooperationists.[50] These conventioneers, Campbell and Yancey conspicuous among them, were no doubt embarrassed that their summons to this meeting prompted the appearance of but ninety-seven delegates. Such a paltry number was hardly reflective of—nor could they speak for—all Alabamians. There were no Whigs in attendance, and the leadership within Alabama's Democracy was so uncompromisingly divided that the convention was almost entirely without effect. Yancey dominated the proceedings with his characteristic bluster and colorful locutions. The fact was, though, that Yancey's once dominant position within Alabama's Democracy had waned considerably by 1851, and his brand of radicalism had lost its luster with the more moderate party members. Furthermore, Yancey was viewed as vacillating by most Alabama radicals and had·therefore alienated nearly all factions within the state.[51]

With Yancey's star so dim, Campbell assumed a more dominant position over the state's radical elements. During the second Southern Rights Convention, held in June, he departed substantially from radicalism by refusing to support the separate state action secessionists in South Carolina. The platform adopted at this meeting warned Congress not to abolish slavery in Washington, D.C., an action that would be viewed as a flagrant violation to southern rights. Congress must also refrain from enacting any legislation threatening the interstate slave trade or measures that refused to admit a new state because it allowed slavery within its borders. Last, the delegates adopted a statement that they considered "the faithful execution of the fugitive slave law, by proper authorities," fundamental to the Union's preservation.[52]

Through Campbell's leadership, the convention also pledged its support for Unionist Henry Collier in the upcoming gubernatorial election. As his rulings in the submerged land cases indicated, Collier was indeed a strong advocate of states' rights. Yet, like Campbell, Collier was no fire-eater, and by no means did he support secession. Campbell, therefore, was at least moderately useful in healing the schism among Democrats that had to varying degrees plagued the party throughout the previous several years. In the end, Campbell supported secession but only in the abstract; when the actual event threatened to occur, he rapidly retreated to the moderate fold and repudiated his often pugnacious rhetoric.

Fortunately for Campbell, his authorship of inflammatory articles—such as those under the auspices of the Southern Rights Association—was not common knowledge. If Campbell's more radical writings had been widely known, his career might have turned out far differently, and he would have remained a relatively obscure lawyer in the Deep South. As noted earlier, he made his first appearance before the United States Supreme Court in 1849, during the same period when the nation tottered on the brink of disaster. Throughout the next three years, Campbell brought eleven more cases before the nation's highest tribunal. There is little doubt that he made a profound impression on the Court with his forceful argumentation and his unmatched knowledge of the law. When a vacancy occurred on the bench in 1852, the justices took the unprecedented step of recommending someone to fill the seat: John Archibald Campbell.

By the summer of 1850 Campbell's political philosophy had matured considerably and had become more focused on states' rights and what he perceived as a diminution of the South's political position in the Union. The crisis at midcentury had indeed played a considerable role in prompting a deterioration of Campbell's once implacable nationalism. This is not to say, however, that he believed that the South had no alternative but to secede from the Union. Though he could engage in considerable rabble-rousing on occasion, he was not interested in destroying the nation. And in that regard Campbell was certainly no fire-eater. He wanted northerners to respect southern rights, southern institutions, and the southern interpretation of the federal Constitution. The fundamental change in Campbell's political philosophy, therefore, was a recognition that states' rights was as applicable in the territories as in states already in the Union. And as the national debate over slavery continued unabated, as the Free Soil movement gained more adherents among the northern population, and as the territory acquired from Mexico filled with settlers, the issue of whether Congress had the authority to prohibit slavery from the Mexican cession imperiled relations between North and South as never before. Such was the situation when Campbell traveled to Washington in 1853 to join his colleagues on the United States Supreme Court.

7 | States' Rights Justice, Part 1: Commerce, Contracts, and Quitman

Campbell's law practice in Mobile became increasingly active throughout the 1840s and early 1850s. He was admitted to the United States Supreme Court bar in 1849, and between 1850 and 1852 he argued twelve cases in Washington. Although he lost seven of these cases, his arguments so impressed the justices that he was regarded as one of the most talented lawyers in the nation. This recognition led in 1853 to his nomination to the United States Supreme Court, quite an accomplishment for a person who had never before sat as a judge. But his knowledge of common and civil law proved so extensive that his lack of judicial experience was of little importance.[1]

Campbell's appointment to the bench strengthened by one the Court's pro states' rights contingent. The new justice unabashedly asserted that the legislative branch of the federal government had exceeded its constitutional boundaries with various laws enacted since the nation's birth. It was no surprise, or it should not have been, when Campbell ruled in a number of significant cases that in certain specified areas the rights of the states superseded those of the federal government. But at the same time, Campbell showed that he would remain vigilant regarding infractions of federal law despite popular sentiment among many southerners to the contrary. Campbell's attempts to arrest filibustering expeditions that were direct violations of American neutrality laws and his stern approach to the illicit trading of slaves were the most obvious examples of his nationalistic jurisprudence. A study of Campbell's eight-year tenure on the Court therefore presents starkly contrasting images of a justice seeking to protect states' rights while striving to balance the authority of the federal and the state governments.

After Campbell successfully argued *Goodtitle v. Kibbe* in 1849, he was one of the most sought-after attorneys throughout the South. His employment in several of the most famous cases in the nineteenth century not only brought him further recognition but greatly increased his wealth. In 1846, he purchased a small parcel of land on the east side of Mobile Bay at Point Clear, Alabama, and over the next few years he constructed a house on this property. But this was not the typical antebellum home of wealthy southerners; it was but a modest, one-story dwelling with a cozy front porch bordered by twelve thin columns. The small size and notable simplicity of this dwelling reflected his simple lifestyle and unpretentious manner.[2]

Campbell's success as an attorney reflected his massive intellect but was brought on mostly by a profoundly strict work ethic. In a speech delivered to the Alabama State Bar Association later in his life, Campbell noted that the duties of an attorney required placing all records and pertinent information "in a distinct and intelligible form." A competent lawyer will also ensure that "the petition, demand, or the opposition, or defense of his client, the appropriate testimony, the principles applicable, the precedents that have been established, the precise and particular question to be decided, and the reasons for a particular decision," will all be of primary concern. "Some cases have seemed to involve the destinies of a nation," Campbell noted, "and some lawyers have appeared at times the personification of Patriotism in pleading her cause." But other lawyers "have sold their words and their anger for pottage."[3] Obviously he felt strongly that attorneys had special obligations to labor as diligently as possible on the client's behalf. This led him to extensive preparation before he entered the courtroom. Campbell may have lost cases on occasion but never from lack of preparation. A longtime associate once said that Campbell, whose "success at the bar was the result of patient laborious industry," "went to the bottom of everything that required his attention, and [he] shrank from no drudgery that was necessary to accomplish his purposes. . . . Yes, sir, it was mainly by labor, incessant labor, that he stood first at the Bar."[4]

The most interesting litigation in which Campbell was involved between 1850 and 1853 was the famous case of Myra Clark Gaines. This courtroom drama lasted for fifty-five years, was not settled until all of the principals in the original case had died, and involved one of the largest claims of the nineteenth century. It was a case that literally enthralled the public and had "all of the incredible drama of bad romantic fiction."[5] The prolonged litigation involved a dispute over the estate of Daniel Clark, a wealthy New Orleans businessman and speculator who had purchased much of the land that would later become downtown New Orleans. Clark died supposedly without heirs in 1813, heavily indebted but still owning considerable valuable real estate. The executors for Clark's estate, New Orleans attorneys Richard Relf and Beverley Chew, sold parts of his property to clear the debts but retained the majority and collected rent from various parties. In 1835, a young woman calling herself Myra Clark Whitney arrived in New Orleans with her husband, William Whitney of New York, claiming that she was the only legitimate daughter of Daniel Clark and had come to town to collect her inheritance.[6]

All indications were that Myra was indeed Clark's daughter. Apparently, Clark had entered into an bigamous affair with a young New Orleans socialite of dubious reputation and character named Zulime Carriére. This woman was married to Geronimo Des Grange, a rather mysterious fellow whose sporadic disappearances from New Orleans evidently caused Zulime to seek affections from other quarters. When Clark was in Philadelphia on business in either 1803 or 1804—the records are unclear on this point—Zulime followed him to the city, where he agreed to marry her. A short time later, Myra was born, and Clark decided to allow a close friend, Samuel B. Davis of Delaware, to raise his child. So Myra grew up believing that she was one of Davis's daughters. Not until her marriage to Whitney in 1835 did she learn the truth about her parentage. Hearing of the vast estate and believing that she was perfectly entitled to all of Clark's property—even that which Relf and Chew had sold—Myra and her husband set out for New Orleans in 1836. Thus began a more than fifty-year battle for this inheritance. With such a flamboyant cast of characters, and considering the enormous value of Clark's property—an appreciated worth of nearly $20 million by midcentury—it was little wonder that the case fascinated the public.[7]

When Campbell agreed to serve as counsel for Mrs. Gaines—Whitney died of fever in 1838 and two years later Myra married General Edmund P. Gaines of Seminole War fame—her claim was already fourteen years old and had been through a series of suits, countersuits, and appeals. The litigation was made more complex because it was governed by the Louisiana civil code, a combination of the Napoleonic Code and a perplexing amalgam of Creole laws and customs. Few people outside the state were sufficiently acquainted with Louisiana law to argue cases there. Campbell, though, had spent at least one day each week reading law at Saunders's Pleading, a Mobile law firm specializing in land disputes arising from conflicting French and American claims. Thus he not only had a mastery of common law, he was also well equipped to argue cases in Louisiana courts.[8]

After being hired by Mrs. Gaines, Campbell began gathering evidence and taking depositions in support of Myra's claims of legitimacy. He needed to show whether Zulime's marriage to Des Grange had been duly consummated, and if so whether her husband's prolonged absences could be viewed as legal abandonment. If the court ruled, as it had on several previous occasions, that the marriage was in fact legitimate, Zulime could not have legally married Clark. Under such circumstances, Myra's illegitimacy would be established and her claims to the estate denied.[9]

When Campbell completed gathering the evidence, the files for the case contained roughly 1,200 pages of material. On 20 January 1850, the Clark case was once again argued before the United States Circuit Court in New Orleans. The presiding judges were federal judge Theodore H. McCaleb and Supreme Court justice John McKinley. They could not agree whether to follow the common law precedents or those established in Louisiana courts under its civil code. McKinley, the "unspeakably weak" man of whom Campbell had complained in 1836, announced halfway through the hearings that McCaleb was far more qualified to rule on the case and that he would render a decision only if the case was remanded to the Supreme Court.[10]

With McKinley's absence, Campbell's case was seriously weakened by McCaleb's insistence that only civil laws governing legitimacy applied. Campbell argued that despite all of the "bar room and brothel" rumors, Zulime and Clark had indeed been legally wed in Philadelphia. He admitted that Zulime was at the time married to Des Grange, but that this marriage should not be recognized because Zulime tried to have it annulled on several occasions but could not legally do so without her husband's consent. "Thus I have shown an unbroken chain of evidence," Campbell stated in his concluding remarks, "reaching from the birth of the child to the death of Clark to establish the legitimacy."[11]

Campbell's closing argument, in the words of the *New Orleans Bee*, "all but immortalized him." One city merchant taking a short break decided to stop in the courthouse and listen to the proceedings. After hearing Campbell speak for only a few moments, the merchant was as enthralled as the other spectators. Hours passed and the merchant remained, listening to the eloquence, the cold, clear logic, and the convincing arguments presented by Campbell. The merchant later explained that he simply could not pull himself away until he had heard the entire speech delivered by Campbell that day.[12] It was later said that when Campbell addressed the Court,

> His striking intellectual characteristics were the breadth of his mind, the cogency of its movements and a capacity to retain, ready for instant use, unusual stores of thought. . . . His stature, his features, his look, his bearing— his whole presence was commanding. His learning, not alone in the law, but also in history, in literature and in the sciences was a marvel for its vastness and exactitude. His memory continually surprised you by its unfailing tenacity. During the longest argument he used no memoranda, but turned to the books and pages of his authorities from his own recollection.[13]

Despite Campbell's argument, despite the witnesses who claimed that Zulime's marriage to Clark was indeed legitimate, and despite the copious notes attending the case, Judge McCaleb was not convinced. He ruled in Relf's behalf as he had done on several previous occasions. Mrs. Clark at once agreed to send the case to the United States Supreme Court.[14]

Campbell was joined in his efforts in Washington by Reverdy Johnson, a prominent Baltimore lawyer whose many appearances before the Supreme Court brought him national acclaim. The opposing lawyers in the case were Greer B. Duncan of New Orleans and, to add substantial weight to the opposition, Daniel Webster, who was then serving as secretary of state in the Fillmore administration. Both sides argued convincingly; Webster's closing presentation was especially noted for its eloquence as well as for its strength. He reminded the Court that Myra was fighting as much for her property as she was for her legitimacy, which he intimated was actually of minor concern. Poor Relf, Webster proclaimed, had for nearly two decades been "persistently besieged by litigation as a rock beaten by ocean waves." Campbell's argument likewise drew wide acclaim as one of the best heard in that tribunal. The justices and members of the packed gallery marveled as he waded through voluminous testimony and evidence without the benefit of notes or script. As one historian notes, "Campbell had captured New Orleans; the Justices of the Supreme Court proved almost as impressed."[15]

But Campbell's efforts to persuade the Court that Zulime's marriage to Clark had not been bigamous failed largely because of the insurmountable evidence to the contrary. Campbell had summoned many individuals who testified that Zulime had been victimized by Des Grange, whose long absences from New Orleans constituted abandonment. He also presented evidence that Des Grange was married even before he married Zulime, thus negating the marriage on those grounds. But the Court nonetheless ruled that Zulime should not have married Clark because she was already married to Des Grange.

A writer for the *Southern Quarterly Review* noted cynically that the decision was "one that has attracted a larger share of public attention and has inspired a stronger feeling of interest, than any other in all the records of the American courts; and this interest is one of a sort permanently to affect society, particularly in a country where law is too little settled, and where society itself is but too little liable to be swayed, to and fro, from the anchorages of fast principles, by every gust of passion, and every wind of doctrine, no matter from what quarter it blows."[16] Despite its overall insignificance, the *Gaines* case fundamentally altered Campbell's career. Combined with his other arguments before the Court, the impression he made on the justices led them to recommend him to fill the next vacancy.

In 1852, Justice McKinley died. He had long suffered a series of illnesses that had kept him away from the bench during much of the previous several years, and the mounting caseload in the Fifth Circuit required that the position be filled as soon as possible. President Fillmore was eager to fill the seat before the 1852 presidential election, and of course he sought a Whig to replace McKinley. Fillmore first nominated Edward A. Bradford of New Orleans, who had built a lucrative practice in that city litigating land disputes. The Democratic majority in Congress, though, stalled Bradford's confirmation with the hope that Franklin Pierce would be elected president and the vacant Supreme Court seat would be open to a Democrat. Fillmore waited until February before naming his second nominee, Whig senator George E. Badger of North Carolina. Thunderous complaints came from all quarters of the South, however, because Badger had supported the Wilmot Proviso and also because he resided outside the Fifth Circuit. Once again the Senate failed to act on Fillmore's nominee, and Badger's candidacy was quietly dropped. Fillmore then sent the name of William C. Micou of New Orleans to the Senate, but as a highly partisan Whig he suffered the same fate as the earlier nominees. Obviously, the Democrats wanted the seat filled by one of their own, and they anxiously awaited Pierce's inauguration so that he could install the new justice on the bench.[17]

Upon assuming office in March 1853, Pierce sought advice from members of the Supreme Court, who unanimously agreed that McKinley's seat should be filled by John Archibald Campbell. The justices explained to the president that Campbell was an eminently qualified, supremely skilled attorney fully adept at the finer points of law. Furthermore, he was a Democrat, he was from Alabama, and he was thoroughly familiar with Louisiana state law, a qualification that McKinley had lacked.[18]

Meanwhile, Pierce received hearty approval for Campbell's nomination from the legislatures of every southern state except Louisiana and Texas—both of which had hopes of seeing one of their native sons placed on the bench. Campbell, of course, was well aware of the lobbying on his behalf. John Bragg, a resident of Mobile who had been elected to the House of Representatives in 1851, pressed for Campbell's appointment from the first day the vacancy became known. "In reference to the movement in favor of my appointment to the Bench," Campbell wrote to Bragg, "I feel greatly obliged to you." He was worried, though, that his nomination, if and when it materialized, might go the way of the earlier nominations. "As the prize comes nearer to me I have greater misgiving upon the subject of securing it." And after politely apologizing for any imposition caused by Bragg's lobbying efforts, he whimsically mused, "A man has perhaps the right to worry himself and I think the theory is that he may worry his wife. . . . that right is absolute, . . . but I do not know that he can disturb his friends."[19]

Campbell asserted privately to Bragg that the person chosen for the bench should reside in the Fifth Circuit. "The distinctions of our profession in our circuit . . . we fairly suppose belong to the men here in our profession." He bitterly complained about Badger's nomination because he was a North Carolinian, although an assumption may be made that Campbell strongly objected to Badger's position on Wilmot's proviso as well. "I have seen Mr. Badger at the bar and in the Senate and I do not consider that he has a right to pronounce upon his title to appear among us as a superior, nor that a Senate has the right to confirm that title." Badger's consideration was "one of insults and outrages" in Mobile and would be ardently opposed.[20]

Bragg's lobbying efforts in Washington on Campbell's behalf added additional support to the flow of enthusiastic accolades for the Alabamian. With recommendations from the Court, from the southern states, and from Congress, therefore, Pierce submitted Campbell's name to the Senate on 21 March

1853. He was confirmed as an associate justice of the Supreme Court just two days later without dissension.[21]

The *New York Times* informed its readers of Campbell's appointment, stating that he "enjoys a high reputation at home for learning and legal ability." But the paper expressed mild misgivings over the nomination. "He is said, by some of the papers, to be a 'fire-eater,' meaning thereby an extremist on the sectional question of North and South, or, in other words, a Nullifier." Yet the article expressed confidence that Campbell's position on the bench would temper any supposed states' rights sentiments he may have harbored. "But there is reason to suppose that his fame on this score is more the result of warm personal and party devotions to Mr. Calhoun than to his own settled convictions on the right of secession." The article continued: "He will doubtless, at all events, in his new estate, prove true to the Constitution and to the Union of States as established by it. The highest toned Federalists now on the same bench have been taken from the Democratic ranks; and it will be strange if the views of a gentleman of first rate legal talents, like Mr. Campbell, should prove less conservative. Past experience has shown that once in this exalted post and for life, the professions of the partisan soon give place to the convictions and sense of high responsibility of the Jurist."[22]

The same newspaper reported the following week that Campbell's mind was "singularly analytic." "[N]either rocks nor metals can stand his crucible. Added to all and crowning all, his private character is of the best stamp." In glowing terms, the paper added that he was exceedingly "modest, amiable, gentle, strictly temperate, and inflexibly just." "Anomalous as it seems in gentlemen of the Green Bag," it continued, "[Campbell] is delicate almost to tremulousness, and with prodigious intellectual power, as shy as a young lady."[23] Even the *New York Tribune,* which normally printed nothing but venomous invective about southern politicians because of their sentiments on slavery, admitted that Campbell was eminently qualified for the post. Characteristically, though, in the same article in which the paper announced Campbell's confirmation, it reported, "The Senate did nothing remarkable" that day.[24]

Campbell received official notice of his confirmation a few weeks into April. A former commissioner in the federal Circuit Court in Mobile, Robert B. Owen—who eventually became a state judge—reported an interesting anecdote concerning Campbell's appointment. Asked by a reporter to recount the day in April 1853 when Campbell arrived at the courthouse to be sworn into office, Owen replied,

> Yes, I remember it as well as if it had only happened yesterday. I was a mere boy then, but had been appointed by the Honorable John Gayle [as] a United States commissioner for the district.

A few days after his appointment, Judge Campbell came into my office with the grave and somewhat solemn demeanor which my previous association with him as a student in his office gave me to understand that no trivial matter was to be attended to. I rose and greeted him respectfully.

In tones of great seriousness he announced, "I have been appointed an Associate Justice of the Supreme Court of the United States, and I have come to take the oath of office before you."

You may imagine my embarrassment, so humble an object in the great judiciary system of the nation, thus being called on to administer the oath of office to a justice of its highest tribunal.

. . . I took the printed form of this oath, which he held out to me, and, steadying my voice as much as possible, proceeded to read it aloud to him. From sheer embarrassment, however, I was unable to proceed, and came almost to a full stop. Looking piteously up to the Judge, to my great surprise I saw that he was, if possible, as deeply embarrassed as myself. There was an awkward pause, but soon, smiling benignantly, he came to my relief by saying, with great kindness, "Well, never mind; I swear to all that is there written," which he did with great solemnity, and thereupon signed his name, and I attested the document in the usual form.[25]

Such was the scene when Campbell took the oath of office and received, as he termed it, the "prize." See photo 2. He was thereafter responsible for all litigation involving federal laws, disputes between states, or cases that reached the highest court on appeal. The Fifth Judicial Circuit, to which Campbell was assigned, encompassed Alabama and Louisiana. While riding circuit—as Supreme Court Justices were then required to do for most of the year—Campbell shuttled back and forth from Mobile to New Orleans. Anne and the children remained in Alabama throughout this period, dividing their time between the home in Mobile and the one at Point Clear. This was perhaps the happiest period of their marriage. Campbell had achieved the pinnacle of success, the post on the Court afforded him a $4,500 yearly salary, and he was warmly regarded as the leading citizen in the community.[26]

Campbell's political and constitutional views, largely explained in previous chapters, well complemented those of the Taney Court in Washington. When Taney became chief justice in 1837, the Court had redirected its focus away from the further extension of federal authority. But to state that the Court was dogmatically states' rights and intent on destroying Marshall's legacy would not only be an overstatement but would be untrue. The Taney Court sought to strike a balance between the two realms of government, which in the chief justice's view existed concurrently and had to be afforded equal consideration. For cases in which the jurisdiction was doubtful, the Court tended to rule in the states' favor, but that was far removed from wanting to destroy the judicial edifice so carefully constructed by Marshall.

Much of the litigation with which the Taney Court was concerned during

Campbell during his tenure on the Supreme Court, ca. 1855.
(Photograph by Havdy Studios, courtesy of the Collection of the
Supreme Court of the United States, Washington, D.C.)

Campbell's tenure involved an application of the commerce clause of the
federal Constitution. Under Marshall's direction, the Court had ruled in a
number of landmark decisions that the federal government's power over commercial regulation was absolute and could in no way be circumvented or ex-
propriated by the states. Taney's view maintained that authority over commerce was shared between the federal and state governments; the paramount
question being exactly where to draw the line between state and federal regulatory power. On this issue the Court remained largely divided. In the 1847
License Cases, for example, the Court upheld the power of states to regulate
the sale of imported liquor; in 1849, on the other hand, the Court struck down

a state statute imposing a tax on foreign passengers arriving in various ports. Such contradictory decisions produced discord on the bench and made litigation involving the nebulous commerce clause less than predictable.[27]

Finally, in the 1852 case *Cooley v. Board of Wardens*, Justice Benjamin R. Curtis, in one of his first formal decisions on the bench, drafted the majority opinion that "like a bolt out of the blue" put forward the doctrine of "selective exclusiveness."[28] Curtis wrote that the Court had earlier erred in deciding disputes over regulatory laws because it had based its decisions solely on the powers involved. He explained that what was necessary was a decision based not on the *power* but rather on the *subject* and whether it could be deemed within the exclusive jurisdiction of state governments. The test that should be applied, according to Curtis, was whether there was a recognized national standard that could be upheld with regard to the various subjects coming under the definition of "commerce." Whenever, therefore, the federal government had failed to enact legislation involving commerce, states had residual power to regulate the subject at their discretion. With the "Cooley Compromise," then, the Court incorporated a decidedly more flexible approach to adjudicating commerce cases.[29]

The second area with which the Court was greatly concerned during the 1850s was the legal status and rights of corporations. The expansion of business interests in the Northeast had produced the nation's dramatic entrance into the Industrial Revolution. Without enormous financial resources it would have been impossible for many industries such as railroads, canal companies, and the banking business to construct the nation's financial, industrial, and transportation infrastructure. The status of corporations was, therefore, of paramount importance throughout the nineteenth century. But one tenet of Jacksonianism was that financial conglomerates were the bulwark of the monied interests in the nation and that these tended to dominate the economy and destroy individualism. The most glaring example of this hostility was, of course, Jackson's destruction of the Bank of the United States in 1836. Significantly, Jackson's chief henchman in this effort was Roger B. Taney, whose subsequent nomination to the Court boded ill for corporate interests.[30]

The Court's fears proved to be without merit. Taney clearly recognized the significant role that corporations played in the development of national industries, but he sought to establish strong regulatory guidelines to reduce his innate mistrust and apprehension over financial conglomerations. In 1839, for instance, *Bank of Augusta v. Earle* was appealed to the Supreme Court from the Fifth Circuit, where Justice McKinley had ruled that states held extensive powers to regulate within their borders the activities of corporations chartered in other states. Such shortsighted logic on McKinley's part, had the decision stood, would have grossly limited various corporations' ability to conduct business across state lines. When the case was brought before the Supreme

Court on appeal, the chief justice delivered the majority opinion, ruling that corporations had, under the rules of comity, full rights to conduct business in states other than in the original chartering state. But the majority also affirmed that states could exclude corporations from their borders or could impose reasonable restrictions on them, provided that all preconditions be clearly stated.[31] Taney, seeking a more balanced approach to corporate rights, did not assert that corporations, which for legal purposes held similar status as individuals, were protected under the privileges and immunities clause and thus afforded rights of full citizenship. Nonetheless, this was a landmark decision that enhanced entrepreneurial enterprises and facilitated the rise of the American industrial behemoth during the latter half of the century.[32]

Contrary to what some contemporaries feared, the Taney Court was not totally pro states' rights. Its hallmarks were a moderate states' rights position often tempered by a more refined definition of the respective rights of the federal and state governments. Given Taney's earlier obedience to Jacksonian dogma, it was little wonder that nationalists lamented for the Marshall legacy. But as the *New York Times* had commented with regard to Campbell's appointment, duty on the Supreme Court tended to temper strong states' rights sentiment and to augment a more nationalistic philosophy and broad construction of the Constitution. As he traveled to Washington in the winter of 1853 to sit with his colleagues for the first time, it remained to be seen whether that prediction would hold true with Campbell's appointment.

According to a publication sponsored by the Supreme Court Historical Society, the Supreme Court handed down decisions on 636 cases from 1853 to 1861. Of these cases, Campbell either wrote or joined in thirty dissenting opinions—only 4.7 percent of the total.[33] This low percentage indicates that Campbell, at least fundamentally, should not be considered a "dissenting judge." Yet, and of extreme significance, a deeper investigation into those cases in which he could not follow the opinion of the Court revealed that he indeed retained the framework of his increasingly inflexible states' rights philosophy. At the same time, however, Campbell contributed to a number of decisions that enhanced federal authority. Thus, no blanket statement can be made that Campbell was either ardently for states' rights or supremely nationalistic. Like Taney, he believed that there should be clearly divisible lines between federal and state authority. The general government, Campbell would argue, had exclusive jurisdiction as sanctioned by the Constitution. But in those many instances where jurisdiction was left ill defined, such as in admiralty, commerce, and contractual obligations, Campbell tended to vote on the side of state authority, which, as we have seen earlier, he believed held the people's sovereignty in trust.

During his first term on the bench, Campbell's decision in the case of *McDonough's Executors v. Murdoch* convinced his colleagues that he had indeed been an excellent choice to fill McKinley's seat.[34] Closely resembling the *Gaines* case in that it dealt with the disposition of a contested will and also in that it was governed by the complex Louisiana civil code, the *McDonough* case involved a holographic will establishing a trust for the education of poor children in New Orleans. Mary Murdoch, McDonough's only daughter, insisted that because the will established a trust in perpetuity and this trust was beyond all bounds of practicality, the will could not be administered and she should receive her inheritance. Campbell's opinion held that the tendency to maintain huge estates through primogeniture laws had long prevailed in Europe and that these laws had had a corrupting effect on society. But primogeniture, Campbell explained, was abolished in France during the Revolution, and this legislation had been transferred to the Louisiana Territory with the adoption of the Napoleonic Code. Thus, by the strict letter of the law, McDonough had no right to invest his entire estate in a single trust.

Campbell concluded, however, that the Louisiana statute banning such financial arrangements did not apply in this case because it could not extend to municipal corporations—such as McDonough had established with his trust. A corporation or trust created entirely "for lawful and honorable purposes, or for public works, or for other objects of piety or benevolence" was a perfectly legitimate enterprise protected by corporate charter. The *McDonough* case is significant only in that it was one of the few cases in which Campbell ruled in favor of corporate rights. In most such instances he ruled against corporations, believing that they were dangerous financial conglomerates that amassed sufficient financial strength to sway public opinion—and in many instances state legislatures—in their favor. In ruling that the trust McDonough had established would have a positive impact on society, however, Campbell displayed a small measure of Benthamite utilitarianism, and he overlooked his normally inherent distrust of corporate enterprises that tended to concentrate wealth.[35]

The most significant case to reach the Supreme Court in the 1850s that involved the rights of corporations to sue or to be sued in federal courts was *Marshall v. Baltimore and Ohio Railroad Company.*[36] Alexander J. Marshall, a citizen of Virginia, brought suit against the Baltimore and Ohio Railroad, alleging that the company owed him $50,000 for lobbying services to the Virginia state legislature. Because the railroad company had been chartered in Maryland and was legally regarded as a citizen of that state, the dispute involved whether a citizen of one state could bring suit against a chartered corporation of another. The Circuit Court presided over by Taney decided against Marshall for breach of contract, and the case was remanded to Washington on writ of error. Justice Grier delivered the opinion of the Court that reversed the circuit court ruling and declared that federal courts had sufficient jurisdiction because the real defendants in the case were the individual stockholders of the company, most of whom resided in Maryland.[37]

Campbell submitted a rather strongly written dissent in this case in which he lauded those earlier precedents, which declared that corporations, although legal entities, were by no means citizens with rights to appear in federal courts. His *Marshall* dissent revealed a strong anticorporation bias and underscored his conservative, strict construction of the Constitution. Campbell quoted Chief Justice Marshall's opinion that "the invisible, intangible, and artificial being, the mere legal entity, the corporation aggregate is certainly not a citizen, and consequently cannot sue or be sued . . . unless the rights of the members . . . can be exercised in the corporate name." He continued by outlining precedents that had been established under the Taney Court he believed went beyond original intent. "I have been specific in the statement of precedents," he claimed, "that it may appear that this dissent involves no attempt to innovate upon the doctrines of the court." He stated that, on the contrary, he merely wanted to "maintain those sustained by time and authority in all of their integrity."[38]

"A corporation is not a citizen," Campbell wrote. "It may be an artificial person, a moral person, a juridical person, a legal entity, a faculty, an intangible, invisible being; but Chief Justice Marshall employed no metaphysical refinement, nor subtlety, nor sophism, but spoke of the common sense, 'the universal understanding,' as he calls it, of the people, when he declared the unanimous decision of this court, 'that it certainly is not a citizen.' " Campbell maintained that the framers of the Constitution had no intention of providing corporations with citizenship rights. Any interpretation that recognized absolute jurisdiction in cases involving corporations, would be "to say no more, a broad and liberal interpretation." He then commented that all rules and "domestic policy" governing corporations must be maintained by the states in which each corporation is chartered.[39]

Campbell feared that if corporations were allowed to sue in federal courts, they would be able to circumvent rules and regulations applied to their activities by state legislatures. A recognition of citizenship rights for "mere legal entities" would further enlarge the jurisdiction of the federal judiciary at the expense of state courts, rendering them incapable of ruling in cases that involved purely local matters. He agreed with a ruling in Kentucky's supreme court, which stated, "The competition for extraterritorial advantages would but aggrandize the stronger to the disparagement of the weaker states." "Weaker States," the ruling maintained, "must either submit to either have their policy controlled, their business monopolized, their domestic institutions reduced to insignificance, or the peace and harmony of the states broken up and destroyed."[40]

Campbell continued that the current decision "applied" to the Constitution "rules of construction which will undermine every limitation [on government], if universally adopted." "A single instance of [this] kind awakens apprehension, for it is regarded as a link in a chain of repetitions." He concluded with a strong warning that an affirmation of corporation rights, originally reserved specifically and exclusively for "real" people, would perilously weaken state legislatures and judiciaries. Corporations, Campbell asserted, "mock at the frugal and stinted conditions of state administration; their pretensions and demands are sovereign; admitting impatiently, interference by state legislative authority. And from the present case we learn that disdainful of 'the careless arbiters' of state interests, they are ready to 'hover about them' in 'efficient and vigilant activity,' to make them a prey, and, to accomplish this, to employ corrupt and polluting appliances."[41]

To Campbell, therefore, corporations presented a clear danger to state sovereignty, especially when they were guaranteed equal protection and citizenship rights by the federal courts. Campbell was by no means antibusiness; he did, however, object to the concentration of money and all aggregate political power in the hands of a few individuals claiming corporate rights, privileges, and immunities under the law. He envisioned that if corporations were given rights to sue in federal courts, states would be subjected to innumerable suits and would be forced to cater to the demands of the nation's corporate interests. Moreover, the establishment of corporations and the subsequent concentration of wealth promoted corruption on an unprecedented scale, and state legislators would fall victim to the vast financial resources controlled by conglomerates. To preserve the powers of the states and to avoid a disruption of their trusteeship over the people's sovereignty, Campbell recommended that corporations had to be strictly limited and their legal status ruled less than equal with regular citizens.

Campbell's pro states' rights, strict constructionist views also guided his decision in a second historic case involving commerce, contracts, and corporations. This case, argued during the December 1855 term, was *Dodge v. Woolsey*.[42] It arose from a dispute between the state of Ohio and that state's banking industry over the ability to collect taxes on bank property regardless of the wording of a law passed in 1845. This legislation, forced through the state house during a brief period of Whig domination, stated that bank profits could be taxed at a rate of only 6 percent. Moreover, all properties owned by the industry would be exempt from taxation. By 1850, when the state suffered financial strains, the Democrat-controlled legislature attempted to nullify the tax provision of the 1845 bank charter and to tax the assessed value of all bank property. In 1851, Ohioans adopted a new state constitution that included an amendment allowing the state to collect taxes on bank property equal to that paid on the property of individuals. A plethora of litigation arose out of this constitution as the bank corporations claimed that the state could not breach the 1845 contract it had made with the banks.[43]

In the first case brought before the Court in 1853, the majority ruled that the provision in the 1851 constitution allowing the state to tax bank property unconstitutionally violated the state's 1845 contractual obligations. Campbell issued a dissent, arguing that the charter was not in fact a contract and that the people of Ohio had full rights to enact new tax provisions at their discretion.[44]

Meanwhile, the banks sought to press the issue further. When in 1853 George C. Dodge, a county treasurer, entered several Cleveland banks and seized property he claimed was due the state in tax revenues, the banks assigned their remaining revenues to a John C. Deshler of New York. Deshler was then ordered by the banks to file a writ of replevin in federal courts to recover its seized property. The Court, with Campbell once again dissenting, ruled that the state could not collect taxes on property held by a citizen of a second state. The banks, although pleased with this nominal victory, wanted the Court to deny that the state had any right whatsoever to collect the tax and thereby nullify the 1845 contract. These events established the background for *Dodge v. Woolsey.*[45]

John M. Woolsey, a Connecticut resident who controlled thirty shares of stock in a Cleveland bank, sought an injunction in the circuit court to prevent Dodge from collecting taxes on bank property. In the circuit court decision, Justice McLean granted the injunction, proclaiming that the state grossly ignored its contractual obligations. Dodge filed suit in the Supreme Court on writ of error to have McLean's injunction overturned.

The Court sustained the circuit court ruling and upheld the injunction. In his dissenting opinion, Campbell vehemently protested the ruling, claiming that the Court was laying the foundation for a dangerous and unprecedented social and economic revolution. With his most striking assertion of states' rights, Campbell stated that the current ruling was even "more fatal to the states than the impotence of Congress" because it encouraged corrupt and mischievous corporate activity that would ultimately destroy the authority of state governments and render legislators mere pawns of an economic elite. This in turn would produce a caste system in the country in which the majority of wealth would be controlled by a few individuals who could dominate state legislatures. "Where, then, [would be] the remedy for the people?" he asked. "They [would] have none in their state governments, nor in themselves, and the federal government [would be] enlisted by their adversary."[46]

Campbell wrote that the case exemplified the "extreme pretensions of corporations" that sought protection in federal courts against state legislation. Such rulings, he wrote, would "establish on the soil of every State a caste made up of combinations of men, . . . who [would] look beyond the institutions of the State to the central government" for "special privileges and exemptions." If extensive rights for corporations were recognized by the Court, Campbell feared, "a new element of alienation and discord between the different classes of society" would surface and introduce "a fresh cause of disturbance in our distracted political and social system." "In the end," he predicted, "the doctrine of this decision may lead to a violent overturn to the whole system of corporate combinations."[47] Such words illustrate Campbell's apprehension over increased powers for a federal government that could be manipulated by corporations asserting rights he believed were not sanctioned by the Constitution. "But, for my part," he wrote,

> when I consider the justice, moderation, the restraints upon arbitrary power, stability of the social order, the security of personal rights and general harmony which existed in this country before the sovereignty of governments was asserted, and when the sovereignty of the people was a living and operative principle, and governments were administered subject to limitations and with reference to the specific ends for which they were organized, and their members recognized their responsibility and dependence, I feel no anxiety nor apprehension in leaving to the people of Ohio a "complete power" over their government, and all the institutions and establishments it has called into existence.[48]

Here again Campbell asserted that sovereignty resided with the people and that states were the original repository of their authority. For the previous two generations, the federal government had been harnessing greater power at the expense of the states, and this he believed needed to be reversed. In those instances where the powers of the federal government were clearly expressed in the Constitution, however, for example in foreign relations and with proclamations of neutrality, Campbell fully agreed that these powers should be upheld.[49]

Campbell's reading of the federal government's expressed powers led him into direct conflict with one of the South's most popular adventurers, John A. Quitman, who in the 1850s was the leading personality behind attempts to wrest Cuba from Spain and add another slave state to the Union. While riding circuit in New Orleans, Campbell made strenuous efforts to stymie Quitman's filibustering schemes, and his actions revealed the "law and order" stand that he adopted in enforcing federal statutes.

Many people regarded the acquisition of Cuba as a goal for the United States throughout much of the nineteenth century. Between 1852 and 1854, this sentiment gained increasing strength, and calls for immediate annexation were more pronounced as one of the major issues during the 1852 presidential election centered on the United States' manifest destiny to acquire new territory. This expansionist impulse blossomed when Franklin Pierce was elected president, and many Americans—southerners in particular—believed that an opportunity to wrest Cuba from an ever-weakening Spanish Empire had finally arrived. Cuba already had a well-established system of slave labor, and a potential "State of Cuba," many southerners reasoned, could restore the balance of power in Congress that had been disrupted since the Compromise of 1850.[50]

When Franklin Pierce took office in March 1853, support for a new filibustering expedition to Cuba reached fever pitch in the South. In his inaugural address delivered 4 March 1853, Pierce declared that "the policy of my Administration will not be controlled by any forebodings of evil from expansion." He also suggested that "the acquisition of certain possessions not within our jurisdiction [is] eminently important for our protection, if not in the future essential for the protection of the rights of commerce and the peace of the world."[51] It was generally believed that by "certain possessions" Pierce directly referred to Cuba, and his speech spawned genuine encouragement among southerners willing to support filibustering expeditions. For the next fourteen months, a planned excursion headed by John A. Quitman, a United States Army general during the Mexican War and governor of Mississippi from 1849 to 1851, gained much support in the United States and seriously threatened Spanish domination of the island. Meanwhile, due to political considerations that could have divided the Democratic party, and sectional strife that seriously threatened the Union, Pierce remained uncharacteristically silent on the acquisition of Cuba. Ironically, the administration's reluctance to formulate a Cuban policy and its unusual silence on possible annexation convinced Quitman that the president tacitly approved his filibuster expedition.[52] As a consequence of Quitman's widely publicized activities, and Pierce's failure to establish a sound Cuba policy, it appeared that the United States would turn a blind eye to an independent invasion of Cuba.

The principal event that forced Pierce to adopt a position regarding the annexation of Cuba was the raging congressional debate over the Kansas-Nebraska bill. By 1854, the Free Soil movement in the United States was growing at an astonishing rate and was threatening to create a schism between northern and southern Democrats. In late May when Congress finally passed the bill with its popular sovereignty provisions, most northern politicians felt that they had made a genuine concession to the South's interests. The Kansas-Nebraska Act, signed by Pierce on 20 May, effectively repealed the Missouri Compromise line—a time-honored settlement to many northerners. Given these considerations, the president felt that if he were to allow an illegal seizure of Cuba, the Democratic party would most certainly split along sectional lines.[53]

A few days after Pierce signed the Kansas-Nebraska Act, he issued a proclamation declaring that filibuster expeditions against Cuba violated existing neutrality treaties between Spain and the United States and would not be tolerated. Pierce sternly warned all Americans to steer clear of such enterprises, as the federal government would "not fail to prosecute with due energy" any United States citizen violating neutrality laws.[54] This proclamation should have diminished Quitman's hopes of invading Cuba, but the Mississippian remained confident that Pierce was similarly disturbed by Cuba's "Africanization" and that the president still hoped to acquire the island.[55] Thus Quitman continued with preparations.

Quitman's campaign, however, suffered a most damaging setback when Campbell decided that Pierce's neutrality proclamation should be enforced to its fullest and that the filibusterers had scoffed at federal laws long enough. During the June 1854 session of the circuit court in New Orleans, Campbell summoned a grand jury and ordered its members, most of whom were apparently enthralled with Quitman and his daring scheme, to investigate the extent of the planned invasion. Campbell stated that if the grand jury found that certain individuals were purchasing Cuban bonds or even making public speeches on the virtues of filibustering, their activities would be infractions of the neutrality law and justification for indictments. In other words, in his zealous attempt to quell any invasion of Cuba, Campbell asserted that a mere intention to invade was as much a violation of the law as would be an actual invasion.[56] "There is a consideration to fortify you in the performance of this duty," he explained to the jurors,

> which is particularly operative at this time. The exercise of some of the powers conferred in the interest of one section of the Union inflicts a wound upon the sensibilities of other sections of the Union. Some of these powers are deemed of vital importance to this portion of the United States. We exact the fulfillment of the compact in which they are formed with strictness, and applaud the power that maintains them. Not long ago, one of the cities (Boston) of the Northern section of the United States was involved in riot and disorder in an attempt to maintain these stipulations. This portion of the Union regards these expeditions with abhorrence, as designed to secure sectional advantages by piratical and lawless outrages; by the sacrifice of the faith of treaties and the prostration of national character. They offend their sense of right, jeopard their material interests, and mortify their national pride.

This passage clearly shows that Campbell was sensitive to sectionalism and that he was concerned that the acquisition of Cuba would seriously offend northerners and would possibly spawn another crisis of 1850 magnitude. He concluded that in his judgment all citizens of the United States had to uphold the laws and to "frown indignantly upon all such lawless enterprises."[57]

The grand jury summoned several of Quitman's closest subordinates and inquired whether they intended to invade Cuba, but each of the witnesses refused to answer on the grounds of self-incrimination. Unable to garner sufficient evidence against the filibusterers, the grand jury informed Campbell on 1 July that the rumors of an expedition were "not altogether without foundation" but that it would be unnecessary to continue the investigation. Campbell strongly suspected, however, that the filibusterers were still making plans for an invasion. Therefore, he ordered that Quitman and two of his associates each post $3,000 bonds to ensure that they would obey the neutrality law. Although the three filibusterers defiantly refused at first to pay the bond— Quitman practically dared Campbell to jail him—the money was eventually paid. The payment seriously drained their finances and stalled any further preparations for the invasion.[58]

Naturally, Quitman was irate at Campbell's order. On 3 July he sent a letter for publication to the *New Orleans Delta* in which he lambasted the justice for his high-handed ruling, made even though the grand jury had no direct evidence that any laws had been broken. Referring to Campbell's orders requiring the bond as "the after-birth of an uneasy mind," Quitman explained that Campbell's ruling was incorrect, said it was based solely on public rumor, and declared it clearly indicative of the justice's personal hatred for filibustering expeditions.[59]

By hindering Quitman's campaign, Campbell was denounced throughout the South. Robert J. Walker, a Mississippi politician and an avid supporter of filibustering missions, complained of Campbell's high-handedness and concluded that the judge was "crazy." The *Vicksburg Whig* declared that Campbell's actions in New Orleans had been based on a "monstrous" doctrine, and a public meeting staged in that city pledged full support for Quitman. Such remonstrances were echoed in many places in the South, and Campbell began to be regarded with suspicion as perhaps less friendly to the South than most people had originally believed him.[60]

Such cases well illustrate Campbell's decisions while on the bench. Though these are but a minute cross section of his entire judicial record, they indicate that he was adamantly for states' rights, particularly with regard to monopolies and the threats they posed to state sovereignty. At the same time, however, Campbell showed that he would enforce federal laws without impunity whenever—and wherever—they were breached. Whereas cases involving commerce and contracts dominated the Court during Campbell's tenure, the Taney Court is best remembered for its verdict in the *Dred Scott* decision of 1857. This ruling, by declaring the Missouri Compromise unconstitutional, afforded Campbell an opportunity for reversing what he perceived as a congressional usurpation of the people's sovereignty and the trend toward increased power for the federal government.

8 | States' Rights Justice, Part 2: *Dred Scott* and *Sherman Booth*

It is unfortunate, but with hindsight clearly understandable, that the Taney Court has been most notably remembered for its fateful decision in the *Dred Scott* case. The Court's ruling in this 1857 litigation spawned the popularly held view that the southern members of the Court comprised a slave power conspiracy intent upon destroying the abolition movement and preserving the political hegemony of slaveowners. Of course, this sentiment was but the popular misunderstanding of the ruling; it was largely the creation of anti-slavery publicists and editors seeking to sway public opinion in their favor. A writer for the *New York Tribune* caustically remarked, "If epithets and denunciations could sink a judicial body, the Supreme Court of the United States would never be heard of again."[1] But Dred Scott's case represented much more than these editors perceived, for it was a clear manifestation of the trend toward judicial activism that had begun in 1803 with the famous *Marbury v. Madison* decision. By glancing at his opinions in a number of cases involving the commerce and contract clauses, it was apparent that Campbell fully intended to be an activist judge. His *Dred Scott* decision was no departure from this stance, for he employed his dogmatic states' rights philosophy to its fullest in ruling that Congress's authority to govern in the territories was limited to external policies that could in no manner affect slavery. On the other hand, Campbell also proved that he harbored a far more nationalistic jurisprudence than his decision in *Dred Scott* revealed. His recognition of the need for a strong central government clearly sanctioned by the Constitution was quite evident when he concurred in *Ableman v. Booth,* an 1859 case in which a state's action to nullify a federal law was abruptly overturned.

On 11 March 1857, five days after the majority opinion in the *Dred Scott* case was read by Chief Justice Taney, the *New York Tribune* stated, "It is impossible to exaggerate the importance of the recent decision of the Supreme Court," because, according to this newspaper, *Dred Scott* established "that *Slavery is National.*" Until the "wicked and false judgement" was reversed, "the Constitution is nothing better than the bulwark of inhumanity and oppression."[2] In popular opinion, this decision symbolized a political struggle between the slave and free states. But in the realm of judicial decision making, the case exemplified the constitutional crisis that had plagued the nation since its inception and had involved almost diametrically opposed interpretations of the Constitution pitting the defenders of states' rights against the power and authority of the federal government.[3]

The facts surrounding Dred Scott's campaign for freedom have been re-counted so often that they may be stated here only briefly.[4] In 1833, an army surgeon named John Emerson purchased Dred Scott from the Peter Blow family of St. Louis, Missouri. Emerson was soon thereafter transferred to Rock Island, Illinois, and Scott accompanied him there despite Illinois state laws prohibiting slavery. In 1836, the surgeon was transferred to Fort Snelling in the Wisconsin Territory (now Minnesota). While at Fort Snelling, Emerson arranged Scott's marriage to Harriet, a slave whom the doctor had recently purchased. In 1838, Emerson and his slaves returned to Missouri.

Emerson died in 1843, and his estate passed to his wife. Meanwhile, the Blow family, many of whom harbored antislavery sentiments, had become re-acquainted with Scott. The Blows convinced their former slave that his residence in Illinois and in the Wisconsin Territory rendered him and Harriet free. In 1846 a suit of trespass was brought against Mrs. Emerson for illegally holding slaves who had been made free by virtue of their residence in free territory. The state court initially ruled against Scott, but on retrial he was granted his freedom in 1850. Mrs. Emerson at once filed suit in the Missouri Supreme Court to have the decision reversed. In 1852, by a count of 2 to 1, the court reversed the earlier decision, and Scott was once again legally a slave. The majority ruled that although some slaves had been granted their freedom in Missouri under similar circumstances, the state had merely recognized such status in a spirit of comity that existed between the states. Such acts granting slaves their freedom were never intended to be universal.[5]

The next logical step for Scott would have been to take the case to the United States Supreme Court on writ of error. Yet Scott's attorney, Roswell M. Field of St. Louis, determined that in light of the recent *Strader v. Graham* ruling, the Court would refuse to accept the case.[6] The *Strader* case, argued before the Taney Court in 1851, involved the status of Kentucky slave musicians who had spent a considerable period north of the Ohio River in free states. The Supreme Court ruled that only Kentucky law need be recognized in determining their status and that antislavery legislation contrary to laws of their home state did not apply. As this ruling was nearly in total agreement with the Missouri Supreme Court decision in Scott's case, Field correctly reasoned that a direct appeal to the highest Court would not be heard.

Meanwhile, the principals in the case had changed somewhat. Mrs. Emerson had moved to Massachusetts, where she married Dr. Calvin C. Chaffee, an influential member of Boston society. She then transferred full control over her departed husband's estate to her brother, John F. A. Sanford of New York.[7]

Because Scott's owner was a resident of another state, Field could file suit in the United States Circuit Court for Missouri claiming federal jurisdiction on grounds of diversity of citizenship.

The defense attorney representing Sanford, Hugh A. Garland, counterfiled a plea in abatement on the grounds that Scott had no right to sue in federal courts.[8] Garland's plea requested the Federal Circuit for Missouri, presided over by Judge Robert W. Wells in St. Louis, to dismiss the case for want of jurisdiction. As Scott was a slave, Garland contended, he was not a United States citizen, and therefore could not sue in federal court. Even if Scott were not a slave, Garland maintained, his African descent prevented him from qualifying for United States citizenship. This tactic, if accepted by the Court, would not only have required the judge to rule whether Scott could sue, but whether blacks, free or slave, could rightfully be considered citizens of the United States.

Field filed a demurrer to the plea in abatement, claiming that Scott's African heritage was insufficient grounds to deny citizenship, and he asked the Court to overrule the defense's delaying tactic. Judge Wells sustained the demurrer and decided to hear the case solely on its merits. After both parties and the judge agreed to a jury trial, Wells instructed the jury that by law they were required to rule in Sanford's favor, which the members promptly did. Scott's attorney then filed an appeal to the United States Supreme Court on writ of error, and the case was first docketed in May 1854. Significantly, Field did not maintain the original demurrer in his appeal to the Supreme Court, which meant that the legal status of the plea in abatement remained obscure and raised the question as to whether the Taney Court had an obligation to rule solely on the plea or to render a decision based on the facts of the case.[9]

Of course, the larger issues involved whether Scott's temporary residence in Illinois and in the Wisconsin Territory rendered him free. Beyond that question, however, the most significant issue was whether Congress had the constitutional authority to prevent slaveowners from carrying their slaves into United States territories, as it had done in 1820 with the Missouri Compromise. At this level, the Court was asked to rule on the constitutionality of a law that had lasted thirty-four years, and although it had been abrogated by the Kansas-Nebraska Act, the heritage of restricting slavery to south of the Missouri Compromise line was regarded as sacrosanct by many northerners.[10]

The case was first argued before the Taney Court in February 1856. After presentations by both sides, the Court postponed a ruling largely because the justices could not agree on the disposition of the plea in abatement. Because of the confusion over the plea, Justice Samuel Nelson of New York asked that the case be reargued to better define the issues involved in the dispute. As a result, *Dred Scott v. Sandford* carried over to the next term.[11]

The second arguments before the Court were completed on 18 December

1856, but the Court again postponed further consideration because the legal points remained unclear. For the next several weeks no decision was handed down; apparently Justices Taney, Wayne, Daniel, and Curtis could not agree as to whether to rule on the plea in abatement or on the merits of the case. Campbell, on the other hand, firmly believed that the case had to be argued solely on its merits and that the plea in abatement had been a manipulative lawyer's trick to avoid a decision based on the issues. In a letter he wrote several years later to Samuel Tyler, one of Taney's early biographers, Campbell stated that the justices held several discussions of the case while in conference. It was readily apparent during these discussions that serious divisions existed between the members regarding the plea in abatement. "The minority of the Court, at that time," Campbell wrote, "were of the opinion that this plea was not open for examination, nor for the judgement on it for review."[12] A few years later Campbell declared in no uncertain terms that he and Justices Catron, Grier, McLean, and Nelson "were unwavering and some denounced the plea, and denounced also the authors of the plea as unscrupulous lawyers who had been astute to frame a plea to catch an opinion upon a mooted question which the facts of the case did not call for."[13] Obviously, Campbell held that the plea in abatement should be ignored altogether.

It was initially decided by a majority of the justices to follow *Strader v. Graham* and rule that the case was governed by Missouri law. Such a decision would have produced a summary dismissal of Scott's case. Of course, it would also have been a supreme dodge of the larger issues involved. On 14 February, Justice Nelson was assigned to write the opinion of the court based on the *Strader* decision. But then suddenly, and almost inexplicably, the Court changed its position and decided to rule on the Missouri Compromise. The most commonly reported explanation for this change was that the southern justices reversed their decision after realizing that Justices John McLean of Ohio and Benjamin R. Curtis of Massachusetts intended to write dissenting opinions declaring that Scott should be freed under the terms of the Missouri Compromise. If the majority said nothing to the contrary, the opinions in the dissent would have been recognized by default. The southern justices, so the story went, were prodded into drafting their more broad rulings.[14]

The problem with this story was that it neglected to consider the anxiety felt by the southern justices over the sectional crisis and the vexing slavery issue. Justices Campbell, Taney, and Peter V. Daniel of Virginia in particular were acutely sensitive to the North's assault on southern institutions as well as the ever-weakening political position of the southern states in the Union. Campbell's denunciation of the plea in abatement clearly indicated that he was anxious to render a decision based solely on the facts. He needed no prodding from two northern justices whose opinions would obviously be in the minority and, he supposed, of little consequence. He believed that the slavery issue, the territory crisis, sectionalism, and the constitutional crisis could all be settled with one fell swoop. Campbell's determination to issue a broad decision epitomized the judicial activism that he employed throughout his tenure on the bench.[15] This ruling, however, also clearly indicates Campbell's remarkable political naiveté and the degree to which he believed that a political—and ethical—question such as slavery could be settled by the judiciary.

On 6 March 1857, just two days after James Buchanan had been sworn in as president,[16] Chief Justice Taney read his four-part opinion, which spoke for the majority. He first declared that Scott was not a citizen and that emancipated slaves or their descendants could not become citizens. He also denied that free blacks were citizens in various states. Second, the Chief Justice stated that if Scott were still a slave, he could not sue. The discussion then considered whether Scott's sojourn in a free state nullified his status as a slave; the conclusion was that the plaintiff's temporary residence in free territory in no manner made him free. The chief justice argued that the Constitution provided that citizens from all states enjoyed the right to take their property into the territories and that Congress had no authority to exclude certain property from the territories. This assertion in effect rendered the Missouri Compromise unconstitutional. Last, Taney interjected an entirely novel interpretation of the Fifth Amendment, providing that citizens not be "deprived of life, liberty, or property without due process of law." Until this ruling, the "due process clause" had been used only in procedural matters, but Taney's interpretation paved the way for substantive due process, whereby congressional laws depriving citizens of freedom of speech or of religion, or the enactment of property laws prejudicial to one section of the nation, "could hardly be dignified with the name of due process of law."[17] So it was that the Missouri Compromise was thereby rendered unconstitutional and Dred Scott was returned to slavery.

The Court's two dissenters in the case, Justices McLean and Curtis, issued opinions that the Missouri Compromise line had been constitutional and that free blacks were citizens. Curtis's dissent seriously weakened Taney's ruling; it argued that blacks were indeed citizens of several states and had full rights to sue in federal courts under diversity of citizenship. He further stated that because the Court had gone far beyond merely deciding the issue of the plea in abatement—the issue to which, he maintained, the case should have been restricted—the Court's opinion had largely been obiter dicta and hardly the law of the land. "A great question of Constitutional law," he wrote, "deeply affecting the peace and the welfare of the country, is not, in my opinion, a fit subject to be thus reached."[18] Antislavery newspapers echoed Curtis's dissent and claimed that the majority opinion should be considered "a stump speech embodied into a judicial decision."[19]

Campbell's opinion, the principal focus of this chapter, represented many years' reflection upon the nature of the Union and the federal-state relationship. He made no use of the due process clause, as Taney had done, but instead focused on a strict construction of the Constitution starting from Congress's lack of authority to prohibit slavery in the territories. "The importance of the case, the expectation and the interest it has awakened, and the responsibility involved in its determination, induce me to file a separate opinion," he wrote.[20] After a brief restatement of the facts in the case, Campbell affirmed that he would rule only on the merits because the issue of jurisdiction raised by the plea in abatement was of no significance.

"[I]n general," he wrote, "the status, or civil and political capacity of a person, is determined, in the first instance, by the law of the domicil [*sic*] where he is born." In this instance, Scott was a slave, and he would remain a slave governed by Missouri law unless his master took appropriate measures through a lawful act of manumission. Campbell then discoursed at length on the history of the legal status of slaves. This portion of the opinion strongly echoed his earlier articles in the *Southern Quarterly Review;* he employed much the same argument, discussed many similar points, and reached identical conclusions.

Campbell next summarized the basic issues involved in Dred Scott's case. He wrote that the Missouri Supreme Court was perfectly within its right to uphold the provisions of the state constitution and not recognize Illinois or Minnesota antislavery laws.[21] Campbell then expounded his fundamental philosophy regarding states' rights and the power and authority of the federal government to legislate in the territories. "It is a settled doctrine of this court," he wrote, "that the Federal government can exercise no power over the subject of slavery within the States, nor control the intermigration of slaves, other than fugitives, among the States. Nor can that government affect the duration of slavery within the States, other than by a legislation over the foreign slave trade."[22] In citing article 4, section 3 of the Constitution ("Congress shall have power to dispose of and make all needful rules and regulations respecting the territory, or other property belonging to the United States"), Campbell admitted that a cursory reading of that sentence seemed to empower Congress to govern slavery in the territories at its discretion. But he adamantly disagreed with this interpretation of article 4.

He maintained that Congress had no powers to regulate purely municipal institutions such as slavery. "[T]he recognition of a plenary power in Congress to dispose of the public domain, or to organize a government over it" was perfectly constitutional. However, he declared, this power "does not imply a corresponding authority to internal polity, or to adjust the domestic relations, or the persons who may lawfully inhabit the territory in which it is situated."[23] Thus Congress had no powers whatsoever to regulate slavery in the territories.

Campbell continued, "The cessions of States to the Confederation were made on the condition that the territory ceded should be laid out and formed into distinct republican States" on an equal footing with the original states. He referred here to his first states' rights argument in the submerged land cases. All states, both the old and those to be added to the Union, "Would be admitted as members to the Federal Union, having the same rights of sovereignty, freedom, and independence as the other States." The inhabitants of the territories were supposed to "form for themselves" temporary state governments that would be made permanent whenever the population sufficiently increased to allow for statehood. This, according to Campbell's argument, had been the framers' intent with regard to territorial governments, but "Congress *assumed* to obtain powers from the States to facilitate this object." "I look in vain, among the discussions" during the Constitutional Convention of 1787

> for the assertion of a supreme sovereignty for Congress over the territory then belonging to the United States, or that they might thereafter acquire. I seek in vain for an enunciation that a consolidated power had been inaugurated, whose subject comprehended an empire, and which had no restriction but the discretion of Congress. This disturbing element of the Union entirely escaped the apprehensive provisions of Samuel Adams, George Clinton, Luther Martin, and Patrick Henry; and in respect to dangers from power vested in a central government over distant settlements, colonies, or provinces, their instincts were always alive.[24]

Obviously, Campbell wrote, if the founders from the southern states had believed that article 4 gave Congress authority to govern the internal affairs of territories, they would have vehemently protested. But he explained that nowhere in the debates could he find such a protest, and the framers must therefore have been in agreement that Congress's authority in the territories was strictly limited to external affairs. Campbell nonetheless recognized that the framers left article 4 too nebulous and ill defined, leading subsequent Congresses to assume powers not intended for the federal government. This was a mistake in the Constitution. It had to be recognized as such, and diligent efforts had to be made to reverse congressional assumption of political power over the territories.[25]

"I find nothing" in the Constitution or in the Convention debates, Campbell wrote, "to authorize [Congress's] enormous pretensions" to govern purely internal matters in either the states or the territories. "Every portion of the United States was provided with a municipal government, which this Constitution was not designed to supersede, but merely to modify as to its conditions." The assertion that Congress could lawfully regulate slavery in the territories "proceeds from a radical error which lies at the foundation of much of this discussion."[26]

Campbell stated that the federal Constitution was at its core a "mere compact among the States." The people of the original states delegated much power to the federal government, but they retained their sovereignty, which was to be held in perpetual trust by their respective states. He claimed that when Congress "imposed" restrictions on slavery in the Louisiana Purchase, it unlawfully affirmed a "concurrent right" that "altered the basis of the Constitution." Under these circumstances "new States [became] members of a Union defined in part by the Constitution and in part by Congress. They [were] not admitted to 'this Union.' Their sovereignty [was] restricted by Congress as well as [by] the Constitution." During the previous four decades, Campbell asserted, "The demand [for greater congressional authority] was unconstitutional and subversive, but was prosecuted with an energy, and aroused such animosities among the people, that patriots . . . began to despair for the Constitution."[27]

Campbell recognized that article 4, section 3 of the federal Constitution provided that Congress had undisputed authority to perform a number of important duties in the territories, including tax assessment and collection, regulation of foreign and interstate commerce, the abolition of the slave trade, protection of copyrights and inventions, operation of the postal service, the establishment of courts of justice, and punishing crimes. But he was uncertain exactly where to set the bounds of congressional authority in the territories, and he admitted that doing so "is a work of delicacy and difficulty." Nonetheless, he maintained that it was not the function of the federal judiciary to define congressional jurisdiction; the Supreme Court could determine only when Congress had overstepped its jurisdiction and enacted legislation in areas in which it was unauthorized to do so. In regard to the validity of the Missouri Compromise, Campbell wrote, Congress had assumed the authority to define property for the territories, and it had acted outside its constitutional bounds. The only true definitions of property were those established by municipal governments, and Congress had the duty to recognize those definitions and to pass no law that altered them. Article 4, he concluded, "confers no power upon Congress to dissolve the relations of the master and slave in the domain of the United States, either within or without any of the States."[28]

Campbell's concurring opinion in *Dred Scott* genuinely reflected the basic foundation for much of his political theory. That he was anxious to have the case decided on the merits cannot be denied, because the case presented an unprecedented opportunity to reassert states' rights and to negate Congress's tendency to overstep its constitutional jurisdiction. What was basically at issue, he contended, was the right of self-government that Congress had denied to the people of the territories—and by inference the people of future states— by passage of the Missouri Compromise. All residents of the territories had the inalienable right to determine their local institutions for themselves.

In contrast to later claims that Campbell employed "extreme Calhounism" in his argument, his ruling in *Dred Scott* actually blended Calhoun's doctrine of nonintervention, the doctrine of original sovereignty that he had so successfully defended in the submerged land cases, and the principle of territorial self-government.[29] Congress could not define property in the territories—and by implication exclude slavery—because such legislation prevented the inhabitants of the territories from expressing their innate sovereignty when establishing their respective state governments. The most salient point of his twelve-page argument was that article 4 did not authorize Congress to define property for the people of the territories, and thus it had had no rights to establish the Missouri Compromise line.

Campbell's position on the bench afforded him an opportunity to render invalid a law he believed wholly unauthorized by the Constitution. Following the tenets of judicial review, Campbell reestablished the doctrine of nonintervention because that was the one weapon within his judicial armory that could be employed to restore municipal control over slavery. In some respects, the *Dred Scott* decision was a truncated form of positive protection because it prevented Congress from legislating with regard to slavery in the territories. Admittedly, this form of protection was quite different from that which Campbell and Yancey had contemplated in 1848, but short of ordering Congress to pass legislation positively protecting slavery—which, of course, Campbell could not do—a statement that Congress had usurped local authority was the next logical line of attack. In the political world, positive protection—however unrealistic—was the only measure that many southern politicians believed could protect southern rights in the territories. In the judiciary, however, where legislation was judged solely on its constitutionality, Campbell's assertion that Congress had no authority to bar slavery from the Louisiana Purchase was his most powerful safeguard against further congressional encroachments on state authority.

From a reading of Campbell's opinion in *Dred Scott,* one gains a clear indication of his staunch states' rights philosophy. But as shown in the previous chapter, Campbell's jurisprudence also recognized that the federal government held supreme authority in many different realms, particularly in foreign policy and in the regulation of the slave trade. In 1858 he sent a lengthy letter in response to an invitation to appear at a public dinner to be held in his honor. "The station I occupy," Campbell wrote, "is one of grave responsibility." Because the Supreme Court was "the final arbiter" of legal controversies, he expressed profound conviction that justices had to remain entirely impartial, had "to disregard [sectional or state] attachments, and [had] to control those affections which would give a preference to special interests of local advantages." Campbell continued, "In favor of the general law [a Supreme Court justice] must restrain the aggressive selfishness, or restless egotism that evade or subvert it; and he can make no compromise with the lawlessness, force, caprice, deceit, or cunning that would overturn a policy of the Union. He can have no other aim than to maintain the Constitution, and the laws and the treaties of the Union that conform to it. . . . This has been the object of my judicial life."[30]

If we are to grasp Campbell's nationalistic philosophy and jurisprudence more fully, we must examine additional cases. The first of these involved the continued filibustering expeditions like that proposed by Quitman in 1854. In 1858, however, it was not Quitman who was causing the trouble but William Walker, whose exploits in Nicaragua had in 1857 led to his seizure and arrest by federal officials. Walker returned to Mobile where, despite President Buchanan's proclamation of 30 October warning that filibustering expeditions would not be tolerated, he established the Mobile and Nicaragua Steamship Company as a front for another planned excursion into Central America.[31]

In November 1858, Campbell arranged for a special session of the circuit court so that Walker's invasion could be stopped. Although he did not have authority to do so during special sessions of the Court, Campbell summoned a grand jury and charged them to investigate violations—or even intentions to violate—the nation's neutrality laws. In other words, despite numerous articles in the *Mobile Register* denouncing Campbell's high-handed actions and reminding its readers of the justice's antisouthern opposition to Quitman's filibustering campaigns, Campbell chose the same method that he had used to stop Quitman four years earlier: Walker and several of his associates were required to post bonds that they would not breach the neutrality laws. At least temporarily, the grand jury's investigation stalled Walker's activities in Mobile, and as a result Campbell was scurrilously denounced throughout the South.[32] The *National Intelligencer,* a decidedly prosouthern organ, announced with considerable derision, "The Campbells are Coming!" "We trust," the article under the headline read, "that none of our Filibuster friends will start at this announcement. We have no allusion to his Honor—the dreaded and dreadful judge of the Supreme Court of the United States."[33] Such denunciations of Campbell and cynical editorials were common. In a paper written several years later, Campbell's brother-in-law, George Goldthwaite, stated that Campbell's rulings with regard to the filibusters and the slave traders led to greatly deepened suspicion and openly hostile condemnations by many southerners. "The excitement against him [Campbell] was so intense," Goldthwaite remarked, "that well-grounded apprehensions of his personal safety were felt."[34]

A second ruling reflecting Campbell's respect for federal jurisdiction where provided by the Constitution involved the state of Wisconsin's nullification of the Fugitive Slave Act and protection for one of its citizens whose activities directly violated that legislation. In 1852, a slave named Joshua Glover owned by Benammi S. Garland of St. Louis escaped to Wisconsin, where for the next two years he was employed at a sawmill in Racine. In 1854, Garland learned of Glover's whereabouts and in March, accompanied by United States

Marshall Stephen V. R. Ableman, seized Glover and placed him in a jail in Milwaukee. On 10 March, a radical abolitionist editor of the *Milwaukee Free Democrat,* Sherman M. Booth, roused an antislavery crowd into a frenzy. The mob soon thereafter battered in the door, seized Glover, and secretly arranged for his passage to Canada.[35]

Booth was arrested for violating the Fugitive Slave Act, and his case was docketed for trial in federal court. Before the case began, however, Booth appealed to the Wisconsin Supreme Court for a writ of habeas corpus. The state court defiantly ordered Booth's release on the grounds that the 1850 Fugitive Slave Act was unconstitutional. Booth was summarily rearrested by federal officials, but once again Wisconsin's Supreme Court intervened and ordered Booth released. The situation grew tense as the Wisconsin judiciary in essence asserted its power to free a prisoner who had been duly tried and convicted in federal court. This act of defiance was perhaps the most explicit example of state nullification of federal law in the nation's history, far exceeding in extent the terms of nullification that Calhoun himself had advocated nearly thirty years earlier.[36]

The disposition of the case remained unsettled for the next four years. But in 1859 arguments for *Ableman v. Booth* were finally heard by the Taney Court.[37] The Court was unanimous in ruling that state courts could in no manner pass judgment on the constitutionality of federal law or issue writs of habeas corpus to remove someone from federal custody. "If the judicial power exercised in this instance," Taney wrote, "has been reserved to the states, no offense against the laws of the United States can be punished by their own courts. . . . [I]f the Supreme Court of Wisconsin possessed the power it has exercised in relation to offenses against" the Fugitive Slave Act, "it necessarily follows that they must have the same judicial authority in relation to any other law of the United States." Taney stated that neither the Wisconsin Supreme Court nor any other state's judiciary had the authority to nullify federal laws. Such laws could be challenged for their constitutionality, but this process could only occur with any finality in the United States Supreme Court.[38] As has recently been stated, the Court's unanimous decision "echoed the broad nationalism of famous decisions of John Marshall's era."[39] That Campbell fully concurred in the majority opinion is further evidence of his strongly nationalistic philosophy.

It should not escape the reader's notice that the *Ableman* case substantially involved the validity of the Fugitive Slave Law adopted in 1850. Taney asserted that that legislation was beyond state reproach. To that extent, *Ableman v. Booth* was considered by many antislavery northerners as a dangerous extension of *Dred Scott* and as further evidence that the Court was a leading actor in the perceived slave power conspiracy. Because Campbell refrained from issuing a separate but concurring opinion and merely voted with the majority, it is impossible to determine where he believed the emphasis in this case should have been placed. In other words, the question arises whether Campbell voted with the majority as a defender of federal authority over state courts or whether his concurrence was but another means of protecting slavery. It would have been interesting to review the outcome of *Ableman* had the case not involved a fugitive slave.

Campbell's eight-year tenure on the Supreme Court encompassed not only his *Dred Scott* opinion, which certainly established him as keenly pro states' rights but also decisions in which he ruled to protect the power and jurisdiction of the federal judiciary and legislature. If Campbell was hated in many portions of the North for his concurring but separate opinion in *Dred Scott,* he also did not endear himself to many southerners by thwarting the Quitman and Walker filibustering campaigns. But because he tempered his states' rights philosophy with a clear recognition of federal jurisdiction, Campbell was viewed by many of his contemporaries as a level-headed political moderate.

As sectional antagonisms reached fever pitch with the schismatic events throughout the 1850s, Campbell's name was circulated in political circles as a possible compromise candidate for the upcoming Democratic nominating convention, someone who could attract support in both the North and the South. In the spring of 1860, an editorial in the *Mobile Advertiser* stated, "[T]he name Mr. Justice Campbell in connection with the next presidency, is attracting very general notice, and is received in many quarters with decided marks of gratification." The article continued that Campbell "would run well at the North, and would not be objected to at the South." "By nominating [Campbell]," counseled the editorialist, "the Convention would nicely escape the difficulties that beset the making of new platforms, and might, with Ulyssean wisdom, pass safely between the Scylla of territorial protection of slavery on the one hand, and the Charybdis of Douglas popular sovereignty on the other."[40]

The writer of this editorial was no doubt disappointed that the Democrats did not nominate Campbell. In fact, the Alabamian did not even attend the convention in Charleston. But William Lowndes Yancey was there, armed with the Alabama Platform. The resulting split in the Democratic party all but assured a Republican victory in November. Lincoln's election in turn precipitated the secession crisis during which Campbell's adopted state of Alabama withdrew from the Union. And though he was staunchly convinced that the South's secession would prove calamitous, he nonetheless felt obliged to resign his seat on the bench and follow his fellow southerners on whatever road lay ahead.

9 | The War Years, Part 1: To Mitigate the Evils upon the Country

As for literally millions of other Americans, the Civil War years were the most tragic in Campbell's life. Not only did he relinquish his coveted position on the Supreme Court, but his family suffered tremendously during the war. Campbell continued to serve on the Court throughout 1860 and into 1861. But by then the South had seceded, Fort Sumter had been bombarded, and President Lincoln had called 75,000 troops into service and had established a naval blockade around the Confederacy. These were ominous events that Campbell had anxiously dreaded, and despite his efforts to stop the secession crisis, the southern states dissolved the Union, and the nation endured four tragic years of Civil War. In May 1861, after resigning his seat on the bench, Campbell moved to New Orleans and established a law firm in that city. In October 1862 he was asked to join the Confederate government in Richmond as the assistant secretary of war, in which capacity he served until April 1865. But Campbell detested the war, he opposed secession, and he believed that the South had all but signed its own death warrant when it broke from the Union. In his own words, Campbell agreed to serve in the War Department solely "to mitigate the evils upon the country." By "country," he was not referring to Alabama; neither was he speaking of the South nor of the Confederacy. He meant the United States, which he believed had been hastily destroyed because radicals in both the North and the South had, after thirty years of agitation and heated rhetoric, convinced southerners that they could no longer remain in the Union.

The apex of agitation over slavery and one of the final wedges of separation occurred in 1859 when John Brown made his infamous raid on Harper's Ferry hoping to spark widespread slave insurrections. To Campbell, Brown's raid was "[t]he most important single event of this time," because as Brown became a martyr to many people in the North, most southerners became convinced that their society and its institutions were under assault and that the South truly no longer held an equal position in the Union.[1] On 19 October, Campbell was invited to attend a cabinet meeting in the White House because "an officer of justice" could perhaps aid in the discussion of Brown's raid. President Buchanan inquired whether the United States should prosecute

Brown or if the incident fell strictly within Virginia's jurisdiction. Campbell advised that Brown's crime was not a violation of federal law, and so Virginia had the sole obligation to prosecute him. He later explained that Brown's raid, once all of the facts were known, was truly of little immediate import. But the reaction in the North against his public execution utterly "destroy[ed] the confidence [in the federal government]—such as had existed."[2]

Seismic events throughout the remainder of 1859 and 1860 occurred with fearful rapidity. The convention in Charleston, the split of the Democrats, and Lincoln's nomination and eventual election in November all precipitated a crisis atmosphere in the South, where people were convinced that the election of a Republican to the presidency portended disaster for their institutions. On 12 June 1860, two months after the Democratic convention in Charleston, Campbell wrote a scolding letter to his cousin, L. Q. C. Lamar, an influential Mississippi politician, conveying his displeasure over the proceedings in that city. "If I had the powers of a Turkish cadi," Campbell wrote, "I should condemn all the Southern actors in that scene to wear veils for four years. Their faces should not be seen among Democrats. I am not sure but what my sentence would comprise certain bastinadoes for all those from whom something better should have come. In that case, you and your friends, . . . would have carried sore feet for a long time."[3]

Campbell was hopeful of silencing demands for immediate secession, especially in Alabama. In mid-November, he received a letter from his brother-in-law and law partner Daniel Chandler soliciting his opinion on Lincoln's election and asking whether he believed that the South should secede.[4] What followed was an exchange of letters in which Campbell fully explained his position on secession and the folly that was certain to follow any impetuous action by southerners.

Campbell wrote that on the night of the election it was apparent before midnight that Lincoln had won. He asserted that Lincoln's election created anxiety but only because few people actually knew what the president-elect intended to do about the extension of slavery. "That question recurs every day, nearly every hour," he informed Chandler. Campbell then lamented that Alabama's General Assembly had hastily summoned a secession convention composed of 100 men to discuss Alabama's reaction to Lincoln's election. He stated that in calling the convention the legislators dispensed with their constitutional obligations to the people of Alabama. "This commission to a single body of one-hundred men is dictatorial, arbitrary, unlimited. . . . Was this what the people of Alabama had asked of their elected representatives?" "The first inquiry that occurs to me," he wrote, "is whence comes the power to convoke so extraordinary a body" in Alabama? "You need not tell me that the power will come directly from the people. This is not true." The secession convention was, therefore, wholly unauthorized and illegal. "I conclude that the people may alter, reform, or abolish their government at pleasure. But the people have done nothing of the sort in this case."[5]

Campbell then explained to Chandler that the South truly had little for which they could rightfully complain.

> I trust that the conservative men of every party will combine and organize for the dangerous conflict to arise in our State. The question of the Union should be discussed anew and at large. The fact that within a third of a century alluded to in the preamble the Statute book of the United States has been purged of every law of which the Southern States has [sic] complained: the Tariff Act for protection; the Act for the Bank of the United States, the Missouri and Oregon slavery restriction acts, have been modified or repealed. We have acquired Texas, established the Independent Treasury and reduced the price of the public lands in favor of actual settlers.[6]

The South should have no grievances, he explained. Campbell concluded that southerners were obviously captives of a radical minority whose power had to be diminished. "I hope you form a Union party and be firm and fearless," he wrote Chandler. He objected strongly "to disunion except for *deliberate, plain, and palpable* violations of the Constitution—violations showing enormity of mischief and where no other form of redress exists." In essence, the South had no reason to secede merely because Lincoln was president-elect.

But what of Lincoln's election, asked Chandler; did that not convince him that the North conspired to destroy southern institutions? Campbell responded that the Republican victory was "calculated to awaken an apprehension," but that was all. There was no discernible threat to the South merely because Lincoln was to be the next president. "I do not doubt that [Lincoln's] administration will be conciliatory," he wrote. Though he believed that the Republicans were not a serious threat to the South, he explained that the radical fire-eaters certainly were. He continued:

> The persons who are raising the cockade of rebellion, who are abandoning public employment without reserve or stint . . . weaken the hands of the South, convert her friends into enemies, and thus precipitate revolution. I cannot believe [that] our people can be carried to sanction such conduct. The cause of the South is not lost. It would be strong and powerful in the Union if we had wise counsels among our representatives and people. The people of the North have been imbued to a large extent with anti-slavery sentiment, but their opposition does not rest upon that alone, nor is the party of Lincoln triumphant from the power of that party sentiment.[7]

Thus the Republicans had not caused the turmoil. But the Democrats, because they had failed to control the fringe elements silencing the more moderate members of the party, had shown that they were incapable of governing. "Supreme disgust for the Democratic rule and rulers is the *causa causans* of this revolution," he explained.[8]

On the twenty-fourth, Campbell drafted a second letter to Chandler. "The election of Mr. Lincoln I regard as a calamity to the country, as it has undermined if not destroyed the confidence—the diminished confidence—of a portion of the Southern States towards the Federal Government." Regardless, he insisted, the framers had never anticipated that the person elected president would always be "capable or virtuous." The Constitution would continue to exist regardless of a weak or incompetent president. In short, Lincoln and the Republicans could do no great harm to the South because the Constitution would prevent them from destroying southern institutions. "No man, no body of men," Campbell forcefully wrote, "is authorized to arouse the evil passions, the restless desires, the factions, proscription hate, revenge incident to revolution, nor to disturb the clear written law, the deep-trod foot-marks of ancient custom, the healthful industry, the confident calculations, the faith, duty, quiet, content and repose of civil society upon grievances, speculative or contingent, or upon the apprehension of evils, that are not imminent and beyond reach of regular and constitutional modes of redress."[9]

Last, Campbell advised that the South should bide its time. Lincoln and the Republicans were but a temporary aberration that would vanish after four years when tempers would cool and moderate voices would prevail. "My inquiries of [the] most respected and reliable gentlemen who know [Lincoln], confirm me in the opinion that he is not an object of fear. But if he were bad, disposed to mischief, I have too much confidence in the Constitution of my country to suppose that it does not afford a sufficient remedy in the case of his wickedness." Given enough time, he suggested, statesmen with the character, good sense, and fortitude of men like Webster, Clay, or Calhoun would rise to the occasion, destroy fanaticism, and restore cordial relations in the country. All that was needed was time.[10]

On 26 November, Campbell drafted a third letter to Chandler, stating that although the antislavery agitation appeared to be an insuperable threat to the South, the abolitionists would be unable to force immediate abolition because the federal government was bound to uphold the laws protecting slavery. As nearly all legislative threats to the institution had been repealed, he suggested, southerners need only demand that the status quo be maintained and southern rights would be protected. He advised southerners to "take counsel together, in a calm, deliberate, impartial and honest inquiry concerning these mighty issues" because "it involves all that we have." The southern radicals had to be silenced; they had for too long destroyed the people's faith in the federal government, and they were now leading the South to destruction. Campbell concluded with four propositions he believed could arrest the secession crisis if they were accepted in good faith by both sections:

First—That the election of Mr. Lincoln does not afford sufficient ground for the dissolution of the Union.

Second—That the great object of disturbance, that of slavery in the Territories, rests upon a satisfactory foundation, and that we have nothing to ask except that the *status quo* be respected.

Third—That the subject of the rendition of fugitive slaves can be adjusted to the satisfaction of the injured property holder and without dishonor to ourselves.

Fourth—That in relation to the maintenance of the rights we have or those that have been defeated or impaired, and in whatever concerns the subjects of contumely and insult we complain of, there may be increased cause for increased vigilance, for preparation for alliance among the Southern States, for the demand of new guarantees, but not for disunion until there is a refusal or redress. In my opinion separate State action will result in discredit and defeat every measure for reparation or security.[11]

Campbell proposed another convention of southern states similar to that held at Nashville in 1850 to articulate the South's grievances. But he well understood that to many southerners the time for talking had ended and that there was nothing left for the South except secession. In the event that Alabama withdrew from the Union, Campbell stated, "My commission would not be affected by the action of the State." Yet, he told Chandler, "I determined many years ago that my obligation was to follow the fortunes of her people. I shall terminate my connection with the Government as a consequence" of Alabama's secession.[12]

On 18 December Campbell met with President Buchanan and tried to persuade him to send federal commissioners to each southern state to placate ill feelings and stymie any further movements toward secession. Buchanan politely listened to Campbell, but did nothing.[13] Early the following morning, Campbell began a letter exchange with former president Pierce suggesting that he should personally visit Alabama; he might even plan to attend the upcoming secession convention, Campbell advised. "There is a wild and somewhat hysterical excitement in all of the Southern States and especially in the tier of States from South Carolina west to the Mississippi [River]," he wrote. Most of the excitement was brought about on account of Lincoln's election, but he did not understand why people had become so upset about an event that "had been anticipated by [all] observant men." Nonetheless, the election "has produced all of the effect of a sudden and direct attack upon the rights of the people." "The object of my writing," he stated, "is to ascertain whether if you were invited or requested by the President (in the mode most agreeable to yourself) to attend the convention in Alabama, you would do so." "I believe that a formal settlement of [the] slavery question should be made, or disunion should follow." He also warned that the ill feelings that had been brewing for thirty years could not continue much longer without the eruption of civil war: "The question is for both sections: shall we part in peace, or shall we make a constitutional settlement of every open question. I think that a constitutional settlement, at all events, is better—far better—than a sudden and violent eruption."[14]

On the twenty-fourth, Pierce replied from Andover, Massachusetts, that he was severely ill and bedridden by doctor's orders. Thus a trip to Alabama at that time was completely out of the question. Pierce did, however, muster the strength to express his consternation over recent developments. "I have striven to cherish something like churning hope," he wrote, "but the gloom which has overshadowed us for the last few weeks, seems to be now shutting down more closely, densely, darkly." Pierce strongly pleaded with Campbell to do everything within his power to remind his fellow southerners that "fraternal regard" still glowed brightly in the hearts of hundreds of thousands of northerners for the people of the South.[15]

On 29 December Campbell drafted a second letter to Pierce that well reflected his mounting anxiety over the secession crisis and his frustration with the apparent inability of the Buchanan administration to prevent the destruction of the nation. "In truth," he wrote, "[Buchanan's] mind has lost its powers of comprehending a complicated situation. He is nervous and hysterical, and I think completely unmannered." But the lame-duck president's inactivity was not the only problem. The "incapacity of Congress, the discredit into which the federal government has fallen, the disloyalty that is pervaded in the highest places, the imbecility of the administration, and the general opinion of its infidelity and corruption, have greatly facilitated the success" of the South's most ardent secessionists. The secession crisis was the culmination of a thirty-year assault on southern institutions, and the southern people were simply reacting to what appeared to them a profound and irreversible victory for the abolitionists. "This controversy in reference to slavery disturbs the foundations of the racial system of the Southern States. It renders not only property insecure, but disturbs the repose and order of the family, as well as of the community," Campbell explained to Pierce. In his opinion the secession crisis, however foolhardy, was undertaken as a natural reaction against the abolitionists, who did not seem concerned that their attacks on slavery ultimately threatened southern society as a whole. "[N]o community can exist and prosper when this sense of uncertainty prevails," he concluded.[16]

Meanwhile, on 20 December, delegates to a special convention called by South Carolina's legislature voted to dissolve that state's relationship with the Union. Their ordinance of secession reverberated throughout the South, and Campbell grew increasingly alarmed that secession fever would sweep the other southern states and lead to civil war. The thought of a broken Union and civil war filled him with such dread that he determined to do everything within his power to prevent Alabama's secession. Campbell correctly believed that antisecession sentiment was strong in that state and that if enough voices could be raised to silence the southern radicals, perhaps Alabama could be kept in the Union. The justice's influence in Alabama had been seriously weakened, however, when, without his knowledge or permission, Chandler published Campbell's three letters denouncing the South for considering secession and advising caution and conciliation.[17] The reaction against the justice was nearly immediate. Many Alabamians reasoned that Campbell was a traitor to the southern cause; perhaps through his appointment on the bench he had become indoctrinated into the mainstream of northern political thought. Had it not been Judge Campbell, many asked, whose actions had restrained filibustering and curbed slave trading? Campbell was not yet aware that people within his own community were rapidly beginning to distrust and despise him.[18]

In north Alabama, though, sentiment toward the justice was quite different. On 2 January, he sent a letter to Henry Tutwiler, a retired professor at the University of Alabama who had written to Campbell applauding his courageous stand against the fire-eaters and asking him to come to Alabama to combat the movement toward secession.[19] The secession convention was scheduled for the sixth, and Tutwiler told Campbell that his services might perhaps stave off the final drastic action that appeared imminent. Campbell thanked the professor for his cordial letter; he explained that since the publication of his correspondence to Chandler in mid-December he had received numerous notes of scorn and disapproval from the people of Alabama. "I have received some with the most opprobrious epithets, applied to me, for expressing opinions, in which I feel the more confirmed by the fact of your approval." Campbell stated to Tutwiler that he would be happy to return to Alabama if he felt it would help to prevent secession. He had authorized Chandler to say that he would serve in the secession convention (in the opposition, of course) as a representative from Mobile. But because his letters had been published, Campbell strongly suspected that the people of south Alabama would never elect him. He informed Tutwiler:

> I am quite willing to serve the State in any capacity in this period of danger, and if elected from Mobile (I am not eligible in any other county) would serve. I am quite at the service of the State in any place in which my services might be needed to secure all her rights in the Union, and being willing to leave when the bulk of the Southern States are. I think that many serious evils are preferable to being the member of a San Marino, or even a separate Alabama republic. . . . I desire peace, security, and a wide field, for my children to develop in, and much real evil and serious grievances I would *bear,* rather than give these up.[20]

Considering his resignation to alleviate the secession crisis, Campbell was willing to go to Alabama in a last-ditch effort to convince Mobilians of the folly of their actions. He also suggested that he would be perfectly amenable to secession once the "bulk" of southern states had seceded. In the meantime, though, Alabama should refrain from precipitous acts and should adopt a wait-and-see posture.[21]

Campbell's letters had thus far done nothing to slow the secession crisis, but he remained determined to dissuade other southern states from dissolving the Union. On 5 January he sent a second letter to his cousin, L. Q. C. Lamar, encouraging him to seek moderation and to avoid hasty actions toward secession in Mississippi. Campbell also unveiled four compromise proposals he believed could satisfy the South and secure cordial feelings between the sections:

> 1. I think that we shall have to depend upon the return of comity or an amendment to the Constitution—I regard this as an important surrender by [northerners].
> 2. I desire to place beyond the power of amendment the provisions for slave representation and taxation and the return of fugitive slaves. If this were done, the Constitution would be placed on stable foundations.
> 3. I believe that the personal liberty bills at the North will be given up. I do not think [that] they prevented slaves from being surrendered but they were an insult and a reproach and I agree that we should demand their repeal.
> 4. The want of the South is not territory but population—We cannot have slave states without slaves, and we cannot fill up new states as territories, until Louisiana, Mississippi, Arkansas, and Texas are filled and that cannot be done for twenty-five years—New Mexico is accidentally slave territory. But from all I have heard of it, it cannot be so permanently. The Republicans will I think agree to disqualify themselves from abolishing slavery there, or [they] will agree to admit New Mexico as a slave state. It is all we can possibly hope. I am willing to take this as a settlement of the territorial question.[22]

Thus he proposed a constitutional amendment forever protecting slavery where it existed, revamping and strengthening the three-fifths compromise of the Constitution, demanding that personal liberty laws be revoked, and settling the territory crisis by admitting New Mexico as a slave state. Most curiously, Campbell believed that the three-fifths clause could be "placed beyond the power of amendment." Certainly he must have realized that to amend the Constitution in such a fashion would have been a blatant denial of people's sovereignty, the very principle on which most of his political philosophy was founded.

Campbell explained to his cousin that secession was undeniably sanctioned by the Constitution. Before any state actually broke from the Union, however, it should first declare its intentions of doing so and "ask the co-states to consent thereto, and to establish relations of comity as consequent thereupon." Separate state action, in other words, was not only ill advised but improper and not sanctioned by the Constitution. Campbell advised Lamar that Mississippians should strive to offset "the precipitate spirit of the politicians in the Southwest." They would then be able to "preserve some of the moral influence and political respectability that was possessed by the southern states before Filibustering, slave trading, and their consequent Disunion became household words among southerners." "I repeat to you," he exclaimed, "that I do not go along with you in this movement any further than I have set down in my letter to Mr. Chandler, and that all my counsel and observations are to be treated as coming from a witness of an opposite way of thinking."[23]

On 11 January, the delegates to the secession convention in Alabama voted to secede from the Union. The vote for this momentous decision, however, was not unanimous. In fact, it was closer than many people believed it would be: 61 ayes to 39 nays. Nonetheless, the state was for the next four years politically separated from the United States. On the thirteenth, Campbell received a telegraph from H. G. Humphries, a secession delegate from Mobile, which read curtly: "I hasten to inform you that Alabama has seceded from the Union and you are expected to resign."[24] Campbell ignored this uncivil message, obviously sent as a rebuke to his published letters to Chandler. Despite his statement to Chandler that he would resign if Alabama seceded, he decided to remain on the bench, believing that a conservative reaction against secession and the radicals who had orchestrated it in Alabama would emerge and would force the state's return to the Union.

Chandler wrote Campbell on the fourteenth that the people of Mobile were literally ecstatic about the dissolution of the Union. The justice replied on the twenty-first, "The exultation and delight of the citizens of Mobile over their secession ordinance [is] edifying." He then reminded his brother-in-law that the ordinance had barely received the required majority and that the state was hopelessly divided, with north Alabamians solidly against secession. He concluded, "[Y]ou are in no condition to bear even the ordinary burdens of social life in a period of peace." "How then carry on a war in which your trade would be stopped by a single steamer?" "If in the heyday of your revolution you can barely get a majority [in the secession convention], what are we to expect in the season of your adversity?" "Take my word for it," he cautioned, "secession is a cake not turned, and there will not be warmth enough to complete the baking." Campbell informed Chandler that he still intended to resign, but only when "circumstances allow me to [leave the Court] without self-reproach or personal discredit." He knew that he could always return to practicing law, but he stated that he would never again practice in Mobile. "I suppose the slave trading and filibustering will be in the ascendent then as they appear to be now. I wish to be a better stranger to them than ever."[25] Campbell then decided to remain in Washington unless all avenues of reconciliation had been closed and hostilities erupted.

During the evening of 10 February, Senator Stephen Douglas hosted a dinner for the French Minister. Campbell and his wife, Anne, attended this event, as did William H. Seward, the nation's most influential Republican and the person many believed would be named secretary of state. During the momentous last months of the Buchanan administration, Seward was as anxious to avoid war and to restore the Union as was Campbell. He had earlier written to Lincoln in Springfield complaining that many people in Washington were "determined to pull the house down," but he emphatically declared, "I am determined not to let them."[26] When Seward was asked to give a toast at Douglas's party, he obliged: "Away with all parties, all platforms, all previous committals, and whatever will stand in the way of restoration of the American Union."[27] After Seward's conciliatory toast, Campbell explained to him that slavery was a transitory institution that would surely die out if only the South could be left to attend to its own affairs. He further intimated that what was needed to placate the South was a constitutional amendment protecting slavery in the states where it existed. The only other issue that would be left to settle, he insisted, was statehood for New Mexico. Campbell stated that the Southwest Territory had been a part of the United States for twelve years, yet only twenty-four slaves had been imported during that period. Obviously, New Mexico's climate, soil, and geography, Campbell noted, would ensure that slavery would pose no threat to free labor. If the North agreed to admit New Mexico as a slave state, southerners would regain much of the faith in the federal government that they had lost through the years. "How, Mr. Seward," Campbell asked, "can you fail to effect an adjustment" when these acts would most assuredly restore the Union? Seward responded that his position in the cabinet was not as yet final, and that although he believed Campbell's ideas sound, there was little he could do at that moment.[28]

As a member of the Supreme Court, Campbell was obliged to attend Lincoln's inauguration on 4 March. His feelings toward the new administration were ambivalent primarily because he—like all other Americans—was uncertain what Lincoln planned to do about the seceded states or, more ominously, about the more immediate problem of Fort Sumter in Charleston harbor, where federal forces under Major Robert Anderson defiantly resisted the Confederate government's demand that the fort be abandoned and surrendered to the South. Campbell wrote to his mother in Mobile on the sixth that "the last week has been full of stir in this city." Lincoln's inaugural address "was a *stump* speech, not an inaugural message." It was "wanting in statesmanship—of which [Lincoln] has none—and of dignity and decorum. I should call it an incendiary message—one calculated to set the country in a blaze." Lincoln "is a conceited man," he told his mother. Although Campbell expressed little faith that the new president could end the crisis peaceably, his cabinet, although "objectionable," was "supremely pacific and not an opportunity will be given for collusion and bloodshed."[29]

Campbell wrote that despite the president's firm stand, outlined in the inaugural address, he believed that the administration would develop a conciliatory policy toward the seceded states. He stated that Lincoln's words were mostly insignificant and were but common expressions "to that class of thieves known as politicians." Despite the inaugural address, therefore, Campbell predicted that Forts Sumter and Pickens would be evacuated within one month and that the new administration would adopt a conciliatory policy regarding the seceded states. "None here are willing to believe that a reunion is impossible," he wrote. "And if peace is sought as the great boon on the one side— and the hope that by conciliation, kindness, and complete assurance of security, a reunion may be affected or be permitted. It will not be difficult for the two conferences to get along for the next three or four years under some agreement as to the terms."[30]

Campbell expressed profound hope that "PEACE, PEACE, PEACE will be the first and the last thought of every responsible person in both sections." He was fully apprised of the admonitions against him since the publication of his letters to Chandler. "But I am aware that I have doen [*sic*] right and that no one has exerted more labor and has been heard more respectfully than myself this season." He explained that he had already prepared his letter of resignation, but that "men of every condition and class from the Border States" urged him to remain on the bench and work toward reconciliation. Last, Campbell stated that Seward, whom he had met the month before at Douglas's dinner party, had sent him a message on the fifth explaining that all would be well "if a little time be given."[31]

With Lincoln's inauguration, William Seward officially became the nation's secretary of state. In that capacity he hoped to bring about an amicable peace and a reconciliation of the Union. Above all, he believed that Fort Sumter should be evacuated by the federal forces holding the installation in order to cool tempers and forge a more agreeable foundation for discussions with the Confederates.[32] Clearly, Seward harbored honorable intentions, yet he was under the impression that he could dominate Lincoln and be the real power in the federal government. But Seward was sadly mistaken if he believed that Lincoln would step aside and allow him to govern. His presumptions about Lincoln were remarkably credulous, perhaps matched only by Campbell's naiveté, which prompted him to intervene in the increasingly dangerous crisis. As Campbell had earlier explained to Chandler, he wished he had resigned immediately after Lincoln's election so that he could have returned to Alabama and ended the secession crisis. This supreme confidence, this overblown perception of their importance, were traits that both Seward and

Campbell shared. As previously stated, both men wanted nothing other than peace and reconciliation, and they both blindly went about trying to procure these objectives without stopping to consider that neither had sufficient influence. After all, final responsibility rested with but two men: Abraham Lincoln in Washington and Jefferson Davis in Montgomery.

On 15 March Campbell was walking along Pennsylvania Avenue when he happened to meet one of his colleagues on the Supreme Court, Justice Samuel Nelson, who explained that he had just come from speaking with Seward. Seward, according to Nelson, appeared most anxious to settle the growing crisis over Fort Sumter. The secretary of state was a man of peace, Nelson insisted, who would "spare no effort to maintain" peaceful relations between the sections. The two justices then proceeded to a nearby hotel, where they discussed the increasingly dangerous crisis. Nelson informed Campbell that there were three commissioners in Washington—Martin Crawford, a former Georgia congressman; John Forsyth, editor of the *Mobile Register;* and André B. Roman, a former Whig governor of Louisiana—sent by the newly created Confederate government in Montgomery to meet with either Seward or Lincoln. But the president refused to receive the commissioners either officially or unofficially because he did not want them to infer that he was indirectly recognizing the legitimacy of secession.[33] Lincoln forbade Seward from meeting with the commissioners as well.

The justices decided that if Lincoln or Seward would agree to hold discussions with the commissioners, it would have a positive effect and at least show that Lincoln could be conciliatory. Campbell and Nelson proceeded directly to Seward's office "to enforce these views upon him." Once they met with the secretary and explained their belief that much relief could be gained through a meeting with the commissioners, Seward explained that such an event was simply impossible because there was too much opposition in Congress. Seward also stated that "if Jefferson Davis had known of the state of things here, he would not have sent those Commissioners." The secretary explained that the vexing Sumter issue occupied nearly all of the president's time, and thus he could not consider a meeting with the Confederates. Unexpectedly, Seward then made an utterly jolting pronouncement: Lincoln was considering abandoning Fort Sumter so that cordial relations could be restored. Campbell at once agreed that if Sumter were to be evacuated, secessionist sentiment in the South would most likely evaporate, particularly in the border states that had not seceded.[34]

Campbell volunteered to act as intermediary between Seward and the commissioners, and he stated that he would write Davis in Montgomery and inform him of these developments. "What shall I say to [Davis] on the subject of Fort Sumter?" Campbell asked. Seward responded, "You may say to him that before that letter reaches him, the telegraph will have informed [Anderson] that Sumter will have been evacuated." As for the other forts—Pickens in Pensacola especially—Seward explained to Campbell that no decision had as yet been made. "We contemplate no action as to [Fort Pickens], we are satisfied with the position of things there."[35] If Campbell's report of this meeting was correct—and his letters to Jefferson Davis certainly indicate nothing to the contrary—then Seward had given him every reason to believe that Sumter would be evacuated. Campbell stated that he would go to the commissioners and persuade them to rescind their ultimatum, that the administration was willing to negotiate in good faith, and that Sumter was going to be evacuated. Campbell later wrote that Seward stated that he wanted their answer as to whether they would rescind the ultimatum as soon as possible. The secretary explained to him that "if [he] were successful, [he] might prevent a Civil War."[36]

Seward's statement that Sumter would be evacuated within a few days was absolutely astonishing news, and Campbell was most anxious to convey the message to the commissioners and to Jefferson Davis. He went immediately to see Crawford and told him of the meeting with Seward. Campbell advised the Georgian that the ultimatum should be abandoned, but Crawford refused, stating that they had been sent to obtain recognition and that they could not assume to change their orders on their own initiative. Campbell nonetheless implored him to reconsider, which Crawford did upon assurances that Sumter would be evacuated. The Georgian then insisted that Campbell place his assurances in writing, and the justice complied.

> I feel perfect confidence in the fact that Fort Sumter will be evacuated in the next five days—and that this is felt to be a measure imposing vast responsibility upon the Administration.
> I feel perfect confidence that no measure changing the existing status of things prejudicial to the Southern Confederate States is at present contemplated.
> I feel entire confidence that any immediate demand for an answer to the communication of the Commissioners will be productive of evil and not of good. I do not believe that it should be pressed.
> I earnestly ask for a delay until the effect of the evacuation of Fort Sumter can be ascertained—or at least for a few days, say ten days.[37]

Crawford obviously believed that what Campbell told him was true and that Seward was sincere in stating that Sumter would be evacuated. After receiving assurances that the commissioners would at least temporarily retract their ultimatum, Campbell left Crawford and immediately wrote to Davis about his meeting with Seward. Obviously buoyant over such startling developments, Campbell was no doubt confident that the crisis over Sumter at least would be settled peaceably.

Five days passed, however, and Sumter was not evacuated. The commissioners immediately went to Campbell for an explanation. The justice requested that they telegraph Beauregard at Charleston and inquire whether preparations for an evacuation were under way. The Confederate commander replied that Sumter had not been evacuated and that Major Anderson was still working on its defenses.[38] Distraught and feeling that they had been duped, the commissioners returned to Campbell and asked him to see Seward at once. Campbell and Nelson took Beauregard's telegraph and went to see the secretary of state on the twenty-first.

Seward was too busy to grant them an interview that day, but he assured them that everything was all right and that nothing had changed with regard to the evacuation of Sumter. He agreed to meet with the justices on the following day. Campbell and Nelson then returned to Crawford and explained that Seward still believed Sumter would be abandoned and that they should be patient. Early on the twenty-second, Campbell and Nelson returned to Seward's office. They later reported that the secretary was "buoyant and sanguine," fully confident that his policy would be carried through by the administration.[39] With Seward's reassurance, Campbell returned to the commissioners convinced that Sumter was to be evacuated.

Campbell wrote a second memorandum for the commissioners, stating that he still had "unabated confidence" that the fort would be abandoned. The fact that the five-day deadline had expired did not "excite any apprehension or distrust" in him. "I counsel inactivity," he wrote, "in making demands on this Government for the present. I shall have knowledge of any change in the existing status."[40] On the thirtieth Crawford showed Campbell a telegraph from Governor Francis W. Pickens of South Carolina inquiring when Sumter would be evacuated. Campbell brought the message to Seward, who agreed to have an answer the following day.

On 1 April Seward and Campbell met again. When the justice asked why Sumter had not been evacuated as promised, Seward replied that the fort had become "a point of honor" to the administration and that its abandonment portended serious political repercussions for Lincoln. The secretary then wrote a message on a small piece of paper and handed it to Campbell. It read: "That the President may desire to supply Fort Sumter, but [he] will not undertake to do so without first giving notice to Governor Pickens."[41] Supply the fort? Campbell had been under the impression that Sumter was to be evacuated, but now it appeared that Seward was retreating from his 15 March promise. "What does this mean?" Campbell asked. "Does the President design to attempt to supply Sumter?" Seward answered, "No, I think not, it is a very irksome thing to [Lincoln] to evacuate it. His ears are open to everyone, and they fill his head for schemes for its supply. I do not think he will adopt any of them. There is no design to reinforce [the fort]."[42]

By that juncture Campbell must have been growing suspicious of Seward's intentions. The five-day deadline had come and gone, Anderson was still building defenses at Sumter, and now the secretary was talking about resupplying the fort. Somewhat perplexed and perhaps believing that he needed to clarify what had transpired between Seward and himself in the event that Sumter would be resupplied, Campbell drafted a letter to Jefferson Davis soon after leaving Seward's office. He wrote that his "contact" in the administration—he felt that he could not name Seward directly—had assured him on the fifteenth that Sumter would be abandoned, and though that had not happened, he had every reason to believe that Lincoln would soon order Anderson to withdraw. "But the President is light, inconstant, variable," he warned, so he could not make the same guarantees he had expressed to Crawford on the fifteenth. Nonetheless, "I do not doubt that Sumter will be evacuated shortly, without any effort to *supply* it."[43]

"I shall remain here for some ten or fifteen days," Campbell informed Davis. "At present I have access to the administration which I could not have, except, under my present relations to the government, and I do not know who could have the same freedom." He would remain in Washington, therefore, until a settlement over Sumter had been reached. Davis responded to Campbell's letter on the sixth, stating his reservations about any further delays. He nonetheless commended the Alabamian for attempting to maintain peace between North and South. "I will gratefully remember your zealous labor in a sacred cause and hope your fellow citizens may at some time give you acceptable recognition of your service and appreciate the heroism with which you have encountered a hazard from which most men would have shrunk."[44] Had Davis's letter to Campbell been published in Mobile newspapers as were Campbell's letters to Chandler, perhaps the people of south Alabama would not have harbored such deep hostility toward Campbell when he returned to Mobile. As it was, all they knew was that he adamantly opposed secession and that he refused to resign from the bench and pledge his allegiance to the Confederacy.

Several more days passed, and yet there were still no signs that the fort would be evacuated. Campbell grew increasingly despondent. War seemed likely, and he no doubt began to believe that Seward had misled him that Sumter would be abandoned to give Lincoln more time to prepare an amphibious assault on Charleston harbor. "During the first week of April," he later wrote, it was apparent that a decision had been made within the administration regarding the forts. Campbell noticed considerable troop movement in and around Washington, and he heard numerous rumors that an assault on Charleston harbor was imminent. Republican politicians, he later recollected, began to resort to more threatening language as if they knew that Lincoln had finally made a decision to take a stand at Sumter. The Democrats, on the other hand, became even more "anxious and despondent."[45]

Thus Campbell's faith in Seward's promises began to fade as it appeared that Lincoln would attempt to resupply Sumter. On Sunday morning, 7 April, the three Confederate commissioners paid Campbell another visit and implored him to speak with Seward about the rumored mission. Campbell decided not to visit Seward, but—as an indication that he was losing faith in the New Yorker—merely wrote a letter asking for an explanation for the delays in the evacuation. "I pray that you will advise me," he wrote. Later that morning, Campbell received an unsigned, undated memorandum—obviously from Seward—stating: "Faith as to Sumter fully kept; wait and see; other suggestions received, and will be respectfully considered."[46] Campbell wrote to the commissioners that he still believed Sumter would be evacuated or that the fort would not be resupplied without Governor Pickens first being notified. As for the rumors of a flotilla of armed vessels leaving New York, Campbell explained that it was most likely heading for Pensacola.

But the commissioners had heard enough of Seward's promises. They now believed that they had been cozened into believing that Sumter would be surrendered and that the delay had allowed Lincoln time to prepare a naval expedition to Sumter. They informed Seward that they expected an answer to their demands, warning that if recognition were not forthcoming, they would "consider the gauntlet of war thrown down," abandon their mission, and return to Montgomery.[47] Events were rapidly reaching a climax, and nothing Campbell or Seward had done had reduced the probability that a clash over Sumter was certain. Most of the blame for this fiasco must rest with Seward, who was obviously giving pledges to Campbell that Lincoln could not honor. The president had never intended to abandon Sumter, and he had no idea that Seward had stated as much. Of course, the Montgomery government believed that Lincoln was fully apprised of the exchanges between Seward and Campbell, but such was not the case. Seward had told Campbell on 15 March that Sumter would be evacuated, firmly believing that he could convince Lincoln to order the fort surrendered. As the next three weeks passed and as Seward failed to convince Lincoln of the necessity to abandon the fort, the secretary of state retreated somewhat from his earlier assurances of conciliation. Seward must not be condemned for his motives; he was after all trying desperately to prevent hostilities. So too was Campbell. But both men failed to realize that the secession crisis had advanced much further than they perceived, and although both anticipated a conservative backlash against secession, this was not forthcoming.[48]

The Confederate commissioners withdrew from Washington on the eleventh, believing that the federal government had refused to negotiate in good faith and had instead arranged a series of lies, delivered through Seward, in order to resupply Sumter. Campbell was truly grief stricken that Sumter had not been surrendered, and when he learned that Beauregard had commenced firing on the fort, he realized that the nation had been thrust into a Civil War from which it might never recover. He later wrote, "Party spirit and sectional ambition and jealousy caused this war in my opinion. . . . [It] was the result of passion, pride, temper, violent quarrel, and unreasoning rage without adequate or justifiable cause on either part of the contending authorities."[49]

He wrote his brother-in-law, George Goldthwaite, on the twentieth that, since the bombardment at Fort Sumter, "events have hurried with great rapidity." "My own belief," he wrote, "is that the administration will recoil before the storm from the South. Oh, that the administration would recollect that there is another audience for what they do and say except the Montgomery [government]."[50] One of Campbell's close colleagues later wrote that "it is scarcely possible now to conceive of a more embarrassing, and at the same time more humiliating, position than [Campbell] was compelled to take at that time."[51] Despite his sincere desire to remain on the Court, Campbell knew that he soon had to resign. Alabama was home; he had started his professional career in the state, he had become its leading attorney, he had married and raised his family there—everything of any true meaning or value was in Alabama, and he simply could not abandon it.[52]

On 26 April he sent a letter of resignation to President Lincoln, and his seat on the bench officially became vacant on 1 May.[53] Mary Boykin Chesnut, wife of Confederate Senator James Chesnut and a woman whose diary contains a wealth of information about the Civil War era, wrote upon learning of Campbell's resignation: "A resigned judge of the Supreme Court of the United States!! Resigned—and for a cause that he is hardly more than half in sympathy with. His is one of the hardest cases."[54]

The Campbell family packed their belongings and returned to Alabama. But when they arrived in Mobile, they found that they were no longer welcome in the community. For the last several months Campbell had been almost universally denounced by south Alabama newspapers questioning his loyalty to the South. Many Mobilians believed that Campbell's letters to Chandler revealed that he was a traitor and should be regarded as the enemy. Many also suspected that Campbell had been involved in deceiving the commissioners.[55] "When I returned to Alabama in May 1861," he wrote,

> it was to receive coldness, aversion, or contumely from the secession population. I did not agree to recant what I had said, or to explain what I had done; and, thus, instead of appeasing my opponents, I aggravated my offense. This was still more aggravated by my opinion that cotton was not king; that privateering would not expel Northern commerce from the ocean, but would affront European opinion, and that privateering and slavery would prevent recognition, and that the war would be long and implacable; that the Northern people were a proud and powerful people that [*sic*] would not endure the supposed insults they have suffered.[56]

Not all Alabama newspapers joined in the anti-Campbell barrage. The *Pickens Republican* of Carrolton, Alabama, for instance, wrote that it was wrong to chastise Campbell "on account of his former anti-secession views." The editorial continued that the Confederacy needed Campbell. "He brings to our aid an intellect massive and gigantic," they reminded their readers. "Intellectually, he has no superior [in the] South."[57]

On 18 May Campbell attended a dinner party in Mobile at the home of Dr. Josiah Nott, one of Mobile's most prominent physicians, who had earlier tried to prove that slaves were mentally inferior to whites because their skulls were smaller. Also in attendance was William Howard Russell, a journalist for the London *Times* who spent much of 1861 and 1862 interviewing Americans about the causes of secession and the Civil War. Russell noted that Campbell was exceedingly embittered over the South's secession and that he spoke scathingly of Seward's "treachery, dissimulation, and falsehood."[58] Although Campbell could attend social engagements like the one at Dr. Nott's, he was increasingly unwelcome in the city. Finally, in July he determined to move to New Orleans and establish a new law practice.

But Campbell's desire to return to the bar in New Orleans was destroyed by the war, especially as federal forces were on the verge of capturing the city. During summer 1862, Campbell worked tirelessly, tending to many of the sick and dying soldiers brought into the city for treatment. "The Southern country had greatly suffered," he wrote, "I had spent much time with the sick and wounded, and had witnessed bereavement, distress, destitution, [and] suffering."[59] In early October, he and his family fled New Orleans and moved to Richmond, where he believed his children would be safe. But Richmond, like every other southern city, was absolutely consumed by the war, and there was little, if any, legal work for an unemployed former Supreme Court justice.

In October, Thomas L. Bayne, a prominent southern attorney who had likewise moved to Richmond, introduced Campbell to George W. Randolph of Virginia, who had recently been named Confederate secretary of war. Randolph explained to Campbell that there was an immediate need in the Department for someone with his vast legal knowledge to assist in day-to-day operations and to offer advice for questions involving legal matters.[60] Randolph encouraged Campbell to accept the position as assistant secretary of war, but he was initially hesitant. "I did not desire a conspicuous place" in the government. "My wish was to be of use in mitigating the evils [that] were upon the country." Campbell accepted the appointment but not enthusiastically. "Under the existing circumstances of the Confederacy," he explained to Randolph, "I do not feel at liberty to decline the appointment."[61] Campbell later explained, "I did not hold the office from avarice, for the annual salary was never worth $500 in specie, and became at last just $100. When I entered the office I supposed that I might become useful in the settlement of a peace if I were connected with the government. There was no opportunity for this in 1863, and not until the year 1864 had nearly expired could the subject [of peace terms] be broached with any advantage."[62]

Campbell served as the assistant secretary of war from mid-October 1862 until 2 April 1865. But as noted above, he did not wish to hold any position that would require him to make decisions regarding strategy, tactics, engagements, or campaigns. In short, he wanted as little to do with the war as possible. His principal objective for accepting the position was to be alert to any peace overtures and then to spring at the first opportunity to end the war. Mary Chesnut commented that Campbell—who had "the saddest face I ever saw"—"jumped down in his patriotism from judge of the Supreme Court, U.S.A, to undersecretary of something or other, I do not know what, C.S.A. No wonder he was out of spirits."[63]

Campbell's role as assistant secretary of war was mostly insignificant. By and large, and as an example of the utmost irony created by the Civil War, Campbell, who had achieved the pinnacle of success in the legal profession—a coveted seat on the Supreme Court—who was touted as having one of the finest minds in the nation, and who many thought would succeed Taney as chief justice, was in 1862 reduced to a mere clerk in the Confederate government.[64] His primary responsibility was to advise the secretary on legal matters that came before the department and to determine the most appropriate course of action. Aside from this function, Campbell was responsible for disseminating all correspondence to the nine bureaus that comprised the War Department and communicating with the heads of the bureaus to ensure unity of purpose and efficient management. In 1863, he was selected to oversee the Bureau of Conscription, but as he delegated most of the power in this role to his son-in-law, Major George W. Lay, his impact was minimal. Last, the assistant secretary had to review all requests for passports to cross Confederate lines and pleas for exemptions from conscription.

On his services to the Confederacy, Campbell wrote in May 1863, "[T]he business of my own particular department is not very congenial, . . . nor does it deal with the great measures of military policy." "[B]ut," he wrote, "it is of great importance in the carrying on of the intercourse of the department, ordering its details, and promoting its efficiency."[65] Campbell wrote several years after the war—when he was perhaps trying to minimize his role at the War Department—that he did not seek the office but was instead talked into accepting the position.

> The country was then suffering all the calamities of invasion. Much of the business and the feelings and the sensibilities of the country were concentered in the War Office, for conscription had placed the whole military population under it, and impressments were doing the same with regard to property. The courts were debilitated. Military rule dominant. The office of

Assistant Secretary did not give to me any control over military operations or organizations. It did not charge me with the subsistence, movement, or employment of troops; or with the conduct of the war. It gave me no control, custody, oversight, care, or responsibility in regard to prisoners of war. I had no charge of regular or irregular enterprises of war, or of any secret service or the employment of money. I decided a vast number of cases for the exemption of citizens from military service. I made details in cases of justice, equity, and necessity, and granted exemptions on that account, on appeal from the subordinate officers. I revised a vast number of cases of arrests by subordinates. I superintended the current correspondence of the office. I made a great variety of orders and decisions in particular cases. The office was one that imposed irksome, uncongenial, and, in most cases, trivial labor. . . . I have no belief that I made any impression upon the great events of the war; or any upon the policy of the Government. All I mean to say is that, under the difficult circumstances of the time, in a subordinate and comparatively unimportant office, I found the means to do a great deal of good. . . . This is my consolation for loss of exalted position [and] competent fortune.[66]

One of Campbell's contemporaries stated that the assistant secretary's "duties and actions" during the war "were little more than clerical and we have the best reasons for knowing that even while holding it he never affiliated with those who were the peculiar representatives of secession but [he] was uniformly desirous of a composition of the unhappy contest." Thomas Bayne, the person most responsible for securing the position for Campbell, later remarked, "All persons connected with the Confederate government know how faithfully he performed his duty."[67]

During Campbell's tenure at the War Department, he developed a close and cordial friendship with Robert Garlick Hill Kean, the head of the Bureau of War and one of Campbell's immediate subordinates. Kean's diary is filled with references to Campbell and tells of the respect that grew between the two men. "Judge Campbell is invaluable," Kean wrote, "his capacity for labor infinite, his breadth of view great. His endorsements are so judicial, deciding questions rather than cases, [that] they perplex the red tapists who complain that they do not decide *the case*."[68] Of course, Campbell's presence in the Confederate government did not please everyone, particularly William Lowndes Yancey, who remained angry with Campbell for having criticized those who advocated secession and also for not having resigned immediately when Alabama withdrew from the Union. Yancey's biographer notes that the Alabama fire-eater adamantly opposed the creation of a Confederate Supreme Court largely because he feared that Campbell would be named chief justice. Yancey was also unhappy that Campbell had been named to the War Department. For several months after he had assumed his duties in the War Office, Campbell's nomination was blocked in the Senate. Finally, on 18 April 1863—six months after he had started on the job—Campbell's position as the assistant secretary was approved.[69]

The four areas in which Campbell played the most significant role were in granting exemptions, issuing passports, reviewing court-martial proceedings, and indirectly controlling the Bureau of Conscripts. Nonetheless, the relative absence of Campbell's name from the *Official Records* indicates that his role in the war was slight.[70] A letter Campbell wrote in 1864 to a petitioner seeking an exemption from service for a "Mr. Williams" was typical of the exemption cases with which he dealt. The assistant secretary explained that much as he would like to allow the petitioner to remain out of the army, the demand for soldiers outweighed any personal reasons for not serving. That petition, Campbell wrote, was "one of a vast number of similar applications that discloses the terrible consequences of the war that now exists."[71]

Many of the letters Campbell received reflect the tremendous hardships generated by the war. Dozens of such letters could be cited, but one specific petition for exemption amply illustrates the heart-wrenching appeals that reached Campbell's desk. In August 1863, the assistant secretary was sent a letter originally addressed to President Davis from a Pickens, South Carolina, resident named Elizabeth Hester. This woman was pleading for her son's discharge from service. She explained that she had had five sons when the war began, all of whom volunteered for service "in defense of their rights and liberties." By summer 1863, four of her sons either had been killed in service or had died of disease. Her last son, the one whom she hoped to see released, was wounded in 1862 and, though crippled, wanted to remain in the army. Elizabeth continued that her husband Carwell had recently died from smallpox. Her only two daughters, made widows by the war, also died and left Elizabeth to raise their six "small and helpless" children. She wrote that her last son was desperately needed at home, for with her twelve slaves, she had thirty people to care for "with no male white person on the premises." Campbell's endorsement on this letter shows that he approved the exemption and ordered that the regimental commander of Elizabeth's last surviving son be notified accordingly.[72]

Not all members of the War Department believed that Campbell performed his duty honorably. John Beauchamp Jones, a clerk in the War Office whose diary reveals a profound lack of respect for Campbell, remarked that the assistant secretary was far too liberal in granting exemptions. Jones complained that scores of certificates for exemptions arrived daily in the War Office requesting special consideration for "rich, young Justices of the Peace, Commissioners of the (County) Revenue, Deputy Sheriffs, clerks, constables, officers and clerks of banks; . . . and they are all 'allowed' by the Assistant Secretary of War." Reflecting the rising "rich man's war—poor man's fight" sentiment that was growing throughout the South, Jones accused Campbell of habitually exempting the wealthy from service, and he pondered whether, "the poor and friendless [would] fight their battles, and win their independence for them." "It may be so," he surmised, "but let not rulers in future wars follow the example!"[73]

Campbell's second principal concern as assistant secretary involved issuing passports for individuals to cross Confederate lines and visit the North. One such case concerned a young woman named Annie Bartlett of St. Louis, Missouri. She had been in Mobile visiting family when the war began. Annie tried to return to Missouri, but she was stranded in Tuskegee, Alabama, where she remained with friends for the next three years. Desperate to return home, she pleaded with state officials in Alabama, who then contacted Campbell's office. The letter Campbell received about Annie described her as a "modest young lady of excellent character. She is tall and quite slender with dark hair and gray eyes and about 25 years of age." What such personal material had to do with whether or not she received a passport is unclear. Regardless, Campbell endorsed the letter with his approval for the passport.[74] Annie Bartlett's case was typical of requests for passports to cross Confederate lines. Many individuals had been in the South when the war began but for various reasons had been unable to return home. Campbell understood this and was quite lenient in approving most of these applications.

But here too Campbell was criticized by Jones, who accused the assistant secretary of aiding the enemy by allowing too many people freedom to cross into the northern states. Many of these people, the clerk concluded, harbored deserters or fugitives from conscription, yet Campbell continued to issue passports liberally. In April 1863, the month that Campbell's appointment was finally approved by the Senate, Secretary of War James A. Seddon "stopped the blockade-running operations of . . . Judge Campbell." Jones accused Campbell of issuing passports to numerous individuals who crossed into Maryland, purchased various dry goods and dried meats, and then slipped back into the Confederacy where they sold their merchandise for enormous profits. The War Department clerk also stated that he suspected Campbell accepted some of the smuggled goods as payment for issuing the passports.[75]

Included among War Department letters were accounts of courts-martial proceedings that Campbell perused and offered recommendations on punishment for those found guilty of various charges. One such case involved a "Lt. Evans" of a South Carolina regiment who was charged with being drunk on duty by a "Captain Farley." The incident occurred in early June 1862. Apparently, Farley excused Evans from duty that day and took no further action until late August, when Evans filed a formal complaint against his captain for abusive treatment. Farley was officially censured. Perhaps seeking to even the score, he filed charges against Evans for being drunk on duty three months earlier. In September Evans's court-martial was held in Charleston. He was found guilty and was sentenced to be executed. The court recommended that Evans be imprisoned until his case could be fully examined by the War Department. Upon reading the proceedings, and perhaps recognizing this case as fundamentally a personal rift between Evans and Farley, Campbell recommended executive clemency for the lieutenant on the grounds that although he had once been drunk on duty, he had since faithfully performed his duty.[76]

A second case, but of a far more serious nature, involved the court-martial of John Miller of Texas, who was charged with "desertion and carrying away his arms and equipment." Though the court found Miller innocent of absconding with his weapons, it recommended that he be "shot dead with musketry" for desertion. Campbell's memorandum indicates that he approved this sentence and suggested that it be carried out immediately.[77]

Campbell's legal expertise was especially useful in handling many conflicts involving the conscription laws. In July 1863, Campbell answered a letter from Mississippi representative Ethelbert Barksdale, who had complained that the Conscript Bureau erroneously forced a Mississippi citizen named Louis Frinkel into active service although he had procured a substitute. Moreover, Barksdale explained, Frinkel's case was heard before a state judge who ruled that several of the Confederacy's conscription laws violated states' rights and were thereby void.

For a man such as Campbell who had spent nearly his entire professional life upholding the doctrine of states' rights, it was supremely ironic in that as the assistant secretary of war he was obliged to administer the conscription laws despite objections from the states and nullifying decrees from state courts. "Some judges," Campbell wrote, "apparently catching the distemper of the time to relieve some of the burden of the military service," had used unconstitutional means of circumventing the conscription laws. "In every state some local judges seemed to have bestirred themselves to withdraw from the service all who by any subtlety could be released. A widespread disaffection has been the consequence, both in and out of the Army."[78] Campbell also explained that while he was on the Supreme Court the justices decided in *Ableman v. Booth* that state courts could not nullify federal laws. If such a determination was necessary in peacetime, Campbell asserted, it was doubly important during times of war. Frinkel's exemption was denied.

In a similar situation, Governor Zebulon B. Vance of North Carolina wrote the War Department, explaining that he had drafted a list of "classes of persons" whom he considered vital state employees exempt from military service. The list, although not part of the official record, was apparently rather extensive and included a variety of state officials, clerks, other employees, and even their "agents." Vance reminded the secretary of war of a state court's recent ruling that, by virtue of state sovereignty, he had the requisite authority to add nearly anyone to the list of exemptions. Secretary Seddon asked Campbell if Vance's claims of state sovereignty had any merit. "I am bound, am I not, to act upon the conscript law without reference to these state decisions?" Seddon inquired. Campbell responded that he had not heard of the case to which Vance referred. Nonetheless, the assistant secretary asserted that the governor "presses the [court's] decision beyond its limits when he claims all the employees and agents, etc. The decision, in my opinion, is erroneous, as militating against that supremacy which the [Confederate] Constitution ordains."[79]

The diarist Jones wrote with scant approbation that "Judge Campbell, has decided in one instance, that a paroled political prisoner, returning to the South, is subject to conscription." The clerk complained that Campbell wielded almost dictatorial powers over the Conscription Bureau but that he concurrently exhibited shameful favoritism in granting exemptions without the least justification for his actions. "It appears that grave justices," Jones cynically noted with reference to Campbell, "are not all inflexibly just, and immaculately legal in their decisions."[80] Even Robert Kean had less than total admiration for Campbell's handling of the Conscription Bureau. "[George] Lay has been the chief man [at the Conscription Bureau], and through Judge Campbell (his father-in-law) has been kept on very sound principles of administration, but there has been little *vim* in the head," Kean wrote.[81]

Of course, Kean's criticism in this case was directed more at Lay than at Campbell, for whom Kean had enormous respect. Jones, on the other hand, obviously detested the assistant secretary—Campbell did have the ability to alienate most people. But Jones's outlandish accusation that Campbell accepted bribes in return for passports was entirely without merit. Apart from the clerk's diary entries, there is no evidence that Campbell engaged in illicit profiteering. It is important to consider the source when assessing Jones's allegations against Campbell. Considering his deep-seated contempt for the assistant secretary, had Jones actually possessed immutable evidence of Campbell's alleged illegal activities, he would certainly have taken his proof to the secretary of war or to some other higher official within the government. That he simply recorded the accusations in his diary suggests that his charges against Campbell were the product of an inherently jealous and suspicious individual and lacked substance.

Campbell's tenure in the War Department was the most mundane experience of his life. Yet he tolerated the boredom and the uneventful day-to-day activity in the department in the hopes of bringing the war to an end. As the assistant secretary, Campbell had access to information from which the normal citizen was barred, and he regularly queried the heads of the various bureaus about the South's ability to maintain the fight. Even before Lee's momentous defeat at Gettysburg, Campbell accepted what he had long suspected: the South could not win the war, regardless of southern patriotism and the Confederate war effort. "I do not know," he wrote his sister-in-law in Mobile,

> that events have taken a different course than what I contemplated in the beginning and which I labor with all of my energy to avert from the country. It does not astonish me that England and France have not been compelled by [their need for cotton] to take our war into their hands; nor that cotton is not king; nor that slavery has not won the affections of Europe to our cause; nor that the northern people have no other motive than money. The shallow and conceited cowards of the leaders in our affairs have borne the fruit that I anticipated, and I believe that the whole country has been satisfied that they were not competent to guide the counsels of a town much less of a great country.[82]

Certain that the South was going to lose the war, Campbell began writing a series of reports and letters to various government officials suggesting that the Confederate government should consider negotiating an end to the struggle. Such suggestions, however, went entirely unheeded until well into 1865 when the South's defeat was all but certain. With very little left to bargain, Campbell realized that the South would have to agree to any reconstruction terms. He hoped that Lincoln would be lenient with the South and allow the southern states to rejoin the Union without completely destroying their few remaining possessions. During the winter of 1864–1865, Campbell once again assumed the role of peacemaker. He only hoped that he would be more successful in ending the war than he had been in preventing the outbreak of hostilities in 1861.

10 | The War Years, Part 2: That We Should Not Be Utterly Destroyed

On the morning of 3 February 1865, a small boat carrying three passengers was rowed across Hampton Roads, Virginia, toward the United States steamer *River Queen*. On board were three Confederate commissioners from Richmond: Vice-President Alexander Stephens, Senator R. M. T. Hunter, and Assistant Secretary of War John Archibald Campbell. Once on board the steamer, the commissioners met with President Abraham Lincoln and Secretary of State William Seward for the only meeting during which representatives of the two governments attempted to negotiate an end to the war. But the conference failed and the war continued as Sherman's forces trekked north into the Carolinas, Wilson raided much of central and eastern Alabama, and Grant carried on with the siege of Petersburg. Perhaps these events could have been avoided and lives could have been saved had the talks at Hampton Roads been successful. The Confederate commissioners, and Campbell in particular, hoped that Lincoln would agree to an armistice and that the southern states could return to the Union under lenient terms. These expectations, however, were dashed largely by Jefferson Davis's refusal to allow the commissioners to negotiate in the absence of recognition that secession and southern independence were legitimate. Lincoln could never agree to these terms, but Campbell, while anxiously awaiting an opportunity to meet with the president, steadfastly continued to believe that a settlement leading to an armistice could be reached.

By winter 1864, Campbell was convinced that the Confederacy was defeated, but he hoped that a suitable peace could be arranged between the two sides and that the South would be readmitted to the Union on lenient terms. On 1 December, Campbell addressed a letter to Justice Samuel Nelson, his former colleague on the United States Supreme Court. The purpose of the letter, Campbell explained, was to "ascertain whether anything could be effected for the amelioration of the [present] conditions." He suggested that "good might follow from a frank and candid interchange of opinions and information between citizens of the different sections" and added, "I believe now that an honorable peace will relieve the country from evils, possibly more permanent and more aggravated than those which have been suffered. I [have never], at any time, hesitated to believe that wise, moderate, [and] magnanimous counsels might result in an honorable peace. . . . If you suppose that any advancement to this end would be made by any communication between us, or between myself and others, I am ready to hold that communication. My object is simply to promote an interchange of views and opinions that might be productive of good and scarcely do harm."[1] Justice Nelson soon replied to Campbell's letter, and he informed his former colleague that the federal government was presently awaiting news concerning a different peace mission already in progress. Nelson therefore suggested that it would be best to delay any further peace offerings.

The other peace mission alluded to by Justice Nelson served as the catalyst for the Hampton Roads Conference. It involved Francis Preston Blair, Sr., the seventy-three-year-old Jacksonian who, in concert with Horace Greeley, had concocted an elaborate scheme he believed would end the war. In a 20 December letter to Greeley, Blair wrote that he had devised a plan that could remedy "the cause of the war, the war itself, and the men and the means essential to carry it on against us." He stated that he would approach Lincoln with his plan at the next available opportunity. As a consummate Jacksonian, Blair well understood the power of public opinion, so he asked Greeley not to publish anything about his mission until a later date.[2]

Blair hoped to persuade Lincoln and Davis to abandon the war, consent to an armistice, agree to combine the Confederate and Union forces, and invade Mexico. As a French army had recently helped to overthrow Mexican President Benito Juárez's government and had installed Austrian Archduke Maximilian as emperor of Mexico, Blair insisted that France had violated the Monroe Doctrine. As a result, Americans had an obligation to oust the French from North America. Blair met with Lincoln on two separate occasions in late December and asked for a passport to cross federal lines in order to seek out Davis's opinion of his plan.[3]

On 28 December, Lincoln gave Blair a card reading "Allow the bearer, F. P. Blair, Sr. to pass our lines, go South, and return."[4] Whether Blair had actually convinced Lincoln that his plan was anything more than a poorly conceived, half-baked scheme remains something of a puzzle. Lincoln later denied ever knowing the full extent of Blair's proposal. The president informed Congress on 9 February 1865 that Blair "was given no authority to speak or act for the government, nor was I informed of anything he would say or do."[5] But Lincoln was just as eager to end the war as Blair, and perhaps he figured that the mission to Richmond could do no harm and might lead to serious talks to end the war. With the newly acquired pass, Blair began his secret, yet wholly unauthorized, mission to Richmond.

After Blair arrived in the Confederate capital, many people speculated as to why the elder statesman was in town. Some claimed that the war had ended, others that Lincoln had agreed to an armistice. Rumors also spread that Richmond was to be evacuated. These uncertainties raised apprehensions and expectations that hostilities would soon end. Although Blair attempted to conduct his "mission" secretly, many southern papers reported that he was acting as a peace negotiator.[6]

Blair met with Davis on 12 January and read a long script detailing his "peace plan." He said that a "secret treaty" could be arranged to combine Union and Confederate forces. According to the Marylander, a joint invasion of Mexico by Confederate and Union armies would reawaken age-old cordial relations between North and South and would provide the Confederates with a face-saving way to reenter the Union. Davis was not interested in rejoining the Union, but he regarded Blair's plan as holding promise nonetheless. Davis thought that a joint invasion would necessitate a postponement of hostilities and would thereby give the South sufficient time to rebuild military strength. Thus he expressed interest in negotiating with the federal government. To initiate an alliance between the Confederacy and the United States, Blair suggested, Davis should appoint commissioners to speak directly with Lincoln. Davis drafted a letter to Lincoln stating that he had "no disposition to find obstacles in forms, . . . and [I] am willing to enter into negotiations for the restoration of peace, am ready to send a commission whenever I have reason to suppose it will be received, or to receive a commission if the United States Government shall choose to send one. [Commissioners could be sent] to renew the effort to enter into conference *with a view to secure peace to the two countries.*"[7]

Blair promptly returned to Washington believing that Davis had found his plan acceptable. He was admitted to see the president on 18 January and read Davis's letter. Lincoln, still unaware that Blair had proposed a joint invasion of Mexico, drafted his reply. "Sir: You having shown me Mr. Davis's letter of the 12th instant, you may say to him that I have constantly been, am now, and shall continue ready to receive any agent whom he or any other influential person now resisting the national authority may informally send to me *with the view of securing peace to the people of our one common country.*"[8]

The last phrases of Davis's letter and of Lincoln's reply struck at the heart of the conflict. Lincoln was as determined to restore the Union as Davis was to continue fighting for southern independence. Obviously, the two governments had reached an impasse, and yet Davis still considered a conference between representatives of both governments potentially advantageous. Exactly why the Confederate president, so intent on gaining southern independence, agreed to send commissioners when the conference reflected assumptions antithetical to his demands has been disputed ever since. There are at least two possible explanations for his actions.

Perhaps, as Davis later claimed, he truly wanted to restore peace, and so he was willing to make concessions leading to an armistice. Blair intimated to him that Lincoln was besieged by radicals and wanted to break free of their influence. He also informed Davis that Lincoln so urgently desired peace that he might allow Grant to meet with Lee and suspend hostilities without demanding unconditional surrender. But if the Confederate president actually believed Lincoln would agree to such terms, he was thoroughly duped by the Maryland statesman. This explanation hardly seems credible in light of Davis's high intellect.[9]

A second, and far more plausible, reason why Davis agreed to a peace conference dealt largely with the political atmosphere in Richmond. By December 1864, Campbell was not the only Confederate official convinced that the South was defeated and that honorable terms should be sought. Vice-President Alexander Stephens and several members of the Confederate Congress held similar opinions. As Stephens voiced his concern for the South and as several peace measures circulated through Congress, Davis sought to defuse these peace efforts. He obviously understood the significant differences between the two letters, and he reasoned that Lincoln would surely demand unconditional surrender as his only terms for ending the war. More than likely Davis believed he could discredit the vice-president and other people willing to concede defeat by sending them to meet with United States officials. Davis conjectured that when the commissioners learned that Lincoln demanded total surrender to federal authority, all conciliatory efforts would cease. Perhaps Davis further believed that such terms would inspire a patriotic rejuvenation of the war spirit in Richmond and stiffen southern resolve to continue the war. Obviously, the selection of the commissioners was of the utmost significance.[10]

During the early afternoon of 27 January, Davis summoned Stephens to a special meeting. After hearing of Blair's plan and reading the correspondence between Davis and Lincoln, Stephens was convinced that Lincoln fully supported Blair's scheme. The vice-president asserted that, in light of the importance of the proposed conference, Davis should personally attend and seek an armistice.[11] Davis rejected this notion outright, however, and declared that three commissioners would be selected. Stephens proposed Henry Benning, a retired justice of Georgia's Supreme Court; Thomas S. Flournoy, a former Whig from Virginia who was well acquainted with Lincoln; and Assistant Secretary of War John Archibald Campbell as commissioners to negotiate with the federal government. Stephens later claimed that Davis agreed with these nominations.[12] Much to his dismay, however, during a cabinet meeting held the following morning Stephens learned that he, Campbell, and Robert M. T. Hunter, president pro tem of the Confederate Senate, had been selected as negotiators. None were considered "die-in-the-last-ditch men," and it was suggested that they were "strong in intellect, but weak in war."[13] Despite protests from Stephens, Davis could not be persuaded to choose different commissioners.

Although Stephens had initially called the conference "humbug," his enthusiasm for it increased during the next two days.[14] The day before the commissioners left Richmond, the vice-president expressed confidentially to a colleague that there was "some prospect of doing *something* if we be received."[15] That night Campbell was notified by an official of the Confederate State Department that he had been selected. After being shown the correspondence between Lincoln and Davis, the assistant secretary immediately noted the differences between the two letters, and he complained to the messenger that this "might make difficulty."[16]

The commissioners' original orders drafted by Davis instructed the three men to "proceed to Washington City for [a] conference with [Lincoln] upon the subject to which [Lincoln's letter] relates." After having second thoughts about these instructions, Davis rewrote the orders: "In conformity with the letter of Mr. Lincoln of which the foregoing is a copy, you are requested to proceed to Washington City for [an] informal conference with him upon the issues involved in the existing war and for the purpose of *securing peace to the two countries.*"[17] Davis's instructions, which directed the commissioners to inquire whether Lincoln would be willing to recognize the South's independence, defeated nearly all chances to negotiate an end to the war.

On the morning of 29 January, Campbell, Stephens, and Hunter departed Richmond by a train en route to Petersburg. After Campbell showed the other two commissioners Davis's instructions, they proceeded as planned, hoping to arrive in Washington within two days. Upon arrival at Petersburg, they sent a message addressed to General Grant through the lines under flag of truce. The commissioners requested permission to proceed through federal lines, travel to Washington, and meet with Lincoln "upon the subject of the existing war, and with a view of ascertaining upon what terms it may be terminated."[18] They also asked to confer with Grant at the earliest convenience to discuss the various peace proposals. Grant, receiving this letter on 30 January, telegraphed Lincoln the following day and awaited instructions. Meanwhile, he ordered that the commissioners be brought to his headquarters at City Point.[19]

The *Richmond Sentinel* reported that as the commissioners passed through the lines "shouting . . . was prolonged and enthusiastic." The reporter said that it "would be delightful if there were any room to hope that the Washington authorities are prepared" for terms that "would allow the soldiers to disperse at once." This account also claimed that shouts of joy could be heard from the Union lines as the commissioners passed. Such stories further raised expectations in Richmond that the commissioners would succeed in orchestrating a negotiated peace.[20]

Grant was enthusiastic about the planned meeting as well, but he remained cautious. He received a telegraph from Lincoln ordering him to "[l]et nothing which is transpiring change, hinder, or delay your military movements or plans."[21] Grant answered that he understood that there would be no armistice as a result of the commissioners' mission, and he informed the president that "troops are kept in readiness to move at the shortest notice if occasion should justify it."[22]

Upon learning that the Richmond government had dispatched commissioners to meet with representatives of the United States, Lincoln summoned Secretary of State Seward and instructed him to travel by steamer to Hampton Roads and meet the Confederates. The president gave Seward explicit instructions on what terms were to be demanded. "As to peace," Lincoln wrote, "three things are indispensable":

1. The restoration of the national authority throughout all of the states.
2. No receding by the Executive of the United States on the slavery question from the position assumed thereon in the late annual message to Congress and in preceding documents.
3. No cessation of hostilities short of an end of the war and the disbanding of all forces hostile to the Government.[23]

Meanwhile, Secretary of War Edwin Stanton persuaded Lincoln to send Major Thomas Eckert, assistant superintendent of the United States Telegraph Office, to rendezvous with the commissioners in order to read their instructions from the Richmond government. Supposedly, Eckert was to meet with the Confederates before they passed through federal lines east of Petersburg, but Grant (who was unaware of Eckert's mission) allowed the men to proceed to City Point before the major's arrival. When he learned of his mistake, Grant expressed regret that he had allowed them to proceed.[24] Actually, as it unfolded, the Hampton Roads Conference would never have taken place had it not been for this breakdown in communication between Grant and Lincoln. Eckert's orders were to intercept the commissioners and determine whether they had been instructed to seek negotiations based on Davis's "peace to the two countries" clause. If those words were part of their orders, Eckert was not to allow the Confederates to cross federal lines, and he was to cancel the conference at once.

While at City Point, Campbell and the commissioners were housed on board a steamer in the James River. They enjoyed comfortable accommodations and were visited by Grant on several occasions. On the thirty-first, Grant held a long interview with Hunter and Stephens. Campbell excused himself because of illness.[25] During the interview, the two commissioners convinced Grant that they were sincere in their desire to end the war. Before the evening ended, however, Major Eckert arrived and asked to read their instructions from Richmond. Eckert informed the commissioners that in his opinion a meeting with federal authorities was impossible due to the wording of their orders. He wired Lincoln of this discovery and the conference was summarily canceled.

Upon hearing of this development, Grant immediately wired Stanton, asking the administration to reconsider seeing the commissioners. Grant explained that he was convinced that the southern commissioners were sincere in their desire to end hostilities and "to restore peace to the Union." He expressed apprehension that to reject their peace overtures "will have a bad influence," and he hoped that Lincoln could meet with all three commissioners.[26] Lincoln was about to recall his secretary of state when Stanton delivered Grant's wire. Upon reading the telegraph, the president reconsidered. On 2 February he asked Grant to transport the commissioners to Hampton Roads, and he told the general, "Say to the gentlemen I will meet them personally at Fortress Monroe, as soon as I can get there."[27] By dawn of 3 February the *River Queen* had steamed into Hampton Roads.

Once the commissioners were on board, they were escorted into one of the steamer's salons. Shortly thereafter, Lincoln and Seward entered and the conference began. The conversation started on a friendly and relaxed basis. Stephens and Lincoln recalled their days in Congress when they "acted together in effecting the election of General Taylor in 1848." They spoke of intimate friends and former associates and asked about their well-being. Stephens then inquired whether there "was any way of putting an end to the present trouble."[28] Realizing that the commissioners were ready to begin addressing important issues, Seward stated that the conference was to be absolutely informal and that no records were to be made. All conversations were strictly off the record, the federal government would not be bound by anything said, and the proceedings were to be held in strictest confidence. The commissioners agreed to these terms, and Stephens asked Lincoln once again how the war could be brought to an end.

In a short but concise reply, Lincoln declared that the war would end when those resisting the laws of the federal government laid down their weapons. It was as simple as that. Somewhat taken aback by the abruptness of the president's response, Stephens asked if there was not "some other question that might divert the attention of both parties. . . . Is there no continental question which might thus temporarily engage their attention? We [the Richmond government] have been induced to believe that there is." According to Stephens, Lincoln responded:

> I suppose you refer to something that Blair has said. Now it is proper to state at the beginning, that whatever he said was of his own accord, and without the least authority from me. When he applied for a passport to go to Richmond, with certain ideas which he wished to make known to me, I told him flatly that I did not want to hear them. If he desired to go to Richmond of

his own accord, I would give him a passport; but he had no authority to speak for me in any way whatever. When he returned and brought me Mr. Davis's letter, I gave him the one to which you alluded in your application for leave to cross the lines. I was always willing to hear propositions for peace on the conditions of this letter and on no other.[29]

The president informed the commissioners outright that Blair's "mission" was unauthorized, and that "the restoration of the Union is a *sine qua non* with me."[30] Lincoln proclaimed that he would not sanction any armistice or cessation of hostilities until southerners agreed to acknowledge the authority of the United States.

Campbell then asked in what manner reconstruction would be implemented if the South agreed to it. Seward responded that Campbell's question should be deferred until the proposal to divert the public's attention from the war was explored more fully. Stephens and Seward then engaged in a lengthy debate about the Monroe Doctrine. Stephens said that both sections had an intrinsic interest in seeing that no European country acquired a political or economic foothold in North America. The southern vice-president proposed "a union of power" comprised of Federal and Confederate forces to oust the French from Mexico. As a result of this union, he believed, old "fraternal feelings" would emerge and a peaceful settlement of the war could more easily be arranged. Seward responded with a series of questions that, he believed, would naturally arise if the two sides agreed to such a union. The secretary inquired about the status quo while the proposed invasion was carried out, problems involving tariffs, and instances when a confederate government and federal authority existed in the same region. Stephens responded that such matters could be settled by military convention, but he also claimed that all state governments recognized by the Confederacy should be dominant over federal authority.[31]

At this juncture, apparently, Lincoln had heard enough of Stephens's half-baked proposal. He informed the commissioners that no further discussion concerning a joint invasion of Mexico would be entertained. According to Campbell, the president explained that "there could be no war [with Mexico] without the consent of Congress, and no treaty [ending hostilities in the United States] without the consent of the Senate of the United States." More important, Lincoln was unwavering in that no armistice could be arranged because he said (as Campbell reported), "that would be a recognition of [the Confederate] states, and this could not be done under any circumstances."[32]

To Stephens's chagrin, Lincoln summarily dismissed the proposal to invade Mexico. Campbell then reiterated his former question concerning Lincoln's plans for Reconstruction. The president responded that Reconstruction would begin as soon as the South disbanded its armies and permitted the national government to resume its functions. Seward expounded on Lincoln's statement by reading a part of the president's annual message to Congress delivered in December. After reciting the portion of the address providing that no laws, statements, or declarations concerning slavery that had previously been enacted would be retracted, Seward read the following lines: "In stating a single condition of peace, I mean simply to say that the war will cease on the part of the government whenever it shall have ceased on the part of those who began it."[33]

But Campbell asserted that many issues would have to be solved before a proper restoration of the former relations could occur. He informed the president that disbanding the southern armies was a most delicate operation and would not be easy or quick to accomplish. He also said that questions regarding confiscated property would likewise have to be addressed. Lincoln replied that all questions involving property would be settled by the courts. In the meantime, he was confident that Congress would be liberal in making restitution for confiscated property.[34]

The next topic arose after Seward showed the commissioners a copy of the Thirteenth Amendment, which had passed Congress on 31 January. Remarkably, Seward suggested that both the Emancipation Proclamation and the Thirteenth Amendment were passed as war measures and that if the South ceased to resist federal authority, "it was probable that the measures of war would be abandoned." Lincoln agreed that the Emancipation Proclamation was a war measure and that as soon as the war ceased it would remain inoperative for the future. This was but his personal opinion, however. The actual disposition of the slaves would have to be determined by the courts, and he did not care to comment on what they might do. Seward then claimed that the southern states could annul the Thirteenth Amendment during the ratification process if they agreed to cease hostilities and recommence their constitutional obligations.[35]

Hunter asked whether Virginia would be established "with her ancient limits." No, Lincoln responded; West Virginia would remain a state unto itself.[36] Irritated at Lincoln's abrupt answer, Hunter suggested that it would be most prudent for the president to negotiate in good faith and in an official capacity with the commissioners, as that would have a positive effect in the South. But Lincoln remained adamant that he could not enter into any arrangements "with parties in arms against the government." Hunter curtly reminded the president that even Charles I had entered into agreements with people in rebellion against the English crown. Lincoln replied that he could not "profess to be posted in history. On all such matters I will turn you over to Seward. All I distinctly recollect about the case of Charles I, is, that he lost his head in the end."[37]

After several remarks by Campbell and Stephens, the commissioners realized that the conference had ended. Hunter recapitulated the different discussions and concluded that the federal government was prepared to agree only to unconditional surrender. Seward at once insisted that neither he nor the president had used the term "unconditional surrender." But Hunter asked what else had they demanded but the South's complete surrender and dismemberment of its armies? The Virginia senator then exclaimed that the South would be humiliated because there could be "no treaty, no stipulation, no agreement, either with the Confederate states jointly, or with them separately, as to their future position or security! What was this but unconditional surrender to the mercy of conquerors?"[38] Seward insisted that an end to the hostilities on Lincoln's terms would in no way humiliate the southern people. They would merely be readmitted to the Union and granted the rights and protection guaranteed by the Constitution.

Lincoln, agreeing fully with Seward's remarks, promised that he would use his powers as president to effect liberal peace terms that would include a fair settlement of all confiscated properties. Furthermore, he stated that the North was as much at fault for slavery as the South, because northerners were the first Americans to trade in African slaves.[39] He continued by declaring that, if the war should cease, he would be willing to compensate southerners for the loss of their slaves and that he could possibly allocate $400 million to be disbursed to former slaveowners. But as with all other topics discussed, Lincoln confessed that he could not guarantee this payment, nor could he enter into any agreement with the commissioners concerning compensation.[40]

When Stephens realized that the meeting was about to end, he suggested that perhaps they could "do something in the matter of the exchange of prisoners."[41] Lincoln agreed to discuss the matter more fully with Grant at a later date. In one final but futile effort, Stephens asked Lincoln to reconsider an armistice to end hostilities. The president consented to think it over but doubted that he would change his mind. After pleasant farewells, the meeting ended, and the commissioners were escorted back to Grant's headquarters at City Point.[42]

So ended the Hampton Roads Conference. The final result was an awareness on the part of its participants that the war had to continue unless the South was willing to abandon its war for independence. Perhaps constructive talks concerning reconstruction would have been able to allay southern fears about reentry into the Union. Campbell had hoped to address this issue in particular, but discussions concerning slavery, the Mexican invasion, and a possible armistice dominated the meeting. As he wrote on the day following the conference: "My own purpose was to ascertain, if possible, the precise views of Messrs. Lincoln and Seward, as to the manner in which reconstruction would be effected, and the rights that would be secured to the southern States in the event that one should take place."[43] Apparently Campbell was the only commissioner willing to accept the South's defeat, and he was hoping to negotiate a lenient and forgiving Reconstruction. Hunter, despite his claims at a much later date, was unwilling to admit that the South was defeated, and he became as resolute as ever to continue the war to its bitter end. Stephens was enamored by the notion of a possible Mexican invasion and certain of the president's willingness to go along with Blair's scheme. As a result, he failed to realize that Lincoln was solely interested in ending the war; all other matters were secondary.

Lincoln and Seward returned to Washington content that they had, if nothing else, at least spoken with high-ranking officials within the Richmond government on courteous, calm, and considerate terms.[44] On 4 February, Lincoln summoned his cabinet to discuss what had transpired at Hampton Roads. Upon hearing of the discussions with the Confederate commissioners, Secretary of the Navy Gideon Welles wrote that although there were no immediate results, the Hampton Roads conference was "likely to tend to peace."[45] On the following Monday, Lincoln announced a plan he believed could expedite an end to the hostilities. The president proposed allocating $400 million to be paid "for the extinguishment of slavery."[46] He even went so far as to write an address to Congress asking for an appropriation but stating, however, that no money would be paid unless "all resistance to the national authority be abandoned." Lincoln concluded that if southerners would surrender, "war will cease and armies be reduced to a basis of peace; that all political offenses will be pardoned; that all property, except slaves, liable to confiscation or forfeiture, will be released therefrom, . . . and that liberality will be recommended to Congress upon all points not lying within executive control."[47]

After reading Lincoln's message to Congress, Secretary of War Stanton ardently protested these measures. Welles likewise warned the president that Congress was not likely to agree to his request and that if it failed in Congress, there would be a negative impact in the South. Furthermore, Welles suggested that "there may be such a thing as so overdoing as to cause a distrust or adverse feeling." Besides, he suggested, southerners would most likely misconstrue Lincoln's offer to recompense slaveowners, and this would only result in further ill feelings between North and South.[48]

The outcry against these measures from cabinet members convinced Lincoln that he should abandon them. Yet in writing the proposal he showed his willingness to appease the South in its moment of defeat and to afford genuine and forgiving reconciliation. He knew that the North had won the war—his proposal was an attempt to win the peace. As Lincoln contemplated peace measures and reconciliation, however, many southerners became even more determined to continue the war. This sentiment was especially evident after the Confederate commissioners returned to Richmond on 5 February.

Soon after their arrival, Campbell, Hunter, and Stephens were summoned to meet with Davis and Secretary of State Judah P. Benjamin. Upon being asked for a full written report, the commissioners asked to report verbally. They stated that, as nothing of any real consequence had transpired at Hampton Roads, a written report was unnecessary.[49] Davis was adamant, however, that a written account should be submitted as soon as possible. Early the following morning Campbell delivered the "Report of the Commissioners" to Davis. The document revealed that Lincoln would not agree to any type of armistice, truce, or peace terms until the Confederate government pledged complete restoration of federal authority. Nevertheless, the commissioners specifically avoided using the phrase "unconditional surrender" to describe Lincoln's terms.[50]

Davis was dissatisfied with the report as written, and he insisted that the commissioners amend it to read that Lincoln had demanded abolition and submission. Although Hunter was willing to concede that point, Stephens and Campbell were adamantly opposed to adding those words. According to Robert Garlick Hill Kean, Campbell told him that he had protested adding "unconditional surrender" because "the [report] stated the exact result of the conference and as written would speak for itself."[51]

On 6 February, the diarist John Beauchamp Jones wrote that "Stephens is in his seat [presiding over the Senate] today, and seems determined. . . . Mr. Hunter is rolling about industriously. . . . [And] Judge Campbell is still acting as Assistant Secretary; but he looks very despondent."[52] Many people in Richmond were greatly excited about the reports of the Hampton Roads Conference. It was announced that a public meeting would be held that afternoon in the African Methodist Church, the largest meeting hall in the city, and excitement mounted as people learned that Davis and other members of the Confederate government were scheduled to speak.

During several highly patriotic orations, the Richmond audience listened as each speaker harangued Lincoln and his demands for "unconditional surrender." After denouncing Lincoln as "His Majesty Abraham the First," Davis read the commissioners' report. He included the phrase "unconditional surrender" in his speech, but he failed to mention that it had not been part of the original document. Amid cheers from the crowd Davis said that Lincoln and Seward "would soon find that they had been speaking to their master when demanding unconditional submission."[53] Stephens reported that Davis's speech "was not only bold, undaunted, and confident in its tone, but had the loftiness of sentiment, as well as magnetic influence in its delivery, by which the passions of the masses of the people are moved to their profoundest depths, and roused to the highest pitch of excitement. . . . The occasion, and the effects of the speech, as well as all the circumstances under which it was made, caused the minds of not a few to revert like appeals by Rienzi and Demosthenes."[54]

Three days later, R. M. T. Hunter and Judah Benjamin addressed another gathering at the African Church. Hunter delivered a speech that was said to "reanimate the people for another carnival of blood."[55] The confederate senator later wrote that he regretted delivering his speech that day but he believed that "if the contest were to be kept up, it was necessary to animate the spirit which could alone sustain it."[56] After Hunter spoke, Secretary Benjamin said that the Confederacy had no other alternative but to enlist blacks into the ranks of their armies. He also asked the people to donate cotton, tobacco, corn, and meat as a sign of their dedication to the South's fight for independence. Speeches similar to those delivered in Richmond on the sixth and the ninth were repeated in many regions of the Confederacy, and for a short period many southerners swore to fight on until the last drop of blood.

Campbell, however, remained as discouraged as ever. Convinced that the patriotic zeal then sweeping Richmond was to be but a short-lived interregnum before the South's inevitable defeat, he continued his campaign to end the war.[57] On 7 February, John C. Breckenridge assumed the duties of the Confederate secretary of war. Breckenridge summoned Campbell to his office, where the two men spoke at length about what could be done to reverse the South's losses. The secretary asked Campbell to petition each of the nine Bureaus of War to determine the Confederacy's ability to conduct another campaign. Several days later his report indicated that the South had completely depleted its ability to fight.[58] This report further convinced the assistant secretary that more vigorous efforts to achieve peace should have been made earlier. Campbell explained that "there was, in my opinion, full justification for the opinion that peace on the precise terms offered at the Hampton Roads Conference, if none better could have been obtained, should have been accepted."[59]

The Hampton Roads Conference failed to initiate negotiations that could have ended the war in February 1865. Davis's instructions to the commissioners, by demanding negotiations to secure peace to the two countries, seriously handicapped talks that might have hastened the end of the war. Realistically speaking, however, Davis was not ready to quit the fight. He obviously believed that the South was not defeated and that, once Lincoln demanded unconditional surrender, southerners would resolve to destroy the North's will to fight. It was a gamble that Davis believed he had to take. As one historian notes, "Had Mr. Davis agreed with the commissioners that peace should be restored upon any basis, the soldiers in the field would have marched over him and them into battle."[60] Considering the political circumstances prostrating the Confederate government and the patriotic zeal that the people of Richmond still harbored, the Civil War was destined to end with one side the victor and the other the vanquished. That Campbell believed Lincoln would be willing to agree to an armistice showed either a remarkable degree of naiveté or a tremendous amount of wishful thinking. He was greatly discouraged that the Hampton Roads Conference had been unproductive, but he continued to hope that victory for the North would not mean utter despair in the South.

In the meantime Campbell still had his normal duties at the War Department, and immediately after returning to Richmond he decided to calculate the Confederacy's remaining resources and to determine how much longer the South could carry on the war. On 23 February, Campbell drafted a memorandum to Secretary Breckenridge in which he suggested that the government should begin making arrangements to evacuate Richmond in the likely event that Lee could not restrain Grant's forces. "We should take instructions from the lessons afforded by Nashville, Memphis, New Orleans, Norfolk, Atlanta, Savannah, Columbia, and Wilmington," he wrote. None of those southern cities had adequately prepared evacuation plans, and when each fell to federal forces, chaos resulted. "It is the part of wisdom to consider what is to be done" if Richmond had to be evacuated, he advised.[61]

Campbell stated that several matters needed to be considered before the city could be evacuated. These included determining where to locate the new seat of government, which of the departments should be relocated, how best to transport the archival material, whether to inform the citizens of Richmond of all evacuation plans, whether to plan for transport of the sick and wounded, and whether vital machinery and workshops would accompany the government. "I do not submit this inquiry under any immediate apprehension, nor with any view to any immediate or hurried action," he wrote, "but upon a calm consideration of the prospects ahead of us, and to avert the evils from which the Confederacy has suffered so much." There was no reason to panic—at least not yet. But the time to prepare had unquestionably arrived. "At no time previously," Campbell advised Breckenridge, "within my knowledge have the military leaders spoken with so much hesitation as to the future; at no time has the embarrassment as to supplies been so great, at no time have the embarrassments attending the holding of Richmond been apparently greater. For these reasons, in my judgement, some policy should be adopted."[62]

After receiving this memo, Breckenridge requested that Campbell investigate nearly every aspect of the Confederacy's financial, economic, and military affairs to determine exactly how long the South could continue fighting. On 5 March, Campbell responded with a preliminary report detailing the decrepit state of the Confederacy. "The present condition of the country requires, in my opinion, that a full and exact examination be made into the resources of the Confederate Government available for the approaching campaign, and that accurate views of our situation be taken." After investigating the Confederacy's financial state, its ability to raise armies, the possibility of impressing slaves, the state of the economy, the condition of the Ordnance Department, the political conditions throughout the South, and the Confederacy's treasury, Campbell concluded, "It is not the part of statesmanship or of patriotism to close our eyes upon" the South's condition.[63]

The Confederacy's financial condition, he asserted, was dire and all but prohibited any immediate military campaigns. The national debt was nearly half a billion dollars, and the government could borrow no more money. The projected expenditures amounted to over $1.3 billion, but there was no indication as to how such a hefty amount could be procured. The Confederate dollar, Campbell explained, had become virtually worthless, and the scant amount of specie held in the national treasury would soon be gone. "It is needless to comment on the facts," he wrote. "When this exchequer becomes exhausted, I fear that we shall be bankrupt, and that the public spirit in the South and in the Southwestern States will fail."[64]

Campbell reported that the condition of the armies was no better. Despite the various Conscription Acts passed over the last two and one-half years, the Confederacy simply could not raise armies large enough to confront more than 1 million men of the United States forces. "The casualties of the war cannot be accurately ascertained. But enough is known to show that no large addition can be made from the conscript population." He explained that desertion had reached epidemic proportions as well. It was estimated that there were over 100,000 deserters "scattered over the Confederacy." "So common is the crime [of deserting]," he wrote, "it has in popular estimation lost the stigma which justly pertains to it." Deserters "are everywhere shielded by their families and by sympathies of many communities" throughout the South. "[T]he evil is one of enormous magnitude, and the means of the Department to apply a corrective have diminished in proportion to its increase."[65]

Since the defeat at Gettysburg in July 1863, there had been much discussion of the need to impress slaves into the Confederate armies. Campbell, however, believed in March 1865 that such talk was nonsense. It was simply too late to consider impressing, training, and arming hundreds of thousands of slaves—Grant's army would obviously not wait until the South could construct such a force. He noted that perhaps if slaves had been used from the outset of hostilities as engineers, teamsters, and laborers, their services would have had a positive impact. But such contingencies so late in the war were impossible. "As a practical measure, I cannot see how a slave force can be collected, armed, and equipped at the present time," he advised.

According to Campbell's report, the South's economy was nearly nonexistent. Moreover, the dire economic situation was compounded by the

subjugation of the most productive parts of the country, the devastation of other portions, and the destruction of railroads. Production has been diminished and the quantity of supplies has been so much reduced that under the most favorable circumstances subsistence for the army would not be certain and adequate. At present these embarrassments have become so much accumulated that . . . the problem of subsistence of the Army of Northern Virginia, is in its present position, insoluble. . . . The remarks upon the subject of subsistence are applicable to the clothing, fuel, and forage requisite for the army service, and in regard to the supply of animals for cavalry and artillery.[66]

In sum, Campbell reported that the Army of Northern Virginia was desperately lacking in food, clothing, munitions, and animals and that the government was all but powerless to assist Lee's struggling forces.

The Ordnance Department was likewise in a perilous state. Most of the South's ironworks and munitions factories had been captured or destroyed. After consulting with General Josiah Gorgas, head of the Ordnance Department, Campbell learned that the South's stockpile of guns had diminished to a mere 25,000 weapons. Gorgas explained that he had relied on the importation of European weapons to maintain the armies throughout the war but that that source had been "nearly cut off" and a shortage of guns would soon become manifest in all of the armies. "The armies in the field in North Carolina and Virginia," Campbell wrote, "do not afford encouragement to prolonged resistance." Because of the high desertion rate, Lee's army and Joseph Johnston's army were rapidly losing strength. Campbell explained that the reasons for such high desertions were understandable, considering that the soldiers were constantly "exposed to the most protracted and violent campaign that is known in history, contending against overwhelming numbers, badly equipped, fed, paid, and cared for in camp and hospital, with families suffering at home." The Army of Northern Virginia, he wrote, "has exhibited the noblest qualities," especially considering the hardships that its soldiers experienced and the sacrifices that the men were asked to make. But he suggested that the government's capacity to supply its armies had evaporated and that it was perhaps time to consider peace terms.

"The political condition is not more favorable" than the economic and supply problems, he wrote.

> Georgia is in a state that may properly be called insurrectionary against the Confederate authorities. Her public men of greatest influence have cast reproach upon the laws of the Confederacy and the Confederate authorities, and have made the execution of laws nearly impossible. A mere mention of the condition in Tennessee, Missouri, Kentucky, Western Virginia, the line of the Mississippi, the sea-board from the Potomac to the Sabine, and of North Alabama is sufficient. North Carolina is divided, and her divisions will prevent her from taking upon herself the support of the war as Virginia has done. With the evacuation of Richmond, the State of Virginia must be abandoned. The war will cease to be a national one from that time.[67]

With these realities, therefore, Campbell concluded that only the most optimistic person would believe that the South could win the war and gain its independence. He counseled that it was still not too late to consider peace negotiations; that was all that was left for the South.

"It is the province of statesmanship to consider these things," he wrote. "The South may succomb [*sic*], but it is not necessary that she should be destroyed." Campbell insisted that the South's defeat was assured, but he asserted that southerners should still hope that a magnanimous peace could be arranged. As he learned at Hampton Roads that Lincoln would agree to no cessation of hostilities without a restoration of the Union, Campbell determined that the southern states should begin to consider canceling their ordinances of secession. "I do not regard reconstruction as involving destruction unless our people should forget the incidents of their heroic struggle and become debased and degraded. It is the duty [of southern] statesmen and patriots to guard [the people] in the future with even more care and tenderness than they have done in the past." Campbell wrote that he had examined every aspect of the Confederacy, and he could not but determine that all hope for victory was lost. "I do not ask that my views be accepted, but that a candid inquiry be made with a view to action." He knew that he alone could not convince President Davis of the need to begin negotiations along the lines proposed at Hampton Roads. He therefore suggested that General Lee's opinions on the state of the Confederacy be sought as well.[68] He was obviously aware that no person commanded more respect and admiration in the South than Lee and that the general was perhaps the only man who could bring an end to the war before the South was completely devastated.

Lee's immediate concern, however, was not surrender but rather figuring out some way to evade Grant's mighty Army of the Potomac. Since July 1864, the haggard Army of Northern Virginia had been entrenched at Petersburg trying to stave off Grant's ferocious assaults. During the nine-month siege, the Confederate forces suffered considerably as supplies ran out and morale diminished. By the end of March 1865, the Army of Northern Virginia numbered fewer than 25,000 men, many of whom were without weapons or decent uniforms.[69] Grant was determined to crush Lee's forces, and he expressed confidence to Lincoln that surrender was imminent. In mid-March 1865, the president traveled to Grant's headquarters at City Point, Virginia, located on the James River several miles south of Richmond. On March 27 and 28, Lincoln held conferences with Grant, General William T. Sherman, and Admiral David D. Porter to discuss plans for the final defeat of the remaining Confederate armies.[70]

Even with the prospects of the South's defeat nearly assured, Lincoln still worried that one or perhaps two major battles remained to be fought. According to Sherman's account, the president asked, "Must more blood be shed?

Cannot this last bloody battle be avoided!"[71] The president desperately wanted to end the fighting without the expected final confrontations.

On the night of 30 March, Lincoln heard bombing in the distance and feared that the final battle against Lee's forces had begun. Actually, the explosions heard that night indicated that General Philip Sheridan was carrying out Grant's orders to destroy the Richmond-Danville Railroad and cut the Confederates' only remaining supply line. Sheridan's success at what became known as the Battle of Five Forks forced Lee to surrender Petersburg and flee west.

On Sunday, 2 April, while attending services at Saint Paul's Episcopal Church, Davis received a telegraph from Lee. The president's face became ashen as he read the note, and he immediately rose and walked briskly out of the church, leaving the congregation bewildered and worried. Lee's dispatch explained that his army could no longer remain at Petersburg; Richmond had to be evacuated at once. For the next several hours, members of the Confederate government loaded their belongings onto a freight train. By 3:00 A.M., Richmond was no longer the capital of the Confederacy, as its government was en route to Danville, Virginia.[72]

Although he was saddened by the sudden evacuation of Richmond, Campbell believed that an opportunity to end the war had at last arrived.[73] Because he had always taken upon himself the role of peacemaker, it was perfectly natural, albeit quite presumptuous, for him once again to plan for negotiations. In effect, but without formality, Campbell resigned his position that night, and he abandoned the Confederacy in the hopes of returning Virginia to the Union.

Meanwhile, Richmond erupted into a series of explosions when fleeing Confederate soldiers destroyed several munitions warehouses. These explosions quickly produced fires that spread to all parts of the city. With the army gone, there was little the people in Richmond could do but stare in amazement as vandals destroyed property and looted stores. To protect the inhabitants of the city, Mayor Joseph Mayo rode out to Federal lines and surrendered to General Godfrey Weitzel. At about eight o'clock that morning Federal troops marched into Richmond and raised the American flag over the capitol while a military band played the "Star Spangled Banner." As Richmond socialite Sallie B. Putnam explained, "[T]hat song was a requiem for buried hopes."[74]

On Tuesday morning Campbell reported to General George F. Shepley, the appointed military governor for Virginia. The two men were well acquainted, for Shepley had argued cases before the United States Supreme Court while Campbell was an associate justice. Campbell told Shepley that he was prepared to surrender himself to Federal authorities because he knew that the war was over. During the conversation, Shepley spoke freely concerning restoration and reconstruction. He explained that Virginia would probably be ruled by a military government but that the governor would be selected by the state's population.[75] Campbell had hoped to avoid such restoration, for it involved implementing martial law in each conquered state. When Shepley informed him that Lincoln was at City Point, Campbell asked if he could meet with the president to argue that martial law would be both unwise and unnecessary.

For reasons not exactly clear, Lincoln had already decided to visit Richmond. Two of his earliest biographers felt that the trip was especially dangerous. But they also wrote, "Never in the history of the world did the head of a mighty nation and the conqueror of a great rebellion enter the captured chief city of the insurgents in such humbleness and simplicity."[76] Actually, Lincoln's trip to Richmond would have seemed somewhat comical had it not been so detrimental to his safety.

On the morning of 4 April, Lincoln boarded the *River Queen* at City Point and, escorted by Admiral Porter's flagship, *Malvern,* began the voyage to Richmond. But the river soon became nearly unnavigable, obstructed by large sections of bridges destroyed by the Confederates. When the *Malvern* became entangled and was blocked from further progress, Lincoln decided to use a twelve-oared barge to complete the journey. Finally, after several hours of treacherous navigation, the group arrived in Richmond.[77]

Because they had departed City Point in haste, no one had remembered to inform Weitzel of Lincoln's visit. There was no one on the banks to meet the president except a group of freed blacks who rejoiced at the sight of the man who had brought them freedom. As Lincoln walked down the streets of Richmond, more and more blacks gathered around. If the one dozen sailors had not been there to protect him, Lincoln could have been mobbed. Even worse, he could easily have been shot from any one of the buildings lining the streets. Porter spotted a Federal cavalryman in the road and ordered him to rush ahead and inform Weitzel that the president had arrived. Much to the admiral's relief, the party reached the Confederacy's presidential mansion without incident.[78]

Shortly after Lincoln's arrival, a staff officer was sent to escort Campbell to the mansion. After pleasant greetings, Campbell informed Lincoln that his visit was completely unofficial and that he could speak for no one other than himself. He then stressed that the war was over and that "all that remained to be done was to compose the country." He hoped Lincoln would consider "a long, liberal, and magnanimous policy" for the defeated states.[79]

Campbell claimed that he was greatly concerned about Virginia because if a harsh policy were established for that state, other seceded states would remain adamant about retaining their independence. In other words, perhaps it would be best to make an example of Virginia so that the other states could witness the president's good intentions and liberal restoration policy. Campbell inquired whether it would be possible for prominent Virginians to hold a meeting and discuss "the restoration of peace, civil order, and a renewal of her [Virginia's] relations as a member of the Union."[80]

Lincoln seemed receptive to all of Campbell's ideas. He gave no indication, however, that he accepted any of them. Their meeting on 4 April ended with Lincoln stating that he would consider Campbell's suggestions and that they should meet again on the following day. The president then proposed that Campbell invite the most influential citizens of Richmond to their next meeting. That evening Campbell sent invitations to six or seven people. Only one response arrived, however, from Gustavus A. Myers, a prominent attorney in Richmond and one of Campbell's closest friends, who agreed to hear Lincoln's views on restoration.[81]

The following morning at seven o'clock Campbell and Myers, escorted by General Weitzel, boarded the *Malvern*. In contrast to their meeting on the previous day, Campbell reported that Lincoln "was prepared for the visit and spoke with freedom and apparent decision." The president explained that his primary objective was to restore the Union without creating undue resentment or animosity. He then produced a document that was neither signed nor addressed. On it were written the three conditions offered to the Confederate commissioners at Hampton Roads.[82] Given the frankness of this memorandum, neither Campbell nor Myers should have expected Lincoln to accept an armistice. For all practical purposes, the meeting could well have ended at that juncture. Campbell's hopes of initiating an armistice were now smashed. And yet Lincoln offered a glimmer of hope for the two southerners.

After allowing Campbell and Myers to read the memo, Lincoln spoke of how it saddened him to see the South so utterly destroyed. He then explained that he was working on a plan to end the fighting in Virginia. According to Campbell's account, this plan required that the members of the Virginia legislature "meet together" so that they "might restore the state to the Union." Lincoln asserted "that it was important for that legislature to do so, that they were in the condition of a tenant between two contending landlords, that the tenant should attorn to the successful party who had his established right."[83] Lincoln advised Campbell that he had not yet worked out all of the particulars of his plan but that he would send orders the following day concerning the convening of Virginia's legislature.

Toward the conclusion of the meeting, despite Lincoln's written statements to the contrary, Campbell suggested that a convention be called so that Grant and Lee could discuss the possibility of an armistice "during which negotiations might be opened and conducted." Lincoln did not comment on Campbell's suggestion but asked if he could have a written copy. At that juncture the interview ended "with entire civility and good humor."[84] Campbell and Myers then returned to Richmond, and Lincoln went back to City Point.

On Thursday, 6 April, Weitzel received the following message from Lincoln:

> It has been intimated to me that the gentlemen who have acted as the legislature of Virginia in support of the rebellion may now desire to assemble at Richmond and take measures to withdraw the Virginia troops and other support from resistance to the General Government. If they attempt it, give them permission and protection, until, if at all, they attempt some action hostile to the United States, in which case you will notify them, give them reasonable time to leave, and at the end of which time arrest any who remain. Allow Judge Campbell to see this, but do not make it public.[85]

Thus Lincoln had set his plan into motion. His thinking, of course, was for Virginia's troops to be withdrawn from the war. If that occurred, Lee's Army of Northern Virginia would disband, the expected bloody battle would be avoided, and, in all likelihood, the war would end.

For the next several days, Campbell made plans to summon the legislature. On 7 April, he wrote to Joseph Anderson and four other members of the legislature concerning his meeting with the president. He explained that numerous topics, including the "establishment of a government for Virginia, the oath of allegiance, and the terms of settlement with the United States," had been discussed. Campbell also wrote, "The object of the invitation is for the government of Virginia to determine whether they will administer the laws in connection with the authorities of the United States. I understand from Mr. Lincoln, if this condition be fulfilled that no attempt would be made to establish or sustain any other authority [in Virginia]."[86] Thus as Campbell believed, Virginia's legislators needed to accept the authority of the federal government. Their state government would then be recognized by Lincoln as legitimate and lawful, all federal troops then occupying Virginia withdrawn, and martial law avoided.

Campbell drafted a letter later that day to a number of influential state politicians explaining that he had met with Lincoln twice since the evacuation of Richmond and had discussed a number of important issues with the president. "My object," he asserted, "was to secure for the citizens of Richmond, and the [people] of Virginia . . . as much gentleness and forbearance as could be possibly extended." Campbell said that Lincoln had agreed to allow Virginia's legislature to convene and to "determine whether they will administer the laws in connection with the authorities of the United States, and under the Constitution of the United States." "I understood from Mr. Lincoln," he continued, "if this condition be fulfilled, that no attempt would be made to establish or sustain any other authority."[87] On the eleventh a handbill written by Campbell titled "To the People of Virginia" was published in the *Richmond Whig*. This message notified Virginia legislators that a general meeting was scheduled for 25 April for the purpose of discussing "the restoration of peace to the state of Virginia, and the adjustment of questions involving life, liberty and property that have arisen in the state as a consequence of the war."[88]

When word of Lincoln's meeting with Campbell reached Washington, many of the more radical congressional leaders within the Republican party were stunned. Charles Sumner of Massachusetts complained that Lincoln's meeting with Campbell had underscored that the president "is full of tenderness to all." "I hope that the complication at Richmond may be got rid of, or, rather, that the whole proceeding may fail," he wrote.[89] Several members of Lincoln's cabinet likewise were greatly distressed when they learned that Lincoln had tacitly sanctioned a meeting of Virginia's legislature. Secretary of War Stanton and Judge Advocate General Joseph Holt especially believed that Lincoln had blundered terribly. After speaking with the secretary of war, Sumner stated that Stanton was fearful that the North "might lose the fruits" of its victories as a result of Lincoln's shortsighted negotiations. Upon Lincoln's return to Washington, therefore, Stanton and Holt implored him to reverse the order of 6 April to Weitzel. Stanton later stated, "The policy of undertaking to restore the government through the medium of rebel organizations was . . . strongly and vehemently opposed by myself." He reported that he held several conversations with Lincoln on the subject and that he finally persuaded the president to cancel Weitzel's orders.[90]

On 12 April, Weitzel received a wire from Lincoln that officially rescinded his permission for the legislators to meet. According to the president, Campbell assumed "that I have called the insurgent Legislature of Virginia together, as the rightful Legislature of the State to settle all differences with the United States. I have done no such thing. I spoke of them not as a Legislature, but as the gentlemen who have *acted* as the Legislature of Virginia in support of the rebellion."[91]

Lincoln also stated that he had intentionally phrased his earlier message to Weitzel "to exclude the assumption that I was recognizing them as a rightful body." He claimed that he only "dealt with them as men having power *de facto* to do a specific thing." Despite Campbell's assertions and letters to the contrary, Lincoln said that he had only authorized the legislature to "withdraw the Virginia troops and other support from resistance to the general government." Because Lee had surrendered on 9 April, Lincoln stated that his offer to Campbell was no longer necessary. Thus notification was given to Weitzel that his orders were countermanded. The president concluded with, "Do not allow them to assemble, but if any have come, allow them safe return to their homes."[92]

For the remainder of his life, Campbell maintained that Lincoln had officially sanctioned the convening of the Virginia legislature. The essential questions were threefold: whether Lincoln actually authorized the meeting, the exact purpose for the meeting, and last, why it was so essential that Lincoln's order be rescinded. If, as Campbell claimed, all aspects of his accounts were true, Lincoln indeed moved well beyond any earlier position on restoration and reconstruction that he had expressed. An officially recognized meeting of the Virginia legislature would have been a precedent-setting act that could well have applied to each seceded state. Campbell surmised that Lincoln's plan of restoration was for each state in the Confederacy to convene its legislature to return to the Union—each state would reenter the Union as each state had left it, individual political entities.

Was this actually Lincoln's plan of restoration as of April 1865? Historians have never been able to agree on exactly what he intended to do with the conquered Confederacy. One historian notes that by war's end Lincoln was searching for a way to end the hostilities and restore the Union for practical political reasons.[93] By the end of the war, the Republican party was deeply divided into two factions: those who wanted liberal terms and uncomplicated Reconstruction and the radicals who wanted to see the South treated as conquered territory.

Because Lincoln never agreed with the latter approach, some historians argue that he attempted to restore the Union before the radicals in Congress could meet and intervene. If restoration had been based on liberal terms, the president would have gained much political support from grateful southerners and Peace Democrats. The result would have been the formulation of a new national organization closely resembling the defunct Whig party.[94] If this was indeed Lincoln's political objective, it may well have been possible that he wanted the Virginia legislature to meet and end the fighting. Each state of the Confederacy would then do likewise and the war would be over.

Two events that occurred before Campbell met with Lincoln suggest that the president sought a liberal and uncomplicated restoration. The first took place during the Hampton Roads Conference in February. According to Alexander Stephens, Lincoln stated that if he were the Confederate vice-president, "I would go home and get the Governor [of Georgia] to call the legislature together, and get them to recall all of the state troops from the war; elect Senators and members to [the United States] Congress, and ratify this Constitutional [Thirteenth] Amendment prospectively."[95] This statement, if accurately reported, revealed that Lincoln at least considered allowing each rebel state legislature to vote their respective states back into the Union.

A second instance of similar circumstances occurred in early March when the president held discussions at City Point with Grant and Sherman concerning the final campaigns. During these meetings, Sherman reported that, "Lincoln assured me that he was already prepared for the reorganization of affairs of the South as soon as the war was over." Furthermore, the general insisted that he had Lincoln's full permission to notify Governor Vance of North Carolina "that to avoid anarchy the State governments then in existence, with their civil functionaries, would be recognized by him [Lincoln] as the government *de facto* until Congress could provide others."[96]

Historians disagree as to whether Lincoln actually made this statement to Sherman. The president had previously instructed Grant to refrain from all political issues in conducting the war, so it seems doubtful that he would instruct Sherman to do otherwise.[97] Yet when Sherman and Johnston consented to negotiate, the terms agreed upon were both liberal and political.

Sherman signed what was in effect a peace treaty providing for a general amnesty, guaranteeing the southern people their political and property rights and recognizing the existing state governments in the South. He later insisted that every point included in his settlement originated during his meeting with the president at City Point. Secretary of the Navy Gideon Welles stated in his diary that "Sherman's terms were based on a liberal construction of Lincoln's benevolent wishes and the order to Weitzel concerning the Virginia Legislature, the revocation of which S[herman] had not heard."[98]

Further evidence showing that Lincoln consented to the session was Gustavus Myers's 5 April account of the meeting on board the *Malvern*. According to Myers, "[Lincoln] said that he was thinking over a plan by which the Virginia Legislature might be brought to hold their meeting in . . . Richmond." Myers also stated that the purpose of the meeting was to "see whether they desired to take any action on behalf [of Virginia] in view of the existing state of affairs."[99] This account, coupled with the evidence shown earlier, demonstrated that Lincoln, despite the wording of his two telegrams to Weitzel, meant for the rebel Virginia legislature to convene. After all, who but the members of Virginia's legislature had the authority to withdraw state troops?

The next question involved what Lincoln expected Virginia's legislators to do once they met. In an account written by Campbell many years later, he quoted Lincoln as having instructed the legislature, "the same legislature as had been 'sitting up yonder'—pointing to the Capitol—to come together and to vote to restore Virginia to the Union, and recall her soldiers from the Confederate army."[100] Apart from Campbell's report, however, there is no additional evidence that Lincoln wanted the legislature to return Virginia to the Union. Myers did not mention it in his account, and such an omission hardly seems inadvertent.

In the telegraph Lincoln sent to Weitzel on 6 April the significant phrase was that the legislators were to "withdraw the Virginia troops and other support from resistance to the General Government."[101] Nowhere in the message did Lincoln authorize the Virginia legislature to vote on a return to the Union and acknowledge federal authority. Thus by summoning the legislature to "determine whether they will administer the laws in connection with the authorities of the United States," Campbell exceeded his instructions.[102]

The third issue was why it was so essential for Lincoln to rescind his orders to Weitzel. First of all, had the Virginia legislature met with Lincoln's approval, it would have constituted de facto recognition of a rebel legislature. Lincoln had always maintained that secession was unconstitutional, and he had to remain extremely careful not to recognize seceded state governments, as doing so would legitimize secession. Even the convening of the Virginia legislature solely to withdraw the troops from the war could have been construed as legal recognition.[103] Moreover, if legislators could vote a state into the Union, they could just as easily vote to secede. If Virginia had been allowed to restore its membership in the Union, and had this act been recognized by the federal government, Lincoln could have been accused of acknowledging at least tacitly the legality of secession.

Another reason why it seemed important—especially to Stanton—that Lincoln rescind the offer to the Virginia legislature was that it would have validated and perpetuated the predominance of the secessionist leadership in the state. In other words, the same men who had voted Virginia out of the Union would have retained political control. Thus Stanton convinced Lincoln that he had to withdraw his offer to Campbell.

There can be no question that Campbell exceeded his authority. Lincoln never permitted the Virginia legislature to meet as a legally recognized political body. But the president did in fact sanction a meeting of the legislature to withdraw Virginia's forces from the war. When Lincoln rescinded his orders to Weitzel, he avoided what could have become a rather embarrassing situation. After Lincoln's assassination, Campbell was arrested ostensibly for exceeding his authority and for misrepresenting the president's orders. Meanwhile, some of the Republican leaders, ever eager to punish the South, sought to implicate southern leaders in the assassination, and Campbell became embroiled in the investigation of that alleged conspiracy.[104]

11 | Reconstruction and Redemption

Campbell spent the remaining twenty-four years of his life practicing law. In many respects, these years were his most productive. Although he had lost virtually all of his possessions during the war, and although he was unemployed after the Confederacy's defeat, Campbell worked diligently to rebuild his once unblemished reputation as a highly successful advocate. Soon after Campbell's arrival in New Orleans, Henry M. Spofford, a former justice of the Louisiana Supreme Court, invited him to join his practice as a full partner. Duncan was soon thereafter asked to join the firm as well. Within two years, Campbell had not only become reestablished in the legal profession but was again considered one of the leading attorneys in the nation. Campbell's primary objective during this period, the one overriding concern above all others, was seeing to his family's financial security. And in this regard he was successful within a few years after the war. At the same time, though, the war had taken an enormous psychological toll on Campbell and his family. After all, his prewar career had been marked with stellar success culminating in his appointment to the nation's highest judicial body. With the loss of his seat on the bench, Campbell was forced to return to the bar—a move many would regard as a mortifying demotion. But Campbell persevered through all of his misfortune. His unremitting tenacity, his unimpeachable character, his devotion to hard work, and his superior intellect allowed him to rebuild his career, his stature, his self-respect, and his once ample income.

Aside from assuring his family's financial security and happiness, Campbell focused on his legal career and, to a lesser extent, on the politics of postwar America. It has been claimed that Campbell exhibited absolutely no interest in political affairs during the postbellum period.[1] This is incorrect. Though Campbell did not hold elective office, he was politically active and acutely interested in dismantling federal policies aimed at "reconstructing" the southern states. During his negotiations with Lincoln in April 1865, Campbell's objective had been to convince the president that military rule in the defeated southern states would be both unwise and counterproductive. For the first year after the war, it appeared that civil state governments would be returned to their prewar status as Campbell wished. Much to his dismay, however, Congress assumed control over reconstruction policies and instituted revolutionary changes in southern politics and society. To Campbell, congressional Reconstruction wrought societal chaos, political disorder, and internecine racial turmoil on an unprecedented scale. He became a rather active critic of Reconstruction and a person who continually assailed what he perceived as the disastrous results of social revolution. Earlier, though, because of allegations in April and May 1865 that officials within the Confederate government had somehow been involved in Lincoln's assassination, Campbell was arrested in late May and detained for the next five months. He suffered tremendous anguish during these months, not from any concerns for himself, but from a genuine desire to rejoin his family and provide for their welfare.

At ten o'clock on the night of 22 May 1865, Campbell and Anne were at home in Richmond when armed soldiers appeared at their front door, placed iron restraints on Campbell's hands and feet, and pulled him off into the darkness without the least explanation as to why he was under arrest. Needless to say, Anne was panic stricken. He was immediately confined on board the U.S.S. *Mosswood*, a steamer in the James River. For the next week Campbell remained on the boat unaware of the reasons for his arrest, but he assumed that it had something to do with his services to the Confederacy. He drafted a request for amnesty and sent it to President Johnson, but he could not be certain that it reached the president or that Johnson read it. Not knowing why he had been arrested, and quite unsure of his fate, Campbell had good reason for concern. Nevertheless, he implored his wife not to worry on his behalf. On the twenty-ninth, Campbell wrote Anne that he experienced no discomfort and was allowed to walk on the banks of the James for about two hours each day. Although he had no idea of its meaning, there were reports that his arrest was due to one specific letter found among those captured by the United States Army and pertaining to the Confederate government.[2]

Apparently, a Lieutenant W. Alston had sent a letter to Jefferson Davis in November 1864 in which he offered "to rid my country of some of her deadliest enemies, by striking at the very hearts [*sic*] blood of those who seek to enchain her in slavery." Little is known about Alston except that his father, William J. Alston, a state representative from Alabama's Fifth Congressional District, had been acquainted with Campbell prior to the war. The most damning part of the letter for Campbell was the endorsement on its reverse side. The letter was first handled by Davis's personal secretary, Burton H. Harrison, who endorsed it and sent it to the War Department. Upon its arrival at Campbell's desk, he wrote "AG [Adjutant General], For Attention, By Order, J. A. Campbell" on the back of the letter and forwarded it to the adjutant general's office. In light of the many conspiracy theories then prevalent and the chaotic investigation concerning Lincoln's assassination, federal officials thought it wise to arrest members of the Confederate government and hold them until the letter—with its supposed offer to assassinate Lincoln—could be fully investigated.[3]

At the end of May, however, Campbell neither remembered the letter nor recalled William Alston's son in Alabama. "I can hardly realize," he wrote, "that my detention is owing to the order in the Austin [*sic*] letter," which like many similar letters received was "wild, chimerical, foolish. [W]icked propositions are constantly made in a time of high excitement and popular exasperation."[4] Although the Alston letter was endorsed by Campbell "For Attention," no action was taken. He asked Anne to write Secretary of War Stanton and explain that all letters received by the Confederate War Department had been endorsed in much the same manner regardless of their contents. Anne complied with Campbell's request, and in July she traveled to Washington and met personally with Stanton. She pleaded for her husband's release, but the secretary curtly explained that he could not oblige her at that time.

Campbell told Anne that she should bring the children to see him on the steamer. "I think visitations," he wrote, "should have the effect upon the children to review their own habits and lives and to induce them to establish solid habits, so as to make efforts and to sustain adverse fortune." He also advised Anne to prepare for difficult times ahead. As for the children, Campbell wrote, "It is not probable that they will ever see as favorable circumstances as they did previously to this war and that they will be required to curtail their indulgences and wishes. The present is a time when firm resolutions may be taken and a new life commenced."[5] Admirably, despite his incarceration and the anxiety of not knowing why he was being held or for how long his detention would last, Campbell thought of his family first and wanted his children to learn from his misfortune. Of all the extant documents concerning Campbell's life, this letter perhaps best illustrates his strength, his character, and his genuine devotion to family. "I have no other desire," he wrote, "than that of availing myself for [the children's] welfare."[6]

It is interesting that in 1865 Campbell continued to refer to his offspring as "children." After all, Henrietta, the eldest, became thirty-three that year, and she had been married to Colonel Lay since before the war. The youngest daughter, Clara, turned eighteen in January 1865, and had certainly surpassed childhood. Yet Campbell always called them children—clearly illustrating his nurturing but rather repressive paternalism. Moreover, Campbell's references to "the children" reflects the commonly held perception throughout the nineteenth century that women were emotionally frail and lingered in perpetual childhood. While Campbell remained detained, he constantly worried about his daughters, believing that they would suffer without his guiding hand. As he explained to Anne, his only concern was with being released and with being allowed to reenter the legal profession so that he could once again provide for his family.[7]

On 30 May, Campbell was transported to Fort Pulaski, a federal installation on an island off the coast of Georgia. For the next several months he wrote numerous individuals, including Stanton, asking why he was being held. But he never completely learned the reasons for his arrest and prolonged imprisonment.[8] Campbell also sent a petition for amnesty under President Johnson's Amnesty Proclamation of 29 May in which he described his opposition to secession in 1861, his minimal role at the War Department, and his efforts to hasten an end to the war.[9] In the meantime, Anne continued writing to influential people pleading for her husband's release. Most significant, former Supreme Court justice Benjamin Curtis sent a letter to the president on 1 August, asking that his former colleague be released. "Though my intercourse with Judge Campbell ceased with my retirement from the Bench," Curtis wrote,

> I have retained a strong regard for him, founded on his purity and strength of character, his intellectual power, his great attainments, and his humane and genial nature.
>
> That such a man should in any way be connected with assassination is as near an impossibility, as the frailty of humanity will allow us to consider anything, respecting any man.
>
> If I had not an entire conviction that he was incapable of entertaining the thought of such a crime, and that his apparent connection with the subject, through the "Alston letter" has been satisfactorily explained to yourself, I should not address you.[10]

Through Anne's diligent and persistent efforts, and because of scores of letters similar to Curtis's, President Johnson finally ordered Campbell's release on 11 October 1865. Although he had lost considerable weight, Campbell still enjoyed good health, and he determined at once to devote his energies to professional pursuits. During Campbell's incarceration, Anne had moved to Baltimore to live with Henrietta and George Lay. Johnson's pardon, however, initially provided that Campbell must return to Alabama and remain in that state unless given permission to leave.[11]

After his release, Campbell saw firsthand the horrible devastation of the southern states. "I have been so long from this world," he wrote, "that things are strange to me. Men do not talk and project as they formerly did. Within four months there seems to be the revelation of a century." On the thirteenth, while passing through Savannah, he wrote Anne that he did "not expect a great deal of law business at present. There is a deadness about this city that fills me with concern. I think that it is but a type of what exists all over the South."[12] Campbell's first concern was seeing to the condition of his property in Mobile, particularly the cotton warehouse that he had purchased several years before the war. During the spring of 1865, a tremendous explosion in a downtown armory destroyed a large section of the city, including much of

Campbell's warehouse. After the explosion and fire, Eliza Witherspoon Goldthwaite, his sister-in-law in Mobile, reported, "The explosion blew down over one-hundred thousand dollars worth of [Campbell's] property." "I desire to save what there may be in the wreck and then to work for the future," Campbell wrote to Anne.[13]

He was no doubt pleased to learn upon his arrival that his warehouse was at least salvageable, but repairs to the structure consumed most of the next year and cost nearly $40,000. He had to borrow $25,000 of that sum almost at once, and the anxiety of incurring such hefty debt made lucrative employment more of a necessity than ever. Having received permission in early November from the War Department to relocate either to Baltimore or to New Orleans, and having determined that the legal business in Mobile would be years in recovering from the war, Campbell decided to move to New Orleans, where he believed his prospects for success were much sounder. Also, his son Duncan and daughter Mary Ellen had recently moved to the Crescent City, so his residence there placed him near family as well.[14]

By the first week of February, Campbell had arrived in New Orleans and had moved in with his daughter Mary Ellen and her husband, Anthony P. Mason. Campbell resented not being able to travel to Maryland and be with his wife. As he explained to Anne, "I am held as one of the selected hostages from the southern states and am treated as if I had been one of the leaders of the so-called rebellion. Yet I am in no condition to escape it, nor can I escape the consequences of it."[15]

For a brief period in 1867 most of Campbell's family was together in New Orleans. But Anne was unhappy; there was simply too much dismay and misery in the South, and the region hardly resembled the place in which she had spent most of her adult life. In early May, Campbell's son-in-law George Lay died suddenly, leaving his wife, Henrietta, inconsolable. Anne was so distraught by Lay's death that she wished to return to Baltimore as soon as possible. Campbell agreed to let Anne move back to Maryland, and though he wanted desperately to accompany her, he decided to remain in New Orleans.[16] Campbell and Anne spent much of the next decade living apart from one another.

On 15 May 1870 tragedy once again struck the family when Mary Ellen grew suddenly and violently ill. She likely contracted the yellow fever that ravaged New Orleans and Mobile on an almost annual basis, and she died later that same day. Campbell grieved considerably for his daughter, and he labored even more intensely, perhaps to recover more quickly from the loss. Mary Ellen's widower, Anthony Mason, decided that he could not look after the children alone, so they were sent to live in Baltimore with Anne and Henrietta. Campbell and Mason then rented rooms at one of the local boardinghouses in town. During the day Campbell labored intensely, while he and Mason passed most evenings relaxing and speaking of the children.

Campbell had much genuine affection for his daughters, but he rarely if ever displayed the same love and affection for his son, Duncan. Aside from Campbell's personal predilection to treat men with sternness and reservation, which precluded his developing a healthy relationship with Duncan, the younger Campbell's performance at the bar greatly disappointed his father. Duncan simply did not want to work as hard as was needed to win cases. In addition, he consumed considerable amounts of alcohol. After he arrived drunk at court on a number of occasions, Campbell decided that his professional relationship with his son had to end. In 1870 he asked Duncan to leave the firm. Campbell tried unsuccessfully to persuade his son to quit drinking, and with great sadness he watched Duncan sink ever deeper into alcoholism. In April 1871, he wrote his daughter Katherine, "Duncan, I suppose, has relapsed, and . . . his habits do not improve."

> Your mother thinks he looks ill, and I have a key to all of his disability as weakness. I do not know what to do with him, or about him. I have not been sanguine of success unless he understood surveillance. He has no power in himself to resist. When he goes where liquor can be had, he will drink. Nor has he any persistency of purpose. He surrenders himself to his habit, and supposes that he can conceal its power and effect. The whole land is filled with such cases. It seems to me that half the young men are enibriates [*sic*]. The difficulty of dealing with [Duncan] operates upon all my conclusions and plans. . . . Duncan's case is the most embarrassing one.[17]

As he was strictly temperate and believed drunkenness to be a sign of weakness, Campbell had little patience for Duncan and his alcoholism. Father and son became estranged after 1871 and rarely spoke. Duncan was certainly one of Campbell's greatest disappointments.

Campbell's life during this period was not without its bright spots. Some events were comical and reveal a lighter side to his normally stolid, businesslike demeanor. For instance, Eliza Goldthwaite's son planned to be married on New Year's Day 1869, and as the bride's father had earlier died, Campbell was asked to give the bride away. He was at first hesitant to accept this task, but he consented after much prodding by his daughter Anna. Campbell arrived at the Goldthwaite home on the day of the wedding to escort the bride to church. When she came out of the house, he was astonished to see that her wedding gown was fitted with an enormous cone that, once she ascended into the carriage, left little room for Campbell. He was thus forced to lie directly across the front seat "in as straight a line as possible [so as] not to incommode the vast cone that was formed with the bride."[18]

Campbell wrote that "two damsels, one ethiopian and one caucasian, [were in] attendance to gather and arrange the draping when we reached the church," where, he reported, they entered "like a cloud." As no one voiced their objection to the marriage, Campbell "resigned the bride to the groom" and went to the reception at Eliza Goldthwaite's home. Campbell wrote his daughter, "I performed so well [giving away the bride], that several young ladies asked me to give them away at once—but being penuriously affected I proclaimed that I did not intend to show any more lights before men that day."[19] At about one o'clock in the afternoon the doors and shutters were firmly closed and many of the candles were kindled so as to give the appearance of night. The guests then began dancing "like bacchantes" for what seemed several hours. Campbell must have truly enjoyed himself, for he lost all track of time. Believing it to be close to midnight, he informed Anna that he was going to retire for the night. She protested loudly that he could not leave the party so early; after all, it was but four o'clock in the afternoon. To his amazement he learned that Anna was right. But he went to bed shortly thereafter anyway.[20]

A few years later Campbell described an incident that happened during his stay at the boardinghouse in New Orleans. He awoke one morning feeling well and had just started to shave when a close friend named Arthur Pendleton burst into the room and announced that a thief had stolen his best pair of shoes. Pendleton was even more upset because, he explained, the thief could have stolen any one of a dozen pairs but had made off with Pendleton's finest shoes, which had been mail ordered from New York City. Campbell then checked on the floor of his room and discovered that his shoes were missing as well. "But they were not my fine shoes—they were shoes that hurt my feet and that I wore from the economical reason[s] of [Benjamin] Franklin—to get the full value of the clothes you have."[21]

Pendleton left the room quite perturbed over his friend's obvious lack of concern for his fine New York shoes. Campbell wrote Katherine that after shaving that morning, he decided to take a bath, and when he had finished bathing he went to get dressed. "But when I came to decorate myself with dress," he explained, "my shirt was gone; so were my under garments; so were my pantaloons; so was my vest; so was my coat; so was my dressing gown; so was my overcoat; my wardrobe was pillaged." The thief had stolen every stitch of Campbell's clothing. "I have read poetry of a woman who had nothing to wear," he lamented, "but no poet has ever had the imagination to depict the misery of a *man* who had nothing to wear. *There* is a woe, greater than woes. . . . Mr. Pendleton is in a state of delight. He lost his shoes awhile ago and I laughed and offered him something to wear. I have lost all my glory."[22] Considering the ample income which he generated from his thriving law practice, Campbell no doubt replaced his clothes that morning and suffered no further embarrassments.

Aside from his family's safety and security, which to Campbell were paramount above all other concerns, his law practice in the Crescent City consumed nearly all of his time. Politics, as will be shown, also interested Campbell considerably. But he had no intention of seeking political office. As he had explained to Anne in May 1865, the experience of being arrested and dragged off into the night had "quite relieved me from any latent desire to mingle in public affairs."[23] Even if Campbell had harbored such ambitions, the "iron-clad test oath," passed during the war and requiring any officeholder to swear that he had never supported the rebellion, clearly excluded Campbell from holding public office. In 1865, the test oath was extended to lawyers who had served the Confederate government in various capacities, and it prevented them from arguing cases in federal courts.[24] With the ratification of the Fourteenth Amendment in 1868, any person who had previously taken an oath of office for an elected or an appointed position but who had "engaged in insurrection or rebellion" against the United States was specifically forbidden to hold any federal or state office. The amendment, however, provided that the exclusion could be countermanded by a two-thirds vote in both houses of Congress.

As Campbell's political ambitions had evaporated after 1842 when he never again ran for public office, this section of the Fourteenth Amendment had little direct bearing on his life. He wrote in 1883 with noteworthy smugness, "This disability [ineligibility to hold office] has not been removed; nor have I asked for the removal. This was my deliberate purpose and has been adhered to without deviation."[25] Of course, Campbell's lack of interest in holding public office neither diminished his concern with political affairs nor his tendency to be politically involved. Within two years of his arrival in New Orleans, Campbell's perceptions of the turbulent political world that characterized postwar Louisiana prompted him to assail what he perceived as the root cause of the state's internal strife: congressional Reconstruction.

A complete history of how the federal government dealt with the defeated southern states is well beyond the scope of this study. Generally speaking, though, any account of the Reconstruction era should underscore the problems inherent in reconstituting a nation that had been rent in half and had been nearly destroyed through four years of unparalleled warfare. Great questions concerning the South created divisions within the federal government that pitted persons (such as President Andrew Johnson) who sought lenient Reconstruction with little or no societal changes against those (such as Pennsylvania representative Thaddeus Stevens and Massachusetts senator Charles Sumner) whose purpose was to effect a social revolution so as to protect the civil rights of blacks forever from recalcitrant former Confederates. Sumner harbored intense hatred for those persons who had served the Confederacy, particularly those from within the Richmond government. During a meeting he held with President Johnson the day following Lincoln's death, Sumner suggested that "none of the old traitors should be allowed to take part in establishing new governments." He also recommended that laws be passed "to

frighten out of the country as many [ex-Confederate officials] as possible."
And in this regard, he continued, "we should begin with Campbell and
Hunter." The senator left the president that day confident that Johnson agreed
with his sentiments and was "discreet, properly reserved, but firm and determined."[26]

If Sumner originally believed that he and President Johnson were of one
mind regarding Reconstruction, he was soon disappointed. The executive
branch proscribed extraordinarily lenient Reconstruction policies during the
first year after the war. During this period, many former Confederate officers
returned to their respective home states and promptly resumed the political
positions that they had held prior to the war. Compounding concern among
many northerners were Black Codes adopted by southern legislatures that reduced former slaves to peonage status. To many congressional Republicans,
Johnson's Reconstruction policies threatened to reverse all of the gains that
had resulted from the war. The nation seemed headed for the political and
social status quo ante bellum.[27]

The schism in the federal government led in early 1866 to congressional
Reconstruction. Johnson's policies were replaced by far more radical measures
designed to punish the South for the Civil War and to usher in a social revolution to protect blacks' political and civil rights. The Civil Rights Act, passed
by Congress in March of that year and providing citizenship rights to all persons born in the United States, was vetoed by the president. That Johnson had
lost nearly all political clout was evident when his veto was promptly overrid-
den in April. From that point on, Congress assumed control over Reconstruction. In the spring of the following year, congressional Republicans enacted the
Military Reconstruction Act, establishing military control over a reconstituted
South divided into military districts.[28]

The Fifth Military District, comprising Louisiana and Texas, was overseen
by Union general Philip Sheridan, who had been one of Grant's most capable
commanders. Sheridan genuinely sympathized with the former slaves, and he
immediately established procedures to ensure that blacks were registered to
vote and that they would participate in the political process. Sheridan also
oversaw elections in September 1867 for a constitutional convention. The result was that over one-half of the delegates elected were black. Most of these
individuals, who had been considered inviolate property less than a decade earlier, would now be largely responsible for drafting a new state constitution.
Congressional Reconstruction was indeed revolutionary and greatly elevated
the political power within the black community—at least temporarily.[29]

The new constitution ushered in substantial social and political changes in
Louisiana. Opposition to the Civil Rights Act and to the constitutional convention galvanized Democrats—who preferred the term, Conservatives—into
a staunchly antiblack, anti-Reconstruction party filled mostly by disenchanted

former Confederates, who believed that the Republicans were "Africanizing" their state. The Conservatives were further concerned by the rise to prominence of Republican carpetbagger Henry Clay Warmoth, a one-time Union colonel serving on John McClernand's staff who was practicing law in New Orleans at war's end. Warmoth can certainly be ranked among those most radical of Republicans who wished to orchestrate a social revolution. His advocacy of black suffrage and his speeches in favor of radical reconstruction made Warmoth an especially hated target for Conservative bluster. According to his enemies, Warmoth could not refrain from political demagoguery to enlist the support of blacks. When he was elected governor later that year, his opponents claimed that Warmoth created a virtual dictatorship in which he controlled the voter registration and election machinery and thereby ensured solid Republican control over state politics. Conservatives also accused Warmoth of gross abuse of office, of unfathomable corruption, and of organizing a system of spoilation that reduced the state "'to unexampled poverty.'"[30]

Such were the most significant political developments in Louisiana during the first two years of Campbell's residence there. His personal letters indicate that he was by no means apathetic about Republican rule; as he explained to Anne in many letters, in his opinion the political, social, and economic revolution inaugurated in Louisiana would lead to increased violence and bloodshed. Campbell also conjectured that the political climate in Louisiana was such that there was little hope for harmonious relations between the races. "Public, as well as private matters in [Louisiana] are in a chaotic state," he wrote.[31]

The Civil Rights Act of 1866 had a profound impact in Louisiana where animosity and resentment toward blacks increased throughout the spring and summer. On 30 July, when a special convention was to be held to revise the state constitution and to initiate reforms in compliance with the Civil Rights Act, whites and blacks rioted outside the meeting hall. Evidently, scores of white thugs had decided to create a disturbance and, according to current scholarship, were assisted in their efforts by the New Orleans police. When the firing began, blacks scrambled into the meeting hall. A two-hour fire fight ensued after the police and the white mob battered open the doors and entered the hall firing at random. The massacre soon spread into the streets, where scenes of terrifying brutality and outright murder were played out for the next three hours. Finally, at about three o'clock that afternoon, federal troops arrived in sufficient numbers to disperse the rioters.[32]

Though his daughters pleaded with him to move the family to New Orleans so that they could be together, this riot further convinced Campbell that the city was simply too dangerous for them. "I do not feel disposed to submit [my daughters] to the experiences [that] they will have here," he explained to his sister-in-law Eliza Goldthwaite. As for the violence and bloodshed during the riot, Campbell seemed to have expected nothing else. "The riots that occurred," he stated, "[are] only what must continuously arise" as long as the radicals continued to gain political power. Campbell later complained that, with the carpetbaggers cajoling blacks into voting for them, "the Yankees have discovered a weak point in our society. . . . I do not see when we may look for peace from their machinations." In May of the following year he complained to his daughter Katherine, "The political complexion of affairs, is such that I have no desire to settle here permanently." But he continued that there was no other place "that I can do so well professionally, and there is no place that I am willing to settle as a professional man but here. I am bound to the Southern States in this calamity and I do not feel like abandoning them."[33]

Despite the mounting civil and political discord in Louisiana, therefore, Campbell decided to remain in New Orleans. See photo 3. But he was unquestionably disturbed by political developments and by the freedmen's political power. "Darkness is the fashionable color in these regions," he explained to his wife in 1868. Campbell later wrote Katherine that white residents of New Orleans "have ascertained that they have been plundered, but they do not know how to find a remedy." "We have the Africans in place all about us," he lamented. "[T]hey are jurors, post office clerks, [and] customhouse officers, and day-by-day they barter away their obligations and duties." "The carpetbaggers," he noted, "are installed in all offices and corruption is the rule. There is nothing to be accomplished without paying some officer for some [service]."[34]

In June 1871 Campbell addressed a letter to his former Supreme Court colleague Nathan Clifford in which he described his perceptions of politics under Republican rule. "The Southern communities," he wrote,

> will be a desolation until there is a thorough change of affairs in all the departments of the government. There is now no responsibility—and we are fast losing all of our ancient notions of what is becoming and fit in administration. The public are tolerant of corruption, maladministration, partiality in courts, worthlessness in juries, and [they] regard government only as a means of exploitation. Indifference to anything wrong, is the common Sentiment. Hope is disappearing from the motives to exertion.
>
> Discontent, dissatisfaction, murmurings, complaints, even insurrection would be better than the insensibility that seems to prevail.[35]

Obviously convinced that Louisiana's Republican-controlled government was shamelessly corrupt, Campbell was even more distressed over the gubernatorial election of 1872. This election was to Campbell the epitome of the incessant wickedness and societal ills in Louisiana that had prevailed since mid-1866.

During Henry Clay Warmoth's tenure as governor, Republican control

Campbell about 1875 in New Orleans. (From Photo File, Box 7, Campbell Portraits, Alabama Department of Archives and History, Montgomery, Alabama.)

over state politics was nearly absolute. One legacy of the Warmoth administration was the governor's creation of and control over the Returning Board, a body of election officials appointed by the governor whose task was to tabulate election returns from each parish. Through Warmoth's influence, the Returning Board had proved most helpful in maintaining Republican control over the state's government; when these individuals were unhappy with the returns, they simply altered them to ensure that members of their party were elected. Until 1871 at least, the Republicans maintained firm control over Louisiana politics. Yet, during that year a feud erupted between Warmoth and President Grant over the appointment of James F. Casey to be collector of customs in New Orleans. Casey and Warmoth had never liked one another, but as the former was the president's brother-in-law, his appointment was nearly assured. The ensuing struggle between Warmoth and what became known as the "Custom House Ring" created deep divisions within the Republican party that eventually undermined its political base. Leadership within the anti-Warmoth faction centered on Casey and the politically powerful and ambitious Senator William Pitt Kellogg. During the election of 1872, this schism manifested itself in an alliance of the Warmoth faction, the moderate Republicans, and the Conservatives that entered the contest as the "Fusion" ticket and placed John McEnery of Ouachita Parish in contention for governor. The custom house faction, numerically weaker than their opponents, ran Kellogg for the state's executive position.[36]

The participation of the Fusionists in 1872 portended serious difficulties for the Kellogg Republicans. Early returns showed that Kellogg was to be defeated, yet these returns were by no means conclusive. Due to political machinations and maneuvers by Warmoth—who wanted to assure Kellogg's defeat—the board underwent extensive personnel changes soon after the election. The result was that by early December two boards emerged, one proclaiming victory for Kellogg and the other maintaining that McEnery had won. Meanwhile, Kellogg had filed suit in federal court to force the Fusion Returning Board to surrender its returns to him and his board. The Kellogg faction then resorted to using federal authority to oust McEnery and the Fusionists.[37]

On 3 December Kellogg received a wire from United States Attorney General George H. Williams instructing him to enforce any mandates that were handed down from federal Circuit Judge Edward H. Durell—an old, infirm, and alcoholic judge who was most likely instructed by the Grant administration to secure Kellogg's victory. On 5 December, Durell issued an order to federal marshal Stephen B. Packard—a prominent member of the Kellogg faction—to prevent the Fusionist government from assembling. This order was carried out the following day, but Warmoth and the Fusionists refused to back down, and a stalemate ensued.

Meanwhile, the Kellogg contingent that held control of the legislature inaugurated impeachment proceedings against Governor Warmoth, whose term was not due to expire until mid-January. Under the Constitution of 1868, Warmoth was immediately suspended from office pending the outcome of the impeachment. P. B. S. Pinchback, an influential black politician allied with the Kellogg faction and the current president pro tem of the senate, became interim governor. A few days later Pinchback received a message from Attorney General Williams stating that the Grant administration had recognized him as the state's lawful chief executive. In effect, therefore, when Kellogg took the oath of office as governor on 14 January, his administration had already been tacitly recognized by the federal government. A few hours later, despite Grant's support for the Kellogg regime, McEnery was sworn into the same office. For the next several months Louisianans lived under two separate state governments, each claiming legitimacy.[38]

The shameful political developments in the state—coupled with sporadic violent eruptions between competing factions—were an outright embarrassment to many Louisianans. Moreover, opponents of congressional Reconstruction pointed to events in Louisiana as ample evidence that national policies affecting the South did nothing other than spawn corruption, instability, and violence. Campbell had earlier expressed great disdain for congressional Reconstruction propped up by military occupation. He had all but predicted the tumultuous events in Louisiana when he spoke with Lincoln in Richmond at the end of the war, and his efforts during that period concentrated on ensuring that martial law would not be imposed on the South. Campbell was not averse to social change, but he was certainly no advocate of the social revolution that was attempted in the South under the auspices of congressional Reconstruction. Since his arrival in New Orleans in early 1866, Campbell had refrained from any public denunciation of Reconstruction and of state politics. But with the fraudulent election of 1872, he could no longer remain idle while—in his judgment at least—the state degenerated into political and social chaos.

On 12 December 1872, a "Committee of Two Hundred Citizens" was organized in New Orleans for the purpose of exposing and denouncing the political fraud that had characterized the recent elections.[39] The two individuals who were most instrumental in the formation of this committee were Thomas A. Adams, a leading Democrat, and Campbell, whose name appears first among those persons selected as the group's five-man "executive committee." Although President Grant had previously recognized the Pinchback government and had in his opinion settled the disputed state election, Campbell, Adams, and forty-two other committee members traveled to Washington in mid-December hoping to instigate formal congressional investigations into the contested election.

Upon their arrival, the committee drafted *An Address of Citizens of Louisiana to the People of the United States* and arranged for this document to be printed and circulated by a Washington publishing company. Clearly written in concise, lawyerlike language, and looking much like a lawyer's court brief, the *Address,* if not entirely penned by Campbell, was most assuredly shaped by him. According to this document, these citizens had come to the capitol "to lay the facts upon the several departments of the [federal] government, and to solicit their aid in repairing the gross wrong which has been done." The committee also hoped to restore "to the people [of Louisiana] the right of self-government which had been wrested from them by the most patent usurpation."[40]

Claiming purely nonpartisan motives, the committee traced the fraudulent events of the Louisiana elections and concluded that "the men who have been foisted into the offices of the State have been not merely irregularly and unlawfully installed, but were not elected by the people, and were not and are not the choice of the majority of the voting population of Louisiana." The committee expressed profound dissatisfaction that Judge Durell had assumed authority to become involved in this affair. After all, the parties to the suit filed by Kellogg were citizens of Louisiana, and the federal court therefore had no jurisdiction in the case whatsoever. "The Circuit Court of the United States is a court of limited jurisdiction," the committee asserted, "and without authority to entertain civil suits between citizens of the same state."[41] Their argument thereby centered on what they perceived as an unlawful, unconstitutional act on the part of the federal court that had preempted state authority.

Campbell and the committee asserted, "We affirm, without fear of contradiction" that Durell's intervention in the recent Louisiana elections was "the most high-handed usurpation of jurisdiction and authority of which the annals of jurisprudence afford any example." They further claimed that prior to Durell's order the election had been legitimately decided, and that the early election returns reflected the will of the people who for too long had suffered under mischievous government officials. As an indictment against Governor Warmoth in particular but also against congressional Reconstruction in general, the *Address* claimed:

> [D]uring the last four years, there has not been good government in Louisiana. There has been extravagance, prodigality, dishonesty, and waste in the public expenditures. The public debt has been enormously increased, with but little corresponding benefit. The credit of the state has been given to speculating corporations, for personal aims. The taxes on property have assumed such proportions that they might appropriately be called rents paid by the proprietors to the State for its occupation and use. . . . The laws to control elections, corporations, and public institutions stimulate these excesses of office-holders, and the consequence is universal depression and discontent.[42]

The election, according to the *Address,* had promised to reverse many of the social and economic ills plaguing Louisiana—at least until the Kellogg Republicans stole the election in a partnership with a federal judge who took intrusive and unlawful action.

The committee members returned to Louisiana just a few days before both political factions were sworn into office on 14 January. On 22 March, the executive committee issued a report to the Committee of Two Hundred.[43] As with the *Address*, there is little doubt that Campbell was instrumental in preparing this document. The members of the executive committee stated that their time in Washington had been productive and that they had been permitted to express the "discontent, pressures, and grievances under which the people of the State were suffering from the unconstitutional and revolutionary action of a portion of the federal authorities." They reiterated earlier statements that Judge Durell's actions had been unconstitutional and beyond federal jurisdiction. Included also were copies of telegraphs sent from Attorney General Williams's office to Marshall Packard revealing that the Grant administration had played no passive role in the governor's race and had in fact instructed Durell on actions to ensure Kellogg's victory. "But we may say," asserted the report's authors,

> that the profound humility of the President of the United States and of his Attorney General Williams, in accepting the decree and mandate of this Circuit Court as entirely infallible, and too sacred to be the subject of any inquiry, and that the secular force of the nation should be spontaneously volunteered to enforce whatsoever mandate or order it might procreate, is, of the scenes in what the committee of the Senate have termed, "the Comedy of Errors and of Frauds" of Federal interference in the domestic affairs of the State of Louisiana.[44]

The administration's connivance, according to the report, unconstitutionally usurped authority reserved specifically for states. "[T]he employment of the army . . . to enforce mandates which exceed the power and jurisdiction of any Court of the United States," the author noted, "must be regarded by every patriot as a great national calamity." And what had this usurpation of state authority wrought? According to the executive committee, "The State of Louisiana may now be likened to a ship which has now been under the command of a reckless and dissolute master, with turbulent, riotous and wasteful mates, and a crew disorderly." After seven years of congressional Reconstruction, federal officials and carpetbaggers in Louisiana were "wrangling and mutinous." The state's leaders "have had quarrels, contentions, and tumults which have ended in revolt, the marooning of the master and some of the mates, the seizure and casting away of the ship, and the pillage of the wreck by the crew and wreckers from the neighboring coast, to the ruin of the owners of the ship, the cargo, and the underwriters." The report, therefore, was much more than an expression of grievances concerning the recent gubernatorial election. It was a wholesale indictment of Reconstruction as ruinous and productive of unprecedented levels of civil discord.[45]

The committee concluded with a series of recommendations to alleviate the crisis. First among these was an emphatic statement that no support or respect should be afforded to the Kellogg government. It was an unlawful assembly that did not deserve recognition by Louisianans. The committee also recommended that a Committee of Seventy be established to compile additional testimony of the "mal-administration under which the State groans from the Federal officers of this State, and of the State, whereby property has been rendered insecure, its value diminished, confidence destroyed, and persons impoverished and oppressed." Their grievances should be compiled and submitted to each state legislature, all persons and groups seeking judicial and administrative reforms in the state government should be encouraged to join them, and reforms to promote "economy, retrenchment, and official responsibility" should be actively pursued by all Louisianans. Last, the committee offered suggestions on the treatment of freedmen. "We recommend that the colored population of this State be protected, encouraged, assisted, and what is needed for their improvement, guidance, and progress, be assured; and that this be a standing principle of act and counsel in the dealings towards them."[46]

The controversy in Louisiana surrounding the 1872 gubernatorial election continued despite Grant's recognition of the Pinchback and Kellogg administrations. As of spring 1873, Louisiana Democrats "writhed in impotent rage" because Republicans remained in power.[47] More important, the Kellogg regime, coupled with local carpetbagger governments throughout the state, created increasing animosity among Louisiana whites, who perceived that their control over the state had vanished. Fears of social revolution among many whites culminated in the formation of the White League, which through violence and intimidation undermined support for the Republicans and eventually led to a resurgent Conservative party fully intent on ousting the Radicals and restoring white control over Louisiana. The political turmoil and social upheaval also generated considerable racially based violence clearly reflecting white Louisianans' disdain for Reconstruction. The most sickening example of this violence occurred in Colfax, where armed whites began a reign of terror on 5 April 1873 that ended with 105 blacks brutally murdered. Such events had a paralyzing impact on Republican rule as many southern blacks—in the interest of personal safety—refrained from political activity altogether.[48]

Reconstruction ended in Louisiana in 1877. But the Republicans' political base had long since evaporated as more and more blacks became too intimidated to vote. There is absolutely no evidence that Campbell was in any way connected either with the White League or with the Knights of the White Camelia—white supremacist groups in Louisiana similar to the Ku Klux Klan. There is also nothing to indicate that he sanctioned their violence or their intimidation tactics. That is not to say that he relished Republican rule and wished it to continue. On the contrary, when Reconstruction ended in Louisiana, Campbell expressed utmost satisfaction that the state had finally broken the yoke of federal control.[49]

Violent events in Louisiana such as the Colfax Massacre and reports of unparalleled corruption within Republican regimes reverberated throughout the nation. Coupled with the public's general disenchantment with the corrupt Grant administration, the Republicans' chances for an 1876 presidential victory appeared especially bleak. The campaign unveiled few differences between the parties on national policies; both sides, for instance, agreed that it was time to end congressional Reconstruction. Two little-known nondescripts were nominated by the national conventions: Rutherford B. Hayes for the Republicans, a locally popular Ohioan whose chief virtue was that he offended neither Radicals nor the reformist wing, and Democrat Samuel J. Tilden, a wealthy corporate lawyer and a former governor of New York.[50]

There was considerable dissension within the national Republican party. In the southern states many former members had since fled to the Conservatives, swelling their numbers and creating high hopes for the upcoming presidential contest. On election day, 7 November 1876, preliminary reports of the popular vote could not have been rosier for Democrats as Tilden enjoyed a 250,000-vote advantage. The New Yorker was similarly well placed in the electoral college, having received 184 votes to Hayes's 165 votes. Tilden's electoral count fell 1 vote short of the required majority, though. During the next week canvassing reports indicated that the combined 19 votes from Louisiana, Florida, and South Carolina were by no means conclusive, as each of those states had rival returning boards. As there was no clear winner in the presidential contest, therefore, the election had to be decided by Congress, which was hopelessly divided between a Democrat-controlled House and a Republican Senate. After nearly two months of partisan bickering, Congress created a fifteen-member Electoral Commission comprised of five representatives, five senators, and five Supreme Court justices whose decision regarding the disputed election would be final.[51]

Meanwhile, the Republican-controlled Returning Board in Louisiana canvassed the votes during several days of open hearings—and a few days of secret deliberations. Finally, on 5 December the board issued its election report, which gave all eight of the state's electoral votes to Hayes. For the board to reach this conclusion, it had to throw out the votes from sixty-nine polling places that had registered over 13,000 votes for Tilden but fewer than 2,500 for Hayes. As one historian writes, "Thus was an apparent Democratic majority converted into a Republican majority."[52] The board also decided that all Republican candidates for the state's elected offices had won a majority of votes and were entitled to be sworn into office.

Louisiana Democrats were livid with the Returning Board's report. As in 1873, by mid-January the state was encumbered with two governors, two legislatures, and two sets of presidential electors. This stalemate would not be settled until the Electoral Commission in Washington settled the presidential dispute. The party that was deemed the victor in the national race would be considered victorious in Louisiana, and citizens of that state—and of the entire country—eagerly awaited the commission's final report. Campbell was likewise distressed over the election results, and as he ardently supported the Democrat Tilden, he sought to interject his thoughts on the presidential crisis and the enormity of the task that awaited the Electoral Commission.

One member of the commission was Senator Thomas F. Bayard, a Democrat from Delaware who had opposed secession and had remained loyal to the Union. At war's end, though, Bayard displayed no vindictiveness toward the defeated states. In fact, during Bayard's early career in the Senate, he was an outspoken champion of the southern states who wholeheartedly rejected congressional Reconstruction.[53] Soon after Campbell learned that Bayard had been named to the Electoral Commission, he drafted a lengthy letter to the Delaware senator reminding him that the Constitution included strict guidelines that had to be followed in the event of a disputed presidential contest. Campbell stated that the recent elections had "startled the people of this land, and most of us are waiting to discover the result with anxiety and concern."[54] He then proceeded to lecture Bayard on the intricate debates concerning the electoral college when the Constitution was being drafted. Campbell explained that there were prolonged discussions involving what to do in the event that no person received a majority vote in the college and that this issue created tremendous discord among the delegates.

Campbell complained in his letter to Bayard that the current arrangement with the Electoral Commission was unconstitutional and clearly beyond the framers' intent. After several days' debate, he wrote, the framers had decided that the House of Representatives was to choose the president. What the framers had not perceived, however, was the "predominance of cabal, intrigue, circumvention, violence, [and] unrestrained and unbridled ambition" that had become so much a part of national politics. Campbell continued that corrupt political parties, absurdly partisan politicians, and mean-spirited radicals had succeeded in disrupting the nation's election process, and the current crisis over the presidency was no better example that the nation was heading toward political disaster unless sober, magnanimous, and reflective statesmen strictly adhered to the Constitution's dictates.

Throughout this letter Campbell observed that the Constitution did not include a provision allowing Supreme Court justices to assist in rectifying disputed presidential elections. Campbell counseled that the decision over who should be the next president rested firmly with the House of Representatives and not with some extraconstitutionally selected body incorporating representatives from the three branches. He complained that the Republicans could in no measure be trusted to follow the Constitution; after all, it had been the members of that party who had converted "the army into a body of Janizaries to enforce the will of the chiefs of the party." In Campbell's opinion, the Republican party cared less for the Constitution than for punishing the South. "I have brought to your notice," Campbell explained to Bayard, "the records of the wisdom of the fathers of the Constitution. In that wisdom I have sought a guide for the Government and the people. In the present crisis the people and the States demand of their Congressional representatives that the Constitution be maintained inviolate."[55] The Electoral Commission, which came formally into being with a law signed by President Grant on 29 January 1877, was to Campbell a dangerous experiment that could imperil free government.

Despite Campbell's appeals that the final decision over the presidency should rest with the Democrat-controlled House—which, of course, would select Tilden over Hayes—his concern that the Constitution be strictly upheld evidently had little impact on those politicians dealing with the crisis. The Electoral Commission convened its first session on 31 January in the Supreme Court's chambers, elected its officers, and began scheduling hearings over the disputed returns from Louisiana, Florida, and South Carolina. There was an impressive array of professional counsel for both Tilden and Hayes: William M. Evarts, one of the most gifted attorneys in the country, lent considerable weight to the Republicans. The Democrats likewise employed lawyers of appreciable talent—former secretary of state Jeremiah S. Black, former postmaster general Montgomery Blair, and former Supreme Court justice John Archibald Campbell. Though Campbell was ardently opposed to the commission and its role in deciding the presidential contest, he was nonetheless quite willing to appear before that body and argue on the Democrat's behalf.[56]

Hearings on Florida's disputed count began on 2 February, and the outcome of these deliberations determined how the commission would proceed on the other two state returns. The most significant issue was whether Congress had the constitutional authority to inspect votes counted and reported by state returning boards. In that regard, the commission's principal concern dealt with states' rights and whether the Constitution afforded the federal government authority to interfere with state election processes. On 8 February, by a partisan vote of 8 to 7, the commission decided that Congress had no authority to investigate the legitimacy of Florida's returns. A similar vote reached two days later gave Florida's electoral votes to Hayes. The commission next prepared for hearings on Louisiana's electoral votes, the legitimacy of both returning boards, and, once again, whether Congress possessed authority to inquire into how that state chose its electors.[57]

The commission reconvened at 10:00 A.M. on 15 February. William Evarts delivered a twenty-minute oration, which asserted that Congress could not investigate state returns without seriously unconstitutionally infringing state sovereignty. "The Constitution has undertaken," Evarts noted, "to determine that the State shall have the power to appoint electors as its legislature may direct, and no authority or argument can disparage or overreach that right of the State. That right is in the State." Of genuine interest and of notable irony, Evarts then began a strong defense of Campbell's original sovereignty argument. With the right to choose its electors in any manner prescribed by its legislature, Evarts declared, "The State of Louisiana stands in this behalf as one of the original thirteen States stood. Whatever was the right of one of the original thirteen States in the election of Washington, is the right of Louisiana now in the election of a President."[58] Evart's argument much resembled one that Campbell had delivered many times throughout his career. The most recent instance was in 1872 during the Louisiana gubernatorial election when he insisted that the federal government—through the actions of a circuit court judge—could in no manner interfere in state elections.

On this occasion, though, Campbell assumed the extreme opposite position and presented a clear and logical defense of federal jurisdiction over state elections to choose presidential electors. As one historian observed, Campbell's presentation that day was characterized by "high-toned nationalism."[59] Campbell alerted the commission that he would temporarily disregard his prepared remarks and address the states' rights issue raised by Evarts, because "I differ so fundamentally with the gentleman who preceded me upon the principle of the generative process by which the electors of President and Vice-President came into the Constitution."[60] Campbell asserted that the process of electing a president in no way originated "in any State constitution . . . or from any reserved fund or power belonging to the State." The power to name electors, he continued, originated exclusively from the people and was incorporated into the Constitution with little deference for state authority. "I do not assert," Campbell stated,

> that the government of the United States came into being only with this Constitution, or that the United States themselves came into being by the ratification of this Constitution. The Constitution came into being by the ratification and acceptance of the States; but if the States had rejected this Constitution, there would still have been a United States. The United States came into existence with the Declaration of Independence. . . . During the period of the Confederation, they were still the United States under confederate articles; but the people of the United States constituted some sort of a Union, a historical Union, stronger than the Union formed by the confederate compact; and so, when they sent delegates to Philadelphia who formed and organized the articles which compose the Federal Constitution, it was a proposition to the States to accept those articles and to form a Union, not for the first time, but, as declared in the very face of the Constitution itself, "a more perfect Union."[61]

Campbell maintained the foundation of his original sovereignty doctrine by insisting that sovereignty rested entirely with the people. He reminded the commission that "We, the People" sanctioned the drafting of the Constitution.

More important, where the Constitution provided that " 'each state shall appoint electors,' " Campbell concluded that "each state is permitted to appoint, each state is charged to appoint, each state is required to appoint, [and] each state is commanded to appoint." In this regard, Campbell argued that the words "shall" and "charged" and "required" were synonymous and should be viewed as part of the federal government's orders to the state governments: they must appoint electors.

If the federal government had authority to require that each state designate electors, Campbell argued, it likewise had the power to investigate the manner in which that process was undertaken. "Do the States come before you in the shape of sovereigns, claiming of you by any title superior to that of the Constitution that their votes shall be counted?" Campbell asked. "Do they come here and tell your President of the Senate, 'lay these votes before these Houses and tell that Senate and tell that House of Representatives to count them at the peril of our displeasure?' " Certainly not, Campbell stated. He asked what would have been Congress's response in 1865 had Virginia's legislature sent electoral lists and demanded that they be counted. "What would have been the answer?" Campbell asked, "It would have been as haughty and as proud as the demand: 'You are no longer entitled to the benefits of this Constitution, because you have attempted to abrogate it, and we will not count your votes and we will not allow you even to come so far as our Houses to present them.' " And now, Campbell asserted, with the fate of the presidency resting with Congress, that body had been reduced "to the poor, feeble, paltry imbecile thing that cannot deal with a certificate of a fraudulent returning board!"[62]

Having established that Congress clearly had authority to investigate election returns that pertained to presidential electors, Campbell next explained that the election in Louisiana was riddled with fraud and that even the most cursory inquiry into the returns would reveal that the Republican Returning Board did not properly canvass the votes and did not report accurate returns. Three-quarters of the way through his argument, Campbell was asked by Justice William Strong, one of three Republican members of the Court appointed to the commission, to clarify his position on the powers of Congress to intervene in state elections. "What is the position you take in regard to the power of the State over the final action of its Returning Board?" Strong inquired. "As I understand you," the commissioner remarked, "the power of judging of the honesty or accuracy of the decision of the returning-board is in the State." "In the case of state officers," Campbell responded. "I am speaking of electors," Strong retorted. "In reference to that," he answered, "my own opinion is that the State has no jurisdiction over the elector. . . . I say that the election is to be reviewed and examined by the two Houses of Congress when their certificates of returns come."[63]

Campbell did not doubt that Congress was vested with full authority to oversee elections for presidential electors, even though those elections were held in conjunction with those for state officers. The fact that these two elections were held simultaneously was only a matter of convenience, and this by no means established state jurisdiction over the electoral college. In the end, Campbell argued, Congress was fully empowered to "create a tribunal [that could ascertain] the validity and truthfulness and regularity of any election for electors for the purpose of determining the question whether the votes cast . . . are cast by the men competent to do so."[64]

Campbell's argument was indeed powerful, but it did not persuade. On 16 February the commission voted—once again along strict party lines, resulting in an 8-to-7 vote—not to allow evidence of fraud allegedly committed during Louisiana's election. Furthermore, as with Florida's returns, the commission argued that Congress had no authority to investigate returning boards. Three days later a vote was taken to recommend that all eight of Louisiana's electoral votes be given to Hayes.[65]

In the final analysis, neither Campbell's argument nor the commission's recommendations had any appreciable impact on the presidential election. On 2 March the House voted to grant all disputed electoral votes to Hayes, thus giving the Ohioan a 185-to-184 majority over Tilden. The principal explanation for this House vote was the defection of moderate Democrats, who, in an agreement with the Republican leadership made on 26 February at the Wormley Hotel in Washington, pledged to support Hayes. In return, congressional Republicans promised that the president-elect would withdraw the remaining Federal troops from Louisiana and South Carolina and would thereby allow southern state Republican administrations to collapse. Also of considerable importance to southern congressmen was Hayes's consent to grant federal subsidies to internal improvements in the South—particularly to the Texas and Pacific Railroad Company. The so-called Compromise of 1877 therefore marks a significant turning point in American history. Reconstruction had ended, and white southerners spent the next several decades "redeeming" their state governments and ensuring that black citizens played as insignificant a political role as possible.[66]

Though Campbell supported Tilden and argued on his behalf to the Electoral Commission, he was genuinely pleased when the Compromise of 1877 was reached. Hayes's election, Campbell wrote, "betoken[s] the dawn of a brighter day than we have had in the Union for some years. It is a measure of high and magnanimous statesmanship which manifests that 'Great men still live among us, Heads to plan and tongues that utter wisdom.' "[67] With the removal of federal troops from Louisiana, Campbell envisioned a rejuvenation of states' rights and, in his estimation, a restoration of the proper federal-state relationship as at least fundamentally intended by the framers.

Campbell's appearance before the Electoral Commission may have led some of his contemporaries to conclude that he had forsaken much of his pre-war states' rights philosophy. From a cursory reading of his argument, it could reasonably be concluded that he had become decidedly more nationalistic during the postwar years. In reality, though, Campbell's address to the commission defending congressional authority to investigate state returning boards applied only with regard to electors. As for the election of state officers, he maintained that these events were not even remotely within the federal government's domain. Now as throughout his professional life, Campbell sought to maintain a delicate balance between the respective powers of the federal and state governments. Although some writers claim that Campbell remained politically inactive after the war, his association with the Committee of Two Hundred and his appearance before the Electoral Commission indicate otherwise. Yet Campbell's political activity was, in the larger scheme of events, almost entirely ineffectual. Though he detested military rule and Reconstruction policies in Louisiana, the impact of his sporadic ventures into the turbulent postwar political arena was minimal and his influence hardly felt during an extremely troubled period in American history when promises made became promises broken.

12 | Postwar Palingenesis

After the war, Campbell's most pressing concern was his family's financial security; all else was of secondary importance to him. In that regard, after his release from Fort Pulaski in October 1865, Campbell plunged himself into the legal profession that had once brought him and his family wealth, security, and no small measure of prominence. Because he was a former Supreme Court justice, Campbell was sought after as an attorney, and he had few difficulties becoming reestablished in the profession. Within several months of his arrival in New Orleans, Campbell informed Anne that he had all of the business that he could handle. His partnership with Spofford was indeed one of the busiest firms in the city, and from 1866 until his retirement two decades later, Campbell represented literally hundreds of clients.

With this consideration, therefore, a complete examination of Campbell's postwar law practice would fill a sizable volume. At the same time, though, such a study would be of little practical use for those wishing to understand John Archibald Campbell. As an attorney, and an exceptionally gifted one, Campbell's job was to argue on behalf of his clients using the most persuasive arguments he could muster. It would be a mistake for the historian to infer Campbell's personal convictions from the arguments he delivered in court. After all, he was paid to win cases regardless of his personal feelings about the implications and the ramifications of his own arguments. By examining a certain portion of the vast array of cases Campbell accepted during this period, and by studying his court arguments, one might justifiably conclude that Campbell had forsaken his prewar pro states' rights philosophy. On the other hand, a survey of other cases would lead one to the opposite conclusion. As will be shown later in this chapter, despite court appearances during which he proffered revolutionary concepts on federalism that proposed appreciably greater power, reach, and authority for the federal government, in actuality Campbell personally remained a staunch defender of states' rights in areas that were not clearly delegated to the federal government. Until his death in 1889, he steadfastly proclaimed the sanctity of state governments as the standard-bearers of the people's sovereignty. But these convictions remained largely unexpressed during many of his court appearances. In short, Campbell's briefs are an inadequate source for determining whether he had become avidly nationalistic, whether he had grown bitter and even more solidly in support of states' rights, or whether he retained the fundamental dual federalism that had been the driving force behind the majority of his judicial decisions while on the Supreme Court.

Before Campbell could argue cases involving federal laws, he had to determine whether he would be allowed to argue cases in federal courts. The problem, as mentioned earlier, was the Test Oath Act. The "iron-clad oath," as it was then known, required all former Confederates to swear an oath that they had never aided in a rebellion against the United States. This legislation was no insignificant matter; it excluded from postwar politics all members of Confederate state governments and those who had served in the Richmond government. In January 1865, the often vindictive Senator Charles Sumner introduced a measure, subsequently signed into law by President Lincoln, that extended the test oath to attorneys wishing to appear in federal courts. On 10 December 1866, Campbell drafted a letter to Daniel W. Middleton, the Supreme Court's clerk, inquiring whether the justices had rendered an opinion on the Test Oath Act and asking to be sent a telegram if the Court made any decision in the matter. Apparently Campbell had a case waiting to be remanded to federal court, or he most likely would have asked Middleton to simply mail his reply.[1]

Campbell also drafted a lengthy argument exposing the inherent unfairness of the test oath that was published as *Observations Respecting the Test Oath, Imposed Upon Attorneys By Congress.* "My object," Campbell wrote, "is to state perspicuously the signification of the statute, and I shall not shrink from stating what I believe to be its plain import."[2] He began by outlining the five provisions of the oath. Individuals had to swear that they had never taken up arms against the United States; had never given aid "countenance, counsel, or encouragement" to persons engaged in armed hostility; had never served in a government openly hostile to the United States; and had never supported or sworn allegiance to another constitution. The fifth requirement was to swear allegiance to the Constitution of the United States without mental reservation.

Campbell explained that the first four provisions were entirely exculpatory, meaning that they were essentially ex post facto provisions pertaining only to past actions that were not illegal when they were performed. He also complained that the law was poorly written particularly in that it did not specify any statute of limitation. He noted that a person who had taken up arms during the Whiskey Rebellion, or who had joined the British assault on New Orleans in 1815, or who had fought with Santa Anna's army during the Mexican War, would be barred from practicing law in federal courts. "More than a half century of sobriety, good conduct, sorrow, and repentance, would not absolve him," he stated.[3]

Campbell wrote that the legislation far exceeded the laws governing treason because these did not include the ordinary act of giving aid or countenance to persons in armed hostility to the United States. Under such circumstances, he chided, those who had aided John Brown in 1859 would be forever barred by the test oath. Even those who had "held friendly intercourse and fellowship with secessionists in 1861" came under the law's provisions.

> The statute imposes disabilities that were not penal under any of the laws of the land, or had ceased to be so, when they were committed. The first four clauses of the act impose a disqualification for acts previously done, and which were not or might not have been cause for disqualification when they were done. I grant that some of the acts specified, under some conditions, would have authorized the court, upon a rule, to strike the offender from the rolls, but the court would have heard the party, have considered the extenuating facts and justifying circumstances; would have enquired whether there was malice in the design, wickedness in the purpose and act, and mischief in the consequences. The court would have accepted proper explanations, and assurances of future good behavior, and in many of the cases would have dismissed the rule.[4]

The Test Oath Act, therefore, prohibited the Court from using its own discretion in approving those attorneys who wished to appear at its bar. This fact, Campbell explained, was a profound humiliation for the Court, and it stripped the justices of jurisdiction over their own internal affairs. He stressed that the Court was in no way dependent on either Congress or the executive branch to regulate strictly internal matters. "My argument is," Campbell wrote, "that this act of Congress strikes a fatal blow at the honor, independence, and stability of the judiciary department." With the Test Oath, "the legislature assumes judicial magistery, pronouncing upon the guilt of the party without any of the common forms and guards of trial. . . . In short, in all such cases, the legislature exercises the highest power of sovereignty and what may be properly deemed an irresponsible, despotic discretion."[5]

Campbell's argument against the test oath was powerful not only in its eloquence and in its logic but also because Campbell was entirely correct in that Congress had exceeded its authority and had written a law empowering itself to oversee the judiciary. Such a gross abuse of power, of course, could not long have operated without a judicial challenge. In 1867, two cases—*Cummings v. Missouri* and Ex Parte *Garland*—were accepted by the Supreme Court to hear arguments on the test oath's constitutionality.[6] By a 5-to-4 vote in the *Cummings* decision, Justice Stephen Field delivered the Court's opinion that the test oath violated article 1, section 9 of the Constitution strictly forbidding ex post facto laws and bills of attainder. Though the act did not specifically punish former Confederates, Field stated, it prevented certain citizens from practicing their occupation without benefit of trial. With the *Cummings* decision, the restriction was lifted, and Campbell and his southern colleagues could thereafter bring cases before federal courts.[7]

After the *Cummings* decision in early January 1867, Campbell at once began petitioning the nation's highest tribunal. For the next two decades he spent considerable time in Washington, averaging six appearances before the Court each year.[8] He rapidly regained the esteem of his colleagues and the confidence of the public. One account of Campbell's stellar postwar career states, "It was legendary that when there was a hard job to do people said, 'Turn it over to God and Mr. Campbell.' "[9] Characteristically, Campbell refused to accept invitations to social engagements, and he devoted nearly all of his time to the practice. One of his colleagues on the New Orleans bar who commented on Campbell's work habits stated:

> [Campbell] threw himself into the contests into which he became engaged, with a degree of intensity which it is difficult to express. He became absorbed in his professional undertakings. He would sit for hours in his great library lost in thought, without turning the leaves of the volume before him. At other times, he would walk in the streets gesticulating, as he went, to the surprise of all who passed him. He spoke in court customarily from the many books spread out before him. His language seemed to be borrowed from the books and was apt to be technical and quaint, as the authorities themselves. His style, for the most part, was measured and grave, as became his years and standing at the Bar. From time to time, however, as he caught fire from the concussion of the debate, he became inflamed and fierce in his assaults upon his adversary's side.[10]

On occasion, after Campbell had "caught fire," his arguments became exceedingly melodramatic, particularly when he discussed Reconstruction and political conditions in the South. During one of his more colorful tirades against radicalism, Campbell exclaimed, "In the Eighth Circle of the Inferno is a place reserved for those people who traffic in the public interest for their own private advantage." He warned that Satan has constructed a special chamber in Hell for those whose " 'no' is quickly changed to 'aye' for lucre." And finally, "The Malebolge is a dark and dreadful lake, of a thick glutinous mass which on every side belimes the shore and demons watch its wretched inmates with seething forks to press them down, should they uplift their heads above the surface, so that if steal they can, it shall be out of view."[11] Such courtroom theatrics no doubt had little impact on the outcome of his cases, but watching Campbell deliver such hellish admonitions most assuredly added atmosphere to an otherwise often stolid Supreme Court chamber.

As throughout the antebellum years—and despite the horrifying Civil War that seemingly inaugurated a revolution in American federalism and reduced state authority to insignificance—cases appealed to the Supreme Court involving states' rights abounded in the postwar era. In the final analysis, the

Supreme Court had to decide just how revolutionary the war had been. Interestingly, many of the cases Campbell brought before the Court were argued in support of the political revolution ostensibly ushered in by the war. On these occasions he often asserted that the federal government had garnered appreciably more power—and responsibility—to protect people's sovereignty and civil rights from encroachment by state authorities. The first of these was *Waring v. Mayor of Mobile,* during which he argued that an import tax imposed by the City of Mobile and sanctioned by the state of Alabama did not accord with the federal Constitution as it violated Congress's power to regulate trade. The Court disagreed in this case, citing the long-established original package doctrine recognized by the Marshall Court in 1827.[12] Campbell was more successful with the *State Tonnage Tax Cases* two years later when he convinced the Court that an Alabama tonnage tax was unconstitutional.[13]

These two cases mark but a sampling of those in which Campbell seemed to have recognized that the Civil War had dramatically altered the political relationship between the states and the federal government. It appeared at least that the Alabamian was now of the opinion that as of 1865 the federal government was supreme in nearly all aspects of government and that it had assumed an exceedingly more proactive role in regulating the nation's internal affairs. In other words, he asserted that the prewar emphasis on dual federalism was no longer relevant. Of the many cases he brought before the Supreme Court in which this theme dominated his argumentation, the *Slaughterhouse Case* offers the foremost expression of his presumed postwar ideology.[14]

In 1869, Campbell was hired by a group of New Orleans butchers indignant over recently passed legislation enacted by Louisiana's Republican government under Governor Warmoth. From this initial meeting rose the famous *Slaughterhouse Case,* which Campbell presented before the United States Supreme Court in 1873.[15] The litigation began when the legislature passed a statute regulating the slaughtering of cattle. Prior to this legislation, much of the livestock was slaughtered in facilities located along the Mississippi River above the intake of the New Orleans water plant, a practice that posed a serious health hazard. The state legislature adopted Act 118 in March 1869, requiring that after 1 June of the following year all cattle would have to be butchered at the Crescent City Slaughterhouse. This requirement meant not that the city's independent butchers were out of business but only that they had to herd their cattle to Crescent City and pay a fee for each animal slaughtered. Immediately upon passage of Act 118 the Butchers' Benevolent Association of New Orleans sought an injunction against the implementation of the law on the grounds that it unlawfully created a monopoly and deprived them of their livelihood.[16] In hiring Campbell, the butchers had clearly found an advocate worthy of assuming their cause. But when in April 1870, the state supreme court ruled against Campbell and the butchers, holding that the granting of the monopoly was necessary to promote public health and that the state of Louisiana, under the doctrine of "police powers," was fully authorized to create the monopoly.[17]

After this decision, the case was immediately remanded to federal court on writ of error. Campbell and his coattorney, John Quincy Adams Fellows of New Orleans, applied to United States Supreme Court Justice Joseph P. Bradley of the Fifth Circuit for an injunction against the 1 June effective date for Act 118. Bradley, then on circuit in Galveston, Texas, consented to the appeal and granted a temporary injunction until full arguments could be heard on 9 June.[18]

It is interesting to note the relationship that developed between Campbell and Justice Bradley. Their personal ideologies differed sharply—the Democrat Campbell, known for his forceful defense of states' rights, and the Republican Bradley, named to the bench by President Grant in 1870 as a strong advocate of federal authority. Despite their fundamental ideological differences, both men developed extraordinary respect for one another. Bradley later said of Campbell that he had "never heard an advocate who brought to his aid so much learning and breadth. The esteem in which [Campbell] was held by the members of the Supreme Court anointed [him] to reverence. For myself, from the first time I heard him in New Orleans, in the Slaughterhouse Case, . . . he was my beau-ideal of forensic perfectness."[19]

Campbell's fondness for Bradley no doubt stemmed from the justice's willingness to hear his appeals and then to agree substantially with his argument on behalf of the butchers. After the first day of arguments presented in New Orleans, though, Bradley refused to continue the injunction. Then, inexplicably, on the following day he reversed himself. He later claimed that after giving both arguments full consideration that evening, he had decided that Campbell was essentially correct.[20] Bradley was well known for his thoughtful and well-reasoned decisions while on the bench, and in view of the revolutionary nature of Campbell's arguments, it is little wonder that Bradley needed to contemplate its ramifications. Campbell had rightly guessed that the case would have to be heard by the full Supreme Court.[21] The state of Louisiana appealed to the Court on writ of error, and after two years of legal maneuvering by both sides in the litigation, the case was heard in Washington during the December 1872 term. Arguments were delivered on 3, 4, and 5 February 1873 and the Court read its decision on 14 April.[22]

Campbell's argument filled thirty single-spaced pages and took two days to deliver. It was based on the assumption that the state of Louisiana had insufficient authority to pass Act 118 because it unlawfully prevented the butchers from freely practicing their trade. The law also deprived them of their property in violation of the due process clause in the Fourteenth Amendment. This amendment to the Constitution was enacted principally as a measure to protect the civil rights of former slaves, but Campbell asked the Court to recognize that the federal government had an obligation to protect the civil rights, including the right to property, of all American citizens.[23] This case was thus the first litigation in which the Court was asked for the judiciary's interpretation of the Fourteenth Amendment.

Section 1 provided: "All persons born or naturalized in the United States, and subject to the jurisdiction thereof, are citizens of the United States and of the State wherein they reside." This section formally remedied the lack of a citizenship clause in the original Constitution and was meant by the amendment's authors as a congressional reversal of Taney's *Dred Scott* decision.[24] The thorny question of the locus of citizenship was thereafter settled in favor of federal jurisdiction. By far the most important sentences of section 1, drafted by Representative John Bingham of Ohio, provided: "No state shall make or enforce any law which shall abridge the privileges and immunities of citizens of the United States; nor shall any State deprive any person of life, liberty, or property, without due process of law." Depending on one's outlook, section 1 could have been interpreted in several ways. The more moderate members of Congress believed that the privileges and immunities clause established the state-action theory of federal legislative power over civil rights. In other words, states retained much of their original sovereignty and police powers, but the federal government was empowered to oversee state legislation to ensure that no citizen's civil rights were violated. As the Fourteenth Amendment was adopted largely in response to the various "Black Codes" enacted by unreconstructed states, moderate Republicans held that the amendment could be used to restrain southern states from denying blacks civil and property rights. But the states retained all residual authority to regulate civil rights. The more radical members of Congress, however, interpreted the amendment far more broadly. They denied the validity of the state-action theory and maintained that states were prohibited by federal statute from enacting any legislation deemed discriminatory against blacks in law, politics, and society.[25]

Campbell's interpretation of the Fourteenth Amendment, oddly enough, surpassed even that of the most radical Republican. He maintained that section 1 applied not merely to former slaves but to all Americans, being fundamentally an extension of federal authority over civil rights legislation. In other words, he suggested that only the federal government had authority to enact civil rights legislation, and that all such laws applied equally to each American citizen regardless of their race or former status. This was truly revolutionary, coming from a man who for nearly all of his life had been a premier defender of states' rights. His argument provided the strongest, most thorough treatise in support of extensive federal authority advanced during the era.[26]

Campbell opened his argument with the words "there are many conditions of servitude in the world in which there is no requirement upon the labor of the slave." Whenever any society became stratified into various castes whereby a small minority controlled the majority of wealth and could dominate the remaining members of society, slavery had in principle at least been reestablished. Under such circumstances, Campbell argued, the lower castes were deprived of their freedom to engage in their chosen vocation and were instead bound to follow the economic and social dictates of the controlling minority. He argued that when the Louisiana legislature adopted Act 118, it had unwittingly instituted a caste system within the state by creating a monopoly protected by law and virtually unimpeachable. Because the butchers were no longer allowed to slaughter their animals in the location and in the manner that they had previously chosen, Act 118 effectively enslaved them and was an outright infringement of the Thirteenth Amendment. Campbell stated:

> The proposition I submit to the Court upon this explanation is this: that in the Crescent City Livestock Landing Charter, every man within the three parishes of Orleans, Jefferson, and St. Bernard is required, if he exercises the trade of preparing animal food for the markets, to do it in the houses of this Company, and not elsewhere; every man in those parishes, if he has a horse, or a mule, or any animal destined for sale, and brings them for that purpose into those parishes, must carry them to the landing places, to the yards, to the stable, to the pens, of that Company. These are personal acts which the owners must perform. . . . I affirm that so far as this Act [118] makes it incumbent upon any one of the defendants, in order to prosecute his industry, that he must do it by force of law in the houses of this Company, that it is a personal servitude affecting each person, . . . just as strong a case . . . as the servitude consisting merely in a dance or a leap before the master on appointed occasions.[27]

There was little difference, Campbell insisted, between a slave who had once labored on the southern plantations and the butchers who were denied freedom of vocation by Act 118. "The 13th Amendment," he remarked, "says that involuntary servitude shall not exist within the jurisdiction of the United States." No government had authority to force a citizen to work "for the mere emolument of another citizen, or to compel by law, or to create conditions of necessity whereby to make it incumbent upon one citizen to work upon the domain of another, or to abandon his lawful avocation."[28]

Needless to say, by claiming that the passage of Act 118 in essence established slavery in southern Louisiana, Campbell advanced a most specious argument. Had he made this claim prior to 1861, he most assuredly would have been branded one of the nation's most radical abolitionists. His amazingly broad and liberal definition of slavery was, however, aimed most pointedly at monopolies, which he contended concentrated wealth, destroyed competition, corrupted governments, and deprived citizens of their right to engage in their chosen professions. His assault on monopolies, however laudable, unfortunately equated the absolutely horrid experiences endured by generations of slaves with a mere inconvenience suffered by a relatively small group of butchers.

Far more plausible, however, was the second portion of Campbell's argument, in which he declared that Act 118 violated the due process and the privileges and immunities clauses of the Fourteenth Amendment. Directing his verbal assault at Louisiana's Republican regime, Campbell asked, "[I]f an ordinance be unreasonable, if it be unequal, if it be unjust because of its inequality, does it not fall within the exact letter of the 14th Amendment of the Constitution?" The civil rights protection afforded by this amendment to former slaves, he asserted, was equally applicable to all American citizens. Campbell continued that any citizen of the United States

> may engage in any lawful pursuit for which he has the requisite capacity, skill, material, or capital. He is entitled to the full enjoyment of the fruits of his labor or industry without coercion or constraint, subject only to legal taxation or contribution. He is entitled to appropriate the proceeds of his undivided industry, and to make a similar appropriation when he has been assisted in his work after deducting the cost of that assistance. These rights not only inhere in the state and condition of the freeman under the amendments to the Constitution, but the common law had maintained them as existing because of the advantage society would receive from their employment.[29]

Because the butchers had no alternative but to slaughter their livestock at Crescent City, and because they were forced to pay a fee to the monopoly, they were unreasonably deprived of their property without due process. Such requirements were as much a denial of equal civil rights as they were restraints of trade. Under either circumstance, Act 118 was unconstitutional.

Before the Civil War and the adoption of the Fourteenth Amendment, Campbell argued, state citizenship superseded United States citizenship. All responsibility to protect civil rights, to maintain equality, and to ensure fairness of competition rested solely with the states. But the war and the subsequent amendments dramatically altered that relationship and transferred the trusteeship over the people's sovereignty from the states to the federal government. All guarantees of civil rights had in 1865 become vested in the federal government, which was then obligated to overturn any state legislation denying property rights without due process. Furthermore, as the Fourteenth Amendment provided that national citizenship was dominant over state citizenship, the federal government was required to extend the protection of civil rights to all American citizens. It was an obligation upon which the federal government had insisted and, therefore, it was one that it was bound to carry out.

Every act of the Legislature that effects any individual member of its population by abridging the privileges and immunities which he claims to have as a citizen, which affects his life, liberty, or property arbitrarily, or which denies him an equal protection of his laws, all those become subject to the control or the revisory power of this Court. The Constitution, by declaring that every member in the empire is its citizen, every person born within its jurisdiction derives his state and condition from its authority, and at the same time stating to those States that this citizen of ours must not be disturbed in his privileges or immunities, or in his life, liberty, or property, brings the government into immediate contact with every person, and gives to every citizen a claim upon its protecting power.[30]

By twentieth-century standards of liberty and equality, the power of Campbell's reasoning cannot be denied. The federal government had assumed a guardianship over civil rights, and it had to accept the responsibility that accompanied the transfer of the trust from the states. This was essentially the same argument used at the turn of the century by progressives wanting the federal government to weaken the nation's powerful industrial monopolies, which were often accused of destroying civil rights and denying people equality under the law. Campbell's 1873 argument was also similar—although under admittedly different circumstances—to that used in the 1954 *Brown v. Board of Education* case and in the enactment of the 1964 and 1965 Civil Rights Acts.[31]

Thus the federal government, according to Campbell, had a fundamental responsibility to protect each American citizen's civil rights. At the same time, though, in an argument that was especially broad and was meant to appeal to all factions of the Court, Campbell employed the privileges and immunities and due process clauses to deny that government could regulate American businesses. Campbell's argument in this regard has been described as an attempt "to marry *laissez faire* capitalism to the Fourteenth Amendment."[32] By claiming that government—and in this case the state of Louisiana—could not enact legislation that would in any manner impede private property rights, Campbell appealed to the Court's emerging conservative elements, who disapproved of governmental encroachment into the business community. Although requiring little prompting from Campbell, the Supreme Court effectively implemented his logic throughout the next two decades when it denied the federal government authority to intervene in America's growing business interests. With regard to civil rights, Campbell's argument is often viewed as enlarging the federal government's powers. Conversely, his logic is regarded as a profoundly convincing exegesis on the virtues of *laissez faire* and a diminution of federal authority.

The Court's majority opinion was read by Justice Samuel F. Miller, a moderate Republican from Iowa. The ruling, he explained, was based on three important observations: first, states have the power to "prescribe and determine the localities where the business of slaughtering" could occur; second, Miller explained that Act 118 did not impose that serious a burden on the butchers, who could quite easily take their livestock to Crescent City for slaughter; third, and most important, the majority opinion held that the Thirteenth, Fourteenth, and Fifteenth Amendments were added specifically to aid the former slaves. "We repeat, then," Miller stated,

> in light of this recent recapitulation of events, almost too recent to be called history, but which are familiar to us all; and on the most casual examination of the language of these amendments, no one can fail to be impressed with the one pervading purpose found in them all, lying at the foundation of each, and without which none of them would have been even suggested; we mean the freedom of the slave race, the firm and secure establishment of that freedom, and the protection of the newly made freedom and citizen from the oppression of those who had formerly exercised unlimited dominion over them.[33]

Thus the Court adopted an extremely narrow and conservative interpretation of the three amendments, one that not only reasserted state police power to regulate purely internal matters but also denied that the federal government had assumed extraordinary new powers. The Court rejected Campbell's contention that civil rights derived from federal citizenship, and it instead applied the dual citizenship theory to deny that federal citizenship rights, privileges, and immunities superseded those afforded to citizens of the various states.[34]

Although Campbell lost the *Slaughterhouse Case,* his argument made an profound impression on the Court; four members dissented from the majority opinion and largely agreed with Campbell's interpretation of the Fourteenth Amendment. Due to his performance during this case, Campbell's practice from 1873 until the end of his career in 1886 was exclusively limited to appeals to the Supreme Court. Of course, this meant that he spent much time in transit between New Orleans and Washington, a difficult journey even under the best circumstances. In early December 1870, soon after he had been commissioned by the butchers, Campbell suffered a serious fall at the boardinghouse in New Orleans when a second-story balcony on which he was standing collapsed to the street. The injury to his legs and back plagued him for the remainder of his life and made travel, especially during the winter months, almost impossible. In order to be closer to Washington, Campbell moved to Baltimore and lived in the family residence on St. Paul Street with Anne, Henrietta, and several grandchildren.[35]

If one were to examine only Campbell's argument in the *Slaughterhouse Case,* one might conclude that he had become an archnationalist. But as previously noted, this would be a misrepresentation. In many cases Campbell presented arguments of a diametrically opposite nature; ones denying that a revolution had occurred with the Civil War and that staunchly upheld the power and authority of state governments. Although there were many cases during which Campbell eloquently defended states' rights, two of the most notable instances were *United States v. Cruikshank* in 1873 and *New Hampshire v. Louisiana* a decade later.[36]

The *Cruikshank* case originated as a criminal prosecution against scores of white Louisianans involved in the Colfax Riot, described in the preceding chapter. After widespread denunciation of the massacre that occurred that Easter Sunday in 1873, the Justice Department opened an investigation that led to indictments of seventy-two persons on charges of violating the Enforcement Act of 1870. Seeking to enforce the civil liberty guarantees of the 14th and 15th Amendments, Congress had enacted this legislation in May 1870. Aside from preventing state election officials from discriminating among voters on the basis of race, the measure also made bribery and the intimidation of voters a federal offense. Finally, in a section directed against the rising threat from white terrorist groups such as the White League and the Ku Klux Klan, the Enforcement Act outlawed conspiracies to prevent citizens from exercising their civil rights. The indictments generated after the Colfax Riot charged the perpetrators "with murder in the commission of offenses punished by the 6th and 7th sections" of the act, which forbade conspiracies and the "banding together of two or more persons" to deny the constitutional rights of any citizen.[37]

Highlighting the difficulties for federal and state officials in prosecuting whites for violence against freedmen in a society that wanted nothing to do with Reconstruction, only nine arrests were made from the original seventy-two indictments. One of the defendants, William J. Cruikshank, was brought to trial in federal circuit court in New Orleans, but the charges against him and two other defendants were dismissed for being too vaguely drawn. United States Attorney General Williams and Solicitor General Samuel Phillips filed for an appeal to the full Supreme Court, and initial arguments were heard in March and November 1875. Williams's presence before the Court in this case clearly indicates the gravity with which the federal government approached the prosecution. The defendants were assisted by a legal "team" of eight attorneys. Among the best known of these men were Philip Phillips of Mobile; David Dudley Field, the brother of Supreme Court justice Stephen J. Field; Reverdy Johnson of Maryland; and John A. Campbell of New Orleans.[38]

Campbell's principal role in the case was to draft the written brief, which he subtitled "Conspiracy and Banding in Grant Parish, La." The fundamental question before the Court, Campbell began, was determining whether the indictments brought against his clients were "good and sufficient in law, and contain charges of a criminal matter indictable under the laws of the United States." Campbell charged that the federal judiciary did not have sufficient jurisdiction in this case. The alleged crimes, he stated, were intrinsically local and thus subject to prosecution only through local statutes.[39] Having argued in the *Slaughterhouse Case* that the Fourteenth Amendment infinitely broadened the federal government's scope, powers, and jurisdiction, Campbell reversed himself entirely in this brief.

Campbell recognized that the federal government may pass laws to prevent conspiracies against the United States, or those with intentions of overthrowing the government, or those that would disrupt the government's constitutional authority. "But beyond this we shall not go," he stated. "The Constitution of the United States delegates no authority to Congress, to define the purposes for which the people may assemble, nor to superintend the conduct of the members at those meetings. . . . These are all concerns, which affect the order, tranquility, and police [powers] of the States."

> The State has the same undeniable jurisdiction over all persons and things within its territorial limits, as any foreign nation, where that jurisdiction is not surrendered or restrained by the Constitution of the U.S. that by virtue of this, it is not only the right, but the solemn and bounden duty of a State, to advance the safety, happiness, and prosperity of its people, and to provide for its general welfare by any and every act of legislation which it may deem conducive to these ends, where the power over the particular subject, or the manner of its exercise is not surrendered or restrained. That all those powers which relate to merely municipal legislation, or what may be termed its *internal police,* are not thus surrendered or restrained; and that consequently, in relation to these, THE AUTHORITY OF THE STATE IS COMPLETE, UNQUALIFIED, AND EXCLUSIVE.[40]

With regard to the indictments served against Cruikshank, Campbell protested that these were so vaguely drawn that they failed to cite a direct crime for which his client could be prosecuted in federal court. According to the authors of the original indictments, Campbell noted, the federal government "has unlimited jurisdiction over all persons and things in the United States, and to vindicate each citizen when injured, oppressed, threatened, or intimidated by two or more persons with the purpose to deprive one or more of life, liberty, or property, by means of a criminal prosecution in its tribunals." Campbell rejected the prosecution's assumption that the due process and equal protection clauses of the Fourteenth Amendment empowered the federal government to prosecute Cruikshank and the others. In this regard, he insisted, Williams and Phillips were entirely incorrect. Campbell wrote that the prosecution's mistake was in assuming that the provisions of the Fourteenth Amendment "were addressed to each and every inhabitant in the [country]." "The entire subversion of the institutions of the States and the immediate consolidation of the whole land into a consolidated empire, is the immediate consequence of such a conclusion being adopted as law." In stark contrast to his claims in *Slaughterhouse* three years earlier, Campbell asserted that the sole purpose of the Fourteenth Amendment was only to "restrain the States from exorbitant, excessive, and tyrannical legislation affecting the privileges and immunities of citizens, their rights to life, liberty, and property, and to equal protection of the laws." He concluded that the Cruikshank case "was one of surpassing interest, and on its determination depends either the maintenance of the government upon its ancient foundation, or a radical change in its entire structure."[41]

On 27 March 1876, Chief Justice Morrison R. Waite delivered the Court's opinion that upheld the circuit court ruling largely on the basis that the indictments were too vague and the prosecution had been unable to prove racial motivation for the crimes. The Court's increasingly conservative interpretation of the Reconstruction Amendments is evident from the fact that, according to the *Cruikshank* decision, the Fourteenth Amendment did not establish national citizenship. Rather, echoing the *Slaughterhouse* ruling, Waite defended the dual citizenship theory, and he emphasized that neither state nor national citizenship was paramount over the other. The *Cruikshank* decision further underscored the Supreme Court's reluctance to apply congressional Reconstruction with its inherent revolution in federalism. The Court was willing to vindicate federal authority to acknowledge and to protect civil rights, but it refused to destroy state police powers by insisting that state governments had exclusive authority to regulate civil rights. Thus the case was a clear victory for Campbell, for the defense, and for states' rights philosophy.[42]

A second illustration of Campbell's postwar states' rights arguments came with *New Hampshire v. Louisiana,* which centered on the provisions of the Eleventh Amendment. This forty-three-word addition to the Constitution, ratified in 1795, was initially intended as protection of state sovereign immunity from certain lawsuits. In reaction to *Chisholm v. Georgia* (1793), during which the Court upheld the right of citizens from one state to sue another state in federal courts, and viewed as a direct threat to state sovereignty, Congress adopted the amendment solely to repudiate the Court's broad decision.[43] In 1883 (see photo 4), Campbell used the provisions within this amendment to protect his client, the state of Louisiana, from suits filed in federal court by the states of New York and New Hampshire.

In 1874, during the Reconstruction period, the Louisiana government sold numerous bonds to individuals and to corporations throughout the country. After the Compromise of 1877 and the Democrats' resurgence to political domination, Louisiana refused to pay maturities on these bonds. In 1879 and 1880, respectively, the New York and New Hampshire legislatures enacted laws empowering the states' attorneys general to file suits in federal courts on

Campbell in the last known photograph, made shortly before his death in 1889. (From Photo File, Box 7, Campbell Portraits, Alabama Department of Archives and History, Montgomery, Alabama.)

behalf of citizens within those states to collect their maturities from Louisiana. By the terms of this legislation, New York and New Hampshire bondholders who wished to seek redress could assign their interest to the state governments, which would then proceed with collection through federal courts.[44] Campbell brought these cases to the Supreme Court during the 1882 and 1883 sessions as the chief advocate for Louisiana. Astonishingly, the three briefs he filed total one hundred and thirty-six single-spaced pages, no small accomplishment for a man seventy-two years old. Campbell's incredible energy and perspicacious intellect had clearly not failed him despite his advanced years.[45]

Simply stated, Campbell argued that the Eleventh Amendment disallowed this litigation, for the actual originators of the suits were citizens of the states and not the state governments themselves. "The first commentary we have to make," Campbell wrote, "is that the Constitution was made for the United States, and the judicial power, like all of the other powers delegated, were designed to serve the interests and welfare of the Union." He also remarked, "By the revolution each State became a perfect and independent Nation."[46] It would be improper for states acting as the collecting agents for its citizens to abuse the nation's judiciary in such an egregious fashion. Campbell admitted that his client had refused to honor the bonds issued through state legislation in 1874.

> Louisiana, through her conventions, Legislature, and people, [and] after a review of the condition of her population, and the calamities resulting from the war, the loss of virile population, a convulsion in property, and social revolution, pestilence, floods, and irresponsible and profligate government imposed on her, decided that the revenues of the State were not adequate to the expenditures needful. There is retrenchment in the Constitution adopted in 1879, and an anxious purpose to prevent misgovernment in the future. There was always an abatement of interest on an issue of bonds under the Acts of 1874.
>
> New York comes like a belligerent, bewailing her loss of capacity to make reprisals, and in lieu demands a receiver or some interdictory process whereby the State shall lose her powers of administration and government, and this Court is for a long period to perform functions not unlike those of a Brigadier in a state reduced to a department, to undergo reconstruction.[47]

In his third and final brief, Campbell reminded the Court that the Eleventh Amendment specifically forbade the Court from claiming jurisdiction in the case. He asserted that the case "thus invited [by New Hampshire] is a fictitious and a simulated controversy imposed upon this Court contrary to the order, rule, and authority of this Court."[48]

Closely following Campbell's argument, the Court's majority ruled that the Eleventh Amendment clearly prevented New York and New Hampshire from "acting as the collecting agents" for their populations.[49] Thus this case is often cited as a landmark ruling with direct bearing on the continuing evolution of the amendment. More to the point, however, Campbell's briefs in this case—particularly with reference to the above cited passages—underscore a common thread that emerges when the cases discussed in this chapter are viewed collectively. Campbell was perfectly capable of powerful and persuasive arguments whether on behalf of the states or the federal government, so that it is difficult to determine from any one particular case to what degree if any Campbell's personal philosophy was altered by the war. Interestingly, however, the one prevalent theme that surfaces when these cases are examined as a composite is Campbell's intense and ardent opposition to Reconstruction and to the Republican-controlled state governments.

In the two cases against the state of Alabama, Campbell attacked a tax imposed by a Reconstruction government. Similar circumstances existed with regard to the *Slaughterhouse Case*. Though Campbell had never supported state-chartered monopolies, which he believed threatened the internal order and the sovereign powers of the states, his argument in *Slaughterhouse* was directed less against the Crescent City Livestock Company than against the Warmoth government. The most effective means of weakening that government, Campbell reasoned, was to attack the source of its authority: the Radical Republicans. And through "watering down" the provisions of the Fourteenth Amendment by insisting that these were applicable to all Americans, Campbell hoped to erode the Republican's political base in the southern states. Though his argument in *Slaughterhouse* was unsuccessful largely because the Court had adopted an inherently more conservative interpretation of the Fourteenth Amendment than Campbell had offered in 1873, in the broader sense states' rights had been vindicated. And in that regard, the *Slaughterhouse Case* offered Campbell a "win-win" scenario. If the Court had followed his argument, the Warmoth government would have suffered a serious defeat. On the other hand, with the Court's conservative ruling, state police powers, state citizenship, and state authority were clearly revitalized. Thus when viewing Campbell's postwar cases collectively, his interest in weakening Reconstruction governments becomes obvious, and his fundamental states' rights philosophy is as evident after 1867 as during any other period.

Throughout the postwar era, therefore, Campbell maintained the same states' rights philosophy that he had developed by midcentury. In 1884, he was asked to be the honored speaker at an Alabama State Bar Association meeting held in Birmingham. Campbell wrote that due to "a recurring contraction of the bounds," he was precluded from attending the dinner.[50] But he promised that he would send a written address that could be read for him. The fifty-one-page document he sent to the bar association shows that Campbell remained ardently in support of states' rights. Far from celebrating the virtues of nationalism and the rights, duties, and role of the federal government, Campbell passionately extolled states' rights, and he denounced those forces that had fundamentally altered the federal-state relationship as originally established by the framers. "Within the United States the contempt for the Constitution as a parchment idol was a part of the legacy of the war," he wrote. Since 1861, the American people had witnessed

> more instances of oppression and tyranny; more of prodigal and profligate expenditure; more of bribery; more of licentiousness. . . . Who shall deliver

us from the body of this death? Stand fast in the liberty wherewith you became free, and which the Constitution has been the witness. Be constant and
firm to insist that the State shall be maintained in the fullness of the powers
reserved by the Constitution which was made by the people of the States.
The State is the repository where the family is formed, and with this the
source of domestic peace; where religion, morality, reverence, honor, hu-
mane affections, are implanted and instruction most purely imbibed. It is the
State that most surely defends life, liberty, reputation, property, family obligations, and rights. It is the State that teaches primary duties of manhood,
and who [*sic*] shields and protects womanhood in her purity and holiness.
. . . On the foundations of the States, the States as united must repose, and
only when the United States invaded the States was there war and the calamities of war.[51]

Campbell's largely ineffectual political activity in opposition to Reconstruction, his legal maneuvers to weaken Republican control over state governments, and his emphatic and emotional 1884 letter provide clear evidence that
his philosophy remained centered on states' rights. In Campbell's estimation
the Constitution was an inviolate document specifically enumerating the powers and rights given to the federal government. All residual authority was to
remain firmly vested in the states, and any attempts to alter the fundamental
federal-state relationship created in 1787 by empowering the federal government at the states' expense further alienated sovereignty from its original
source: the American people. As most issues directly impacting people's lives
were intrinsically local, Campbell held that the states should have a more fundamental role in governing. In the final analysis, the preservation of states'
rights was the measure of his career.

Campbell closed his practice in 1886 shortly after his seventy-fifth birthday. Sadly, he had been alone during the previous three years—after nearly
fifty-three years of marriage, Anne Goldthwaite Campbell died 13 February
1883. Later that afternoon, Campbell wrote "Incidents in the Life of John A.
Campbell," much of which is devoted to Anne's life. "There was always an
overflowing fountain of love for her family and she at the last, and to the last
commanded their reverence and their love." He continued, "[O]n this day, the
first day of her new life beyond the grave," he would record "this memorial of
her excellence."[52]

Her husband had entire and implicit confidence in her management of the
household and confided to her whatever concerned their domestic affairs.
She enjoyed the gradual rise of her husband in the profession he had chosen
and contributed her help and aid to his improvement. The Civil War in the
United States was a blight upon her enjoyments. Their household was broken up. The prospects of the family dimmed. The members were separated
and herself experienced sorrow and disappointment. The elasticity of her

nature, her proud hopes and calculation were not fulfilled, and as age advanced, her natural vigor was infirmed and finally lost.[53]

After Anne's death, Campbell continued to reside at the family residence in Baltimore. Henrietta and her two children lived there as well and looked after Campbell as his health declined. As noted earlier, when Campbell's daughter Mary Ellen died in 1870, her three children were sent to Baltimore to live with Anne. In September 1877, tragedy struck again as Mary Ellen's two daughters, Mary and Betsey, died of diphtheria within one day of each other. Both girls were buried next to their mother in Greenmount Cemetery in Baltimore.[54] Mary Ellen's only other child was John A. C. Mason, who was but four years old when his mother died and was, therefore, raised by Campbell and Anne.

When John was sixteen, he asked his grandfather about his mother's estate and whether he was the benefactor to any of her property. Campbell informed him that his mother had died leaving but a small estate that was encumbered with debts owed to the Bank of Mobile. Soon after Mary Ellen's death, Campbell began making investments for her children, and he informed John that his share of the investments was nearly $20,000. "I consider that this is a very fair advancement for a young man," Campbell lectured, "and with providence and economy a young man could not measurably ask for more." Perhaps echoing his disappointment over Duncan's failures, Campbell told his grandson that he had "very little" respect for any young man who did not constantly strive for personal and professional improvement. He also expressed little tolerance for youthful indulgences "to gratify [one's] appetites." He advised John to concentrate on "establishing a character for rectitude and propriety" and to avoid "prodigal living."[55] Campbell explained that John would receive the money—but not until he turned twenty-one years old. Thus, he employed much of the same strictness in raising his grandson that he had with Duncan. He, of course, hoped that the outcome in John's case would be different. He could no longer help Duncan, whose condition continued to worsen. Campbell's only son died 13 March 1888 in Baltimore tragically dependent on alcohol.[56]

These deaths obviously devastated Campbell, and he never recovered emotionally from Anne's loss. Though his incredible intellect and remarkable memory continued to serve him well—for example in the *New Hampshire v. Louisiana* litigation—during the five years following Anne's death, Campbell suffered periodic bouts of both mental and physical illnesses. There is some evidence to suggest that Campbell's massive intellect declined somewhat during the last year of his life. One close associate stated that by 1888 Campbell was "much abstracted, and while in that mood, he became unconscious of surrounding objects and indulged in vehement and loud argumentation with himself."[57]

Despite such periodic mental lapses, Campbell nonetheless retained much of his bountiful intellect. But his physical condition continued to decline. In January 1889, he was asked to attend the centennial celebration of the establishment of the federal judiciary. He returned the invitation, explaining that he was simply too weak to make the trip to Washington. "Tell the Court that I join daily in the prayer," Campbell wrote on the reply card, "God Save the United States and its Honorable Court."[58] These were his last words to the Supreme Court. John Archibald Campbell died 12 March 1889 at the age of seventy-seven.

13 | Conclusion

On Saturday, 6 April 1889, two memorial meetings were held in honor of John Archibald Campbell. The first was conducted at Washington, D.C., in the United States Supreme Court, and the second was held in the Fifth Circuit Courthouse in New Orleans. The purpose of these meetings was to pay tribute to Campbell's life and accomplishments and to recognize his superior intellect, his unimpeachable character, and his remarkable talents as a lawyer. The various speakers at both meetings agreed that Campbell was one of the nation's most gifted attorneys of that century, second perhaps only to Daniel Webster. They praised his vast learning in and mastery of both the common law and the civil law; no other person, it was said, could have accomplished the feat. Campbell's remarkable gift, his main asset, and—for those attorneys in opposition—his principal weapon while delivering his arguments in court was his uncanny ability to recall a seemingly endless amount of information pertinent to his case. But the speakers also lauded Campbell for his thorough research, and one suspects that Campbell's memory was made to appear that much more remarkable by his intense preparation, organization, and strategy. This was the key to Campbell's success.

Given that he commanded such heartfelt admiration and respect from his peers, that he was viewed as one of the South's leading citizens both before and after the Civil War, and that his accomplishments and talents at the bar led to his position on the Supreme Court, surprisingly little has been written about Campbell since that Saturday afternoon in April 1889. The only biography was published in 1920, not by a professional historian but by federal district judge Henry Groves Connor of North Carolina. Although this study is praiseworthy for its emphasis on Campbell's legal career, other aspects of the Alabamian's life are omitted or merely glossed over. Three-fifths of this work covers but eight of Campbell's seventy-seven years, and this imbalance makes it less a biography than a specialized study of Campbell's years on the Supreme Court.

Campbell's long life can in many respects be viewed as a near perfect mirror of the era in which he lived. He was involved in various degrees with nearly every significant event and development of the nineteenth century: Indian wars and removal, nullification, the economic mayhem of 1837, the rise of abolitionism, the annexation of Texas, the Mexican War, the Nashville Convention, the *Dred Scott* decision, John Brown's raid, the Civil War, Reconstruction, and Redemption. Campbell's political philosophy had always been one tinged with nationalistic overtones. Yet he was a profound supporter of states' rights, and by the 1850s Campbell's anxiety over the South's waning political influence prompted him to seek broader guarantees of state equality. Despite later claims that he molded or fashioned his ideology to meet certain exigencies or expedients, for example during the *Dred Scott* case, these are largely untrue. The essential premise of Campbell's philosophy, the fundamental basis for all of his thoughts, words, and deeds concerning both political and judicial events, was his unwavering conviction that all citizens of the United States possessed inalienable sovereignty that guaranteed to them rights and privileges all previous societies and civilizations had mostly chosen to ignore. He borrowed extensively from the political theorist John Locke, whose social contract theory is often reflected in Campbell's writings, briefs, and court decisions. He accepted the basic foundation of Lockean political philosophy early in his career—as evident in the submerged land cases—that all sovereignty rested exclusively with the American people and that all powers exercised by government originated in the people who, in their quest for social peace, agreed to surrender a portion of their sovereignty to the government for the good of society.

To Campbell, the United States was the beacon of hope, the engine propelling the rest of the world toward freedom and equality. He understood the necessity for the evolutionary nature of such progress, and he deplored all people—such as the abolitionists—who sought to revolutionize a process he believed had to develop slowly so as to prevent societal and economic mayhem. At the same time, though, he condemned those individuals—such as the filibusters and the slave traders—who sought to damper humanity's natural progression toward freedom and equality.

Though Campbell believed that social change was inevitable, he eschewed any revolutionary changes such as those that occurred too rapidly, before proper measures could be taken to offset inevitable dislocations. What he despised most of all about the abolitionists was, first, their open contempt for the Constitution. Second, and more important, Campbell believed that the abolitionists who demanded immediate emancipation were unconcerned that such a radical revolution would produce disastrous social, political, and economic chaos. His midcentury articles in *Southern Quarterly Review* are the most profound statement of Campbell's progressivism with regard to slavery. These also highlight, however, his inherent fear of rapid change. In this regard in particular Campbell embodied classical Burkean conservatism.

Any study of Campbell must include both the judicial and the political aspects of his life. In the latter realm, Campbell watched with ever-intensifying dread as the issues of slavery and its expansion into the territories, coupled with the unwavering determination of the country's abolitionist and Free Soil interests, drove a wedge deeper and deeper between North and South. These opposing forces, although largely insignificant movements in their infancy when Campbell began his career, entered the mainstream of American life and thought during the 1840s and 1850s. And when the dichotomy inherent in each movement became fundamentally attached to the democratic process, politicians were gauged no longer on their character or on their abilities but rather on their allegiance to each respective section and their position on the most divisive issue of the antebellum era: slavery. Campbell genuinely lamented the rise of single-issue politics in the country; he believed that it lent impetus to sectional political parties and ultimately destroyed the Democratic party when its North-South coalition divided on slavery.

Concurrently, Campbell realized that the sectional crisis was as much a product of the Industrial Revolution as of slavery. The South, therefore, had an obligation to modernize and to industrialize so that southerners could compete economically and politically with the North. If, he warned in the early 1850s, southerners refused to accept the rising tide of industrialization and steadfastly retained their agricultural foundation, their outmoded labor system, and their provincial mentality, they might well witness the downfall of southern society in as little as one generation. Campbell clearly recognized that slavery was a dying institution, and he suggested that the South had to acknowledge this and take measures to prevent the further degeneration of southern society. Therefore, he suggested that slaves be treated less harshly, that they should be educated, that they should be allowed to maintain strong family relationships, and that their legal status should be changed so that they could not be used as capital or credit. When slavery became no longer acceptable, when it was deemed counterproductive and anathema to American concepts of liberty and freedom, and when the institution gradually withered away, the South would have been long prepared and its former slave population could blend into southern society as productive and responsible citizens.

As the sectional crisis intensified throughout the 1840s and 1850s, Campbell likewise implored northerners to refrain from radicalism and to afford the South sufficient time to institute reforms that could rid the nation of slavery without utterly destroying the South's economy and society. He warned that if the abolitionists who demanded immediate emancipation without regard for the consequences became overly prominent in the North, the sectional crisis and the vexing slavery issue could destroy the nation. His most immediate concern at midcentury, however, was not slavery but rather the South's waning political position in the Union. He therefore advised northern politicians to acknowledge the necessity of maintaining the political equilibrium in Congress. Campbell agreed that due to climactic and environmental differences, plantation agriculture as practiced in the southern states was simply an impossibility in most of the territory acquired from Mexico. Thus he believed that slavery was genuinely peculiar to the South and could have but limited influence in the western territories. Even if new slave states were carved out of the Mexican Cession, this would have been but a temporary arrangement and would have provided the South the time it needed to institute reforms leading to gradual emancipation.

Campbell wished to be politically influential, but he despised politics, he had neither the inclination nor the fortitude for political campaigns, and he deplored the lack of principles he believed characterized most American politicians—"that class of thieves," as he once referred to them. Of course, it cannot be denied that Campbell was a wretched politician—as his affiliations with Yancey in 1848, Seward in 1861, and Lincoln in 1865 attest. He lacked the practicality and the willingness to compromise that marked the successful political careers of men such as Henry Clay and Abraham Lincoln, and he instead hovered in the ever-nebulous world of political philosophy. For these reasons, Campbell was no politician, and yet his penetrating anxiety over the sectional crisis drew him into the political arena on a number of occasions. Each time that he ventured from the bar and into the politician's domain, his naiveté and poor judgment of character made him appear ridiculous and foolish. Campbell clearly recognized that there was no place in American politics for one of his temperament and for a person with a proclivity to apply abstract principles to political crises. Such a man was best suited for the judiciary, and when he was invited to join the Supreme Court in 1853, he knew that he had indeed found his proper place in the American government.

His eight-year tenure on the Supreme Court was without question the happiest period of his life. This position allowed Campbell to implement his political philosophy, one that focused on states' rights and the nature of the federal Union. Campbell reasoned that normal, day-to-day life for most Americans was influenced almost exclusively by local concerns, and thus the states had the greatest responsibility to the people and retained their sovereignty in a trust. The powers of the federal government derived originally and solely from the states. The Constitution was a compact among states creating and empowering the federal government to preserve and promote the common interests among the community of states. The fundamental role for the federal government above all else was to ensure that no one state or group of states gained ascendancy over the others, and it was to ensure that political power at the national level be evenly divided among the states. To Campbell, the sectional discord tearing at the Union was fundamentally a constitutional crisis in which the federal government was allowing one section of the country to become politically dominant over the others. The near perfect balance created with the adoption of the Constitution in 1787 had been circumvented not only by the economic hegemony of the northern states but also by unprincipled politicians willing to thwart the Constitution and fundamentally alter the federal government's role in American society. While a member of the Supreme Court, therefore, Campbell sought to redefine the powers, duties, and responsibilities of the federal and the state governments and to make the balance of power not near perfect but more perfect.

In legal disputes where states had usurped powers exclusively reserved to the national government, such as in *Ableman v. Booth,* Campbell had little difficulty in deciding against the states. And in cases where American citizens violated national neutrality laws or those forbidding the importation of slaves, he likewise proved to be an avid guarantor of national authority. Conversely, whenever he believed that the federal government exceeded its constitutional boundaries, such as with the enactment of the Missouri Compromise line, Campbell sought to reestablish the constitutional dominion and political relationship between the federal government and the states. His decision in *Dred Scott v. Sandford* was fundamentally a treatise designed to reaffirm states' rights. Of course, what Campbell did not recognize—or simply refused to acknowledge—was that slavery was fundamentally a political and emotional issue that could not be solved by the judiciary. Slavery had so manifestly permeated southern society that Campbell's ruling, based solely on the abstract principles of constitutionalism and federalism, proved most unsatisfactory and merely confused the issues. For his efforts in *Dred Scott,* Campbell—and the other concurring justices—were chastised throughout the North as radical fire-eaters intent upon extending slavery not only to the territories but throughout the nation.

But Campbell was no fire-eater. The application of such a label to him is entirely unwarranted. He never sanctioned or encouraged secession, but he always maintained that states had the inherent right to dissolve the Union whenever they believed that their continued relationship with the federal government was detrimental to their safety. At the same time, though, he could barely imagine a situation that would necessitate secession. Campbell harbored a deep respect for the nation and an even deeper respect for the Constitution. He believed that that document was humanity's salvation, for it was based on principles of freedom and liberty and protected people from tyrannical government. He somewhat obsessively maintained that the Constitution was under direct assault first from the abolitionists, who claimed that it was a compact with Satan and who swore to destroy it, and, second and more ominously, from politicians and political theorists who championed the supremacy of the federal government over the power and influence of the states. But the South should not secede, Campbell maintained. Instead, southerners should diligently work to maintain the Constitution and the rights of the states. Only then could tyranny be avoided and the people's sovereignty protected.

Campbell's postwar political activity and legal career suggest that despite the horrible four-year Civil War that the nation underwent in the 1860s, he remained an unreconstructed advocate of states' rights. His philosophy at his death in 1889 was as much a part of the antebellum period as it had been in the 1830s. And during the postwar period when the United States rapidly developed into an industrial behemoth, Campbell's states' rights philosophy was undoubtedly antiquated, wholly impractical, and antithetical to the nation's continued development.

America in 1889 was far different from the place that Campbell had known for most of his life. The United States was undergoing changes that would soon make it one of the world's most powerful and advanced countries. Such rapid development was unquestionably disconcerting to people like Campbell who strove to maintain the nation of their youth—one with a small central government that did not intrude on state and local authority. Campbell harbored profound reverence for the past and a seemingly inborn fear of rapid change—again, classic examples of Burkean philosophy—that reflected his lifelong desire for order and stability. His father's death and the subsequent dissolution of the family estate in 1828 when Campbell was at a young and most impressionable age fostered considerable insecurities within him that he battled to overcome throughout his life. His unbridled fear of poverty—something that he experienced twice during his lifetime—was the principal impetus behind his unquenchable desire to succeed. And once his talent and genius in the courtroom brought him wealth and fame, any event—such as the abolition movement or the secession crisis—that portended instability or that encouraged rapid social, economic, or political change endangered Campbell's innate desire for order.

Finally, any label for Campbell that hints at radicalism would be inappropriate. He defies clear, uncluttered, or definitive typecasting. He was liberal in his unwavering love for individual freedom and liberty, yet he was conservative when social or political changes threatened to occur too rapidly. Campbell was progressive in his views toward the institution of slavery, but he was a reactionary toward Reconstruction. His residence in Mobile gave him a commercial outlook largely removed from the mostly agrarian South. In that regard, Campbell certainly welcomed the emergence of new industries such as railroads, banks, canals, and gas companies, and he invested in all of these. Conversely, while serving as an associate justice (photo 5), Campbell sought to protect states from the financial powers and corrupting influences of corpora-

The official portrait of Campbell in the U.S. Supreme Court Archives. This portrait was clearly painted from a photo of Campbell made well after his years on the bench. (Eric John Campbell, artist, courtesy of the Collection of the Supreme Court of the United States, Washington, D.C.)

tions and monopolies. During the crisis at midcentury, Campbell's affiliation with Yancey and his publications through the Southern Rights Association lent considerable credence to the contention that he was a fire-eating radical hell-bent on provoking secession. Yet his moderating influences at the Nashville Convention and during Southern Rights Association conventions indicate that he was by no means a southern radical. For Campbell, as for many social and political moderates, the principal guiding maxim that seemed to dominate every thought and action was perhaps rooted in the Aristotelian ideal of *sophrosyne*—"nothing in excess."

Notes

1. Ancestry and Antecedents

1. Susan Campbell Rowland, "Records Copied From the Family Bible of Mr. Archibald Campbell and His Wife Rebecca (Kirk) Campbell," Papers of John Archibald Campbell, Record Box 1, Alabama Department of Archives and History, Montgomery, Alabama. Hereafter cited as ADAH; Rowland was Archibald and Rebecca Campbell's granddaughter; A document by an unknown author in the Campbell Family Papers, Southern Historical Collection, Library of the University of North Carolina at Chapel Hill (hereafter cited as Campbell Family Papers, SHC-UNC) states: "The family tradition (supported by imperfect records) is that the original ancestors came from Scotland with Flora MacDonald and with her settled in North Carolina, but Judge Campbell's ancestors emigrated thence to Georgia"; Alabama State Bar Association, "An Address on the Life of John Archibald Campbell, by Henry G. Connor, Delivered at Birmingham, Alabama, 12 July 1917," *Minutes of the Fortieth Annual Meeting of the Alabama Bar Association* (Birmingham: Alabama Bar Association, 1917), 105–6.

2. Henry Groves Connor, *John Archibald Campbell, Associate Justice of the United States Supreme Court, 1853–1861* (Boston: Houghton Mifflin, 1920), 2.

3. Rowland, "Records Copied From the Family Bible," Campbell Papers, ADAH.

4. Kenneth Coleman, ed., *A History of Georgia*, 2d ed. (Athens: University of Georgia Press, 1991), 49–50; George R. Gilmer, *Sketches of Some of the First Settlers of Upper Georgia, of the Cherokees, and the Author* (Americus, Ga.: Americus Book, 1926), 141–42; Writers' Program of the Works Projects Administration, *The Story of Washington-Wilkes* (Athens: University of Georgia Press, 1941), 10–14; Eliza A. Bowen, *The Story of Wilkes County, Georgia* (Marietta, Ga.: Continental Book, 1950), 2–3.

5. Gilmer, *Sketches of Some of the First Settlers*, 161–63; Rowland, "Records Copied From the Family Bible," ADAH; Mary B. Warren and Sarah F. White, comps., *Marriages and Deaths, 1820–1830, Abstracted From Extant Georgia Newspapers* (Danielsville, Ga.: Heritage Papers, 1972), 20.

6. Writer's Program, *Story of Washington-Wilkes*, 26.

7. Ibid.; Lucian Lamar Knight, *Georgia's Landmarks, Memorials, and Legends*, vol. 2 (Atlanta: Byrd Printing, 1914), 1042.

8. John Clark, by all contemporary accounts, was an ostentatious, boisterous, and colorful person whose many antics included public drunkenness, fighting, and dueling. At the same time, however, Clark had adroit political instincts that enabled him to parlay his well-earned odious reputation into political power. Clark's political ambitions soon brought him up against the supporters of George M. Troup. Factions formed around these two individuals, and nearly all political struggles became personal attacks on one faction or the other for the first three decades of the nineteenth century. Having Clark in the family was probably a mixed blessing for the Williamsons. Despite Clark's political power and personal popular-

ity, his reputation and caustic temperament often led to heated arguments, physical violence, and dueling. Duncan Greene seems to have had the good sense to remain as politically neutral as possible despite his marriage into the Williamson clan.

9. John Archibald Campbell, therefore, was Sarah Williamson's grandson. He was also a first cousin to L. Q. C. Lamar, with whom he exchanged personal letters on occasion.

10. "Names of Col. Micajah Williamson's Children, Whom They Married, and Their Records," Campbell Papers, Box 1, ADAH.

11. William J. Northen, ed., *Men of Mark in Georgia,* vol. 2, "Duncan G. Campbell" (Spartanburg, S.C.: Reprint, 1974), 223.

12. Connor, *John Archibald Campbell,* 3.

13. Robert Scott Davis, Jr., comp., *The Wilkes County Papers, 1772–1833* (Easley, S.C.: Southern Historical Press, 1979), 179–82.

14. John Archibald Campbell, "Incidents in the Life of John A. Campbell, Recorded 13 March 1883," Campbell Family Papers, SHC-UNC; Rowland, "Records Copied From the Family Bible," Campbell Papers, ADAH.

15. Rowland, "Records Copied From the Family Bible, Campbell Papers," ADAH.

16. Ibid.

17. Northen, *Men of Mark in Georgia,* 223–24; Gilmer, *Sketches of Some of the First Settlers,* 161; Elbert W. G. Boogher, "Secondary Education in Georgia, 1732–1858" (Ph.D. dissertation, University of Pennsylvania, 1933), 221; Dorothy Orr, *A History of Education in Georgia* (Chapel Hill: University of North Carolina Press, 1950), 19.

18. U.S., Congress, House, *Report of the Select Committee of the House of Representatives, To Which Were Referred The Messages of the President U.S. of the 5th and 8th February, and 2nd March, 1827, With Accompanying Documents and a Report and Resolutions of the Legislature of Georgia,* H. R. 98, 19th Congress, 2d Session, 1827 (Washington, D.C.: Gales and Seaton, 1827), 129–30; hereafter H. R. 98, 19/2. A transcribed copy of this treaty is located in the Campbell Family Papers, SHC-UNC.

19. Benjamin W. Griffith, Jr., *McIntosh and Weatherford, Creek Indian Leaders* (Tuscaloosa: University of Alabama Press, 1988), 221–22; Michael D. Green, *The Politics of Indian Removal: Creek Government and Society in Crisis* (Lincoln: University of Nebraska Press, 1982), 98–99; Mary Young, "Racism in Red and Black: Indians and Other Free People of Color in Georgia Law, Politics, and Removal Policy," *Georgia Historical Quarterly* 73 (Fall 1989): 502–3.

20. Commissioners' Report, 10 February 1825, H. R. 98, 19/2, 127–28.

21. "Treaty of Indian Springs," Campbell Family Papers, SHC-UNC; "Report of the Commissioners Appointed to Treat With the Creek Indians," H. R. 98, 19/2, 88. Despite Campbell's charges, most historians agree that Crowell and Walker acted in what they believed to be the Indians' best interest. As Creek Indian agent, Crowell had as part of his duties to distribute any funds or supplies that the federal government allocated to the Creeks. Apparently Campbell did not want Crowell to be responsible for such a large amount of money. Griffith, *McIntosh and Weatherford,* 238, 266–68.

22. Green, *Politics of Indian Removal,* 98; Griffith, *McIntosh and Weatherford,* 250–51.

23. "Major Andrews' Report to the Secretary of War," H. R. 98, 19/2, 315–16.

24. During the third week of January 1826, Secretary of War James Barbour negotiated and signed the Treaty of Washington with a deputation of Creeks clearly representative of the entire Nation. This treaty, in wording similar to that of Campbell and Meriwether, provided for the cession of nearly all Creek lands within Georgia's boundaries. The only

difference between the two cessions was that the latter provided that the Creeks retain a relatively small strip of land in northwestern Georgia of about 1 million acres.

25. Griffith, *McIntosh and Weatherford,* 231.

26. Young, "Racism in Red and Black," 503; Green, *Politics of Indian Removal,* 103; Coleman, ed., *A History of Georgia,* 130–31.

27. Stephen F. Miller, *The Bench and Bar of Georgia: Memoirs and Sketches,* vol. 1 (Philadelphia: J. B. Lippincott, 1858), 136.

28. Henry G. Connor states that Duncan Greene would unquestionably have been elected had he not died on the eve of the gubernatorial election. The election was held in November 1827, however, and Duncan Greene did not die until July 1828. Connor's mistake has prompted several subsequent historians to err on this point.

29. Gilmer, *Sketches of Some of the Early Settlers,* 162.

30. Connor, *John Archibald Campbell,* 6–7; Rowland, "Records Copied From the Family Bible," Campbell Papers, ADAH.

31. Bowen, *Story of Wilkes County Georgia,* 56–57; Writer's Project, *Story of Washington-Wilkes,* 52–53.

32. Campbell, "Incidents in the Life of John Archibald Campbell," Campbell Family Papers, SHC-UNC.

33. Thomas G. Dyer, *The University of Georgia: A Bicentennial History, 1785–1965* (Athens: University of Georgia Press, 1985), 10–23; E. Merton Coulter, *College Life in the Old South* (Athens: University of Georgia Press, 1951), 34–36.

34. Dyer, *University of Georgia,* 49; Coulter, *College Life in the Old South,* 36–37.

35. Campbell, "Incidents in the Life of John Archibald Campbell," Campbell Family Papers, SHC-UNC.

36. Coulter, *College Life in the Old South,* 36; Dyer, *University of Georgia,* 48.

37. Coulter, *College Life in the Old South,* 36.

38. Connor, *John Archibald Campbell,* 7; Gilmer, *Sketches of Some of the Early Settlers,* 162.

39. U.S., Supreme Court, Fifth Circuit, Edward C. Billings, *A Summary of the Life and Characteristics of Hon. John A. Campbell Contained in the Remarks of Judge Edward C. Billings Upon the Occasion of the Presentation to the United States Courts of Resolutions, and in Response to Addresses, by the Bar of New Orleans in Honor of Judge Campbell's Memory, New Orleans, April 6, 1889* (Washington, D.C.: Government Printing Office, 1889), 2.

40. Coulter, *College Life in the Old South,* 130.

41. Moses Waddel to Rev. Turner Saunders, 6 November 1823, in James Edmonds Saunders, *Early Settlers of Alabama,* vol. 1 (New Orleans: L. Graham and Son, 1899), 8.

42. Connor, *John Archibald Campbell,* 7.

43. *Macon Telegraph,* 12 December 1826; Warren and White, *Marriages and Deaths,* 20.

44. Campbell, "Incidents in the Life of John Archibald Campbell," Campbell Family Papers, SHC-UNC.

45. *Macon Telegraph,* August 11, 1828.

46. Campbell, "Incidents in the Life of John Archibald Campbell," Campbell Family Papers, SHC-UNC.

47. Rowland, "Records Copied From the Family Bible," Campbell Papers, ADAH.

48. Campbell, "Incidents in the Life of John Archibald Campbell," Campbell Family Papers, SHC-UNC.

49. Knight, *Georgia's Landmarks, Memorials, and Legends,* 2:139–40.

50. Some sources note that he taught school while in Florida. This information is probably incorrect; Campbell reported that he earned money solely by tutoring his cousin. Campbell, "Incidents in the Life of John Archibald Campbell," Campbell Family Papers, SHC-UNC.

51. Ibid.

52. Rowland, "Records Copied From the Family Bible," Campbell Papers, ADAH; John Archibald's grandfather and namesake moved to Montgomery with his daughter, Margaret Jane, shortly after the death of his wife in 1816. John Archibald, Sr., died in Montgomery in November 1820. Margaret Jane married George W. Towns, who served as the governor of Georgia from 1847 to 1851.

53. For more detailed appraisals of the Broad River residents, see J. Mills Thornton, *Politics and Power in a Slave Society: Alabama, 1800–1860* (Baton Rouge: Louisiana State University Press, 1978), 7–8, 11–20; and Albert B. Moore, *History of Alabama* (Tuscaloosa: Alabama Book Store, 1951), 75–81.

54. Thornton, *Politics and Power in a Slave Society,* 11–12.

55. Henry DeLeon Southerland, Jr., and Jerry Elijah Brown, *The Federal Road Through Georgia, the Creek Nation, and Alabama, 1806–1836* (Tuscaloosa: University of Alabama Press, 1989), 136.

56. Campbell, "Incidents in the Life of John Archibald Campbell," Campbell Family Papers, SHC-UNC.

57. Clanton W. Williams, "Early Ante-Bellum Montgomery: A Black Belt Constituency," *Journal of Southern History* 7 (1941): 500–501.

58. Ibid., 498; J. Wayne Flynt, *Montgomery: An Illustrated History* (Woodland Hills, Calif.: Windsor Publications, 1980), 5.

59. Clanton, "Early Ante-Bellum Montgomery," 498; Flynt, *Montgomery,* 5.

60. Flynt, *Montgomery,* 5.

61. Moore, *History of Alabama,* 320–21; Flynt, *Montgomery,* 6–7.

62. Flynt, *Montgomery,* 7–8.

63. Arthur F. Howington, "Violence in Alabama: A Study of Late Ante-bellum Montgomery," *Alabama Review* 27 (July 1974): 213.

64. Williams, "Early Ante-Bellum Montgomery," 502; Howington, "Violence in Alabama," 215.

65. Campbell, "Incidents in the Life of John Archibald Campbell," Campbell Family Papers, SHC-UNC.

66. Montgomery County, Alabama, *White Marriage Licenses Index,* vol. A-18, 1817–1919, Book 2, C–E, ADAH.

67. Campbell, "Incidents in the Life of John Archibald Campbell," Campbell Family Papers, SHC-UNC.

68. Untitled document, Campbell Family Papers, SHC-UNC; Campbell, "Incidents in the Life of John Archibald Campbell," Campbell Family Papers, SHC-UNC; Connor, *John Archibald Campbell,* 8.

69. Alfred W. Goldthwaite to David L. Bagwell, 10 May 1983, John Archibald Campbell File, John Archibald Campbell Federal Courthouse, Mobile, Alabama.

70. William Garrett, *Reminiscences of Public Men in Alabama For Thirty Years* (Atlanta: Plantation Publishing, 1872), 475; Willis Brewer, *Alabama: Her History, Resources, War Record, and Public Men From 1540 to 1872* (Montgomery, Ala.: Barrett and Brown, 1872), 399–400; Campbell, "Incidents in the Life of John Archibald Campbell," Campbell Family Papers, SHC-UNC.

71. Garrett, *Reminiscences,* 475.

72. Ibid., 476.

73. Ibid., 549; Connor, *John Archibald Campbell,* 8.

74. John Archibald Campbell to P. C. Cameron, September [?], 1887, Cameron Family Papers, Southern Historical Collection, Wilson Library, University of North Carolina-Chapel Hill.

2. Professional Career, 1830–1842

1. Connor, *John Archibald Campbell,* 9; George W. Duncan, "John Archibald Campbell," *Studies in Southern and Alabama History,* vol. 5, *Transactions of the Alabama Historical Society* (Montgomery: Alabama Historical Society, 1905), 8; David A. Bagwell, "The John Archibald Campbell United States Courthouse in Mobile," *Alabama Lawyer* 43 (May 1983): 154.

2. Joseph G. Baldwin, *The Flush Times of Alabama and Mississippi: A Series of Sketches* (Americus, Ga.: Americus Book, 1853).

3. Garrett, *Reminiscences,* 287; Connor, *John Archibald Campbell,* 10.

4. H. C. Semple, *In Memoriam: Addresses Delivered on the Occasion of the Presentation to the United States Circuit Court Sitting at Montgomery, Alabama, of Portraits of Judge John A. Campbell and Judge William Burnham Woods* (n.p., n.d.), 3.

5. Garrett, *Reminiscences,* 287.

6. Campbell was offered a seat on Alabama's Supreme Court in 1836 by Governor Clay and in 1852 by Governor Collier; he declined both offers. He also turned down an offer from the Jackson administration in 1836 to become secretary to the American legation in London. Campbell, "Incidents in the Life of John Archibald Campbell," Campbell Family Papers, SHC-UNC; "Remarks of Thomas L. Bayne," in U.S., Supreme Court, Fifth Circuit, *Memorial Meeting in Honor of the Late Judge John A. Campbell, United States Circuit Court, New Orleans, Louisiana, 6 April 1889* (Washington, D.C.: Government Printing Office, 1889), 15.

7. Semple, *In Memoriam,* 3.

8. Ibid.

9. Ibid., 9, 14–15.

10. Garrett, *Reminiscences,* 286.

11. John Archibald Campbell, "The Creek Indian War of 1836," *Transactions of the Alabama Historical Society* 3 (1899): 162; Brewer, *Alabama,* 51–53; Moore, *History of Alabama,* 30–32; Peter A. Brannon, "Creek Indian War, 1836–1837," *Alabama Historical Quarterly* 13 (1951): 156; William Warren Rogers, Robert David Ward, Leah Rawls Atkins, and Wayne Flynt, *Alabama: The History of a Deep South State* (Tuscaloosa: University of Alabama Press, 1994), 90–91.

12. Campbell, "The Creek Indian War of 1836," 163.

13. Kenneth L. Valliere, "The Creek War of 1836: A Military History," *Chronicles of Oklahoma* 57 (Winter 1979): 464.

14. Campbell, "The Creek Indian War of 1836," 162.

15. Ibid., 163; Green, *Politics of Indian Removal,* 184; Moore, *History of Alabama,* 32; Rogers et al., *Alabama,* 136–37.

16. John Gayle to Lewis Cass, 27 May 1835, Governor's Papers: John Gayle, Executive Letter Book, ADAH, 167.

17. Valliere, "The Creek War of 1836," 465; Campbell, "The Creek Indian War of 1836," 162; Creek Agent Sanford should not be confused with his son, John William Augustus Sanford, who became state Attorney General in 1865. Brewer, *Alabama,* 473; Garrett, *Reminiscences,* 727–29.

18. Sanford to Cass, 22 June 1835, in Valliere, "The Creek War of 1836," 466.

19. Campbell, "The Creek Indian War of 1836," 165.

20. Valliere, "The Creek War of 1836," 481.

21. Ibid., 466; John K. Mahon, *History of the Second Seminole War, 1835–1842*, rev. ed. (Gainesville: University of Florida Press, 1991), 190–91.

22. Valliere, "The Creek War of 1836," 468, 470; Moore, *History of Alabama*, 32; Campbell, "The Creek Indian War of 1836," 163.

23. *Huntsville Southern Advocate*, 7 June 1836.

24. Clement Comer Clay, "Annual Message for 1835," *Journal of the House of Representatives of the State of Alabama, Begun and Held at the Town of Tuscaloosa on the Third Monday of November 1835* (Tuscaloosa: Meek and McGuire, 1836), 53.

25. C. C. Clay to Lewis Cass, 19 March 1836, Governor's Papers: C. C. Clay, Executive Letter Book, ADAH, 189.

26. Campbell, "The Creek Indian War of 1836," 163.

27. "Proclamation of C. C. Clay, Governor of the State of Alabama, to the Chiefs and Warriors of the Creek Tribe of Indians," 20 May 1836, *Huntsville Southern Advocate*, 31 May 1836.

28. Campbell, "The Creek Indian War of 1836," 163.

29. Cass to Thomas S. Jesup, 19 May 1836, *American State Papers: Military Affairs*, 6:622–23; Green, *Politics of Indian Removal*, 185.

30. Mahon, *History of the Second Seminole War*, 190; Valliere, "The Creek War of 1836," 474–75.

31. Valliere, "The Creek War of 1836," 474.

32. Ibid., 475–78.

33. *Montgomery Advertiser*, 11 June 1836; Campbell, "The Creek Indian War of 1836," 164.

34. *Huntsville Southern Advocate*, 17 June 1836; Valliere, "The Creek War of 1836," 477.

35. Mahon, *History of the Second Seminole War*, 190; Valliere, "The Creek War of 1836," 477–78; Campbell, "The Creek Indian War of 1836," 164.

36. Jesup to Scott, 17 June 1836, *American State Papers, Military Affairs* VII: 334; Valliere, "The Creek War of 1836," 478.

37. *Huntsville Southern Advocate*, 5 July 1836.

38. Campbell, "The Creek Indian War of 1836," 164.

39. Ibid.

40. Ibid.

41. Ibid., 165; Valliere, "The Creek War of 1836," 481; Jesup to Cass, 25 June 1836, *American State Papers, Military Affairs*, 7:348.

42. L. D. Miller, *History of Alabama* (n.p.: By the Author, 1901), 115.

43. Campbell, "Incidents in the Life of John Archibald Campbell," Campbell Family Papers, SHC-UNC; Garrett, *Reminiscences*, 286; Connor, *John Archibald Campbell*, 9.

44. For a lucid and often insightful introduction to the origins of politics in antebellum Alabama, see Thornton, *Politics and Power in a Slave Society;* Theodore H. Jack, *Sectionalism and Party Politics in Alabama, 1819–1842* (Spartanburg, S.C.: Reprint, 1975), 34–36.

45. Jack, *Sectionalism and Party Politics*, 37–54; Moore, *History of Alabama*, 165–70; Thornton, *Politics and Power in a Slave Society*, 28–31; Frank Lawrence Owsley, Jr., "Francis Scott Key's Mission to Alabama in 1833," *Alabama Review* 23 (July 1970): 181–92.

46. Thornton, *Politics and Power in a Slave Society*, 29–30.

47. Campbell to Henry Goldthwaite, 20 November 1836, Campbell Family Papers, SHC-UNC.

48. Garrett, *Reminiscences*, 287.

49. Campbell to Henry Goldthwaite, 20 November 1836, Campbell Family Papers, SHC-UNC; Campbell to Henry Goldthwaite, 27 November 1836, Campbell Family Papers, SHC-UNC.

50. Campbell to Henry Goldthwaite, 20 November 1836, ibid.

51. Campbell to Henry Goldthwaite, 27 November 1836, ibid.

52. Thornton, *Politics and Power in a Slave Society,* 33–34; Garrett, *Reminiscences,* 377–78; Moore, *History of Alabama,* 172; Campbell to Henry Goldthwaite, 20 November 1836, Campbell Family Papers, SHC-UNC.

53. Campbell to Henry Goldthwaite, 27 November 1836, Campbell Family Papers, SHC-UNC.

54. Ibid.

55. Ibid.

56. Thornton, *Politics and Power in a Slave Society,* 78–79.

57. Campbell to C. C. Clay, 10 May 1837, C. C. Clay Papers, Administrative File, ADAH.

58. Garrett, *Reminiscences,* 286.

59. Ibid.; Thornton explains that the effects of the relief measure were disastrous, for this law required the state banks not only to circulate another $5 million dollars of loans but also to suspend the collection of $5 million of debts. In many respects, Thornton states, the relief measure of 1837 made bank reform, another Campbell legislative effort, necessary by 1842. Thornton, *Politics and Power in a Slave Society,* 79.

60. Garrett, *Reminiscences,* 286.

61. Campbell, "Incidents in the Life of John Archibald Campbell," Campbell Family Papers, SHC-UNC.

62. David Abrams, "The State Bank of Alabama, 1841–1845" (M. A. thesis, Auburn University, 1965), 1.

63. William H. Brantley, *Banking in Alabama, 1816–1860,* vol. 1 (Birmingham, Ala.: Oxmoor Press, 1967), 352–55.

64. Rogers et al., *Alabama,* 144; Moore, *Alabama,* 1:303.

65. Thornton, *Politics and Power in a Slave Society,* 113–14.

66. Brantley, *Banking in Alabama,* 1:194–97.

67. Garrett, *Reminiscences,* 259.

68. *Mobile Register,* 29 June 1842 in Brantley, *Banking in Alabama,* 1:184.

69. Ibid.

70. Brantley, *Banking in Alabama,* 1:180–81.

71. Rogers et al., *Alabama,* 144.

72. Governor's Annual Message, 5 December 1842, *Journal of the House of Representatives of the General Assembly of the State of Alabama Begun and Held in the City of Tuscaloosa, on the First Monday in December 1842* (Tuscaloosa: Phelan and Harris, 1843), 14.

73. *House Journal,* 15 December 1842, 11.

74. Ibid., 12.

75. Ibid., 19 December 1842, 94–95.

76. Brantley, *Banking in Alabama,* 1:193–94; *House Journal,* 19 December 1942, 98.

77. Brantley, *Banking in Alabama,* 1:193–94.

78. Garrett, *Reminiscences,* 588–90.

79. Campbell to J. L. M. Curry, September 1886, published as J. L. M. Curry, *Hon. Francis Strother Lyon as Commissioner and Trustee of Alabama, A Sketch* (n.p.: n.d.), 30.

3. Submerged Lands and States' Rights

1. Moore, *History of Alabama*, 46–47; Harriet E. Amos, *Cotton City: Urban Development in Antebellum Mobile* (Tuscaloosa: University of Alabama Press, 1985), 1.

2. Amos, *Cotton City*, 2; Paul Wallace Gates, "Private Land Claims in the South," *Journal of Southern History* 22 (1956): 184.

3. Of course, New Orleans had been the region's leading port city for a number of decades. With Alabama's river system emptying directly into Mobile Bay, though, in the 1820s south and central Alabama planters began transporting their cotton crops directly through Mobile, where export fees were lower. North Alabama planters largely continued to ship their agricultural products through New Orleans.

4. Amos, *Cotton City*, 2.

5. Ibid.

6. Lucille Griffith, *Alabama: A Documentary History to 1900* (University: University of Alabama Press, 1987), 186; Erwin Craighead, *Mobile: Fact and Tradition, Noteworthy People and Events* (Mobile, Ala.: Powers Printing, 1930), 128.

7. Ernest R. Bartley, *The Tidelands Oil Controversy: A Legal and Historical Analysis* (Austin: University of Texas Press, 1953), 45.

8. Amos, *Cotton City*, 21; Griffith, *Alabama*, 189.

9. Campbell, "Incidents in the Life of John Archibald Campbell," Campbell Family Papers, SHC-UNC.

10. Ibid.

11. Boogher, "Secondary Education in Georgia," 221–22; Orr, *History of Education in Georgia*, 149–50.

12. Garrett, *Reminiscences*, 394.

13. U.S., Supreme Court, Fifth Circuit, "Life and Characteristics," 2.

14. Bernard A. Reynolds, *Sketches of Mobile* (1868; reprint ed., Bossier City, La.: Tipton Printing, 1971), 23–24.

15. Craighead, *Mobile: Fact and Tradition*, 216.

16. Campbell once wrote to his daughter Katherine: "Duncan so entirely failed in the Supreme Court that I cannot trust him again to go there. He went into court and behaved badly under liquor. You can well understand how I feel about such things. I ought to have anticipated it, but hoped against hope." This letter was written during a period when Campbell was attempting a reconciliation with his son. Unfortunately, Duncan could not refrain from drinking, and his relationship with his father grew strained once again. John Archibald Campbell to Katherine C. Groner, 15 June 1874, Campbell Family Papers, SHC-UNC.

17. Connor, *John Archibald Campbell*, 257.

18. Edward W. Faith, "Great Law Suits Affecting Mobile," *Alabama Lawyer* 1 (October 1940): 320; James Robert Maxwell Alston, "John Archibald Campbell, States' Rights, and the Federal Union" (Senior thesis, Princeton University, 1958), 15.

19. *Mayor and Aldermen of the City of Mobile v. Miguel D. Eslava*, 16 Peters 260 (U.S. 1842).

20. Faith, "Great Law Suits Affecting Mobile," 330; Bartley, *Tidelands Oil Controversy*, 46.

21. Frederick E. Hosen, *Unfolding Westward in Treaty and Law: Land Documents in United States History from the Appalachians to the Pacific, 1783–1934* (Jefferson, N.C.: McFarland, 1988), 112.

22. The full title of this legislation was "An Act to Enable the People of the Alabama Territory to Form a Constitution and State Government, and for the Admission of Such Gov-

ernment into the Union *on an Equal Footing with the Original States,* March 2, 1819," in Hosen, *Unfolding Westward,* 118. Italics mine.

23. Faith, "Great Law Suits Affecting Mobile," 331; Bartley, *Tidelands Oil Controversy,* 46.

24. *The Mayor and Aldermen of the City of Mobile v. Eslava,* 9 Porter 579–80, 583 (Ala. 1839).

25. Faith, "Great Law Suits Affecting Mobile," 336.

26. 9 Porter 577–605 (Ala. 1839).

27. *Heirs of Pollard v. Kibbe,* 9 Porter 712–27 (Ala. 1839).

28. Ibid., 713–15.

29. Edward S. Corwin, *National Supremacy: Treaty Power v. State Power* (Gloucester, Mass.: Peter Smith, 1965), 102–3; Robert R. Russel, "Constitutional Doctrines with Regard to Slavery in Territories," *Journal of Southern History* 32 (1966): 467–68.

30. Garrett, *Reminiscences of Public Men in Alabama,* 718; Thornton, *Politics and Power in a Slave Society,* 182, 192. Although Collier was a staunch states' rights advocate on most issues, Thornton correctly shows that his views on fiscal matters were for the most part moderate. With the submerged land cases, however, Collier advanced what should be considered a radical version of states' rights philosophy.

31. 9 Porter 589 (Ala. 1839).

32. Ibid., 600–601.

33. *Heirs of Pollard v. Kibbe,* 9 Porter 721 (Ala. 1839).

34. Garrett, *Reminiscences of Public Men in Alabama,* 267–68.

35. 9 Porter 723 (Ala. 1839).

36. The full text of the Adams-Onis Treaty is found in Hosen, *Unfolding Westward,* 109–115.

37. 9 Porter 726 (Ala. 1839); italics mine.

38. *Lessee of William Pollard's Heirs, etc. v. Gaius Kibbe,* 14 Peters 353–429 (U.S. 1840).

39. Ibid., 366.

40. *The Mayor and Aldermen of the City of Mobile v. Miguel D. Eslava,* 16 Peters 232–58 (U.S. 1842).

41. Sargeant's affiliation with the submerged land cases perfectly illustrates why special care should be taken not to infer personal positions from those argued in court. Sargeant was a close friend of Nicholas Biddle's and, one may suppose, ardently anti states' rights. Yet he argued these cases solely on the basis of Campbell's reasoning, which he obviously believed sound. The Oliver Wendell Holmes Devise, *History of the Supreme Court of the United States,* vol. 5, *The Taney Period, 1836–64,* by Carl B. Swisher (New York: Macmillan Publishing, 1974), 24, 752–53.

42. 16 Peters 241 (U.S. 1842); italics mine.

43. Ibid., 243; italics mine.

44. *Lessee of John Pollard, William Pollard, John Fowler and Harriet, His wife, Henry P. Ensign and Phebe, his Wife, Joseph Case and Eliza, His Wife v. Joseph F. Files,* 2 Howard 591–606 (U.S. 1844).

45. Swisher, *Taney Period,* 1–2.

46. Ibid., 753.

47. *John Pollard et al. v. John Hagan et al.,* 3 Howard 210–34 (U.S. 1845).

48. Ibid., 220; Bartley, *Tidelands Oil Controversy,* 46.

49. 3 Howard 214–15 (U.S. 1845); Faith, "Great Law Suits Affecting Mobile," 338; italics mine.

50. 3 Howard 219–21 (U.S. 1845).

51. Ibid., 224.

52. Clare Cushman, ed., *The Supreme Court Justices: Illustrated Biographies, 1789–1993* (Washington, D.C.: Congressional Quarterly, 1993), 128; Bartley, *Tidelands Oil Controversy*, 47; 3 Howard 231 (U.S. 1845); italics mine.

53. 3 Howard 232 (U.S. 1845); italics mine.

54. Cushman, ed., *Supreme Court Justices*, 128–29; 3 Howard 235 (U.S. 1845).

55. Bartley, *Tidelands Oil Controversy*, 49; Swisher, *Taney Period*, 753.

56. *John Goodtitle Pollard's Heirs ex dem. v. Gaius Kibbe*, 9 Howard 471–78 (U.S. 1849).

57. 9 Howard 478 (U.S. 1849).

58. Bartley notes that the *Pollard* rule was followed with approval in 52 Supreme Court decisions and 244 lower court rulings. Bartley, *Tidelands Oil Controversy*, 49.

59. Tax Roll, 1841, City of Mobile Municipal Archives; Campbell's Conception Street home was razed many years ago. The lot on which the house once stood is today a privately owned parking facility. Chandler's former home has undergone extensive renovations; the slave quarters were removed several decades ago, but the main house remains mostly unchanged.

60. Tax Rolls, 1843, 1845, 1848, 1850, City of Mobile Municipal Archives, Mobile, Alabama.

4. Campbell and the Peculiar Institution

1. John Archibald Campbell, "Slavery in the United States," *Southern Quarterly Review* 34 (July 1847): 94.

2. Ibid., 95, 102.

3. Ibid., 94–95.

4. Ibid., 103–6, 106–7, 111–12.

5. Ibid., 115.

6. Ibid., 115, 132.

7. Ibid.

8. Ibid., 122, 132, 133.

9. Ibid., 133.

10. Ibid., 134.

11. John Archibald Campbell, "Slavery Among the Romans," *Southern Quarterly Review* 35 (October 1848): 405, 407, 413.

12. Ibid., 414, 425.

13. Ibid., 425.

14. John Archibald Campbell, "British West India Islands," *Southern Quarterly Review* 37 (January 1850): 342–46.

15. John Archibald Campbell, "Slavery Throughout the World," *Southern Quarterly Review* 38 (April 1851): 305–15, 317 (quotation).

16. Ibid., 324.

17. Ibid., 337–38.

18. Ibid., 338.

19. Ibid.

20. Ibid., 339.

21. Campbell to Benjamin R. Curtis, 20 July 1865. Published as "A View of the Confederacy From the Inside," *Century Illustrated Monthly Magazine* 38 (October 1889): 953; hereafter cited as "Letter to Curtis."

22. The probate records that would reveal whether Campbell sold or manumitted these slaves were unavailable at the time of this writing. Hundreds of boxes containing thousands

of documents were discovered during recent renovations to the Mobile County Courthouse. It will be years, however, before these records are properly categorized and available to the researcher.

23. Register of Sale, 1 April 1858, Miscellaneous Book "G," Page 18, Mobile County Probate Courthouse, Mobile, Alabama.

24. Bill of Sale, 22 June 1858, Mobile County Probate Courthouse, Mobile, Alabama.

25. Campbell did not sell his warehouse, and though it suffered extensive damage during the war, this structure provided much needed income for the Campbell family during the postwar period.

5. The Crisis at Midcentury

1. On Wilmot's Proviso and southern reaction, see David S. Heidler, *Pulling the Temple Down: The Fire-Eaters and the Destruction of the Union* (Mechanicsburg, Pa.: Stackpole Books, 1994), 13–15; David M. Potter, *The Impending Crisis, 1848–1861* (New York: Harper Torchbooks, 1976), 22–25; Allan Nevins, *Ordeal of the Union,* vol. 1, *Fruits of Manifest Destiny, 1847–1852* (New York: Charles Scribner's Sons, 1975), 9; James G. Randall and David Herbert Donald, *The Civil War and Reconstruction,* 2d ed. (Lexington, Mass.: D. C. Heath, 1969), 83–84; William W. Freehling, *The Road to Disunion: Secessionists at Bay, 1776–1854* (New York: Oxford University Press, 1990), 459–60.

2. Campbell to John C. Calhoun, 20 November 1847, "Correspondence Addressed to Calhoun," *Annual Report of the American Historical Association, 1899* (Washington, D.C.: Government Printing Office, 1899), 1141.

3. Potter, *Impending Crisis,* 23.

4. John Archibald Campbell, "Slavery in the United States," *Southern Quarterly Review* (July 1847): 91–134; This article, examined more closely in the previous chapter, includes many of Campbell's perceptions of the sectional crisis, the abolition movement, the proper southern response, and his recommendations for reform.

5. Ibid., 91.

6. Ibid.

7. Ibid., 92.

8. John Niven, *John C. Calhoun and the Price of Union: A Biography* (Baton Rouge: Louisiana State University Press, 1988), 323–24.

9. Campbell to John C. Calhoun, 20 November 1847, *Annual Report,* 1139; In his second letter to Calhoun dated 20 December 1847, Campbell wrote, "I made it a point to go over the different offices of publication of the [Massachusetts Anti-Slavery] Society and to examine their publications. I should say that their press was not very active" (Campbell to John C. Calhoun, 20 December 1847, *Annual Report,* 1143).

10. Campbell to John C. Calhoun, 20 December 1847, *Annual Report,* 1141.

11. Ibid., 1142.

12. The "Nicholson letter," written by Cass to Senator A. O. P. Nicholson of Tennessee, was the first clear formulation of popular sovereignty. See Nevins, *Ordeal of the Union,* 1:30; Russel, "Constitutional Doctrines with Regard to Slavery," 473, states that Cass's constitutional theory of popular sovereignty should not be confused with what was termed "squatter sovereignty," a doctrine applied during the 1850s as a political expedient principally to remove the vexing slavery issue from Congress.

13. "The Prospect Before Us," *Mobile Herald,* 5 January 1848.

14. Campbell to John C. Calhoun, 20 November 1847, *Annual Report,* 1141.

15. Ibid., 1139–45.

16. Ibid., 1141–42.

17. Henry Mayer, " 'A Leaven of Disunion:' The Growth of the Secessionist Faction in Alabama, 1847–1851," *Alabama Review* 22 (April 1969): 89.

18. Campbell to John C. Calhoun, 20 December 1847, *Annual Reports,* 1154; Holman Hamilton, *Zachary Taylor: Soldier in the White House* (New York: Bobbs-Merrill, 1951), 70, 97; K. Jack Bauer, *Zachary Taylor: Soldier, Planter, Statesman of the Old Southwest* (Baton Rouge: Louisiana State University Press, 1985), 226. In fact, Campbell had decided to join the growing movement to nominate Zachary Taylor as early as July 1847, when he was the most distinguished speaker at a Taylor rally held in Mobile. Campbell denounced the current political atmosphere in which politicians were irresponsibly using the slavery issue to bolster their careers. He exclaimed that "no man can view the present condition of relations between the northern and southern states without apprehension for the safety of our government." To stem the rising sectionalism, Campbell advised that Alabamians unite in support of Taylor who was free from sectional ties and who could rally Americans around his brilliant military record. Malcolm C. McMillan, "Taylor's Presidential Campaign in Alabama, 1847–1848," *Alabama Review* 13 (April 1960): 85.

19. Campbell to John C. Calhoun, 20 December 1847, *Annual Reports,* 1155.

20. Ibid.

21. Campbell to John C. Calhoun, 1 March 1848, *Annual Reports,* 431.

22. Ibid.

23. E. I. McCormac, "Justice Campbell and the Dred Scott Decision," *Mississippi Valley Historical Review* 19 (March 1933): 565–71.

24. Ibid., 568–70; Campbell to John C. Calhoun, 1 March 1848, *Annual Report,* 430–34.

25. James P. McPherson, "The Career of John Archibald Campbell: A Study of Politics and the Law," *Alabama Review* 19 (January 1966): 53–63.

26. Ibid., 55.

27. Swisher, *Taney Period,* 5:626.

28. Potter, *Impending Crisis,* 277.

29. Ibid., 435.

30. Ibid., 431.

31. The only full biography of Yancey to date remains John Witherspoon Dubose, *The Life and Times of William Lowndes Yancey,* 2 vols. (New York: Peter Smith, 1942); For a useful historiographical essay, see Malcolm C. McMillan, "William L. Yancey and the Historians: One Hundred Years," *Alabama Review* 20 (1967): 163–86.

32. Heidler, *Pulling the Temple Down,* 33–34.

33. Dubose, *Life and Times of William Lowndes Yancey,* 1:245; Heidler, *Pulling the Temple Down,* 15–16; Eric Walther, *The Fire-Eaters* (Baton Rouge: Louisiana State University Press, 1992), 58–59.

34. Nevins, *Ordeal of the Union,* 1:12; Potter, *Impending Crisis,* 80–81.

35. *Journal of the Democratic Convention Held in the City of Montgomery on the 14th and 15th February, 1849* (Montgomery: McCormick and Walshe, 1849), 10–11.

36. Campbell·to John C. Calhoun, 1 March 1848, *Annual Reports,* 431.

37. *Journal of the Democratic Convention,* 12; Ralph B. Draughon, Jr., "William Lowndes Yancey: From Unionist to Secessionist, 1814–1852" (Ph.D. dissertation, University of North Carolina-Chapel Hill, 1968), 188–89. Draughon was the first historian to cite Campbell as a coauthor of the Alabama Platform. He does not, however, specify which of the planks Campbell contributed.

38. Walther, *The Fire-Eaters,* 57; Heidler, *Pulling the Temple Down,* 15; Draughon, Jr., "William Lowndes Yancey," 188–89.

39. Campbell to John C. Calhoun, 20 December 1847, *Annual Reports,* 1154.

40. DuBose, *Life of William Lowndes Yancey,* 1:216.

41. Ibid., 1:216; Potter, *Impending Crisis*, 81; Heidler, *Pulling the Temple Down*, 16–17.

42. Heidler, *Pulling the Temple Down*, 144–53.

6. States' Rights Triumphant

1. Avery Craven, *The Coming of the Civil War* (New York: Charles Scribner's Sons, 1947), 259; Potter, *Impending Crisis*, 87–88; Holman Hamilton, *Prologue to Conflict: The Crisis and Compromise of 1850* (Lexington: University of Kentucky Press, 1964), 96–98.

2. Merrill D. Peterson, *The Great Triumvirate: Webster, Clay, and Calhoun* (New York: Oxford University Press, 1987), 454–55; Nevins, *Ordeal of the Union*, 1:255–56.

3. Cleo Hearon, *Mississippi and the Compromise of 1850* (New York: AMS Press, 1972), 45–47.

4. Thelma Jennings, *The Nashville Convention: Southern Movement for Unity, 1848–1851* (Memphis, Tenn.: Memphis State University Press, 1980), 63–64; Clarence Phillips Denman, *The Secession Movement in Alabama* (Montgomery: Alabama State Department of Archives and History, 1933), 22–26; Thomas S. McFerrin, "Southern Sentiment and the Nashville Convention" (M.A. thesis, Florida State University, 1965), 38–47; Lewy Dorman, *Party Politics in Alabama From 1850 Through 1860* (Montgomery: Alabama State Department of Archives and History, 1935), 43; Abram John Foster, "The Nashville Convention of 1850" (M.A. thesis, Duke University, 1947), 30–32.

5. Jennings, *Nashville Convention*, 157–79; Foster, "The Nashville Convention of 1850," 66.

6. Heidler, *Pulling the Temple Down*, 41, 44.

7. McFerrin, "Southern Sentiment and the Nashville Convention," 62–68.

8. Nevins, *Ordeal of the Union*, 1:254–55.

9. Peterson, *Great Triumvirate*, 455.

10. Heidler, *Pulling the Temple Down*, 48–49; Jennings, *Nashville Convention*, 124, 134; J. H. Ingraham, ed., *The Sunny South; or, The Southerner at Home, Embracing Five Years' Experience of a Northern Governess in the Land of the Sugar and the Cotton* (Philadelphia: G. G. Evans, 1860), 131.

11. *Resolutions, Address, and Journal of Proceedings of the Southern Convention Held at Nashville, Tennessee, June 3rd to 12th Inclusive in the Year 1850* (Nashville: Harvey M. Watterson, 1850), 29; italics mine.

12. Ibid., 29.

13. Ibid., 29–30.

14. Ibid.; italics mine.

15. Ibid., 30.

16. Ibid.

17. Though Campbell supposedly took offense at northern attacks on southern filibustering expeditions, as chapters 7 and 8 will show, during his tenure on the Supreme Court, he staunchly upheld American neutrality legislation and dealt sternly with anyone who attempted to circumvent those laws.

18. *Resolutions, Addresses, and Journal of Proceedings*, 31–32.

19. Ibid., 32

20. Ibid., 32–33.

21. Ibid., 5; italics mine.

22. Jennings, *Nashville Convention*, 210.

23. Harris, a native of Georgia and a graduate of Franklin College, migrated to Alabama in 1838, settled in Wetumpka, and in 1847 was elected to the United States House of Representatives for the Third District (Garrett, *Reminiscences*, 387).

24. Campbell to Prattville Dinner, 10 November 1850, Montgomery *Advertiser and State Gazette*, 11 December 1850; reprinted in Duncan, "John Archibald Campbell," 42.

25. John Archibald Campbell, *Substance of the Remarks of John A. Campbell, At the Organization of the Southern Rights Association* (Mobile: Dade, Thompson, 1850): 5.

26. Ibid., 6; italics mine.

27. Ibid., 10.

28. Ibid., 6–7, 10, 14.

29. Ibid., 13.

30. Ibid.

31. Ibid., 14.

32. Ibid.

33. John Archibald Campbell, *The Rights of the Slave States By a Citizen of Alabama* (Mobile: Southern Rights Association, 1850), 3.

34. Ibid., 8.

35. Ibid., 5–7.

36. Ibid., 8–9.

37. Ibid., 9.

38. Ibid., 11, 12, 15–19.

39. Ibid., 24–25.

40. Ibid., 25.

41. Ibid.

42. Ibid., 23–25.

43. John Archibald Campbell to John C. Calhoun, 20 December 1848, *Annual Report*, 433.

44. John Archibald Campbell, *Address by John A. Campbell, Esq., to the Alabama State Bar Association, at their Annual Meeting at Birmingham, Alabama, 7th August, 1884* (Baltimore: John Murphy, 1884): 13; hereafter cited as Campbell, *Address to the Alabama State Bar Association, 1884.*

45. Campbell, *Rights of the Slave States,* 39–40.

46. Ibid., 47.

47. Ibid., 40, 43, 47.

48. Heidler, *Pulling the Temple Down,* 88–90.

49. *Alabama Weekly Journal,* 8 February 1851.

50. *Alabama Weekly Journal,* 15 February 1851; Denman, *Secession Movement in Alabama,* 54.

51. Dorman, *Party Politics in Alabama,* 53; Heidler, *Pulling the Temple Down,* 89.

52. *Alabama Weekly Journal,* 7 June 1851.

7. States' Rights Justice, Part 1: Commerce, Contracts, and Quitman

1. The twelve cases Campbell argued before the Taney Court were: *Doe ex dem. Farmer's Heirs v. Eslava* 9 Howard 421 (U.S. 1850); *Doe ex dem. v. City of Mobile,* 9 Howard 451 (U.S. 1850); *Hallett v. Collins,* 10 Howard 174 (U.S. 1850); *Dundas v. Hitchcock,* 12 Howard 256 (U.S. 1851); *Saltmarsh v. Tuthill,* 12 Howard 387 (U.S. 1851); *Gaines v. Relf,* 12 Howard 472 (U.S. 1851); *Darrington v. Branch Bank of Alabama,* 13 Howard 212 (U.S. 1851); *Doe ex dem. Kennedy's Executors v. Beebe,* 13 Howard 25 (U.S. 1851); *Parish v. Murphee,* 13 Howard 92 (U.S. 1851); *Rogers v. Lindsey,* 13 Howard 441 (U.S. 1851); *Hagan v. Walker,* 14 Howard 29 (U.S. 1852); and *Wiswall v. Simpson,* 14 Howard 52 (U.S. 1852).

2. Campbell sold the house and property during the Civil War for $2,500 Confederate.

3. Campbell, *Address to the Alabama State Bar Association, 1884*, 5–6.

4. U.S., Supreme Court, *Proceedings of the Bench and Bar of the Supreme Court of the United States: In Memoriam John Archibald Campbell* (Washington, D.C.: Government Printing Office, 1889), 11–12.

5. Swisher, *Taney Period*, 5:757.

6. Nolan B. Harmon, Jr., *The Famous Case of Myra Clark Gaines* (Baton Rouge: Louisiana State University Press, 1946), 3–42; Swisher, *Taney Period*, 5:756–60.

7. Harmon, *Myra Clark Gaines*, 180–81; Swisher, *Taney Period*, 5:758.

8. Connor, *John Archibald Campbell*, 10–11.

9. Swisher, *Taney Period*, 5:763; Swisher mistakenly cites the circuit court case as occurring in January 1863.

10. Harmon, *Myra Clark Gaines*, 342.

11. Ibid., 348.

12. Quoted in Connor, *John Archibald Campbell*, 11–12.

13. U.S., Supreme Court, Fifth Circuit, *Summary of the Life and Characteristics of Honorable John A. Campbell*, 2.

14. *Gaines v. Relf*, 12 Howard 472 (U.S. 1851).

15. Harmon, *Myra Clark Gaines*, 355.

16. "The Gaines Case," *Southern Quarterly Review* 18 (1854): 274.

17. Henry J. Abraham, *Justices and Presidents: A Political History of Appointments to the Supreme Court*, 3d ed. (New York: Oxford University Press, 1992), 111–12; Charles Warren, *The Supreme Court in United States History*, vol. 2 (Boston: Little, Brown, 1937), 245–47; Martin Siegel, *The Taney Court, 1836–1864*, Supreme Court in American Life Series, vol. 3 (New York: Associated Faculty Press, 1987), 292; Tom W. Campbell, *Four Score Forgotten Men: Sketches of the Justices of the U.S. Supreme Court* (Little Rock, Ark.: Pioneer Publishing, 1950), 189.

18. Swisher, *Taney Period*, 5:242–43.

19. Campbell to John Bragg, 3 January 1853 and 12 January 1853, Campbell Family Papers, SHC-UNC.

20. Ibid., 12 January 1853.

21. Swisher, *Taney Period*, 5:243; Connor, *John Archibald Campbell*, 16–18.

22. *New York Times*, 23 March 1853.

23. Ibid., 29 March 1853.

24. *New York Tribune*, 23 March 1853.

25. *Mobile Daily Register*, 25 March 1889.

26. *New York Times*, 23 March 1853.

27. 5 Howard 504 (U.S. 1847); *Passenger Cases*, 7 Howard 283 (U.S. 1849).

28. David P. Currie, *The Constitution in the Supreme Court: The First Hundred Years, 1789–1888* (Chicago: University of Chicago Press, 1985), 231.

29. *Cooley v. Board of Wardens of the Port of Philadelphia*, 13 Howard 299 (U.S. 1852); Bernard Schwarz, *A History of the Supreme Court* (New York: Oxford University Press, 1993), 83–86; Swisher, *Taney Period*, 5:405–6; Siegel, *Taney Court*, 189–93. Kermit L. Hall, ed., *The Oxford Companion to the Supreme Court of the United States* (New York: Oxford University Press, 1992), 197.

30. Carl B. Swisher, *Roger B. Taney* (New York: Macmillan Publishing, 1935), 160–256.

31. Hall, ed., *Oxford Companion to the Supreme Court*, 60–61.

32. *Bank of Augusta v. Earle*, 13 Peters 519 (U.S. 1839); Swisher, *Taney Period*, 5:116–21.

33. Linda A. Blandford and Patricia Russell Evans, *Supreme Court of the United*

States, 1789–1980: An Index to Opinions Arranged by Justice, vol. 1: 1789–1902 (Millwood, N.Y.: Kraus International Publications, 1983), 151–54; Mann, "Political and Constitutional Thought of John Archibald Campbell," 300.

34. *McDonough's Executors v. Murdoch,* 15 Howard 367 (U.S. 1853).

35. Ibid., 564; Siegel, *Taney Court,* 201; John R. Schmidhauser, "Jeremy Bentham, The Contract Clause, and Justice John Archibald Campbell," *Vanderbilt Law Review* 11 (1959): 801.

36. *Marshall v. Baltimore and Ohio Railroad Company,* 16 Howard 314 (U.S. 1853).

37. Ibid., 312; Swisher, *Taney Period,* 5:466–69.

38. *Marshall v. Baltimore and Ohio Railroad Company,* 16 Howard 348–49 (U.S. 1853).

39. Ibid., 350–53.

40. Ibid., 353.

41. Ibid.

42. *Dodge v. Woolsey,* 18 Howard 331 (U.S. 1856).

43. Swisher, *Taney Period,* 4:473–79.

44. *Piqua Branch of the State Bank of Ohio v. Knoop,* 16 Howard 369 (U.S. 1853).

45. Swisher, *Taney Period,* 5:475–77; Warren, *Supreme Court in United States History,* 2:253–58.

46. *Dodge v. Woolsey,* 18 Howard 371–72 (U.S. 1856).

47. Ibid., 372.

48. Ibid., 378; Siegel, *Taney Court,* 204.

49. Siegel, *Taney Court,* 204.

50. C. Stanley Urban, "The Abortive Quitman Filibustering Expedition, 1853–1855," *Journal of Mississippi History* 18 (1956): 183; Robert E. May, *John A. Quitman, Old South Crusader* (Baton Rouge: Louisiana State University Press, 1985), 271, 274–75; Basil Rauch, *American Interest in Cuba, 1848–1855* (1948; reprint ed., New York: Octagon Books, 1974), 263–64.

51. U.S., Congress, House, *Inaugural Addresses of the Presidents of the United States from George Washington 1789 to Harry S. Truman 1949,* House Doc. 540, 82d Cong., 2d sess., 1952, 95–101.

52. Urban, "The Abortive Quitman Filibustering Expedition, 1853–1855," 183; May, *Quitman, Old South Crusader,* 274–75.

53. Potter, *Impending Crisis,* 498.

54. James D. Richardson, ed., *Compilation of the Messages and Papers of the Presidents, 1789–1897,* vol. 5 (Washington, D.C.: Government Printing Office, 1907), 272–73.

55. For more detailed analyses of Quitman's schemes and the then prevalent fears that Cuba was undergoing "Africanization," see C. Stanley Urban's articles, "The Africanization of Cuba Scare, 1853–1855," *Hispanic American Historic Review* 37 (1957): 29–45; and "The Ideology of Southern Imperialism: New Orleans and the Caribbean, 1845–1860," *Louisiana Historical Quarterly* 39 (1956): 48–73.

56. May, *Quitman, Old South Crusader,* 285–86.

57. Quoted in Ronald Sklut, "John Archibald Campbell: A Study in Divided Loyalties," *Alabama Lawyer* 20 (July 1959): 236.

58. May, *Quitman, Old South Crusader,* 285–86.

59. J. F. H. Claiborne, *Life and Correspondence of John A. Quitman,* vol. 2 (New York: Harper and Bros., 1860), 198–206.

60. Quoted in ibid., 286.

8. States' Rights Justice, Part 2: *Dred Scott* and *Sherman Booth*

1. *New York Tribune*, 7 March 1857.

2. *New York Tribune*, 11 March 1857.

3. The most extensive and authoritative secondary study of *Dred Scott* remains Don E. Fehrenbacher, *The* Dred Scott *Case: Its Significance in American Law and Politics* (New York: Oxford University Press, 1978), 595. Although Fehrenbacher called Campbell an "unreserved defender of slavery," he was correct only in that the Alabamian was indeed "unreserved" in his role as a Supreme Court justice. As earlier chapters showed, Campbell was less a "defender of slavery" than an idiosyncratic defender of states' rights. Carl Swisher remarked, "Campbell was an ardent southerner in all respects, including his attitude toward slavery." Carl B. Swisher, *Roger B. Taney* (New York: Macmillan Publishing, 1935), 446.

4. There is certainly no shortage of secondary works covering the *Dred Scott* decision. For excellent versions of the facts in the case, see Fehrenbacher, Dred Scott *Case*, 239–304; Vincent C. Hopkins, *Dred Scott's Case* (New York: Russell and Russell, 1967), 1–60; Swisher, *Taney Period*, 5:599–622; Warren, *Supreme Court in United States History*, 2:279–85; Potter, *Impending Crisis*, 267–70; Allan Nevins, *The Emergence of Lincoln: Douglas, Buchanan, and Party Chaos, 1857–1859*, vol. 1 (New York: Charles Scribner's Sons, 1950), 90–95; Schwartz, *History of the Supreme Court*, 111–15.

5. *Scott v. Emerson*, 15 Missouri 577 (1852). Professor Fehrenbacher's article "The *Dred Scott* Case" provides an instructive abridged version of the case that he presented in his much larger work on Dred Scott. Don E. Fehrenbacher, "The Dred Scott Case," in John A. Garraty, ed., *Quarrels That Have Shaped the Constitution* (New York: Harper and Row, 1987), 87–99.

6. *Strader v. Graham*, 10 Howard 82 (U.S. 1851).

7. In the case listed in the official court records, the defendant's last name was erroneously spelled "Sandford." Consequently, this spelling has been used in a number of various sources through the years.

8. The plea in abatement, one of many procedural and often purposefully dilatory pleas, is closely related to today's motion to dismiss.

9. Swisher, *Taney Period*, 5:602.

10. James G. Randall and David Herbert Donald, *The Civil War and Reconstruction*, 2d ed. (Lexington, Mass.: D. C. Heath, 1969), 113–14.

11. Campbell to George T. Curtis, 30 October 1879, Campbell Family Papers, SHC-UNC. Campbell wrote that in the spring of 1856 "there was no conclusion attained by the Judges upon any question in the case which could be embodied in an opinion" (ibid.).

12. Campbell to Samuel Tyler, 24 November 1870, in Samuel Tyler, *Memoir of the Life of Roger Brooke Taney* (Baltimore: J. Murphy, 1872), 382.

13. Campbell to George T. Curtis, 30 October 1879, Campbell Family Papers, SHC-UNC; see also Swisher, *Taney Period*, 5:607.

14. Frank H. Hodder, "Some Phases of the Dred Scott Case" *Mississippi Valley Historical Review* 16 (June 1929): 10. Charles Warren wrote, "To Judge Nelson was assigned the duty of writing the opinion of the Court. Within a few days, however, it was found that the two dissenting Judges—McLean and Curtis, intended to write opinions discussing at length and sustaining the constitutionality of the Compromise Act. This action *forced* the majority of the Judges to reconsider the necessity of discussing that point as well themselves." Warren, *Supreme Court in United States History*, 2:293; italics mine.

15. Fehrenbacher, Dred Scott *Case*, 309–10; for a lucid discussion of Campbell's perceptions of judicial restraint and judicial activism, see Justine Staib Mann, "The Political and

Constitutional Thought of John Archibald Campbell" (Ph.D. dissertation, University of Alabama, 1966), 115–19.

16. Soon after Buchanan's inauguration, an altogether untrue story circulated that, moments before the oath of office was administered, Taney leaned over and whispered to the president-elect what he knew would be the outcome of the *Dred Scott* decision. Buchanan then supposedly altered his inaugural speech to make political use of the information. This popular myth was but one of many that arose from the case.

17. *Dred Scott v. Sandford,* 19 Howard 393 (U.S. 1857). The Court's record for the case fills 240 pages of Howard's *Reports.* For an excellent compilation of Taney's decisions, see Swisher, *Taney Period,* 5:622–25.

18. 19 Howard 589–90 (U.S. 1857). Historians have generally agreed that Curtis's opinion was the most reasonably argued, for the justice proved not only that the Missouri Compromise was constitutional but also that Scott had been freed because of his residence in free territory. Fehrenbacher, Dred Scott *Case,* 403–14; Swisher, *Taney Period,* 5:627–30. For a dated but nonetheless convincing argument that Taney's opinion was not dicta, see Edward S. Corwin, "The *Dred Scott* Decision in Light of Contemporary Legal Doctrines," *American Historical Review* 17 (October 1911): 54–56.

19. *New York Tribune,* 10 March 1857.

20. 19 Howard 393 (U.S. 1857).

21. 19 Howard 500 (U.S. 1857).

22. Ibid.

23. Ibid., 501.

24. Ibid., 505; italics mine.

25. Ibid., 505–506.

26. Ibid., 505.

27. Ibid., 509.

28. Ibid., 517.

29. Corwin, "*Dred Scott* Decision," 59. Corwin states that Campbell's decision was the "extremest Calhounism" of all the opinions. Faith, "Great Law Suits Affecting Mobile," 341, writes that Campbell's decision in *Dred Scott* was founded principally in the original Alabama Supreme Court case *Pollard v. Hagan,* which Campbell cited in his *Dred Scott* opinion. Fehrenbacher claims that Campbell's argument "was based less upon the Calhoun principle of equal rights for all states within the territories than upon . . . territorial self-government" (Fehrenbacher, Dred Scott *Case,* 400).

30. Campbell to Hons. A. McKinstry, J. M. Withers, and J. A. Hitchcock, 28 June 1858, Campbell Family Papers, SHC-UNC.

31. Connor, *John Archibald Campbell,* 100–104; Swisher, *Taney Period,* 5:709–11; Potter, *Impending Crisis,* 193–95.

32. Connor, *John Archibald Campbell,* 101.

33. *National Intelligencer* (Washington), 18 December 1858; Swisher, *Taney Period,* 5:711.

34. George Goldthwaite, "Untitled document," Miscellaneous File, Campbell Family Papers, SHC-UNC.

35. Alfred H. Kelly, Winfred A. Harbison, and Herman Belz, *The American Constitution: Its Origins and Development,* 6th ed. (New York: W. W. Norton, 1983), 287–88; Schwartz, *History of the Supreme Court,* 92–93; Swisher, *Taney Period,* 5:653–62.

36. Swisher, *Taney Period,* 5:660.

37. *Ableman v. Booth,* 21 Howard 506–626 (U.S. 1859).

38. Ibid., 514.

39. Hall, ed., *Oxford Companion to the Supreme Court*, 2.

40. Quoted in Duncan, "John Archibald Campbell," 19.

9. The War Years, Part 1: To Mitigate the Evils upon the Country

1. Campbell, *Address to the Alabama State Bar Association, 1884*, 27–28.

2. Ibid.

3. Campbell to L. Q. C. Lamar, 12 June 1860, in Edward Mayes, *Lucius Q. C. Lamar: His Life, Times, and Speeches, 1825–1893* (Nashville: Publishing House of the Methodist Episcopal Church, 1896), 84.

4. Campbell to Daniel Chandler, 12 November 1860, "Papers of Honorable John Archibald Campbell," *Southern Historical Society Papers*, n.s., 4 (October 1917), 3; hereafter cited as *SHS Papers*.

5. Ibid.

6. Campbell to Daniel Chandler, 12 November 1860, *SHS Papers*.

7. Ibid.

8. Ibid.

9. Campbell to Daniel Chandler, 24 November 1860, *SHS Papers*.

10. Ibid.

11. Campbell to Daniel Chandler, 26 November 1860, *SHS Papers*.

12. Ibid.

13. Potter, *Impending Crisis*, 520–22; Kenneth M. Stampp, *And the War Came: The North and the Secession Crisis, 1860–1861* (Baton Rouge: Louisiana State University Press, 1950), 56.

14. Campbell to Franklin Pierce, 19 December 1860, Campbell Family Papers, SHC-UNC.

15. Franklin Pierce to Campbell, 24 December 1860, Campbell Family Papers, SHC-UNC.

16. Campbell to Franklin Pierce, 29 December 1860, Campbell Family Papers, SHC-UNC.

17. There was no malicious intent on Chandler's part in publishing Campbell's letters. He likewise wanted to avert secession and believed that Campbell's letters might have helped calm tempers and assuage the crisis.

18. Connor, *John Archibald Campbell*, 120.

19. Campbell to Henry Tutwiler, 2 January 1861, Campbell Papers, Box 2, ADAH.

20. Ibid.

21. Ibid.

22. Campbell to L. Q. C. Lamar, 5 January 1861, in James Murphy, "Justice John Archibald Campbell on Secession," *Alabama Review* 28 (January 1975): 51.

23. Ibid., 57–58.

24. Malcolm C. McMillan, *The Alabama Confederate Reader* (1963; reprint ed., Tuscaloosa: University of Alabama Press, 1992), 33; H. G. Humphries to Campbell, 11 January 1861, Campbell Papers, Box 2, ADAH.

25. Campbell to Daniel Chandler, 21 January 1861, *SHS Papers*.

26. Allan Nevins, *The War for the Union*, vol. 1, *The Improvised War: 1861–1862* (New York: Charles Scribner's Sons, 1959), 22.

27. Campbell, "Memoranda Relative to the Secession Movement in 1860–61," *SHS Papers*, 43.

28. Ibid., 44.

29. Campbell to Mary Campbell, 6 March 1861, Campbell Papers, Box 2, ADAH.

30. Ibid.

31. Ibid.

32. Gideon Welles, *The Diary of Gideon Welles,* vol. 1 (Boston: Houghton Mifflin, 1911), 24–26; Potter, *Impending Crisis,* 572–73; Nevins, *War for the Union,* 1:50; Richard N. Current, *Lincoln and the First Shot* (Philadelphia: J. P. Lippincott, 1963), 71.

33. Campbell, "Facts of History," *SHS Papers,* 31; Ludwell H. Johnson, "Fort Sumter and Confederate Diplomacy," *Journal of Southern History* 26 (1960): 445.

34. Campbell, "Facts of History," *SHS Papers,* 31.

35. Ibid.

36. Ibid., 32.

37. Campbell to William H. Seward, 13 April 1861, *SHS Papers,* 38.

38. Campbell, "Facts of History," *SHS Papers,* 33.

39. Ibid.; Current, *Lincoln and the First Shot,* 89.

40. Campbell, "Facts of History," *SHS Papers,* 33.

41. Ibid., 34.

42. Ibid.

43. Campbell to Jefferson Davis, 3 April 1861, in Lynda Lasswell Crist, ed., *The Papers of Jefferson Davis,* vol. 7 (Baton Rouge: Louisiana State University Press, 1992), 88–89.

44. Jefferson Davis to Campbell, 6 April 1861, in ibid., 92–93.

45. Connor, *John Archibald Campbell,* 136.

46. Campbell, "Facts of History," *SHS Papers,* 38.

47. Johnson, "Fort Sumter and Confederate Diplomacy," 451.

48. Nevins, *War for the Union,* 1:50.

49. Campbell, "Incidents in the Life of John Archibald Campbell," Campbell Family Papers, SHC-UNC.

50. Campbell to George Goldthwaite, 20 April 1861, Campbell Family Papers, SHC-UNC.

51. U.S., Supreme Court, Fifth Circuit, *Memorial Meeting in Honor of the Late Judge John A. Campbell,* "Remarks by Thomas L. Bayne" (Washington, D.C.: Government Printing Office, 1889), 13.

52. Connor, *John Archibald Campbell,* 152–57.

53. Thad Holt, Jr., "The Resignation of Mr. Justice Campbell," *Alabama Review* 12 (April 1959): 105. Campbell wrote Chief Justice Taney on the twenty-ninth, informing him of his resignation. "From your hands," he explained to the Chief Justice, "I have received all that I could have desired, and in leaving the Court I carry with me feelings of mingled reverence, affection, and gratitude." Campbell to Roger B. Taney, "Papers of Roger B. Taney," *Maryland Historical Magazine* 5 (1910): 35.

54. C. Vann Woodward, ed., *Mary Chesnut's Civil War* (New Haven: Yale University Press, 1981), 92.

55. Bayne, "Remarks of Thomas L. Bayne," 13; Connor, *John Archibald Campbell,* 157.

56. Campbell to Benjamin R. Curtis, 20 July 1865, published as "A View of the Confederacy From the Inside," *Century Illustrated Monthly Magazine* 38 (October 1889): 950; hereafter cited as "Letter to Curtis."

57. *Pickens Republican* (Carrolton, Ala.), 20 May 1861.

58. Eugene H. Berwanger, ed., *My Diary North and South,* by William Howard Russell (Philadelphia: Temple University Press, 1988), 156.

59. Letter to Curtis, 950.

60. Bayne, "Remarks of Thomas L. Bayne," 13.

61. Campbell to George W. Randolph, 20 October 1862, National Archives, Letters Received by the Confederate Secretary of War, 1861–1865, Record Group 149, M-437.

62. Letter to Curtis, 950–51; italics mine.

63. Woodward, *Mary Chesnut's Civil War,* 479.

64. Connor, *John Archibald Campbell,* 158; Campbell, "Incidents in the Life of John Archibald Campbell," Campbell Family Papers, SHC-UNC; Letter to Curtis, 951; Duncan, "John Archibald Campbell," 13.

65. Campbell to Eliza Witherspoon Goldthwaite, 23 May 1863, Campbell Family Papers, SHC-UNC.

66. Quoted in Connor, *John Archibald Campbell,* 158–60.

67. Unknown, "Honorable J. A. Campbell, [as] submitted to George Goldthwaite in 1865," Campbell Family Papers, SHC-UNC; Bayne, "Remarks of Thomas L. Bayne," 13.

68. Edward Younger, ed., *Inside the Confederate Government: The Diary of Robert Garlick Hill Kean* (New York: Oxford University Press, 1957), 33.

69. Dubose, *Yancey,* 2:346; Younger, *Inside the Confederate Government,* 305.

70. Campbell's name is listed in the *Official Records* dozens of times with reference to his role in trying to prevent the outbreak of hostilities in 1861, again during the Hampton Roads Conference, and last when he met with Lincoln in Richmond. The profuse number of letters during these periods compared with the scant number elsewhere certainly indicates that his significance as assistant secretary of war was minimal. See *The War of the Rebellion: A Compilation of the Official Records of the Union and Confederate Armies,* ser. 1, pt. 2 (Washington, D.C.: Government Printing Office, 1895), hereafter cited as *Official Records.*

71. Campbell to William Letcher Mitchell, 14 March 1864, Campbell Family Papers, SHC-UNC.

72. Elizabeth Hester to Jefferson Davis, 15 August 1863, Letters Received, M-437.

73. John Beauchamp Jones, *A Rebel War Clerk's Diary at the Confederate States Capital,* vol. 2 (Philadelphia: J. P. Lippincott, 1866), 305.

74. M. C. Cruikshank to Campbell, 3 March 1864, Letters Received, M-437.

75. Howard Swiggett, ed., *A Rebel War Clerk's Diary at the Confederate States Capital by John Beauchamp Jones,* vol. 1 (New York: Old Hickory Bookshop, 1935), 300, 271.

76. Campbell's "Memoranda" on *Confederate States v. Lt. Evans,* Letters Received, M-437.

77. Campbell's "Memoranda" on *Confederate States v. John Miller,* Letters Received, M-437.

78. *Official Records,* ser. 4, 2:656.

79. Ibid., 3:755.

80. Swiggett, *A Rebel War Clerk's Diary,* 1:287–88.

81. Younger, *Inside the Confederate Government,* 84–85.

82. Campbell to Eliza Witherspoon Goldthwaite, 23 May 1863, Campbell Family Papers, SHC-UNC.

10. The War Years, Part 2: That We Should Not Be Utterly Destroyed

1. Campbell to Justice Samuel Nelson, 1 December 1864, in Connor, *John Archibald Campbell,* 161–62.

2. Elbert B. Smith, *Francis Preston Blair* (New York: Free Press, 1980), 304.

3. "Memorandum of a Confidential Conversation Held This Day With F. P. Blair, of

Montgomery County, Maryland," in Jefferson Davis, *The Rise and Fall of the Confederate Government*, vol. 2 (New York: D. Appleton, 1881), 612.

4. John G. Nicolay and John Hay, eds., *Abraham Lincoln: Complete Works, Comprising his Speeches, Letters, State Papers, and Miscellaneous Writings*, vol. 2 (New York: Century, 1907), 623.

5. Ibid., 2:640.

6. Sallie B. Putnam, *Richmond During the War: Four Years of Personal Observation* (New York: G. W. Carleton, 1867), 349; Swiggett, *A Rebel War Clerk's Diary*, 2:384; Younger, *Inside the Confederate Government*, 184.

7. Dunbar Rowland, ed., *Jefferson Davis, Constitutionalist: His Letters, Papers, and Speeches* (Jackson: Mississippi Department of Archives and History, 1923), 7:542; Davis, *Rise and Fall of the Confederate Government*, 616; italics mine.

8. Lincoln to Blair, 18 January 1865, *Official Records*, ser. 1, vol. 46:506; italics mine.

9. For a contrasting view of Davis's reasons for naming these particular men, see William C. Davis, *Jefferson Davis: The Man and His Hour* (New York: Harper Collins, 1991), 591–92.

10. For an interpretation markedly different from that presented by William C. Davis, see James M. McPherson, *Battle Cry of Freedom: The Civil War Era* (New York: Oxford University Press, 1988), 822–24.

11. Alexander H. Stephens, *A Constitutional View of the Late War Between the States: Its Causes, Character, Conduct, and Results*, vol. 2 (Philadelphia: National Publishing, n.d.), 592–93.

12. Ibid.

13. Fitzhugh Lee, "The Failure of the Hampton Conference," *Century Illustrated Monthly Magazine* 52 (July 1896): 476–77.

14. Thomas E. Schott, *Alexander H. Stephens of Georgia: A Biography* (Baton Rouge: Louisiana State University Press, 1988), 442.

15. Ibid.; italics mine.

16. Campbell to Hunter, 31 October 1877, in Rowland, *Jefferson Davis*, 7: 585.

17. Rowland, *Jefferson Davis*, 7:542; Rembert W. Patrick, *Jefferson Davis and His Cabinet* (Baton Rouge: Louisiana State University Press, 1944), 191.

18. *Official Records*, ser. 1, pt. 42:296; John Y. Simon, ed., *The Papers of Ulysses S. Grant*, vol. 13 (Carbondale, Ill.: Southern Illinois University Press, 1985), 333–34.

19. Simon, *Papers of Ulysses S. Grant*, 13:333–35.

20. *Official Records*, ser. 1, pt. 46:318.

21. Simon, *Papers of Ulysses S. Grant*, 13:345.

22. Ibid., 345.

23. Nicolay and Hay, *Complete Works*, 2:633; John Archibald Campbell, *Reminiscences and Documents Relating to the Civil War During the Year 1865* (Baltimore: John Murphy, 1887), 39–40; Joseph W. Rich, *The Hampton Roads Conference* (Iowa City: State Historical Society of Iowa, 1903), 15.

24. Simon, *Papers of Ulysses S. Grant*, 13:345.

25. Rowland, *Jefferson Davis*, 7:586.

26. Simon, *Papers of Ulysses S. Grant*, 13:345.

27. Nicolay and Hay, *Complete Works*, 2:635.

28. Stephens, *Constitutional View*, 2:599.

29. Ibid., 600.

30. Ibid., 601.

31. John Archibald Campbell, "Memorandum of the Conversation at the Conference at Hampton Roads, February 1865," in *Reminiscences and Documents*, 12.

32. Ibid.

33. Nicolay and Hay, *Complete Works*, 2:615. An excellent summation of Lincoln's annual address appears in J. G. Randall and Richard N. Current, *Lincoln the President: Last Full Measure* (New York: Dodd, Mead, 1955), 324–26.

34. Seward to Charles Francis Adams, 7 February 1865, *Official Records*, ser. 1, pt. 46:473.

35. In a memorandum written less than twenty-hours after the conference, Campbell stated that Seward suggested that the Emancipation Proclamation and the Thirteenth Amendment were "passed as a war measure, and under the predominance of revolutionary passion, and if the war were ended, it was *probable* that the measures of war would be abandoned." In the same document Campbell asserted that when pressed concerning these issues, Lincoln said that all cases concerning property would have to be settled in the courts. Stephens's account agrees with Campbell's. Campbell, "Memorandum," 12; Stephens, *Constitutional View*, 2:612.

36. R. M. T. Hunter, "The Peace Commission of 1865," *Southern Historical Society Papers*, 3:412.

37. Rich, *The Hampton Roads Conference*, 21.

38. Hunter, "The Peace Commission of 1865," 175.

39. Campbell, "Memorandum," 17.

40. Hunter, "The Peace Commission of 1865," 174; Stephens, *Constitutional View*, 2:617. Campbell made no mention of $400 million as the sum Lincoln proposed. He reported that Lincoln was willing "to be taxed on his little property for indemnities to the masters of slaves." Campbell, "Memorandum," 17.

41. As a result of the Conference, Stephens's nephew was released from a northern prison and a Union officer of similar rank was released by the Richmond government. Stephens, *Constitutional View*, 2:618; Nicolay and Hay, *Complete Works*, 2:651.

42. According to one humorous anecdote, Lincoln asked Grant if he had seen Stephens take off his coat when the vice-president was under his care at City Point. Smiling, Grant said that indeed he had and that he had been astonished as the thinness of Stephens's body. Lincoln asked Grant, "[D]idn't you think that it was the biggest shuck and the littlest ear that you ever did see?" E. B. Long, *Personal Memoirs of U.S. Grant* (New York: World Publishing, 1952), 524.

43. Campbell, *Reminiscences and Documents*, 16.

44. Seward to Adams, 7 February 1865, Nicolay and Hay, *Complete Works*, 2:651.

45. Welles, *Diary of Gideon Welles*, 2:236.

46. Ibid., 2:237.

47. Nicolay and Hay, *Complete Works*, 2:636.

48. Welles, *Diary of Gideon Welles*, 2:237.

49. Younger, *Inside the Confederate Government*, 202.

50. The full text of the commissioners' report can be found in Campbell, "Report of the Commissioners," *Reminiscences and Documents*, 18–19.

51. Younger, *Inside the Confederate Government*, 202.

52. Swiggett, *A Rebel War Clerk's Diary*, 2:412.

53. Ibid., 2:411.

54. Stephens, *Constitutional View*, 2:623–24.

55. Swiggett, *A Rebel War Clerk's Diary*, 2:414.

56. Lee, "The Failure of the Hampton Conference," 478.

57. Campbell was not alone in his belief that the speeches would only produce a brief period of heightened patriotism. Sallie Putnam, a Richmond socialite, claimed that the speeches resulted in "a spasmodic enthusiasm." "But," she lamented, "despondency rested too heavily on the hearts of many to permit more than a momentary and convulsive effort to shake off the incubus." Putnam, *Richmond During the War,* 350.

58. Campbell to John C. Breckenridge, 5 March 1865, *SHS Papers,* 52–57.

59. Campbell, *Reminiscences and Documents,* 21.

60. Lee, "The Failure of the Hampton Conference," 477.

61. Campbell to John C. Breckenridge, 23 February 1865, *Official Records,* ser. 1, vol. 46:1252.

62. Ibid.

63. Campbell to John C. Breckenridge, 5 March 1865, *Official Records,* ser. 1, vol. 51:1064–65.

64. Ibid., 1065.

65. Ibid.

66. Ibid.

67. Ibid.

68. Ibid.

69. James McPherson, *Battle Cry of Freedom: The Civil War Era* (New York: Oxford University Press, 1988), 844.

70. Ulysses S. Grant, *Personal Memoirs of U.S. Grant,* vol. 2 (New York: Charles L. Webster, 1886), 459; John G. Nicolay and John Hay, *Abraham Lincoln: A History,* vol. 10 (New York: Century, 1890), 168.

71. William T. Sherman, *Memories of General William T. Sherman,* vol. 2 (New York: D. Appleton, 1875), 324.

72. Campbell, *Recollections of the Evacuation of Richmond* (Baltimore: John Murphy, 1880), 4.

73. Ibid.; Letter to Curtis, 952.

74. Putnam, *Richmond During the War,* 367.

75. Campbell, *Recollections,* 6.

76. Nevins, *War for the Union,* 4:301; Nicolay and Hay, *Abraham Lincoln,* 10:218.

77. Nevins, *War for the Union,* 4:301.

78. Ibid., 302; Nicolay and Hay, *Abraham Lincoln,* 10:218.

79. Campbell to Horace Greeley, 26 April 1865, unsent, *SHS Papers,* 61.

80. Campbell, *Recollections,* 8.

81. Gustavus A. Myers, "Memoranda," in "Abraham Lincoln in Richmond," *Virginia Historical Magazine* 41 (1933): 320.

82. Nicolay and Hay, *Complete Works of Abraham Lincoln,* 2:668; Campbell, *Recollections,* 9–10; Mann, "Political and Constitutional Thought of John Archibald Campbell," 215.

83. Letter to Curtis, 953.

84. Myers, "Memoranda," 322; see also Swiggett, *A Rebel War Clerk's Diary,* 2:472.

85. Nicolay and Hay, *Complete Works,* 10:669.

86. Campbell to Joseph Anderson, 7 April 1865, in Campbell, *Recollections,* 24.

87. Campbell to General Joseph R. Andrews and Others, Committee, etc., 7 April 1865, *SHS Papers* 24 (1896): 351.

88. "To the People of Virginia," in Campbell, *Recollections,* 26.

89. Charles Sumner to Salmon P. Chase, 10 April 1865, in Beverly Wilson Palmer, ed.,

The Selected Letters of Charles Sumner, vol. 2 (Boston: Northeastern University Press, 1990), 282.

90. Fletcher Pratt, *Stanton: Lincoln's Secretary of War* (Westport, Conn.: Greenwood Press, 1970), 421; Sumner to Chase, 12 April 1865, in Palmer, ed., *Selected Letters of Charles Sumner,* 2:283.

91. Nicolay and Hay, *Complete Works,* 10:676.

92. Ibid.

93. Ludwell H. Johnson, "Lincoln's Solution to the Problem of Peace Terms, 1864–65," *Journal of Southern History* 34 (1968): 583.

94. Ibid., 585.

95. Stephens, *Constitutional View,* 614.

96. Sherman, *Memoirs,* 2:327.

97. Stanton to Grant, 3 March 1865, in Nicolay and Hay, *Complete Works,* 10:656.

98. Welles, *Diary of Gideon Welles,* 2:296.

99. Myers, "Memoranda," 321–32.

100. Campbell, *Reminiscences and Documents,* 42.

101. Nicolay and Hay, *Complete Works,* 10:669.

102. Campbell to Joseph Anderson, 7 April 1865, in Campbell, *Recollections,* 24.

103. Connor, *John Archibald Campbell,* 198.

104. Seymour J. Frank, "The Conspiracy to Implicate the Confederate Leaders in Lincoln's Assassination," *Mississippi Valley Historical Review* 40 (June 1953): 631.

11. Reconstruction and Redemption

1. Connor, *John Archibald Campbell,* 273, states that Campbell abstained entirely from any political activity, preferring instead to wait "patiently for the passions of the day to pass away." Mann, "Constitutional and Political Thought of John Archibald Campbell," 223–32, shows that Connor's portrayal of Campbell's postwar political activity was inaccurate.

2. Campbell to Anne Campbell, 29 May 1865, Campbell Family Papers, SHC-UNC.

3. Richard H. Leach, "John Archibald Campbell and the Alston Letter," *Alabama Review* 11 (January 1958), 64–66. For a more detailed account of the investigation into the alleged Confederate connection to Lincoln's assassination, see Frank, "The Conspiracy to Implicate the Confederate Leaders," 629–56.

4. Campbell to Anne Campbell, 20 June 1865, Campbell Family Papers, SHC-UNC.

5. Campbell to Anne Campbell, 29 May 1865, Campbell Family Papers, SHC-UNC.

6. Ibid.

7. Ibid.

8. The exact reasons for Campbell's detention are unclear. The Alston letter undoubtedly was instrumental in prompting his arrest but does not fully explain why Campbell remained at Fort Pulaski until October 1865. Henry Connor suggests that because Lincoln had divulged a most lenient reconstruction plan to Campbell in April 1865, the more radical members of the Republican party wished to "put him away" so that he could not insist that the martyred president would have disagreed with Radical Reconstruction. Connor, *John Archibald Campbell,* 187; Richard Leach does not conjecture on the motives of Campbell's jailors, but he recognizes the doubtful credibility of the Alston letter, and he asks why it took so long for federal authorities to release Campbell when there was no evidence that Alston had anything to do with Lincoln's assassination or that the Confederate government had had anything to do with Alston. Leach, "The Alston Letter," 73–74.

9. Campbell to Andrew Johnson, "Petition for Amnesty," 22 June 1865, Campbell Family Papers, SHC-UNC.

10. Benjamin Robbins Curtis to Andrew Johnson, 1 August 1865, Paul H. Bergeron, ed., *The Papers of Andrew Johnson,* vol. 9 (Knoxville: University of Tennessee Press, 1991), 524.

11. Ibid., 9:414; J. T. Dorris, "Pardoning the Leaders of the Confederacy," *Mississippi Valley Historical Review* 15:1 (June 1928): 15.

12. Campbell to Anne Campbell, 13 October 1865, Campbell Family Papers, SHC-UNC.

13. Eliza Witherspoon Goldthwaite to William A. Graham, 31 August 1865, Campbell Family Papers, SHC-UNC; Campbell to Anne Campbell, 13 October 1865, Campbell Family Papers, SHC-UNC.

14. Campbell to Anne Campbell, 6 November 1865, Campbell Family Papers, SHC-UNC. Though he complained about the lack of legal work in Mobile, Campbell reported to his wife on 8 February 1866 that during the previous three months, despite being "unsettled," he had earned $11,000. He evidently believed that New Orleans could yield even larger sums. Campbell to Anne Campbell, 8 February 1866 and 9 March 1866, Campbell Family Papers, SHC-UNC.

15. Campbell to Anne Campbell, 8 February 1866, Campbell Family Papers, SHC-UNC.

16. Campbell to Katherine Campbell Groner, 12 May 1867, Campbell Family Papers, SHC-UNC.

17. Ibid., 9 April 1871, Campbell Family Papers, SHC-UNC.

18. Ibid., 1 January 1869, Campbell Family Papers, SHC-UNC.

19. Ibid.

20. Ibid.

21. Ibid., 20 January 1874, Campbell Family Papers, SHC-UNC.

22. Ibid.

23. Campbell to Anne Campbell, 29 May 1865, Campbell Family Papers, SHC-UNC.

24. The Oliver Wendell Holmes Devise, *History of the Supreme Court of the United States,* vol. 6, pt. 1, Charles Fairman, *Reconstruction and Reunion, 1864–1888* (New York: Macmillan, 1971), 58.

25. Campbell, "Incidents in the Life of John Archibald Campbell," Campbell Family Papers, SHC-UNC.

26. Sumner to Francis Lieber, 17 April 1865, in Palmer, ed., *Selected Letters of Charles Sumner,* 2:293–94.

27. Books covering Reconstruction are numerous, and interpretations of this turbulent era vary widely. Four recent and reliable works that should be consulted are Eric Foner, *Reconstruction: America's Unfinished Revolution, 1863–1877* (New York: Harper and Row, 1988); Kenneth M. Stampp, *The Era of Reconstruction, 1865–1877* (New York: Vintage Books, 1965); C. Vann Woodward, *Origins of the New South, 1877–1913* (Baton Rouge: Louisiana State University Press, 1971); and Richard Nelson Current, *Those Terrible Carpetbaggers* (New York: Oxford University Press, 1988).

28. Foner, *Reconstruction,* 228–32; Stampp, *Era of Reconstruction,* 93–118.

29. Ted Tunnell, *Crucible of Reconstruction: War, Radicalism, and Race in Louisiana, 1862–1877* (Baton Rouge: Louisiana State University Press, 1984), 107, 113; Joe Gray Taylor, *Louisiana Reconstructed, 1863–1877* (Baton Rouge: Louisiana State University Press, 1974), 138–42.

30. Tunnell, *Crucible of Reconstruction,* 117–22, 132–34; Richard Nelson Current,

Three Carpetbag Governors (Baton Rouge: Louisiana State University Press, 1967), 36–37, 40.

31. Campbell to Anne Campbell, 9 March 1866, Campbell Family Papers, SHC-UNC.

32. For a full discussion of the tragic events in New Orleans on 30 July, see Gilles Vandal, *The New Orleans Riot of 1866: Anatomy of a Tragedy* (Lafayette: University of Southwestern Louisiana Press, 1983), 171–80; Taylor, *Louisiana Reconstructed,* 109–13.

33. Campbell to Eliza Witherspoon Goldthwaite, 8 August 1866, Campbell Family Papers, SHC-UNC; Campbell to Katherine Campbell Groner, 12 May 1867, Campbell Family Papers, SHC-UNC.

34. Campbell to Anne Campbell, 13 June 1868, Campbell Family Papers, SHC-UNC; Campbell to Katherine Campbell Groner, 9 April 1871, Campbell Family Papers, SHC-UNC.

35. Campbell to Nathan Clifford, 25 June 1871, in Charles Fairman, *Mr. Justice Miller and the Supreme Court, 1862–1890* (New York: Russell and Russell, 1939), 180.

36. Current, *Three Carpetbag Governors,* 50; Current, *Those Terrible Carpetbaggers,* 277–78; Stampp, *Era of Reconstruction,* 193; Taylor, *Louisiana Reconstructed,* 227–40.

37. Taylor, *Louisiana Reconstructed,* 241–44.

38. Ibid., 245, 248–49.

39. Mann, "Political and Constitutional Thought of John Archibald Campbell," 226–27.

40. Committee of Two Hundred Citizens, *Address of Citizens of Louisiana to the People of the United States* (Washington, D.C.: McGill and Witherow, 1872), 1.

41. Ibid., 2, 9.

42. Ibid., 11.

43. Executive Committee, *Report of the Committee of Two Hundred Citizens Appointed at a Meeting of the Resident Population of New Orleans on December 12, 1872* (New Orleans: Picayune Steam Press, 1873).

44. Ibid., 1, 9.

45. Ibid., 11, 21–22.

46. Ibid., 25–27.

47. Taylor, *Louisiana Reconstructed,* 255.

48. Current scholarship indicates that Reconstruction policies in several regions of Louisiana generated moderately successful reforms such as fair elections, proportionate black representation, and the fundamental protection of civil rights. Contrary to accounts claiming that Reconstruction was an unmitigated disaster that did little other than enrich hordes of carpetbaggers and scalawags, most present-day scholarship demonstrates that Reconstruction in Louisiana experienced various degrees of success—at least temporarily. The violence and rioting by white supremacist groups was not a reaction against the allegedly corrupt Republican governments, but rather a reflection of white Louisianans' fears that Reconstruction would succeed. Thus, it was the promise of further reforms that spawned fierce resistance from white supremacists determined to preserve white society. Tunnell, *Crucible of Reconstruction,* 188, 189–93; Taylor, *Louisiana Reconstructed,* 281–86, 267–73.

49. Although objectionable to most white Louisianans, including Campbell, what would have most benefited the freedmen of Louisiana was not an end to congressional Reconstruction but rather a strengthening of it coupled with sufficient support from the federal government.

50. There is no shortage of studies detailing the Election of 1876. A dated yet detailed examination of the election is Paul L. Haworth, *The Hayes-Tilden Disputed Presidential Election of 1876* (Cleveland: Burrows, 1906). A useful biography of Tilden is Alexander C.

Flick, *Samuel Jones Tilden: A Study in Political Sagacity* (New York: Dodd, Mead, 1939). Of the more reliable recent histories of the 1876 election, see Foner, *Reconstruction, 565–69, 575–82*; and William Gillette, *Retreat from Reconstruction, 1869–1879* (Baton Rouge: Louisiana State University Press, 1979), 302–5.

51. Flick, *Samuel Jones Tilden,* 365–83.

52. Taylor, *Louisiana Reconstructed,* 493.

53. For a brief but instructive biographical sketch of Bayard, see the introductory chapter in Charles C. Tansill, *The Foreign Policy of Thomas F. Bayard, 1885–1897* (New York: Fordham University Press, 1940), xiv–xvi.

54. Campbell, *A Letter from Hon. John A. Campbell to Senator Bayard, of Delaware, Upon the Powers of Congress over the Returns from Electors of President and Vice-President* (n.p.: Clark and Hofeline, 187?), 1–8, 18–20. Although this letter is undated, the subject matter indicates that it was written during December 1876 or January 1877.

55. Ibid.

56. Flick, *Samuel Jones Tilden,* 387–88.

57. U.S., Electoral Commission, *Proceedings of the Electoral Commission and of the Two Houses of Congress in Joint Meeting Relative to the Count of Electoral Votes Cast December 6, 1876, for the Presidential Term Commencing March 4, 1877* (Washington, D.C.: Government Printing Office, 1877), 325; Flick, *Samuel Jones Tilden,* 388–90; Fairman, *Mr. Justice Miller,* 289–90.

58. *Proceedings of the Electoral Commission,* 372–74.

59. Fairman, *Mr. Justice Miller,* 290.

60. *Proceedings of the Electoral Commission,* 395.

61. Ibid., 394–95.

62. Ibid., 395–96.

63. Ibid., 407.

64. Ibid., 408.

65. Ibid., 400; Foner, *Reconstruction,* 580; Flick, *Samuel Jones Tilden,* 392.

66. On the Wormley Hotel agreement and how the southern railroad industry figured prominently in persuading southern representatives to support Hayes, see C. Vann Woodward, *Reunion and Reaction: The Compromise of 1877 and the End of Reconstruction* (Boston: Little, Brown, 1951), 6–10, 89–100, 196–97.

67. Campbell, *John A. Campbell to Senator Bayard,* appendix, 21.

12. Postwar Palingenesis

1. Campbell to Daniel W. Middleton, 10 December 1866, in Fairman, *Reconstruction and Reunion,* 241.

2. Campbell, *Observations Respecting the Test Oath, Imposed Upon Attorneys By Congress* (n.p., n.d.), 11.

3. Ibid., 1–3.

4. Ibid., 11–12.

5. Ibid., 35–36.

6. *Cummings v. Missouri* 71 U.S. 277 (1867); Ex Parte *Garland* 71 U.S. 333 (1867).

7. Fairman, *Reconstruction and Reunion,* 58–59; Hall, ed., *Oxford Companion to the Supreme Court,* 52, 210, 867–68.

8. Sklut, "John Archibald Campbell," 254.

9. Benjamin R. Twiss, *Lawyers and the Constitution: How Laissez Faire Came to the Supreme Court* (New York: Russell and Russell, 1962), 43.

10. Connor, *John Archibald Campbell*, 207.

11. Sklut, "John Archibald Campbell," 256.

12. *Waring v. Mayor, Alderman and Common Council of the City of Mobile*, 19 L.Ed. 342 (U.S. 1869).

13. *State Tonnage Tax Cases*, 12 Wall. 204 (U.S. 1870).

14. Mann, "Political and Constitutional Thought of John Archibald Campbell," for instance, argues extensively that Campbell's *Slaughterhouse* argument provides unimpeachable evidence that he had dramatically altered his states' right philosophy and had in effect abandoned it altogether.

15. The term "Slaughterhouse Cases" refers to several cases in state and federal courts involving the granting of a monopoly by the Louisiana legislature. These are listed collectively in the *Lawyers Edition* as *Slaughterhouse Cases*, 21 L. Ed. 394 (1873). The case Campbell argued before the United States Supreme Court was docketed as *The Butchers' Benevolent Association of New Orleans v. The Crescent City Live-Stock Landing and Slaughterhouse Company*, 16 Wallace 36 (U.S. 1873).

16. Fairman, *Reconstruction and Reunion*, 1321–22.

17. Eva Doris Adams, "The *Slaughterhouse Cases*: The First Interpretation of the Fourteenth Amendment" (Ph.D. dissertation, Miami University, 1992), 26.

18. Ruth Ann Whiteside, "Justice Joseph Bradley and the Reconstruction Amendments" (Ph.D. dissertation, Rice University, 1981), 159.

19. Fairman, *Mr. Justice Miller*, 113; Joseph P. Bradley to Editor, *New Orleans Picayune*, 17 March 1889, Campbell Family Papers, UNC-SHC.

20. Whiteside, "Justice Joseph Bradley," 163–64.

21. Campbell to Philip Phillips, 22 March 1871, Phillips and Meyers Family Papers, SHC-UNC.

22. *The Butchers' Benevolent Association of New Orleans v. The Crescent City Live-Stock Landing and Slaughterhouse Company*, 16 Wallace 36 (U.S. 1873); Adams, "The Slaughterhouse Cases," 40–49.

23. John Archibald Campbell, Untitled Brief, *Slaughterhouse Cases*, Campbell Family Papers, SHC-UNC; hereafter cited as Campbell, *Slaughterhouse* Brief; see also Philip B. Kurland and Gerhard Casper, eds., *Landmark Briefs and Arguments of the Supreme Court of the United States: Constitutional Law*, vol. 6 (Arlington, Va.: University Publications, 1984), 733–63.

24. Kelly, Harbison, and Belz, *American Constitution*, 341–43; Fairman, *Reconstruction and Reunion*, 1118–19; William E. Nelson, *The Fourteenth Amendment: From Political Principle to Judicial Doctrine* (Cambridge, Mass.: Harvard University Press, 1988), 155–58.

25. Nelson, *Fourteenth Amendment*, 48–50.

26. Campbell, *Slaughterhouse* Brief, 25–28; Mann, "The Political and Constitutional Thought of John Archibald Campbell," 237.

27. Campbell, *Slaughterhouse* Brief, 6, 12.

28. Ibid., 23, 15.

29. Ibid., 23.

30. Ibid., 28.

31. Nelson, *Fourteenth Amendment*, 173; Mann, "Political and Constitutional Thought of John Archibald Campbell," 247.

32. William Gillette, "John A. Campbell," Leon Friedman and Fred I. Israel, eds., *The Justices of the United States Supreme Court, 1789–1969: Their Lives and Major Opinions*, vol. 2 (New York: Chelsea House, 1969), 938.

33. 16 Wallace 71 (U.S. 1873).

34. Nelson, *Fourteenth Amendment*, 158–59; Fairman, *Reconstruction and Reunion*, 1349–54; Adams, "*Slaughterhouse Cases*," 93–95.

35. Campbell to Philip Phillips, 2 December 1870, Campbell Family Papers, SHC-UNC.

36. *United States v. William J. Cruikshank et. al.*, 23 L.Ed. 588 (U.S. 1875); *New Hampshire v. Louisiana* 208 U.S. 76 (U.S. 1883). The state of New York was also a litigant in the latter case.

37. Kelly, Harbison, and Belz, *American Constitution*, 356–58; Whiteside, "Justice Joseph Bradley," 205–6.

38. *United States v. William J. Cruikshank et al.*, 23 L. Ed. 588 (U.S. 1875). The other four attorneys for the defendants were R. H. Marr, David S. Byron, William R. Whitaker, and E. John Ellis.

39. Campbell, *United States v. Cruikshank et al.*, "Conspiracy and Banding in Grant Parish, La.," in Kurland and Casper, *Landmark Briefs and Arguments*, 7:382.

40. Ibid., 386, 388–89.

41. Ibid., 385, 407, 409.

42. Hall, ed., *Oxford Companion to the Supreme Court*, 209; Fairman, *Reconstruction and Reunion*, 1379.

43. John V. Orth, *The Judicial Power of the United States: The Eleventh Amendment in American History* (New York: Oxford University Press, 1987), 7–11.

44. Mann, "Political and Constitutional Thought of John Archibald Campbell," 261.

45. Campbell, "Briefs," *The State of New York v. The State of Louisiana, The State of New Hampshire v. The State of Louisiana;* "Argument of John A. Campbell, of Counsel for the Defendants," *The State of New Hampshire, No. 4, The State of New York, No. 6, [and] John Elliott* et al. *v. The State of Louisiana and Her Executive Officers;* "The Answer Made to Points Filed the 11th April, 1882, By These Several Plaintiffs, On Behalf of the Defendants in the Suits Aforesaid," Campbell Family Papers, SHC-UNC; hereafter cited as Campbell, "Brief 1," Campbell, "Brief 2," and Campbell, "Brief 3," respectively.

46. Campbell, "Brief 1," 39.

47. Campbell, "Brief 2," 71–72.

48. Campbell, "Brief 3," 2.

49. Orth, *Judicial Power of the United States*, 37.

50. Campbell, *Address to the Alabama State Bar Association, 1884*, 51.

51. Ibid., 46–47.

52. Campbell, "Incidents in the Life of John Archibald Campbell," Campbell Family Papers, SHC-UNC.

53. Ibid.

54. Ibid.

55. Campbell to John A. C. Mason, 20 February 1886, Campbell Family Papers, SHC-UNC.

56. Campbell, "Incidents in the Life of John Archibald Campbell," Campbell Family Papers, SHC-UNC.

57. Bayne, "Remarks by Thomas L. Bayne," 9.

58. Connor, *John Archibald Campbell*, 280.

Bibliography

Published Writings, Letters, and Speeches of John Archibald Campbell

Address by John A. Campbell, Esq., to the Alabama State Bar Association, at their Annual Meeting at Birmingham, Alabama, 7th August, 1884. Baltimore: John Murphy, 1884.

A Letter from Hon. John A. Campbell to Senator Bayard, of Delaware, Upon the Powers of Congress over the Returns from Electors of President and Vice-President. N.p.: Clark and Hofeline, 187?.

"A View of the Confederacy From the Inside." *Century Illustrated Monthly Magazine* 38 (1889): 950–54.

"British West India Islands." *Southern Quarterly Review* 37 (January 1850): 342–77.

"The Creek Indian War of 1836." *Transactions of the Alabama Historical Society* 3 (1899): 162–66.

"Facts of History." *Southern Historical Society Papers* 4 (October 1917): 30–38.

Francis Strother Lyon as Commissioner and Trustee of Alabama. Printed for private circulation, 1886.

Letter to John C. Calhoun, 20 November 1847. "Correspondence Addressed to Calhoun." *Annual Report of the American Historical Association, 1899,* 1139–45.

Letter to John C. Calhoun, 20 December 1847. "Correspondence Addressed to Calhoun." *Annual Report of the American Historical Association, 1899,* 1152–55.

Letter to John C. Calhoun, 1 March 1848. "Correspondence Addressed to Calhoun." *Annual Report of the American Historical Association, 1921,* 430–34.

"Memoranda Relative to the Secession Movement in 1860–61." *Southern Historical Society Papers* 4 (October 1917): 43–45.

Observations Respecting the Test Oath, Imposed Upon Attorneys By Congress. n.p.: n.d.

"Papers of Honorable John Archibald Campbell 1861–1865." *Southern Historical Society Papers* 4 (October 1917): 3–81.

Recollections of the Evacuation of Richmond. Baltimore: John Murphy, 1880.

Reminiscences and Documents Relating to the Civil War During the Year 1865. Baltimore: John Murphy, 1887.

The Rights of the Slave States By a Citizen of Alabama. Mobile: Southern Rights Association, 1850.

"Slavery Among the Romans." *Southern Quarterly Review* 35 (October 1848): 391–432.

"Slavery in the United States." *Southern Quarterly Review* 34 (July 1847): 91–134.

"Slavery Throughout the World." *Southern Quarterly Review* 38 (April 1851): 305–39.

Substance of the Remarks of John A. Campbell, At the Organization of the Southern Rights Association. Mobile: Dade, Thompson, 1850.

Manuscript Collections

Cameron Family Papers, Southern Historical Collection, Wilson Library, University of North Carolina, Chapel Hill.

Campbell Family Papers, Southern Historical Collection, Wilson Library, University of North Carolina, Chapel Hill.

John Archibald Campbell File, John Archibald Campbell Federal Courthouse, Mobile, Alabama.

John Archibald Campbell Papers, Alabama Department of Archives and History, Montgomery, Alabama.

C. C. Clay Papers, Alabama Department of Archives and History, Montgomery, Alabama.

Governor's Papers, C. C. Clay, Executive Letter Book, Alabama Department of Archives and History, Montgomery, Alabama.

Governor's Papers, John Gayle, Executive Letter Book, Alabama Department of Archives and History, Montgomery, Alabama.

Groner Family Papers, Southern Historical Collection, Wilson Library, University of North Carolina, Chapel Hill.

Miscellaneous Books, Mobile (Ala.) County Probate Courthouse.

Mobile City Tax Rolls, Mobile (Ala.) Municipal Archives.

Phillips and Meyers Family Papers, Southern Historical Collection, Wilson Library, University of North Carolina, Chapel Hill.

Cases Cited

Ableman v. Booth, 21 Howard 506 (U.S. 1859).

Bank of Augusta v. Earle, 13 Peters 519 (U.S. 1839).

The Butchers' Benevolent Association of New Orleans v. The Crescent City Live-Stock Landing and Slaughterhouse Company, 16 Wallace 36 (U.S. 1873).

Cooley v. Board of Port Wardens, 13 Howard 299 (U.S. 1852).

Cummings v. Missouri, 71 U.S. 277 (U.S. 1867).

Darrington v. Branch Bank of Alabama, 13 Howard 212 (U.S. 1851).

Dodge v. Woolsey, 18 Howard 331 (U.S. 1856).

Doe ex. dem. v. The City of Mobile, 9 Howard 451 (U.S. 1850).

Doe ex. dem. Farmer's Heirs v. Eslava, 9 Howard 421 (U.S. 1850).

Doe ex. dem. Kennedy's Executors v. Beebe, 13 Howard 25 (U.S. 1851).

Dred Scott v. Sandford, 19 Howard 393 (U.S. 1857).

Dundas v. Hitchcock, 12 Howard 256 (U.S. 1851).

Ex Parte *Garland,* 71 U.S. 333 (U.S. 1867).

Gaines v. Relf, 12 Howard 472 (U.S. 1851).

The Genesee Chief v. Fitzhugh, 12 Howard 443 (U.S. 1852).

John Goodtitle ex dem. Pollard's Heirs v. Gaius Kibbe, 9 Howard 471 (U.S. 1849).

Hagan v. Walker, 14 Howard 29 (U.S. 1852).

Hallett v. Collins, 10 Howard 174 (U.S. 1850).
The Heirs of Pollard v. Kibbe, 9 Porter 344 (Ala. 1839).
Lessee of John Pollard, William Pollard, John Fowler and Harriet, His wife, Henry P. Ensign and Phebe, His Wife, Joseph Case and Eliza, His Wife v. Joseph F. Files, 2 Howard 591 (U.S. 1844).
Lessee of William Pollard's Heirs, etc. v. Gaius Kibbe, 14 Peters 367 (U.S. 1840).
License Cases, 5 Howard 504 (U.S. 1847).
McDonough's Executors v. Murdoch, 15 Howard 367 (U.S. 1853).
Marshall v. Baltimore and Ohio Railroad Company, 16 Howard 314 (U.S. 1853).
The Mayor and Aldermen of the City of Mobile v. Eslava, 9 Porter 425 (Ala. 1839).
The Mayor and Aldermen of the City of Mobile v. Miguel D. Eslava, 16 Peters 434 (U.S. 1842).
New Hampshire v. Louisiana, 108 U.S. 76 (U.S. 1883).
Parish v. Murphee, 13 Howard 92 (U.S. 1851).
Passenger Cases, 7 Howard 283 (U.S. 1849).
Piqua Branch of the State Bank of Ohio v. Knoop, 16 Howard 369 (U.S. 1853).
John Pollard et al. v. John Hagan et al., 3 Howard 210 (U.S. 1845).
Rogers v. Lindsey, 13 Howard 441 (U.S. 1851).
Saltmarsh v. Tuthill, 12 Howard 387 (U.S. 1851).
Scott v. Emerson, 15 Missouri 577 (Mo. 1852).
Slaughterhouse Cases, 21 L.Ed. 394 (U.S. 1873).
State Tonnage Tax Cases, 12 Wallace 204 (U.S. 1870).
Strader v. Graham, 10 Howard 82 (U.S. 1851).
United States v. William J. Cruikshank et al., 23 L.Ed. 588 (U.S. 1875).
Waring v. Mayor, Alderman and Common Council of the City of Mobile, 19 L.Ed. 342 (U.S. 1869).
Wiswall v. Simpson, 14 Howard 52 (U.S. 1852).

Newspapers

Alabama Weekly Journal, 8 February 1851.
Alabama Weekly Journal, 15 February 1851.
Alabama Weekly Journal, 7 June 1851.
Huntsville Southern Advocate, 31 May 1836.
Huntsville Southern Advocate, 7 June 1836.
Huntsville Southern Advocate, 17 June 1836.
Huntsville Southern Advocate, 5 July 1836.
Macon Telegraph, 12 December 1826.
Macon Telegraph, 11 August 1828.
Mobile Daily Register, 25 March 1889.
Mobile Herald, 5 January 1848.
Mobile Register, 29 June 1842.
Montgomery Advertiser, 11 June 1836.
National Intelligencer (Washington, D.C.), 18 December 1858.
New York Times, 23 March 1853.
New York Times, 29 March 1853.
New York Tribune, 23 March 1853.

New York Tribune, 7 March 1857.
New York Tribune, 10 March 1857.
New York Tribune, 11 March 1857.
Pickens Republican (Carrollton, Ala.), 20 May 1861.

Other Primary Sources

Acts Passed at the Annual Session of the General Assembly of the State of Alabama Begun and Held in the City of Tuscaloosa on the First Monday in December, 1842. Tuscaloosa: Phelan and Harris, 1843.

Baldwin, Joseph G. *The Flush Times of Alabama and Mississippi: A Series of Sketches.* Americus, Ga.: Americus Book, 1853.

Bergeron, Paul H., ed. *The Papers of Andrew Johnson.* 10 vols. Knoxville: University of Tennessee Press, 1991.

Berwanger, Eugene H., ed. *My Diary North and South,* by William Howard Russell. Philadelphia: Temple University Press, 1988.

Committee of Two Hundred Citizens. *Address of Citizens of Louisiana to the People of the United States.* Washington, D.C.: McGill and Witherow, 1872.

Crist, Lynda Lasswell, ed. *The Papers of Jefferson Davis.* 8 vols. Baton Rouge: Louisiana State University Press, 1992.

Curry, J. L. M. *Hon. Francis Strother Lyon as Commissioner and Trustee of Alabama, A Sketch.* N.p.: n.d.

Davis, Jefferson. *The Rise and Fall of the Confederate Government.* 2 vols. New York: D. Appleton, 1881.

Executive Committee. *Report of the Committee of Two Hundred Citizens Appointed at a Meeting of the Resident Population of New Orleans on December 12, 1872.* New Orleans: Picayune Steam Press, 1873.

Garrett, William G. *Reminiscences of Public Men in Alabama for Twenty Years.* Atlanta: Plantation Publishing, 1872.

Gilmer, George R. *Sketches of Some of the First Settlers of Upper Georgia, of the Cherokees, and the Author.* Americus, Ga.: Americus Book, 1926.

Grant, Ulysses S. *Personal Memoirs of U.S. Grant.* 2 vols. New York: Charles L. Webster, 1886.

Hunter, R. M. T. "The Peace Commission of 1865." *Southern Historical Society Papers* III: 168–76.

Ingraham, J. H., ed. *The Sunny South; or, The Southerner at Home, Embracing Five Years' Experience of a Northern Governess in the Land of the Sugar and the Cotton.* Philadelphia: G. G. Evans, 1860.

Jones, John B. *A Rebel War Clerk's Diary at the Confederate States Capital.* 2 vols. New York: Old Hickory Bookshop, 1935.

Journal of the Democratic Convention Held in the City of Montgomery on the 14th and 15th February, 1848. Montgomery, Ala.: McCormick and Walshe, 1848.

Journal of the House of Representatives of the State of Alabama, Begun and Held at the Town of Tuscaloosa on the Third Monday of November, 1835. Tuscaloosa: Meek and McGuire, 1836.

Journal of the House of Representatives of the State of Alabama, Begun and Held at Tuscaloosa on the Third Monday of December 1842. Tuscaloosa: Phelan and Harris, 1843.

Kurland, Philip B., and Gerhard Casper, eds. *Landmark Briefs and Arguments of the Supreme Court of the United States: Constitutional Law.* Arlington, Va.: University Publications, 1984.

Long, E. B., ed. *Personal Memoirs of U.S. Grant.* Cleveland: World Publishing, 1952.

Montgomery County, Alabama. *White Marriage Licenses Index.* Vol. A-18, 1817–1919, Book 2, C–E. Alabama Department of Archives and History.

Myers, Gustavus A. "Memoranda." In "Abraham Lincoln in Richmond." *Virginia Historical Magazine* 41 (1933): 320–22.

Nicolay, John G., and John Hay, eds. *Abraham Lincoln, Complete Works.* 2 vols. New York: Century, 1907.

Putnam, Sallie B. *Richmond During the War, Four Years of Personal Observation.* New York: G. W. Carleton Co., 1867.

Resolutions, Address, and Journal of Proceedings of the Southern Convention Held at Nashville, Tennessee, June 3rd to 12th Inclusive, in the Year 1850. Nashville: Harvey M. Watterson Printers, 1850.

Reynolds, Bernard A. *Sketches of Mobile.* 1868. Reprint ed., Bossier City, La.: Tipton Printing and Publishing, 1971.

Richardson, James D., ed. *Compilation of the Messages and Papers of the Presidents, 1789–1897,* 53d Congress, 2d sess. 10 vols. Washington, D.C.: Government Printing Office, 1907.

Rowland, Dunbar, ed. *Jefferson Davis, Constitutionalist: His Letters, Papers, and Speeches.* 10 vols. Jackson: Mississippi Department of Archives and History, 1923.

Saunders, James Edmonds. *Early Settlers of Alabama.* New Orleans: L. Graham and Son, 1899.

Semple, H. C. *In Memoriam: Addresses Delivered on the Occasion of the Presentation to the United States Circuit Court Sitting at Montgomery, Alabama, of Portraits of Judge John A. Campbell and Judge William Burnham Woods.* n.p., n.d.

Sherman, William T. *Memoirs of General William T. Sherman.* 2 vols. New York: D. Appleton, 1875.

Simon, John Y., ed. *The Papers of Ulysses S. Grant.* Carbondale: Southern Illinois University Press, 1985.

Stephens, Alexander H. *A Constitutional View of the Late War Between the States.* 2 vols. Philadelphia, Pa.: National Publishing, n.d.

Swiggett, Howard, ed. *A Rebel War Clerk's Diary at the Confederate States Capital.* 2 vols. New York: Old Hickory Bookshop, 1935.

Taney, Roger B. "Papers of Roger B. Taney." *Maryland Historical Magazine* 5 (1910): 35.

Tyler, Samuel. *Memoir of the Life of Roger Brooke Taney.* 2 vols. Baltimore: J. Murphy, 1872.

U.S., Congress, House. *American State Papers, Indian Affairs.* 2 vols. Washington, D.C.: Government Printing Office, 1832–1834.

U.S., Congress, House. *American State Papers: Military Affairs.* 7 vols. Washington, D.C.: Government Printing Office, 1832–1834.

U.S., Congress, House. *Inaugural Addresses of the Presidents of the United States From George Washington 1789 to Harry S. Truman 1949.* House Doc. 540, 82d Congress, 2d sess. Washington, D.C.: Government Printing Office, 1952.

U.S., Congress, House. *Report of the Select Committee of the House of Representatives, To Which Were Referred The Messages of the President U.S. of the 5th and 8th*

February, and 2nd March, 1827, With Accompanying Documents and a Report and Resolutions of the Legislature of Georgia, H. R. 98, 19th Congress, 2d. Session, 1827. Washington, D.C.: Gales and Seaton, 1827.

U.S., Electoral Commission. *Proceedings of the Electoral Commission and of the Two Houses of Congress in Joint Meeting Relative to the Count of Electoral Votes Cast December 6, 1876, for the Presidential Term Commencing March 4, 1877.* Washington, D.C.: Government Printing Office, 1877.

U.S., National Archives. *Letters Received by the Confederate Secretary of War, 1861–1865.* Record Group 149, M-437. Washington, D.C.: National Archives Microforms and Records Service, 1965.

U.S., Supreme Court. *Proceedings of the Bench and Bar of the Supreme Court of the United States: In Memoriam John Archibald Campbell.* Washington, D.C.: Government Printing Office, 1889.

U.S., Supreme Court, Fifth Circuit. *Memorial Meeting in Honor of the Late Judge John A. Campbell, United States Circuit Court, New Orleans, Louisiana, 6 April 1889,* "Remarks of Thomas L. Bayne." Washington: Government Printing Office, 1889.

U.S., Supreme Court, Fifth Circuit, Edward C. Billings. *A Summary of the Life and Characteristics of Honorable John A. Campbell Contained in the Remarks of Judge Edward C. Billings Upon the Occasion of the Presentation to the United States Courts of Resolutions, and in Response to Addresses, By the Bar of New Orleans in Honor of Judge Campbell's Memory, New Orleans, April 6, 1889.* Washington, D.C.: Government Printing Office, 1889.

War of the Rebellion: A Compilation of the Official Records of the Union and Confederate Armies. Washington, D.C.: Government Printing Office. 1895.

Warren, Mary B., and Sarah F. White, comps. *Marriages and Deaths, 1820–1830, Abstracted From Extant Georgia Newspapers.* Danielsville, Ga.: Heritage Papers, 1972.

Welles, Gideon. *The Diary of Gideon Welles.* 3 vols. Boston: Houghton Mifflin, 1911.

Woodward, C. Vann, ed. *Mary Chesnut's Civil War.* New Haven: Yale University Press, 1981.

Younger, Edward, ed. *Inside the Confederate Government: The Diary of Robert Garlick Hill Kean.* New York: Oxford University Press, 1957.

Published Secondary Works

Abraham, Henry J. *Justices and Presidents: A Political History of Appointments to the Supreme Court.* 3d. ed. New York: Oxford University Press, 1992.

Amos, Harriet E. *Cotton City: Urban Development in Antebellum Mobile.* Tuscaloosa: University of Alabama Press, 1985.

Bartley, Ernest R. *The Tidelands Oil Controversy: A Legal and Historical Analysis.* Austin: University of Texas Press, 1953.

Bauer, K. Jack. *Zachary Taylor: Soldier, Planter, Statesman of the Old Southwest.* Baton Rouge: Louisiana State University Press, 1985.

Blandford, Linda A., and Patricia Russell Evans. *Supreme Court of the United States, 1789–1980: An Index to Opinions Arranged by Justice,* Vol. 1: *1789–1902.* Millwood, New York: Kraus International Publications, 1983.

Bowen, Eliza A. *The Story of Wilkes County, Georgia.* Marietta, Ga.: Continental Book, 1950.

Brantley, William H. *Banking in Alabama, 1816–1860.* 2 vols. Birmingham, Ala.: Oxmoor Press, 1967.

Brewer, Willis. *Alabama: Her History, Resources, War Record, and Public Men From 1540 to 1872.* Montgomery: Barrett and Brown, 1872.

Campbell, Tom W. *Four Score Forgotten Men: Sketches of the Justices of the U.S. Supreme Court.* Little Rock, Ark.: Pioneer Publishing, 1950.

Claiborne, J. F. H. *Life and Correspondence of John A. Quitman.* 2 vols. New York: Harper and Brothers, 1860.

Coleman, Kenneth, ed. *A History of Georgia.* 2d ed. Athens: University of Georgia Press, 1991.

Connor, Henry Groves. *John Archibald Campbell, Associate Justice of the United States Supreme Court, 1853–1861.* Boston: Houghton Mifflin, 1920.

Corwin, Edward S. *National Supremacy: Treaty Power vs. State Power.* Gloucester, Mass.: Peter Smith, 1965.

Coulter, E. Merton. *College Life in the Old South.* Athens: University of Georgia Press, 1951.

Craighead, Erwin. *Mobile: Fact and Tradition, Noteworthy People and Events.* Mobile, Ala.: Powers Printing, 1930.

Craven, Avery O. *The Coming of the Civil War.* New York: Charles Scribner's Sons, 1947.

Current, Richard N. *Lincoln and the First Shot.* Philadelphia: J. P. Lippincott, 1963.

———. *Those Terrible Carpetbaggers.* New York: Oxford University Press, 1988.

———. *Three Carpetbag Governors.* Baton Rouge: Louisiana State University Press, 1967.

Currie, David P. *The Constitution in the Supreme Court: The First Hundred Years, 1789–1888.* Chicago: University of Chicago Press, 1985.

Cushman, Clare, ed., *The Supreme Court Justices: Illustrated Biographies, 1789–1993.* Washington, D.C.: Congressional Quarterly, 1993.

Davis, William C. *Jefferson Davis: The Man and His Hour.* New York: Harper Collins Publishers, 1991.

Denman, Clarence Phillips. *The Secession Movement in Alabama.* Montgomery: Alabama State Department of Archives and History, 1933.

Dorman, Lewy. *Party Politics in Alabama from 1850 Through 1860.* Montgomery: Alabama State Department of Archives and History, 1935.

DuBose, John Witherspoon. *The Life and Times of William Lowndes Yancey.* 2 vols. New York: Peter Smith, 1942.

Duncan, George W. "John Archibald Campbell," *Studies in Southern and Alabama History,* Vol. 5, *Transactions of the Alabama Historical Society.* Montgomery, Ala.: Alabama Historical Society, 1905.

Dyer, Thomas G. *The University of Georgia: A Bicentennial History, 1785–1965.* Athens: University of Georgia Press, 1985.

Fairman, Charles. *Mr. Justice Miller and the Supreme Court, 1862–1890.* New York: Russell and Russell, 1939.

Fehrenbacher, Don E. *The* Dred Scott *Case: Its Significance in American Law and Politics.* New York: Oxford University Press, 1978.

Flick, Alexander C. *Samuel Jones Tilden: A Study in Political Sagacity.* New York: Dodd, Mead, 1939.

Flynt, J. Wayne. *Montgomery: An Illustrated History.* Woodland Hills, Calif.: Windsor Publications, 1980.

Foner, Eric. *Reconstruction: America's Unfinished Revolution, 1863–1877.* New York: Harper and Row, 1988.

Freehling, William W. *The Road to Disunion: Secessionists at Bay, 1776–1854.* New York: Oxford University Press, 1990.

Friedman, Leon, and Fred I. Israel, eds. *The Justices of the United States Supreme Court, 1789–1969: Their Lives and Major Opinions.* New York: Chelsea House, 1969.

Garraty, John A., ed. *Quarrels That Have Shaped the Constitution.* New York: Harper and Row, 1987.

Gillette, William. *Retreat from Reconstruction, 1869–1879.* Baton Rouge: Louisiana State University Press, 1979.

Green, Michael D. *The Politics of Indian Removal: Creek Government and Society in Crisis.* Lincoln: University of Nebraska Press, 1982.

Griffith, Benjamin W., Jr. *McIntosh and Weatherford, Creek Indian Leaders.* Tuscaloosa: University of Alabama Press, 1988.

Griffith, Lucille. *Alabama: A Documentary History to 1900.* University: University of Alabama Press, 1987.

Hamilton, Holman. *Prologue to Conflict: The Crisis and Compromise of 1850.* Lexington: University of Kentucky Press, 1964.

———. *Zachary Taylor: Soldier in the White House.* New York: Bobbs-Merrill, 1951.

Harmon, Nolan B., Jr. *The Famous Case of Myra Clark Gaines.* Baton Rouge: Louisiana State University Press, 1946.

Haworth, Paul L. *The Hayes-Tilden Disputed Presidential Election of 1876.* Cleveland: Burrows, 1906.

Hearon, Cleo. *Mississippi and the Compromise of 1850.* New York: AMS Press, 1972.

Heidler, David S. *Pulling the Temple Down: The Fire-Eaters and the Destruction of the Union.* Mechanicsburg, Pa.: Stackpole Books, 1994.

Hopkins, Vincent C. *Dred Scott's Case.* New York: Russell and Russell, 1967.

Hosen, Frederick E. *Unfolding Westward in Treaty and Law: Land Documents in United States History from the Appalachians to the Pacific, 1783–1934.* Jefferson, N.C.: McFarland, 1988.

Jack, Theodore H. *Sectionalism and Party Politics in Alabama, 1819–1842.* Spartanburg, S.C.: Reprint, 1975.

Jennings, Thelma. *The Nashville Convention: Southern Movement for Unity, 1848–1851.* Memphis: Memphis State University Press, 1980.

Kelly, Alfred H., Winfred A. Harbison, and Herman Belz. *The American Constitution: Its Origins and Development.* 6th ed. New York: W. W. Norton, 1983.

Knight, Lucian Lamar. *Georgia's Landmarks, Memorials, and Legends.* 2 vols. Atlanta: Byrd Printing, 1914.

Lander, Ernest McPherson. *Reluctant Imperialists: Calhoun, the South Carolinians, and the Mexican War.* Baton Rouge: Louisiana State University Press, 1980.

McMillan, Malcolm C. *The Alabama Confederate Reader.* 1963. Reprint ed. Tuscaloosa: University of Alabama Press, 1992.

McPherson, James M. *Battle Cry of Freedom: The Civil War Era.* New York: Oxford University Press, 1988.

Mahon, John K. *History of the Second Seminole War, 1835–1842.* Rev. ed. Gainesville: University of Florida Press, 1991.

May, Robert E. *John A. Quitman, Old South Crusader.* Baton Rouge: Louisiana State University Press, 1985.

Mayes, Edward. *Lucius Q. C. Lamar: His Life, Times, and Speeches, 1825–1893.* Nashville: Publishing House of the Methodist Episcopal Church, 1896.

Miller, L. D. *History of Alabama.* N.p.: By the author, 1901.

Miller, Stephen F. *The Bench and Bar of Georgia: Memoirs and Sketches.* 2 vols. Philadelphia: J. B. Lippincott, 1858.

Moore, Albert B. *History of Alabama.* Tuscaloosa: Alabama Book Store, 1951.

Nelson, William E. *The Fourteenth Amendment: From Political Principle to Judicial Doctrine.* Cambridge, Mass.: Harvard University Press, 1988.

Nevins, Allan. *Ordeal of the Union.* 2 vols. *Fruits of Manifest Destiny, 1847–1852,* vol. 2. New York: Charles Scribner's Sons, 1947.

——. *The War for the Union.* 4 vols. *The Improvised War, 1861–1862,* vol. 1. New York: Charles Scribner's Sons, 1959.

——. *The War for the Union.* 4 vols. *The Organized War to Victory, 1864–1865,* vol. 4. New York: Charles Scribner's Sons, 1971.

——. *The Emergence of Lincoln.* 2 vols. *Douglas, Buchanan, and Party Chaos, 1857–1859,* vol. 1. New York: Charles Scribner's Sons, 1950.

Nicolay, John G., and John Hay. *Abraham Lincoln: A History.* 10 vols. New York: Century, 1890.

Niven, John. *John C. Calhoun and the Price of Union: A Biography.* Baton Rouge: Louisiana State University Press, 1988.

Northen, William J., ed. *Men of Mark in Georgia.* 7 vols. Spartanburg, S.C.: Reprint, 1974.

The Oliver Wendell Holmes Devise. *History of the Supreme Court of the United States.* 9 vols. *The Taney Period, 1836–64,* vol. 5, by Carl B. Swisher. New York: Macmillan Publishing, 1974.

——. *History of the Supreme Court of the United States.* 9 vols., *Reconstruction and Reunion, 1864–88,* vol. 6, by Charles Fairman. New York: Macmillan Publishing, 1971.

Orr, Dorothy. *A History of Education in Georgia.* Chapel Hill: University of North Carolina Press, 1950.

Orth, John V. *The Judicial Power of the United States: The Eleventh Amendment in American History.* New York: Oxford University Press, 1987.

Owen, Thomas McAdory. *History of Alabama and Dictionary of Alabama Biography.* Spartanburg, S.C.: Reprint, 1978.

Patrick, Rembert W. *Jefferson Davis and His Cabinet.* Baton Rouge: Louisiana State University Press, 1944.

Peterson, Merrill D. *The Great Triumvirate: Webster, Clay, and Calhoun.* New York: Oxford University Press, 1987.

Potter, David M. *The Impending Crisis, 1848–1861.* New York: Harper and Row, 1963.

Pratt, Fletcher. *Stanton: Lincoln's Secretary of War.* Westport, Conn.: Greenwood Press, 1953.

Randall, James G., and Richard N. Current. *Lincoln the President: Last Full Measure.* New York: Dodd, Mead, 1955.

Randall, James G., and David Herbert Donald. *The Civil War and Reconstruction,* 2d ed. Lexington, Mass.: D. C. Heath, 1969.

Rauch, Basil. *American Interest in Cuba, 1848–1855.* 1948. Reprint ed. New York: Octagon Books, 1974.

Rich, Joseph W. *The Hampton Roads Conference.* Iowa City: State Historical Society of Iowa, 1903.

Rogers, William Warren, Robert David Ward, Leah Rawls Atkins, and Wayne Flynt. *Alabama: The History of a Deep South State.* Tuscaloosa: University of Alabama Press, 1994.

Schott, Thomas E. *Alexander H. Stephens of Georgia: A Biography.* Baton Rouge: Louisiana State University, 1988.

Schwarz, Bernard. *A History of the Supreme Court.* New York: Oxford University Press, 1993.

Siegel, Martin. *The Taney Court, 1836-1864.* Supreme Court in American Life Series, vol. 3. New York: Associated Faculty Press, 1987.

Smith, Elbert B. *Francis Preston Blair.* New York: Free Press, 1980.

Southerland, Henry DeLeon, Jr., and Jerry Elijah Brown. *The Federal Road Through Georgia, the Creek Nation, and Alabama, 1806-1836.* Tuscaloosa: University of Alabama Press, 1989.

Stampp, Kenneth M. *And the War Came: The North and the Secession Crisis, 1860-1861.* Baton Rouge: Louisiana State University Press, 1950.

———. *The Era of Reconstruction, 1865-1877.* New York: Vintage Books, 1965.

Swisher, Carl B. *Roger B. Taney.* New York: Macmillan Publishing, 1935.

Tansill, Charles C. *The Foreign Policy of Thomas F. Bayard, 1885-1897.* New York: Fordham University Press, 1940.

Taylor, Joe Gray. *Louisiana Reconstructed, 1863-1877.* Baton Rouge: Louisiana State University Press, 1974.

Thornton, J. Mills. *Politics and Power in a Slave Society: Alabama, 1800-1860.* Baton Rouge: Louisiana State University Press, 1978.

Tunnell, Ted. *Crucible of Reconstruction: War, Radicalism, and Race in Louisiana, 1862-1877.* Baton Rouge: Louisiana State University Press, 1984.

Twiss, Benjamin R. *Lawyers and the Constitution: How Laissez Faire Came to the Supreme Court.* New York: Russell and Russell, 1962.

Vandal, Gilles. *The New Orleans Riot of 1866: Anatomy of a Tragedy.* Lafayette, La.: University of Southwestern Louisiana Press, 1983.

Walther, Eric. *The Fire-Eaters.* Baton Rouge: Louisiana State University Press, 1992.

Warren, Charles. *The Supreme Court in United States History.* 2 vols. Boston: Little, Brown, 1937.

Woodward, C. Vann. *Origins of the New South, 1877-1913.* Baton Rouge: Louisiana State University Press, 1971.

———. *Reunion and Reaction: The Compromise of 1877 and the End of Reconstruction.* Boston: Little, Brown, 1951.

Writers' Program of the Works Projects Administration. *The Story of Washington-Wilkes.* Athens: University of Georgia Press, 1941.

Journal Articles

Alabama State Bar Association. "An Address on the Life of John Archibald Campbell, by Henry G. Connor. Delivered at Birmingham, Alabama, 12 July 1917." *Minutes of the Fortieth Annual Meeting of the Alabama Bar Association.* Birmingham: Alabama Bar Association, 1917.

Bagwell, David A. "The John Archibald Campbell United States Courthouse in Mobile." *Alabama Lawyer* 43 (May 1983): 154-55.

Brannon, Peter A. "Creek Indian War, 1836–1837." *Alabama Historical Quarterly* 13 (1951): 156–58.

Corwin, Edward S. "The *Dred Scott* Decision in Light of Contemporary Legal Doctrines." *American Historical Review* 17 (October 1911): 52–69.

Dorris, J. T. "Pardoning the Leaders of the Confederacy." *Mississippi Valley Historical Review* 15 (June 1928): 3–21.

Faith, Edward W. "Great Law Suits Affecting Mobile." *Alabama Lawyer* 1 (October 1940): 320–44.

Foster, Herbert D. "Webster's Seventh of March Speech and the Secession Movement, 1850." *American Historical Review* 27 (1921–1922): 245–70.

Frank, Seymour J. "The Conspiracy to Implicate the Confederate Leaders in Lincoln's Assassination." *Mississippi Valley Historical Review* 40 (June 1953): 629–56.

Gates, Paul Wallace. "Private Land Claims in the South." *Journal of Southern History* 22 (1956): 183–204.

Hodder, Frank H. "Some Phases of the *Dred Scott* Case." *Mississippi Valley Historical Review* 16 (June 1929): 3–22.

Holt, Thad, Jr. "The Resignation of Mr. Justice Campbell." *Alabama Review* 12 (April 1959): 105–18.

Howington, Arthur F. "Violence in Alabama: A Study of Late Ante-bellum Montgomery." *Alabama Review* 27 (July 1974): 213–31.

Johnson, Ludwell H. "Fort Sumter and Confederate Diplomacy." *Journal of Southern History* 26 (1960): 441–79.

———. "Lincoln's Solution to the Problem of Peace Terms, 1864–1865." *Journal of Southern History* 34 (1968): 576–86.

Leach, Richard H. "John Archibald Campbell and the Alston Letter." *Alabama Review* 11 (January 1958): 64–75.

Lee, Fitzhugh. "The Failure of the Hampton Conference." *Century Illustrated Monthly Magazine* 52 (July 1986): 476–78.

McCormac, E. I. "Justice Campbell and the Dred Scott Decision." *Mississippi Valley Historical Review* 19 (March 1933): 565–77.

McMillan, Malcolm C. "Taylor's Presidential Campaign in Alabama, 1847–1848." *Alabama Review* 13 (April 1960): 83–108.

———. "William L. Yancey and the Historians: One Hundred Years." *Alabama Review* 20 (July 1967): 163–86.

McPherson, James P. "The Career of John Archibald Campbell: A Study of Politics and the Law." *Alabama Review* 19 (January 1966): 53–63.

Mayer, Henry. " 'A Leaven of Disunion': The Growth of the Secessionist Faction in Alabama, 1847–1851." *Alabama Review* 22 (April 1969): 83–116.

Murphy, James. "Justice John Archibald Campbell on Secession." *Alabama Review* 28 (January 1975): 48–58.

Owsley, Frank Lawrence, Jr. "Francis Scott Key's Mission to Alabama in 1833." *Alabama Review* 23 (July 1970): 181–92.

Russel, Robert R. "Constitutional Doctrines with Regard to Slavery in Territories." *Journal of Southern History* 32 (1966): 466–86.

Schmidhauser, John R. "Jeremy Bentham, The Contract Clause, and Justice John Archibald Campbell." *Vanderbilt Law Review* 11 (1959): 801–20.

Sklut, Ronald. "John Archibald Campbell: A Study in Divided Loyalties." *Alabama Lawyer* 20 (July 1959): 233–64.

Urban, C. Stanley. "The Abortive Quitman Filibustering Expedition, 1853–1855." *Journal of Mississippi History* 18 (1956): 175–96.

——. "The Africanization of Cuba Scare, 1853–1855." *Hispanic American Historic Review* 37 (1957): 29–45.

——. "The Ideology of Southern Imperialism: New Orleans and the Caribbean, 1845–1860." *Louisiana Historical Quarterly* 39 (1956): 48–73.

Valliere, Kenneth L. "The Creek War of 1836: A Military History." *Chronicles of Oklahoma* 57 (Winter 1979): 463–85.

Williams, Clanton W. "Early Ante-Bellum Montgomery: A Black Belt Constituency." *Journal of Southern History* 7 (1941): 495–523.

Young, Mary. "Racism in Red and Black: Indians and Other Free People of Color in Georgia Law, Politics, and Removal Policy." *Georgia Historical Quarterly* 73 (Fall 1989): 492–518.

Theses and Dissertations

Abrams, David. "The State Bank of Alabama, 1841–1845." M.A. thesis, Auburn University, 1965.

Adams, Eva Doris. "The Slaughterhouse Cases: The First Interpretation of the Fourteenth Amendment." Ph.D. dissertation, University of Miami, 1992.

Alston, James Robert Maxwell. "John Archibald Campbell, States' Rights, and the Federal Union." Senior thesis, Princeton University, 1958.

Boogher, Elbert W. G. "Secondary Education in Georgia, 1732–1858." Ph.D. dissertation, University of Pennsylvania, 1933.

Draughon, Ralph B., Jr. "William Lowndes Yancey: From Unionist to Secessionist, 1814–1852." Ph.D. dissertation, University of North Carolina at Chapel Hill, 1968.

Foster, Abram John. "The Nashville Convention of 1850." M.A. thesis, Duke University, 1947.

McFerrin, Thomas Sumner. "Southern Sentiment and the Nashville Convention of 1850." M.A. thesis, Florida State University, 1965.

Mann, Justine Staib. "The Political and Constitutional Thought of John Archibald Campbell." Ph.D. dissertation, University of Alabama, 1966.

Whiteside, Ruth Ann. "Justice Joseph Bradley and the Reconstruction Amendments." Ph.D. dissertation, Rice University, 1981.

Index

About the Author

Robert Saunders, Jr., is Assistant Professor in the History Department at Troy State University, Dothan, Alabama. He received his bachelor's and master's degrees from Salisbury State University, Maryland, and his doctorate from Auburn University. His other publications include numerous short articles and book reviews on antebellum American history.